HORSHAM TOWNSHIP LIBRARY
435 BABYLON RD., HORSHAM, PA 19044-1224
3 1224 1015 7047 0

D0810874

Biography Today

Profiles of People of Interest to Young Readers

Volume 18—2009
Annual Cumulation

Cherie D. Abbey
Managing Editor

P.O. Box 31-1640
Detroit, MI 48231-1640

Cherie D. Abbey, *Managing Editor*

Brian Baughan, Peggy Daniels, Joan Goldsworthy, Laurie DiMauro, Jeff Hill, Kevin Hillstrom, Laurie Hillstrom, and Diane Telgen,, *Sketch Writers*

Allison A. Beckett and Mary Butler, *Research Staff*

* * *

Peter E. Ruffner, *Publisher*
Matthew P. Barbour, *Senior Vice President*

* * *

Elizabeth Collins, *Research and Permissions Coordinator*
Kevin M. Hayes, *Operations Manager*
Cherry Stockdale, *Permissions Assistant*
Shirley Amore, Martha Johns, and Kirk Kauffman, *Administrative Staff*

Special thanks to Frederick G. Ruffner for creating this series.

ISBN 978-0-7808-1055-6

Library of Congress Cataloging-in-Publication Data

∞

This book is printed on acid-free paper meeting the ANSI Z39.48 Standard. The infinity symbol that appears above indicates that the paper in this book meets that standard.

Printed in the United States

Manufactured by Edwards Brothers, Ann Arbor, MI, United States of America, November 2009, 119832

Contents

Preface

Biography Today is a magazine designed and written for the young reader—ages 9 and above—and covers individuals that librarians and teachers tell us that young people want to know about most: entertainers, athletes, writers, illustrators, cartoonists, and political leaders.

The Plan of the Work

The publication was especially created to appeal to young readers in a format they can enjoy reading and readily understand. Each issue contains approximately 10 sketches arranged alphabetically. Each entry provides at least one picture of the individual profiled, and bold-faced rubrics lead the reader to information on birth, youth, early memories, education, first jobs, marriage and family, career highlights, memorable experiences, hobbies, and honors and awards. Each of the entries ends with a list of easily accessible sources designed to lead the student to further reading on the individual and a current address. Retrospective entries are also included, written to provide a perspective on the individual's entire career.

Biographies are prepared by Omnigraphics editors after extensive research, utilizing the most current materials available. Those sources that are generally available to students appear in the list of further reading at the end of the sketch.

Indexes

Cumulative indexes are an important component of *Biography Today*. Each issue of the *Biography Today* General Series includes a Cumulative Names Index, which comprises all individuals profiled in *Biography Today* since the series began in 1992. In addition, we compile three other indexes: the Cumulative General Index, Places of Birth Index, and Birthday Index. See our web site, www.biographytoday.com, for these three indexes, along with the Names Index. All *Biography Today* indexes are cumulative, including all individuals profiled in both the General Series and the Subject Series.

Our Advisors

This series was reviewed by an Advisory Board comprising librarians, children's literature specialists, and reading instructors to ensure that the concept of this publication—to provide a readable and accessible biographical magazine for young readers—was on target. They evaluated the title as it developed, and their suggestions have proved invaluable. Any errors, however, are ours alone. We'd like to list the Advisory Board members, and to thank them for their efforts.

Gail Beaver
Adjunct Lecturer
University of Michigan
Ann Arbor, MI

Cindy Cares
Youth Services Librarian
Southfield Public Library
Southfield, MI

Carol A. Doll
School of Information Science and Policy
University of Albany, SUNY
Albany, NY

Kathleen Hayes-Parvin
Language Arts Teacher
Birney Middle School
Southfield, MI

Karen Imarisio
Assistant Head of Adult Services
Bloomfield Twp. Public Library
Bloomfield Hills, MI

Rosemary Orlando
Director
St. Clair Shores Public Library
St. Clair Shores, MI

Our Advisory Board stressed to us that we should not shy away from controversial or unconventional people in our profiles, and we have tried to follow their advice. The Advisory Board also mentioned that the sketches might be useful in reluctant reader and adult literacy programs, and we would value any comments librarians might have about the suitability of our magazine for those purposes.

Your Comments Are Welcome

Our goal is to be accurate and up-to-date, to give young readers information they can learn from and enjoy. Now we want to know what you think. Take a look at this issue of *Biography Today,* on approval, and send me your comments. We want to provide an excellent source of biographical information for young people. Let us know how you think we're doing.

Cherie Abbey
Managing Editor, *Biography Today*
Omnigraphics, Inc.
P.O. Box 31-1640
Detroit, MI 48231-1640
www.omnigraphics.com
editorial@omnigraphics.com

Congratulations!

Congratulations to the following individuals and libraries who have received a free copy of *Biography Today for* suggesting people who appear in this volume.

Alexis, student, Groveport, OH

Carol Arnold, Hoopeston Public Library, Hoopeston, IL

Ayanna Black, Southfield Public Library, Southfield, MI

Erica Carasquillo, Woodward Parkway School, Farmingdale, NY

Susannah Chase, Englewood High School, Jacksonville, FL

Judi Chelekis, Vassar Junior/Senior High School, Vassar, MI

Ashley Daly, Ardmore High School, Ardmore, AL

Sonja Durham, Central Middle School, Dover, DE

Liz Keaton, Columbus, TN

Nancy Keenan, Glenvar High School, Salem, VA

A. Kennedy, Ardmore High School, Ardmore, AL

Emily Larman, Marymount School, Santa Barbara, CA

Andrea Lopez, Oxnard, CA

Jasmine McKinney, Westwood School, Stockton, CA

Shavonne Singleton, Queens Village, NY

Shreya Subramanian, Martell Elementary School, Troy, MI

Thomas, student, McKenna School, NY

Necee White, C.H. Price Middle School Library, Interlachen, FL

Judy Yamane, Aliamanu Middle School, Honolulu, HI

Christy Zhao, Brooklyn, NY

BRIEF ENTRY

Elizabeth Alexander 1962-

American Poet and Professor
Featured Poet at the Inauguration of President
Barack Obama

EARLY YEARS

Elizabeth Alexander was born on May 30, 1962, in Harlem, a section of New York City. Her father, Clifford Alexander, was a civil rights advisor to President Lyndon B. Johnson and also became the first African-American Secretary of the Army. Later he established his own political consulting business. Her mother, Adele Alexander, was a writer and professor who became professor of African-American women's history at

George Washington University. The family also included a younger brother, Mark, a professor of constitutional law and politics who served as an advisor to Barack Obama during his presidential campaign.

Alexander's parents moved to Washington DC shortly after her birth. She was just a toddler when her parents brought her to the 1963 March on Washington. Although she doesn't remember any of it, she was a witness to Martin Luther King Jr.'s famous "I Have a Dream" speech. Her family was dedicated to the causes of civil rights and public service. "[Politics] was in the drinking water in my house," she recalled. Education was important, but so were the arts. "I grew up taking ballet," Alexander revealed. "Very seriously and quite regularly. I think that listening to music and trying to learn how to make my body do things with music and trying to be, as our teachers would say, sensitive to the music, have a lot to do with trying to have and utilize an ear in poetry." She was also fascinated by words and the way people spoke. She had family from Alabama, Jamaica, and New York City, and they could "tell you [the same thing] in such different ways," she said. "I was intrigued that there were so many variations and possibilities in the language."

EDUCATION

Alexander went to Sidwell Friends School, the private school in Washington DC attended by many children of prominent politicians, including the daughters of President Barack Obama. She graduated in 1980 and entered Yale University, where she received a Bachelor of Arts (BA) degree in 1984. She studied poetry at Boston University under Nobel Prize-winning poet Derek Walcott and received her Master of Arts (MA) degree in 1987. She received a doctorate (PhD) in English from the University of Pennsylvania in 1992.

MAJOR ACCOMPLISHMENTS

Becoming a Poet and Professor

Although Alexander would become famous worldwide for the poem she composed for President Barack Obama's inauguration, she didn't graduate from Yale intending to become a poet. She worked as a reporter for the *Washington Post* from 1984 to 1985 before realizing "it wasn't the life I wanted," she recalled. "My mother said, 'That poet you love, Derek Walcott, is teaching at Boston University. Why don't you apply." Alexander entered the program to study fiction writing, but Walcott looked at her diary and showed her the poetry within. "He gave me a huge gift," the author said. "He took a cluster of words and he lineated it. And I saw it." At this

Miss Crandall's School for Young Ladies, *a book of poetry that Alexander co-wrote with Marilyn Nelson, was her first book for young readers.*

time she also discovered a love for teaching and began working towards a career as a professor.

While she was finishing her doctoral degree (PhD) at the University of Pennsylvania, Alexander taught at nearby Haverford College from 1990 to 1991. In 1991 she also published her first poetry collection, titled *The Venus Hottentot.* The title poem is from the point of view of Sarah Baartman, a 19th-century South African woman of the Khoikhoi ethnic group. Baartman agreed to travel to Europe as part of a traveling exhibit so that people could marvel at the shape of her buttocks, which were unusually large but normal for her tribe. In other portions of the book Alexander writes about her family and some of her artistic heroes. Reviewing the collection in *Poetry* magazine, Stephen Yenser remarked, "I am sure, or as sure as I can be, that it will be a landmark in American poetry, and that *The Venus Hottentot* is a superb first book, and that Elizabeth Alexander can be about as good a poet as she cares to be."

Alexander began teaching at the University of Chicago in 1991, serving as an assistant professor of English. There she first met Barack Obama, who was a senior lecturer at the university's law school from 1992 until his election to the U.S. Senate in 2004. She lived near Obama and his wife, Michelle, and introduced them to her brother,

Mark, a law professor who later worked on Obama's presidential campaign and transition team.

Alexander continued growing as a writer while in Chicago. In 1992 she won a creative writing fellowship from the National Endowment for the Arts, and in 1996 she produced both a volume of poetry, *Body of Life,* and a verse play, *Diva Studies,* which was staged at Yale University. Alexander also continued to advance her academic career during this time. In 1996 she became a founding faculty member of the *Cave Canem* workshop, which helps develop African-American poets. The following year she received the University of Chicago's Quantrell Award for Excellence in Undergraduate Teaching. In 1997 Alexander moved to Massachusetts to work at Smith College, one of the country's most prestigious women's colleges. She served as the Grace Hazard Conkling Poet-in-Residence and became the first director of the college's Poetry Center.

In 2000 Alexander returned to Yale University, where she became a professor in African-American studies and English. The following year she published a third poetry collection, *Antebellum Dream Book.* Her poems once again explored topics that were personal, popular, and historical. In some poems she remembers growing up in the civil rights movement; in others she imagines interacting with novelist Toni Morrison, basketball player Michael Jordan, singer Nat King Cole, and comedian Richard Pryor. The poem "Narrative: Ali" imagines the voice of boxing legend Muhammad Ali. According to Jace Clayton, a critic for the *Washington Post,* the collection "sports the page-turning pull of a good story, the intimacy of personal verse, and an unforced braininess that so few smart poets can get right."

Developing as a Writer

Alexander continued developing her reputation as a poet and scholar in the new century. She won a Guggenheim Foundation fellowship in 2002 and published her first collection of essays in 2004. A *Booklist* reviewer called *The Black Interior* an "original and electrifying collection [that] greatly enriches and extends understanding of African-American culture and its essential role in American culture as a whole." In 2005 she won one of the first Alphonse Fletcher Sr. fellowships, a $50,000 award supporting people who further the goals of civil rights and racial understanding. That same year she published another book of poetry, *American Sublime.* It was another combination of personal and historical themes, with one section in particular exploring the true story of the slave ship *Amistad.* In 1839, more than 50 African captives took control of *Amistad* as it sailed from Cuba to America and successfully won their freedom in a Connecticut court. *American Sublime* was a finalist for the 2005 Pulitzer Prize in Poetry.

Alexander explained her fascination with using American and especially African-American history in her poems: "Our history is so rich, but there are so many stories within it that haven't yet been told, or have been improperly told, or that can yield something particular when explored through poetry." One such story can be found in Alexander's first poetry collection for young readers, written with Marilyn Nelson and published in 2007. *Miss Crandall's School for Young Ladies and Little Misses of Color* is based on the true story of Prudence Crandall, a Connecticut school teacher who opened the first school for African-American girls in New England. Through 24 poems—all in sonnet form—Alexander and Nelson give the students voice as they relate how their school is shunned and eventually destroyed by racial hatred.

By 2008, Alexander had achieved renown as a poet and professor. In 2007 she had published a second volume of essays, *Power and Possibility*, and received the first $50,000 Jackson Poetry Prize. This award recognizes a poet who has published at least one book of poems but has not received "major national acclaim."

"I continue to advocate for the necessity of the arts in everybody's day-to-day life," Alexander asserted. "If [the inaugural poem] means those things that I'm trained to talk about will get more hearing, that would be fantastic."

An Inaugural Honor

In 2008, Barack Obama was elected the 44th President of the United States. At that time, Alexander was not widely known outside of academic circles, but then the president-elect selected her to write a poem to be read at his inauguration. She was thrilled that President Obama had commissioned her to write a poem. "I think that he is showing that moments of pause and contemplation in the midst of grand occasion and everyday life are necessary," she said.

Alexander believed she was chosen not because of her friendship with Obama—he and his wife know several poets—but because of her voice. To be chosen to read at the inauguration made her feel "very, very, very humble," although she wasn't scared of having to read in front of an estimated audience of two million people. "Not only is the audience enormous, but unimaginably diverse," she explained. "Paradoxically, what is freeing is

Alexander reciting her poem, "Praise Song for the Day," at the 2009 inauguration of President Barack Obama.

when you really don't know [the audience], you have to listen to and trust your own voice." Poet Maya Angelou, one of only three other poets to read at a presidential inauguration, expressed confidence in the selection of Alexander: "She seems much like Walt Whitman," Angelou told the *New York Times*. "She sings the American song."

On January 20, 2009, Alexander shared the stage with the newly inaugurated President Obama and read her 341-word poem, "Praise Song for the Day." Her poem spoke of everyday American lives, the sacrifices that led to this historic moment, and the power of language: "We encounter each other in words, words/ spiny or smooth, whispered or declaimed;/ words to consider, reconsider." Her concluding lines reflected the sense of hope and inspiration many felt on the occasion: "In today's sharp sparkle, this winter air,/ any thing can be made, any sentence begun./ On the brink, on the brim, on the cusp,/ praise song for walking forward in that light."

"Words matter. Language matters. We live in and express ourselves with language, and that is how we communicate and move through the world in community," Alexander explained. "Poetry is not meant to cheer; rather, poetry challenges.... Language distilled and artfully arranged shifts our experience of the words—and the worldviews—we live in."

Readers around the world critiqued Alexander's poem—some found it too prosaic, others thought it suited to the occasion—but what mattered to Alexander was the visibility her role on Inauguration Day gave to her work and literature in general. "I continue to advocate for the necessity of the arts in everybody's day-to-day life," she asserted. "If [the inaugural poem] means those things that I'm trained to talk about will get more hearing, that would be fantastic." In addition, she looked forward to becoming chairperson of Yale's African American Studies department beginning in summer 2009, and bringing poetry to more people. "Words matter. Language matters. We live in and express ourselves with language, and that is how we communicate and move through the world in community," she explained. "Poetry is not meant to cheer; rather, poetry challenges, and moves us towards transformation. Language distilled and artfully arranged shifts our experience of the words—and the worldviews—we live in."

MARRIAGE AND FAMILY

Alexander married Gustavo A. Paredes, a salesman, on September 18, 1993. They have two sons and live in the New Haven, Connecticut, area.

SELECTED WRITINGS

The Venus Hottentot, 1990 (poetry)
Body of Life, 1996 (poetry)
Diva Studies, 1996 (play in verse)
Antebellum Dream Book, 2001 (poetry)
The Black Interior, 2004 (essays)
American Sublime, 2005 (poetry)
Miss Crandall's School for Young Ladies and Little Misses of Color, 2007 (young adult poetry, with Marilyn Nelson)
Power and Possibility, 2007 (essays)
"Praise Song for the Day," 2009 (inaugural poem)

HONORS AND AWARDS

George Kent Prize (*Poetry* magazine): 1992, 1997
Pushcart Prize for Poetry (Pushcart Press): 1998, 2000, 2001
Guggenheim Foundation Fellowship: 2002
Alphonse Fletcher Sr. Fellowship: 2005
Jackson Poetry Prize (Poets & Writers): 2007

FURTHER READING

Periodicals

Booklist, Jan. 1, 2004, p.794
New York Times, Dec. 21, 2008; Dec. 25, 2008, p.C1; Jan. 18, 2009, p.CT5
New York Times Book Review, Sep. 30, 1990
Poetry, July 1991, p.214
Radcliffe Quarterly, Summer 2008
Wall Street Journal, Dec. 20, 2008, p.W4
Washington Post, Oct. 21, 2001, p.T13; Dec. 18, 2008, p.A1; Jan. 21, 2009, p.C10

Online Articles

http://www.pbs.org/newshour
(PBS, "Poet Elizabeth Alexander Reflects on Inaugural Reading," Jan. 13, 2009)

http://www.poetryfoundation.org
(Poetry Foundation, "Poet Elizabeth Alexander," 2009)
http://www.time.com
(Time, "Q&A: Inauguration Poet Elizabeth Alexander," Jan. 20, 2009)

ADDRESS

Elizabeth Alexander
Department of African American Studies
Yale University
81 Wall Street
New Haven, CT 06510

WORLD WIDE WEB SITE

http://www.elizabethalexander.net

Will Allen 1949-

American Urban Farmer and Activist
Pioneer in the Development of Community-Based Urban Farming

BIRTH

William Edward Allen was born on February 8, 1949, to Willie Mae and O.W. Allen. His mother worked as a housekeeper, and his father was a former sharecropper. The second youngest of seven kids, Allen grew up on a farm in Rockville, Maryland, outside Washington DC. His parents had purchased the farm after moving from South Carolina.

YOUTH

As a boy, Allen had plenty of farming chores. He learned early on that farming was physically demanding yet rewarding work. He and his siblings would put in long hours tilling the soil and pulling weeds. Come harvest time, they enjoyed the fruits of all their labor. The farm produced 85 percent of the food the family ate, and Allen enjoyed his share. "There was always food on the stove. And Willie ate more than anybody," his older brother Joe remembered.

"My parents were the biggest influence on my life," said Allen. "We didn't have a TV and we relied on a wood stove, but we were known as the 'food family' because we had so much food."

The Allens didn't live in luxury, but Willie Mae and O.W. provided their children with plenty of guidance and other essentials. "My parents were the biggest influence on my life," said Allen. "We didn't have a TV and we relied on a wood stove, but we were known as the 'food family' because we had so much food."

When Allen was 13, he started playing basketball. He wasn't an all-star right away, but he knew that he could build on his athleticism and his size. "I could run like a deer, and I was really strong," he said. He was also dedicated to improving his game. He even fashioned a makeshift court by flattening out some ground on the farm and hanging a bushel basket on an oak tree. By pointing a flashlight at the basket, he ensured that he could play into the evening.

EDUCATION

The late-night sessions served Allen well as he continued to improve and grow taller. While attending Julius West Junior High in Rockville, he became the star of the eighth-grade team. Rival teams feared him as the only player who could dunk the ball. By the time he began playing for Richard Montgomery High School, he towered over most players, standing at six feet seven inches tall and weighing 230 pounds.

When Allen was only a sophomore, the *Washington Post* selected him for the All-Metropolitan team, placing him among the best-ranked players in Washington DC and surrounding counties. In 1966, his junior year, Allen led his team to win the Maryland state championship. His squad lost in the state finals the following year, but he was selected for the All-American team, one of the highest distinctions in high school athletics. He also received a scholarship to play for the University of Miami in Coral Gables, Florida.

Allen majored in physical education at the University of Miami, and he made school history as the Hurricanes' first African-American basketball player. He attended college during the late 1960s, a time of deep divisions in race relations in the United States. Allen even received death letters from Ku Klux Klan members, showing that some Floridians had no tolerance for black athletes playing for the university. But Ron Godfrey, the coach at the time, saw a determination in Allen that helped him handle opponents on and off the court. "He put his heart and soul into everything he did," Godfrey said, "and encouraged other young black players to come to Miami at a time when schools were just integrating."

Along with excelling on the court, Allen also proved he was an activist who could rally support for a cause. During his junior season, the school's Board of Trustees issued a sudden announcement that it was about to cancel the basketball program, which spelled disaster for the players since they did not have enough time to transfer to another school. Allen quickly organized his teammates to wage a player strike and hold a press conference. The campaign attracted the attention of the national press, which forced the Board to extend the basketball program for another year. Allen was thus able to play in his senior year. He graduated from the University of Miami in 1971.

CAREER HIGHLIGHTS

Playing Professional Basketball

Allen left college prepared for a bright future. Not only was he on track to play basketball professionally, but he was also married already. He had met his wife, Cynthia, early in his college years, and they were married on February 8, 1969.

Allen was drafted to play for the Baltimore Bullets (the former name of the Washington Wizards), but he quickly transferred to the Miami Floridians, a team that was part of the short-lived American Basketball Association. After finishing the 1971-1972 season with the Floridians, Allen decided to play with the European Professional League.

While living in Belgium and playing in the European Professional League, Allen made friends with some local farmers. He found that the more time

Allen developed a love of farming as a child and then returned to that early love as an adult.

he spent with them, the more they brought him back to his family roots. "They farmed a lot like we used to," Allen recalled. "It must have released a hidden passion in me, because before I left Belgium, I had a garden and some chickens of my own."

In 1977, Allen ended his basketball career and returned to the United States. By that time he and Cynthia were the parents of three children under the age of eight: Erika, Jason, and then Adriana. Allen and the family settled in Cynthia's hometown of Milwaukee, Wisconsin, where some of her family lived.

Allen took a series of full-time jobs, first as an executive at Marcus Corp. and then as a technology salesperson for Procter & Gamble. The work paid well, but over time farming became more attractive to him. "I needed the farm—it's so real and so satisfying," he said. "Mostly, I wanted that life for my kids."

Preserving the Family Farming Legacy

In 1982, Allen quit his job at Procter & Gamble and picked up the vocation he had forsaken years ago. "I remember when I left for Coral Gables, telling my father, 'I will never work on a farm again.' I guess you should never say never." With money from a hefty settlement package with Procter & Gamble, he bought a junkyard tractor and 100 acres of land in Oak Creek, a suburb south of Milwaukee.

Using the sales skills he acquired during his corporate career, Allen sold his vegetables at local markets. He also asked his kids to work on the farm, just as his father did with him. It wasn't a rich life, but by preserving the legacy of the older generation, Allen and his family were learning self-reliance—and enjoying all the good food that came with it. Erika remembered, "My dad would always say, 'You'll thank me someday 'cause you know how to work and grow food.'"

While living in Belgium and playing in the European Professional League, Allen made friends with some local farmers. He found that the more time he spent with them, the more they brought him back to his family roots. "They farmed a lot like we used to," Allen recalled. "It must have released a hidden passion in me, because before I left Belgium, I had a garden and some chickens of my own."

Nine years into his new enterprise, Allen was eager to expand his operations. He set his sights on a two-acre parcel of land on the north side of Milwaukee. The plot was on a busy street, making it an optimal spot for business. Allen was also happy to know he was saving what was the last remaining farmland in the city, in a low-income neighborhood that was once known for its agricultural activities but now provided minimal access to healthy, affordable food.

Settling in what was once called Greenhouse Alley, he constructed a greenhouse of his own. Will's Roadside Stand soon became a popular stop for organic produce. During that time he also established the Rainbow Grower's Cooperative, which connected family farmers outside Milwaukee to consumers in the city.

Soon, Allen was receiving several requests for help to start up gardening projects. In 1995 a group from a nearby YWCA came to him for ideas on how neighborhood youths could make a small organic garden profitable. He offered them a one-half acre of unused land behind his greenhouse. The kids got to work and soon were producing a healthy crop. Having the children nearby provided an opportunity for Allen to do some mentoring.

"I talked to them about how the garden was teaching basic life skills: how to get up in the morning, how to be responsible for growing something," he said.

Developing a Nonprofit Farming Group

An idea for a nonprofit organization began forming in discussions between Allen and other local urban farming enthusiasts with whom he had begun partnering. He was certain he wanted to use sustainable practices to grow crops and distribute them in what he calls "food deserts," urban areas where there is plenty of junk food for sale but not much affordable produce. He also wanted his organization to include a mentoring program for Milwaukee's youth. Finally, no matter what, his collaborators got a clear message that he needed his approach to remain hands-on. "I told them the only thing I wanted to do was to have my hands in the soil and help teach these kids," he said.

Allen started mentoring the kids who came to his farm. "I talked to them about how the garden was teaching basic life skills: how to get up in the morning, how to be responsible for growing something," he said.

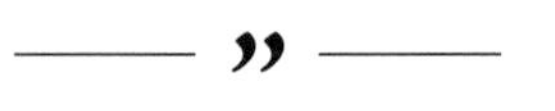

Under Allen's leadership, Farm City Link formed in 1995. A year later, he was approached by Heifer Project International, a charitable organization that helps to relieve hunger through old and new agricultural techniques. The Heifer Project had several ideas on how Farm City Link could expand its operations, including setting up a fish farm of 150 tilapia; bringing in a large supply of red worms to enrich the soil of the vegetable beds; and implementing a hydroponics system, which uses a nutrient-rich solution to grow plants in water. Allen eagerly used all of Heifer Project's ideas at Farm City Link.

In those first years, Farm City Link struggled financially. One of the major challenges for Allen was figuring out how to grow a large amount of crops in the facility's tight quarters, which, along with the raised vegetable beds, had to make room for chickens, ducks, goats, and farmed fish. He also felt divided between remaining productive and keeping his commitment to training new farmers. Those concerns were addressed in 1998, when he met Hope Finkelstein. An organizer and activist, Finkelstein had recently formed Growing Power, a nonprofit group with a similar focus. Impressed

When children got involved at the farm, Allen's role grew to include mentorship.

with Farm City Link's work, Finkelstein suggested they increase their capacity by merging the two organizations, with Allen as co-director.

Allen agreed wholeheartedly with the proposal. He immediately identified with the name Growing Power, which aligned with his goal to "grow communities by growing sustainable food sources." In 1999, the building once known as Will's Roadside Stand became Growing Power's Community Food Center, where farmers young and old received training and assistance in farming practices.

The group's mission became to support people from diverse backgrounds by providing equal access to healthy, high-quality, safe and affordable food. To reach this goal, Growing Power provides hands-on training, on-the-ground demonstrations, outreach, and technical assistance—all with the goal of helping people grow, process, market, and distribute food in a sustainable manner. According to the group's web site, "Our goal is a simple one: to grow food, to grow minds, and to grow community. Growing Power began with a farmer, a plot of land, and a core group of dedicated young people. Today, our love of the land and our dedication to sharing knowledge is changing lives."

Involving kids in the farming community is an important part of the Growing Power mission. The organization promotes the Growing Power Youth Corps, a youth development apprenticeship program that gives academic and professional experience to kids from low-income backgrounds. Kids in the Youth Corps can learn about different farming methods, develop leadership experience, build entrepreneurial skills, and learn to work with diverse groups of people.

Branching Out

As Allen's vision became a reality in Milwaukee, he and his organization decided to start another program in a nearby city. Growing Power selected Chicago for the new program and asked Allen's eldest daughter, Erika, to lead it. Now an adult and an art teacher, Erika had a special bond with kids, along with plenty of farming know-how. The new branch opened in February 2002 and began establishing more Community Food Centers. From the beginning, Allen showed confidence that his daughter could handle the challenges of the job. "People admire Erika's intelligence and grasp," he said. "But her commitment and passion are incredible, and that's what it really takes."

"Will Allen is an urban farmer who is transforming the cultivation, production, and delivery of healthy foods to underserved, urban populations," according to the award statement from the John D. and Catherine T. MacArthur Foundation. "Allen is experimenting with new and creative ways to improve the diet and health of the urban poor."

In 2002 the Growing Power farm was producing over 100,000 pounds of chemical-free vegetables and continually adding more staff and volunteers to its operations. To remain productive, Allen needed to locate more funding, and he did that in 2005 when he won the Ford Foundation Leadership for a Changing World Award, which included a $100,000 grant from the Ford Foundation.

Three years later, in 2008, Allen received the highly prestigious "genius grant" from the John D. and Catherine T. MacArthur Foundation. The $500,000 award for MacArthur Fellows is presented to "individuals across all ages and fields who show exceptional merit and promise of continued creative work." In the award statement, the organization said that "Will

The Growing Power Youth Corps is an apprenticeship program that involves neighborhood kids in farming, entrepreneurship, and leadership activities.

Allen is an urban farmer who is transforming the cultivation, production, and delivery of healthy foods to underserved, urban populations.... Allen is experimenting with new and creative ways to improve the diet and health of the urban poor." To Allen, the award helped signify that public attitudes about his line of work were dramatically changing. "I think it's really a recognition that will really help push this movement forward so people start eating healthier," he said.

News of Allen's award led to a string of interviews with "Good Morning America," CNN, National Public Radio, and the *New York Times*. By that time, Growing Power had literally gone global. Over the course of distant travels, Allen had conducted trainings in Africa, Europe, and South America. The Growing Power headquarters had become massive, now with three dozen full-time employees working in five large greenhouses and annually producing half a million dollars worth of fresh, organic food. Now the leader of a large organization, Allen could still experience the simple joy of getting kids excited about farming. "You just see the enthusiasm in the young people grow right along with the tomatoes and peppers," he said.

Future Plans

Allen's enterprises have been ambitious thus far, but his future ideas for Growing Power could surpass them all. His dream for the main facility includes a five-story, glass-walled building that would act as a vertical farm. Allen and other pioneers see vertical farming as a powerful solution to today's challenges of large-scale agriculture. Like the present facility, the building would devote resources to farming instruction. "Three-fourths of the building would be used for growing, and the other part would be classrooms for teaching," he explained.

As wild as Allen's idea sounds, he has the support of the organization. Said Growing Power board president Jerome Kaufman: "Yes, it will be a major shift. But Will is an innovator. He has started new ventures. He has done this all of his career."

Now the leader of a large organization, Allen could still experience the simple joy of getting kids excited about farming. "You just see the enthusiasm in the young people grow right along with the tomatoes and peppers," he said.

MARRIAGE AND FAMILY

Allen has been married to his wife Cynthia for over 40 years. They have three children: their daughter Erika works for Growing Power; their son Jason is a lawyer; and their daughter Adriana is a model/actress.

Of the three children, Allen spends the most time with Erika, since they work together. "I had my kids when I was very young, so I grew up with them," he explained. "But we've made that transformation from father/daughter to friends.... Now it's more equal." In collaborating with and teaching Erika what he knows, Allen knows she will in turn pass on the tradition to other farmers. As she explained, "I have that legacy—that generational appreciation—because my dad sacrificed so much of his time to develop something."

HOBBIES AND OTHER INTERESTS

Because Growing Power has become such a large organization, serving as its director takes up most of Allen's time. He does, however, set aside time to watch basketball. He sometimes flies down to the University of Miami to attend home games at his alma mater. An enthusiastic eater and cook,

Allen also will stop his work routine to fix a tasty meal for his employees using ingredients from Growing Power's greenhouses.

HONORS AND AWARDS

Leadership for a Changing World Award (Ford Foundation): 2005
MacArthur Fellowship Award (MacArthur Foundation): 2008

FURTHER READING

Periodicals

Better Homes and Gardens, Summer 2007, p.64
Christian Science Monitor, Jan. 29, 2009, p.17
Madison Capital Times, Sep. 25, 2008
Milwaukee Journal Sentinel, Apr. 19, 2008; Sep. 23, 2008; Oct. 6, 2008; Jan. 27, 2009
Money, Sep. 2002, p.30
New York Times, Oct. 1, 2008, p.6
Yes! Magazine, Spring 2009

Online Articles

http://www.biztimes.com
(Biztimes, "Growing Power: The Farm in the City," May 30, 2008)
http://www.macfound.org
(The John D. and Catherine T. MacArthur Foundation, "2008 MacArthur Fellows: Will Allen," Sep. 2008)
http://www.progressillinois.com
(Progress Illinois, "A Growing Movement: Urban Farming in Chicago," Sep. 9, 2008)
http://www.urbanitebaltimore.com
(Urbanite, "MacArthur Award Winner Will Allen on Raising Food—and Farmers—in the Inner City," Nov. 2008)

ADDRESS

Will Allen
Growing Power
5500 West Silver Spring Drive
Milwaukee, WI 53218

WORLD WIDE WEB SITES

http://www.growingpower.org

2005 © SPARC *www.sparcmurals.org*

Judy Baca 1946-

American Mural Artist, Educator, and Community Arts Pioneer

Creator of the Collaborative Murals *The Great Wall of Los Angeles* and *The World Wall: A Vision of the Future without Fear*

BIRTH

Judith Francisca Baca was born on September 20, 1946, in Los Angeles, California. She never knew her father, Valentino Marcel, who was a musician. She was raised by her mother, Ortencia, who worked in a tire factory. Baca has a half-brother, Gary, who was born in 1952, and a half-sister, Diane, who was born in 1957.

YOUTH

Baca grew up in a Spanish-speaking household in Watts, a predominantly Mexican-American neighborhood in south central Los Angeles. She lived with her mother, her grandmother Francisca, and her aunts Rita and Delia. While her mother worked to support the family, Baca was cared for mostly by her grandmother. Known as the neighborhood healer, Baca's grandmother practiced *curanderismo,* a form of Mexican folk medicine that combines traditional beliefs and herbal remedies to cure illness.

In a household of independent, self-sufficient women, Baca learned to form her own opinions at an early age. "The formative years, the most important years, were really good for me because, first of all, I didn't have any sense of the limits of what women could do," she recalled. "I did not have the appropriate role models of what girls were supposed to do or not do." Baca has said that she was very happy during these early years.

"The formative years, the most important years, were really good for me because, first of all, I didn't have any sense of the limits of what women could do," Baca recalled. "I did not have the appropriate role models of what girls were supposed to do or not do."

In 1952, when Baca was six years old, her mother married Clarence Ferrari. Baca, her mother, and her new stepfather moved to Pacoima, a suburb of Los Angeles in the San Fernando Valley. Baca's whole world changed with that move. Mexican Americans were the minority in her new neighborhood, and her Italian stepfather did not allow Spanish to be spoken at home. Her grandmother and aunts stayed behind in the old neighborhood, and Baca missed them very much.

EDUCATION

Baca had a difficult time when she started school. She was not allowed to speak Spanish at school, even though she didn't understand very much English. Some of her teachers and classmates treated her unfairly because she was Mexican American. Baca struggled with her classes and worked hard to learn English quickly so that she could understand her textbooks and what was being said around her.

As Baca improved in English, her schoolwork became easier. She did well in every class, but her favorite was art. With the encouragement of her art teacher, she began to spend as much time as she could painting and drawing. In 1964, Baca graduated from Bishop Alemany High School in Mission Hills, California.

After high school, Baca attended California State University at Northridge, where she continued studying art. At that time, abstract modern art was very popular in art schools and galleries. Abstract art does not portray objects and people as they actually are. Instead, abstract artists use different colors and shapes to show how they imagine things to be, or to tell a story with pictures. Sometimes abstract art looks so unusual that people may not understand it at first. Abstract modern art is usually displayed in galleries, museums, or inside other buildings. Baca liked painting abstract art, but she also wanted to make art that was easy for people to understand and available for everyone to see.

"I thought to myself, if I get my work into galleries, who will go there? People in my family had never been in a gallery in their entire lives. My neighbors never went to galleries. All the people I know didn't go to galleries.... And it didn't make sense to me at the time to put art behind some guarded wall."

Baca knew that she wanted to make art for the people in her life, like her grandmother, her aunts, and others in the neighbhorhood where she grew up. But they did not go to galleries to look at art. "I thought to myself, if I get my work into galleries, who will go there? People in my family had never been in a gallery in their entire lives. My neighbors never went to galleries. All the people I know didn't go to galleries.... And it didn't make sense to me at the time to put art behind some guarded wall." Baca decided that she would make art that was somehow connected to her Mexican-American background. She would combine the abstract artist's way of seeing the world with the bright colors and bold shapes that were traditionally found in Mexican folk art.

In 1969, Baca received a bachelor of arts (BA) degree in art from California State University at Northridge. She earned a master of arts (MA) degree in art education in 1979 from the same university.

CAREER HIGHLIGHTS

After more than 40 years as an artist, Baca is best known for her murals in public places. She has created murals in a wide variety of forms, including painting, tile mosaic, digital imaging, and collages incorporating

Baca has often involved the community in creating her art work, particularly young people. Here she is shown with the mural crew at The Great Wall of Los Angeles, *1983. © SPARC www.sparcmurals.org*

such different materials as photographs, letters, and original artwork. Her murals cover a range of subjects, often reflecting her commitment to social justice and her heritage as a Chicana. These subjects have included the history of California, the journey of immigrants from Mexico to Colorado, civil rights, visions of world peace, and memorials to such renowned individuals as Dr. Martin Luther King Jr., Robert F. Kennedy, and Cesar Chavez.

Baca's work is founded on time-honored mural techniques established by generations of Mexican and Mexican-American artists, and many art experts see echoes of this artistic tradition in her murals. But she has also expanded this tradition, experts say, moving it a step forward. For example, she has developed new ways to design murals using computers and new methods of installing murals in public spaces so the artwork can be better preserved over time. As a result, Baca is considered a pioneer in the field of mural-making.

Becoming an Artist

Baca first began making murals in 1969. She had just graduated from California State University and found her first job teaching art at her former high school. She liked her job, but she found that different groups of students did not get along with each other very well. This was causing problems throughout the school. It was difficult for teachers to manage their classrooms, and students often fought outside of class.

Baca had an idea that she thought would help students learn to cooperate with each other. She decided to have a group of students work together to paint a mural on one of the school's walls. She explained to the group of students that they would have to figure out how to get along with each other and work together on the mural. Everyone wanted to participate in the mural project, so they learned to work with each other without fighting. Baca hoped that by helping the students work together on the mural, they might also be able to learn to cooperate with people in other areas of their lives. This was her first attempt at a cooperative art project, with many people working together to make art, and also her first attempt at a project involving young people. It was a success.

Baca's success in teaching at that high school was short-lived, however. Around the same time that she started teaching, she became involved in *El Movimiento* ("the movement"). In the mid-1960s and early 1970s, people who participated in *El Movimiento* worked for civil rights, peace, and an end to discrimination against Hispanic Americans. Baca took part in demonstrations and protests against the Vietnam War. The principal of the school where she taught believed that teachers should not take part in these protest marches. Baca and several other teachers were fired for their participation.

Working for the City of Los Angeles

At first Baca was worried that she would never find another teaching job because she had taken part in the controversial anti-war protests. However, she was soon hired by the city of Los Angeles to work in their Parks and Recreation Department. In her new job, Baca taught art for a summer program in the city's public parks. There she worked with people of all ages, in many different neighborhoods.

One neighborhood, known as Boyle Heights, had the most Mexican Americans as well as the highest number of gangs in the country at that time. Members of different gangs hung out in each of the parks where she worked, and there was gang graffiti everywhere. Baca knew that the graffiti marked the territory of each gang. The graffiti was a way for the gang members to feel like the neighborhood belonged to them, and that they belonged in that neighborhood. "You could read a wall and learn everything you needed to know about that community." One of her favorite graffiti markings was "I'd rather spend one day as a lion than a hundred years as a lamb."

As Baca traveled from one park to another teaching in the art program, she started to see the deep divisions within the community of Boyle Heights. She had begun getting to know many of the teeanagers who spent time in each of the parks where she worked. Baca saw that she had the freedom to go to any park in the neighborhood, but these teenagers did not. Each gang stayed in its own park or faced the consequences of fighting with a rival gang in another park.

> *"It seemed to me that the only real answer if art was not to be an elitist practice was to bring it to the people, to paint in the places where people lived and worked."*

Baca wanted to find a way to use art to bring the neighborhood together, instead of dividing the community the way the gang's graffiti did. She decided to create a mural in Boyle Heights. She wanted to use the mural as a positive way for people to feel that the neighborhood was theirs. To do this, the mural would be a cooperative art project, with many people working together on it.

Las Vistas Nuevas and *Mi Abuelita*

In the summer of 1970, Baca created her first mural team. She included 20 members of four different gangs and named the team *Las Vistas Nuevas* ("New Views"). The mural created by Las Vistas Nuevas would show images that would be familiar to the Mexican Americans who lived in the neighborhood. Baca wanted the mural to reflect the community's Mexican heritage. "I want to use public space to create a public voice for, and a public consciousness about people who are, in fact, the majority of the population but who are not represented in any visual way," she declared. In the process of making the mural, she hoped that team members would learn to share public spaces and respect each other, and, most importantly, that they could get along with people from different gangs. In this way, Baca hoped the team members would get a new view of themselves, their neighborhood, and their lives.

The first mural created by Las Vistas Nuevas was on the three walls of an outdoor stage in Hollenbeck Park. Titled *Mi Abuelita* ("My Grandmother"),

Mi Abuelita *was Baca's first collaborative mural, and the grandmother's outstretched arms made it a welcoming image in the community. Located in Hollenbeck Park band shell, the mural was developed with a youth team, Las Vistas Nuevas, from four neighborhoods in East Los Angeles. 20 ft. x 35 ft., acrylic on cement. © SPARC www.sparcmurals.org*

the mural's central image was a typical Mexican-American grandmother with her arms outstretched as if to give a hug. "This work recognized the primary position of the matriarch [female leader] in Mexican families," she observed. "It also marked the first step in the development of a unique collective process that employs art to mediate between rival gang members competing for public space and public identity."

Baca faced many challenges with this first mural. She had to help her team members learn to work together in spite of their differences. Every day, there were problems with gang members who were not on the mural team and didn't like what she was doing. They tried to interfere with the project by threatening team members and vandalizing the work site. The local police didn't like the idea of Baca encouraging rival gang members to gather together because they thought it would increase gang violence. Also, she had started to work on the mural without permission from the city or the manager of Hollenbeck Park, which raised questions from her supervisor and other city officials.

In spite of all this, Baca was dedicated to completing the mural, so she handled problems as they arose. She posted lookouts who would signal the mural team if rival gang members were headed toward the work site. Another signal let the team know if police officers were approaching. One day, a city official came to Hollenbeck Park because he had been getting complaints about Baca's project. After seeing the progress that the team had made, and how well everyone was getting along with each other, he told Baca that she could finish the mural with the city's permission. "The city was amazed at the work I was doing," she stressed, "making murals with kids who scared directors out of neighborhood centers."

"This work [Mi Abuelita] *recognized the primary position of the matriarch [female leader] in Mexican families," Baca observed. "It also marked the first step in the development of a unique collective process that employs art to mediate between rival gang members competing for public space and public identity."*

Response to *Mi Abuelita*

When *Mi Abuelita* was completed, the community loved it. The mural brought the neighborhood together, and the grandmother figure with its outstretched arms became a symbol for unity. "Everybody related to it," Baca recalled. "People brought candles to that site. For 12 years people put flowers at the base of the grandmother image." During the rest of that summer, Las Vistas Nuevas completed a total of three murals in Boyle Heights.

After proving herself with the success of her independent mural project, Baca was offered a job in 1970 as the director of a new citywide mural program. She was put in charge of creating the program from the ground up, including choosing where murals would go, designing the murals, and supervising the mural painting teams. Team members were teenagers who had been in trouble with the police. Members of the original Las Vistas Nuevas team were hired to help run the multi-site program. The program included hundreds of young people representing many different ethnic and cultural backgrounds, and ultimately they painted more than 500 murals under Baca's direction.

While running the citywide mural program, Baca had her first problems with censorship. People in the communities where the murals were being

A view of The Great Wall of Los Angeles, *a 13 ft. x 2,400 ft. mural located in the Tujunga Wash, a flood control channel. The world's longest mural depicts a multi-cultural history of California from prehistoric times. This section of the wall shows the later panels depicting the 1950s. Acrylic on cast concrete. © SPARC www.sparcmurals.org*

made wanted the murals to show all the parts of life in their neighborhood—both good and bad. The city government, however, did not want the murals to show anything controversial. For example, the city objected to part of one mural that showed people struggling with police. The city threatened to stop funding the mural program if Baca did not remove these images. She did not think that the city should censor public art created by residents of the community. "I really liked the idea that the work could not be owned by anyone," Baca explained. "So, therefore it wasn't going to be interesting to the rich or to the wealthy, and it didn't have to meet the caveats of art that museums would be interested in." Rather than give in to the city's demands, Baca founded the Social and Public Art Resource Center (SPARC) in 1976 to continue funding the creation of murals in public spaces.

The Great Wall of Los Angeles

SPARC began work on its first cooperative mural project in 1976. The U.S. Army Corps of Engineers hired Baca to help them improve the area around a San Fernando Valley flood control channel known as the Tujunga

Wash. This channel was basically a ditch that contained a large concrete retaining wall. The Army Corps of Engineers wanted to put a public park in the space, and they asked Baca to plan a mural for the wall.

The wall was 13.5 feet high and a half mile long—2,435 linear feet of concrete standing just below ground level. Baca's idea for the mural was to paint a history of the city of Los Angeles, but not the version found in history books. She wanted to show the events that were usually overlooked or forgotten and to include the stories of everyday people who lived and worked in Los Angeles as the city grew over time. "It was an excellent place to bring youth of varied ethnic backgrounds from all over the city to work on an alternate view of the history of the U.S. which included people of color who had been left out of American history books," she commented. The mural was to be titled *The Great Wall of Los Angeles.* According to Baca, the mural's defining metaphor would be the statement "It is a tattoo on the scar where the river once ran."

"Making a mural is like a big movie production," Baca said about creating The Great Wall, *which took seven summers to complete and is thought to be the world's longest mural. "It can involve 20 sets of scaffolding, four trucks, and food for 50 people."*

In her work on murals, Baca was inspired by the book *Los Tres Grandes (The Three Greats).* This book was about three of the most influential Mexican muralists: Diego Rivera, David Alfaro Siqueiros, and José Clemente Orozco. These three artists had modernized the centuries-old Mexican tradition of mural painting by pioneering new techniques, ideas, and styles. In 1977, Baca traveled to Mexico to see their murals first-hand. Although none of the three famous muralists were still living at that time, she was able to work with some former students of Siqueiros. From them she learned about advanced mural painting methods and the materials that she ultimately applied to the large-scale outdoor project *The Great Wall.*

Baca decided that the design of *The Great Wall* mural should be a cooperative project. She interviewed people about their lives, family histories, ancestry, and stories they remembered hearing from their older relatives. She also consulted many other artists as well as history experts. Putting together everything that she learned from these conversations, Baca began creating the design for the mural. It would include many different scenes illustrating the development of Los Angeles, with panels depicting these scenes arranged chronologically along the wall. One section showed dinosaurs in a tar pit. Another section featured Spanish explorers arriving in their ships. There were images of Chinese workers building the railroad, Mexican farm workers in the fields, and other immigrants arriving in California with hope for a better life. Baca also illustrated such controversial events as the great Dust Bowl Journey, the Zoot Suit Riots of 1942, Japanese Americans being taken to internment camps during World War II, and the Freedom Bus Rides. Some of these sections of *The Great Wall* represented the first time the events had ever been acknowledged in such a public way.

Baca also decided that the painting of *The Great Wall* mural should be a cooperative project. Painting was done by groups of teenagers and adults of all ages and backgrounds. Some were scholars and artists, but many were simply community members. Some were paid workers, while others were volunteers. "Making a mural is like a big movie production," Baca said, "it can involve 20 sets of scaffolding, four trucks, and food for 50 people." In the end, 400 people contributed to the mural, which took seven summers to complete. *The Great Wall,* completed in 1984, is thought to be the world's longest mural. It has been called "the largest monument to interracial harmony in America" and a "landmark pictorial representation of the history of ethnic peoples of California from their origins to the 1950s." It stands as one of Baca's greatest accomplishments.

The World Wall

In the early 1980s, while still working on *The Great Wall,* Baca took a teaching position at the University of California at Irvine. In 1981, she developed the Muralist Training Workshop to teach other artists the techniques she had learned. Around this time, she was reminded of a comment from one of the young people who worked on *The Great Wall,* who said to her, "Wouldn't it be great if we could take this project all over the world?" Baca began to think about expanding the idea of *The Great Wall* mural to include a worldwide scope. She thought that if the concepts of cooperative mural making could be successful in Los Angeles communities, the same idea might be successful on a global scale.

In 1987, Baca began painting *The World Wall: A Vision of the Future Without Fear.* She envisioned this new mural as a far-reaching depiction of a world without violence. Baca believed that the first step toward world peace was to imagine it, and she wanted to involve artists from around the world in the creation of that vision. She also realized that in order to be seen by as many people as possible, in as many countries as possible, this new mural would have to be portable. She decided that the mural would be created in panels

Begun in 1990, The World Wall *is an international traveling mural installation consisting of numerous transportable panels with the theme "a vision of the future without fear." When the piece was shown in Mexico City, the panels were separated and mounted as individual artworks. Eight panels totaling 10 ft. x 240 ft., acrylic on canvas. © SPARC www.sparcmurals.org*

that could be moved around to different places. The piece is also adaptable, since the individual panels can be shown as one continuous work, in traditional mural form, or as separate works, with the panels arranged in a variety of ways. *The World Wall* is an attempt to push the state of arts in muralism so that the mural creates its own architecture," she explained. "It makes its own space and can be assembled by any people anywhere."

After several years of planning, and with the contributions of many different artists, *The World Wall* had its debut in Finland in 1990. As the mural traveled on to be shown in other countries, the artist team in each country would add their panel to the display. Currently, *The World Wall* includes panels from Finland, Russia, Israel/Palestine, Mexico, and Canada, along with four panels from Baca and her Los Angeles team. *The World Wall* will grow to 14 panels, and perhaps more.

Meanwhile, in 1988 the mayor of Los Angeles wanted Baca to create a new mural program for the city. Once again, she agreed to lead a mural program for Los Angeles. The program, known as Great Walls Unlimited:

Neighborhood Pride, was given the goal of painting a mural in almost every ethnic neighborhood of Los Angeles. To meet this goal, Baca and SPARC trained hundreds of artists and young people. Over the course of many years, the Neighborhood Pride program painted 105 murals throughout the city, commissioned works from 95 established or emerging artists, and employed over 1,800 young apprentices.

Creating the Future of Murals

"I am a Mexican mural painter in the true sense, but I took it to the next level," Baca declared. "To keep an art form living, it has to grow and change."

In addition to creating countless murals in public spaces, Baca has devoted her career to teaching others how to make murals. While working at SPARC, she has taught at several universities in California. Baca began her academic career at the University of California-Irvine, where she worked as a professor in the Studio Arts department from 1981 to 1994. From 1994 to 1996 she was a professor at California State University-Monterey Bay, where she co-founded the Visual and Public Art Institute Program. In 1996 she moved to the University of California-Los Angeles (UCLA), where she has taken on multiple roles. While serving as a professor in UCLA's Cesar Chavez Center for Interdisciplinary Instruction in Chicana and Chicano Studies, she has also served on the Center's board and has taught in UCLA's World Arts and Cultures department.

In addition, Baca created the UCLA/SPARC Cesar Chavez Digital Mural Lab. The lab is a research, production, and teaching facility that uses modern technology in community-based art programs. The lab offers opportunities for those in low-income communities to have access to state-of-the-art technology. It brings local youth and their families together with students at UCLA to create community-based public art. At the same time, it brings UCLA students together with Baca so they can learn how to use computer technology to create murals.

Through work in this lab, Baca has pioneered several new techiques in mural-making. She developed one technique that uses digital imaging in murals, combining traditional mural-painting techniques with computer-generated imagery. "I draw hundreds and hundreds of sketches, look at things from thousands of different perspectives to make sure that I'm preparing a site well," she said. "With the computer I am able to see the work ... from a variety of perspectives and directions, thus eliminating the need for hundreds of sketches.... I could also eliminate hours and hours of work." Baca also developed a technique for creating murals on thin sheets of aluminum that can be attached to the interior or exterior walls of buildings. These murals can then be easily removed for cleaning or restoration, or saved in the event that the buildings are torn down. "I am a Mexican mural painter in the true sense, but I took it to the next level," she declared. "To keep an art form living, it has to grow and change."

"I struggle not to be lost from my culture because I think it is the very spirit of how I work," Baca affirmed. "My work is informed by my connection. There's force in the connection. It is the base from which the work flows."

One example of the way that Baca combines these two new techniques in mural-making is her work titled *La Memoria de Nuestra Tierra* (*Our Land Has Memory*), which she created for the Denver International Airport in Colorado. This mural shows the history of the land that is now Colorado and the people who lived there. The project was a very personal one for Baca, because her grandparents fled Mexico during the Mexican revolution and traveled to Colorado to escape the war. Baca wanted to use this mural "not only to tell the forgotten stories of people who, like birds or water, traveled back and forth across the land freely, before there was a line that distinguished which side you were from, but to speak to our shared human condition as temporary residents of the earth.... The making of this work was an excavation of a remembering of their histories."

Completed in 2000, *La Memoria de Nuestra Tierra* is 10 feet high and 50 feet long. The mural combines painting with digital images and historical documents and is printed on a sheet of bronze-colored aluminum. "With the use of computer technology I have incorporated these images and documents into the mural," Baca explained. "The landscape imagery was hand painted at a small scale and then scanned into the computer at a very high resolution for inclusion into the mural ... a meticulously hand painted landscape with historic photographs in a seamless blend." It has been called "a breakthrough in digital murals."

In 2008, Baca's work in murals took on a new form. For the *Cesar Chavez Monument Arch of Dignity, Equality, and Justice,* she designed a 25-foot arch with individual digital mural panels. The monument is located at San Jose

For the 2008 Cesar Chavez Monument Arch of Dignity, Equality, and Justice, *shown here, Baca designed a 25-foot arch with individual digital mural panels. This monument at San Jose State University consists of murals of farm workers, Cesar Chavez, Mahatma Gandhi, and Dolores Huerta. The monument was designed by Baca and the UCLA/SPARC Cesar Chavez Digital Mural Lab. © SPARC www.sparcmurals.org*

State University in San Jose, California. It consists of farm workers featured in two murals painted and printed digitally, a portrait of Cesar Chavez painted and then produced in full color Venetian tile, along with portraits of Mahatma Gandhi and Dolores Huerta. The monument, which was designed by Baca and the UCLA/SPARC Cesar Chavez Digital Mural Lab, commemorates Chavez through his ideals and beliefs, carried out in his actions to improve the conditions of the farm workers, which inspired so many to join his efforts to achieve social justice. A key element to the monument is to teach members of the next generation how to choose to live a life in the center of their values and beliefs, as Cesar Chavez did.

Saving the Murals of LA

In recent years, a movement has been underway to save the murals of Los Angeles—those created by Baca, as well as those created by many other artists. Over the years, many murals have been damaged by sunlight, water, and exposure to the elements, while some have been ravaged by vandalism. To address this problem, SPARC began a new campaign called

Save LA Murals (SLAM) to raise funds, to act as advocates for this public art, and to organize people to take action.

One mural affected in this way is *The Great Wall of Los Angeles,* which has been extensively damaged. The 35th anniversary of the project's start is approaching in 2011, and Baca and SPARC are now working to restore the mural to its original condition. They are also adding new sections illustrating the decades after the 1950s, where the original mural ended. Unlike most art restoration, which involves experienced experts, the restoration of *The Great Wall* is being done in the same way that the work was originally created—by *Great Wall* alumni, youth, and community members.

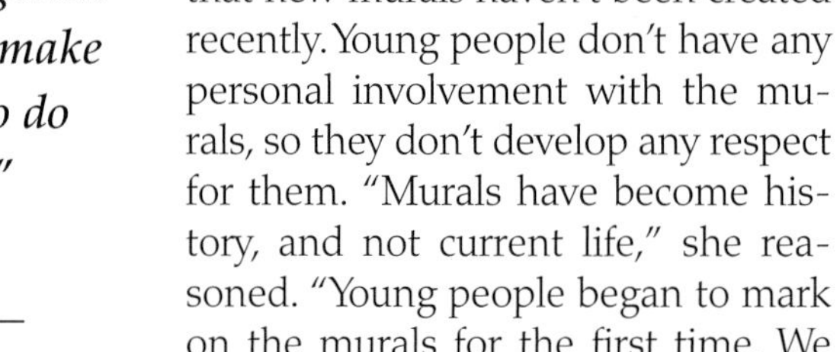

> *"I have had a very blessed life," Baca said. "I've gotten to dream dreams and make them be. Who gets to do that? Pretty cool."*

Baca has argued that one reason for the damage to the existing murals is that new murals haven't been created recently. Young people don't have any personal involvement with the murals, so they don't develop any respect for them. "Murals have become history, and not current life," she reasoned. "Young people began to mark on the murals for the first time. We need to reeducate the young people about the importance of the murals. A generation has not worked on them—their brothers, their sisters, their friends, have not been on a mural. Painting is really just one step for making a dream real. You imagine it, you visualize it, you create it, and then it becomes more tangible, and it becomes important to the people because they can see it on a daily basis. And then put it where the people live, put it where they work. It becomes embedded in the consciousness, and it becomes part of the fabric of a community. That's why the murals are important—and that's why they're important to be preserved."

For Baca, creating art shouldn't be limited to artists. She believes that everyone can create art and that art can be a tool for social change and self-transformation. "Break the mold! Have the biggest vision you can! If you can't dream it, it cannot occur." Reflecting on her own work as an artist, Baca said, "I have had a very blessed life. I've gotten to dream dreams and make them be. Who gets to do that? Pretty cool."

MARRIAGE AND FAMILY

Baca married when she was 19 years old and still in college. The marriage ended in divorce six years later. She continues to live in Venice, California.

SELECTED WORKS

Mi Abuelita, 1970
Medusa Head, 1973
Las Tres Marias, 1976
History of Highland Park, 1977
Hitting the Wall: Women in the Marathon, 1984
The Great Wall of Los Angeles, 1984
Guadalupe Mural Project, 1990
The World Wall: A Vision of the Future without Fear, 1990 (ongoing)
Danzas Indigenas, 1994
Raspados Mojados, 1994
Local 11, 1998
La Memoria de Nuestra Tierra: Colorado, 2000
Durango Mural Project: Recollections, 2002
Digital Tile Murals on the Venice Boardwalk, 2003
Migration of the Golden People, 2003
Cesar Chavez Monument Plaza, 2008

SELECTED HONORS AND AWARDS

Educator of the Year (National Association of Art Educators): 1988
Rockefeller Fellowship Award (UCLA Chicano Studies Research Center): 1991
Lifetime Achievement Award (National Hispanic Magazine): 1997
Influential Woman Artist Award (Women's Caucus for Art): 1998
Master Artist and Senior Scholar (Harvard University): 1998
Creative Vision Award (Liberty Hill Foundation): 2001
Hispanic Heritage Award (National Hispanic Heritage Foundation): 2001, for Educator of the Year
Montgomery Fellowship (Dartmouth College): 2002
John Simon Guggenheim Fellowship): 2003
Named One of 100 Most Influential Hispanics (Hispanic Business Magazine): 2005
Self-Help Graphics Master Artist Series: 2008
Champions of Change Award (Escuela Tlatelolco Cenro de Estudios): 2009
Elizabeth "Betita" Martinez Activist Scholar Award (InnerCity Struggle): 2009
Judy Chicago's Through the Flower Awards: 2009, for contribution to feminist art movement
White House Briefing on Arts, Community, Social Justice, and National Recovery: 2009

FURTHER READING

Books

Fernandez, Mayra. *Judy Baca: Artist,* 1994 (young adult)
Isenberg, Barbara. *State of the Arts: California Artists Talk about Their Work,* 2000
Liu, Eric. *Guiding Lights: The People Who Lead Us Toward Our Purpose in Life,* 2004
Olmstead, Mary. *Judy Baca,* 2005 (young adult)

Periodicals

Hispanic Magazine, May 1991, p.17
Los Angeles Daily News, Oct. 21, 2007, p.N1
Los Angeles Times, Aug. 10, 1993, p.8; Dec. 1, 1997, p.3; Aug. 19, 2001; Jan. 6, 2009
New York Times, Sep. 19, 1997, p.A18; Apr. 28, 1998; May 26, 2002, sec. 2, p.29
People, May 24, 2004, p.98
Wall Street Journal, Sep. 29, 2000

Online Articles

http://www.pbs.org/americanfamily/mural.html
(PBS, "The Art of the Mural," 2004)
http://www.aaa.si.edu/collections/oralhistories
(Smithsonian Institution, "Judith Baca Interviews," Aug. 5, 1986)
http://latino.si.edu/virtualgallery/ojos/bios/bios_Baca.htm
(Smithsonian Institution, "Judith F. Baca," 2004)

ADDRESS

Judy Baca
SPARC
685 Venice Blvd.
Venice, CA 90291

WORLD WIDE WEB SITES

http://www.judybaca.com
http://www.sparcmurals.org
http://www.savelamurals.org

Joe Biden 1942-

American Political Leader and Six-Term U.S. Senator
Vice President of the United States

BIRTH

Joseph Robinette Biden Jr. was born on November 20, 1942, in Scranton, Pennsylvania. His father, Joseph Robinette Biden, worked as a boiler cleaner and car salesman and later owned his own car dealership. His mother, Jean (Finnegan) Biden, was a homemaker. He has two younger brothers, James and Francis, and one younger sister, Valerie.

YOUTH

Biden grew up in a working-class neighborhood in Scranton, an industrial city located in the northeastern corner of Pennsylvania. The Biden home was modest, and the family never had much money. Biden recalled that he even used to put cardboard in his shoes to cover up holes in the soles. But his parents created a loving and supportive home for all their children, and Biden has many fond childhood memories.

Biden says that his mother taught him many valuable lessons about life as he was growing up. She taught him to believe in himself and in the importance of family. In his autobiography, *Promises to Keep,* he recalled that she often said, "Remember, Joey, you're a Biden. Nobody is better than you. You're not better than anybody else, but *nobody* is any better than you."

> *"The one thing my mother could not stand was meanness," Biden recalled. "She doesn't have a mean bone in her body, and she couldn't stand meanness in anybody else. She once shipped my brother Jim off with instructions to bloody the nose of a kid who was picking on smaller kids, and she gave him a dollar when he'd done it."*

Biden also noted, however, that his mother believed deeply that all people deserved respect and consideration. "The one thing my mother could not stand was meanness," he said. "She doesn't have a mean bone in her body, and she couldn't stand meanness in anybody else. She once shipped my brother Jim off with instructions to bloody the nose of a kid who was picking on smaller kids, and she gave him a dollar when he'd done it."

Biden's father also played a major role in shaping the children's moral character and outlook. "There was no daylight between my mom's philosophy of life and my dad's," Biden wrote in his autobiography. "She was just more vocal about it.... Dad was the keeper of the rules at the table—our manners were to be impeccable—and he liked to nudge the conversation toward big issues like morality, justice, and equality."

Joe Biden Sr. also provided a shining example to his children of how to handle disappointments and setbacks in life with grit and grace. During the 1930s and early 1940s he had been a successful businessman who raced cars, flew in private planes, and wore expensive business suits. His wealth vanished during the late 1940s, though, due to a thieving business partner. This turn of events was difficult for Biden Sr. to absorb, especially because he had a growing family to support. But he refused to wallow in bitterness or despair about the downturn in his fortunes. Instead, he dusted himself off and quietly worked long hours as a used car salesman to support his family. "He never, ever gave up, and he never complained," Biden wrote of his father. "He had no time for self-pity. He didn't judge a man by how many times he got knocked down but by how fast he got up."

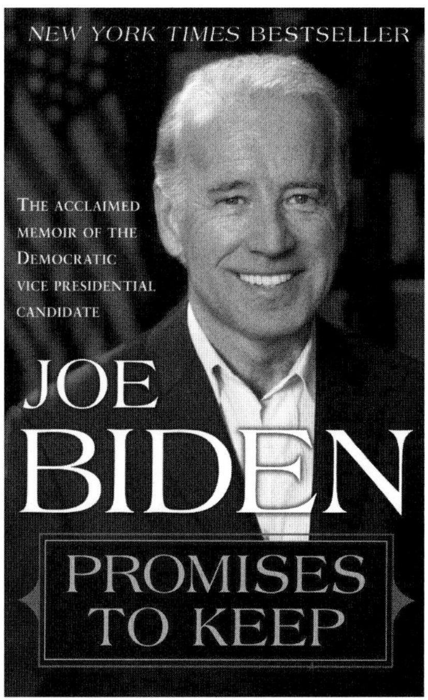

In his memoir, Biden includes stories about his early life and career, showing the guiding principles that helped him overcome the many setbacks he faced along the way.

Overcoming a Speech Problem

The general happiness that marked Biden's childhood was marred by one problem that tormented him on a daily basis. He struggled with a stutter, a speech disorder in which normal sentence flow is disrupted by repeated expressions of the same sounds, syllables, and words. People who experience these speech "roadblocks" are no less intelligent than people who can converse without any problems. But they often become the target of teasing and taunting in childhood.

Stuttering problems vary greatly from person to person, and Biden's disorder was not as severe as some cases. "When I was at home with my brothers and sister, hanging out with my neighborhood friends, or shooting the bull on the ball field, I was fine," he recalled in *Promises to Keep.* "But when I got thrown into a new situation or a new school, had to read in front of the class, or wanted to ask out a girl, I just couldn't do it.... Even today I can remember the dread, the shame, the absolute rage, as vividly as the day it was happening."

Sports provided a welcome escape for Biden. "As much as I lacked confidence in my ability to communicate verbally, I always had confidence in my athletic ability," he recalled in his autobiography. "Sports was as natural to me as speaking was unnatural. And sports turned out to be my ticket to acceptance—and more. I wasn't easily intimidated in a game, so even when I stuttered, I was always the kid who said, 'Give me the ball.' Who's going to take the last shot? 'Give me the ball.' We need a touchdown now. 'Give me the ball.' I'd be eight years old, usually the smallest guy on the field, but I wanted the ball. And they gave it to me."

Biden had a problem with stuttering when he was young. "When I was at home with my brothers and sister, hanging out with my neighborhood friends, or shooting the bull on the ball field, I was fine," he recalled. "But when I got thrown into a new situation or a new school, had to read in front of the class, or wanted to ask out a girl, I just couldn't do it.... Even today I can remember the dread, the shame, the absolute rage, as vividly as the day it was happening."

In 1953 the Biden family moved from Scranton to Claymont, Delaware, where his father continued to work as a car salesman. It was in Claymont that young Joe Biden finally conquered his stutter. He practiced public speaking for hours in front of a mirror at home and gradually learned to "beat" the disorder. By the time he graduated from high school, he was an accomplished and confident public speaker. Biden even gave the commencement address at his high school graduation in 1961.

EDUCATION

Biden attended Roman Catholic parochial schools in Scranton and Claymont for his elementary education. He attended high school at Archmere Academy, a private Catholic prep school in Claymont, on a special work-study program that helped his family with the tuition. He was a solid B student in high school who was popular with his classmates. "In almost any group I was the leader," he recalled. "I was class representative my sophomore year and class president my junior and senior years. I might have been student body president, but Father Diny [who headed Archmere] wouldn't let me run—too many demerits."

After graduating, Biden enrolled at the University of Delaware in the fall of 1961. He played safety on the football team and loved the social whirl on campus. He later admitted that he was not very disciplined about his studies, but college roommates recall that he was never in danger of flunking out. "He had a talent for getting it done when it had to get done," recalled one college roommate. Another friend from his college days added that "Joe was the kind of guy who could read someone else's notes and do better on the exam than the guy who made the notes."

During his junior year at Delaware, Biden went to the Bahamas for spring break. During his stay he met Neilia Hunter, an attractive college student from Syracuse University who was also on spring break. The two of them quickly struck up a close relationship, and Biden later admitted that in his case it was "love at first sight." Their love affair became so intense that he quit the football team to spend more time with her. And after earning his Bachelor of Arts (BA) degree from Delaware in 1965, he decided to attend law school in Syracuse, New York, where Hunter had secured a teaching job.

Biden entered Syracuse University College of Law in the fall of 1965, and one year later he married Hunter. He was not a particularly good student at Syracuse—he graduated 76th in a class of 85—but he excelled in the courses that really engaged his interest. In addition, he discovered at Syracuse that he possessed an actual talent for speaking before audiences. "What had terrified me in grade school and high school was turning out to be my strength," he recalled in his autobiography. "I found out I liked speaking in public.... I fell in love with the idea of being able to sway a jury—and being able to see it happen right before my eyes." In 1968 Biden earned his Juris Doctor or Doctor of Law (JD) degree from Syracuse. He and Neilia then promptly moved back to Delaware, where he had received a job offer from a prominent legal firm.

FIRST JOBS

Biden had worked a wide range of jobs as a youngster, from lifeguarding to landscaping. He knew after leaving Syracuse that he was entering the "real" world; the careless approach that he had taken to college classwork would get him fired in a law office. As a result, Biden had little trouble adjusting to the long hours required of a young attorney, and he passed the Delaware bar exam on his first try in 1968. But he disliked the conservative political orientation of the big firm, and in 1970 he established his own small legal firm in downtown Wilmington.

Biden developed a reputation as a strong and sympathetic defender of accused criminals and poor people trapped in expensive legal cases. But in

Biden is shown with his two sons, Beau and Hunter, and his wife, Neilia, while campaigning for a seat in the U.S. Senate. This shot was taken in 1972, just a few months before his wife and young daughter were killed in a terrible car accident. Shown here on the left are governor-elect Sherman Tribbitt and his wife, Jeanne Tribbitt.

the early 1970s he became even better known around Wilmington as a member of the New Castle County Council. Biden won a seat on the council in 1970 as a Democrat, even though the district was mostly Republican. He spent the next two years developing a reputation as "the guy who took on the builders and the big corporations," in his own words. Biden supported new job-creating businesses, but he also challenged projects that he thought were damaging to the environment or the welfare of the wider community.

CAREER HIGHLIGHTS

Biden's performance as a county councilman captured the attention of Democratic Party leaders across Delaware. Taking note of his energy, good humor, and liberal political beliefs, they saw him as a rising young star in Delaware politics. They were horrified, though, when the 29-year-old Biden announced his intention to seek the U.S. Senate seat held by

J. Caleb Boggs. Party leaders thought he was crazy to challenge Boggs, who had been a popular governor in Delaware in the 1950s, then gone on to win two terms as a U.S. senator.

Biden defied their predictions and pulled out a narrow victory in the November 1972 election. One factor in his surprise win was a strong set of positions in support of environmental protection, civil rights, labor unions, and new health care and mass transit programs. But Biden never would have succeeded without the help of his family. In addition to his wife Neilia, who took care of their three young children and encouraged and counseled him every day, Biden got help from his sister, Valerie, who served as his campaign manager. Her husband volunteered to be the campaign's budget director, and Jean Biden organized dozens of small "coffee hour" speaking engagements for her son all across Delaware.

“

"The moment exceeded all my romantic youthful imaginings," Biden said about election night. "I was a United States senator-elect at age 30. Our family was together under one splendid roof. The doors were just beginning to swing open on the rest of our lives. Neilia and I had done this amazing thing together, and there was so much more we would do. Neither of us was sure exactly what the rest of our lives would bring, but we couldn't wait to see."

Biden's victory made him the youngest senator in U.S. history to win by popular election. Political observers noted that, when he took his oath of office in January 1973, he would become the fifth-youngest senator in the history of the U.S. Congress. Years later, he recalled savoring his victory on election night with his wife in front of the big crackling fireplace at their home. "The moment exceeded all my romantic youthful imaginings," he later wrote. "I was a United States senator-elect at age 30. Our family was together under one splendid roof. The doors were just beginning to swing open on the rest of our lives. Neilia and I had done this amazing thing together, and there was so much more we would do. Neither of us was sure exactly what the rest of our lives would bring, but we couldn't wait to see."

Family Tragedy Strikes

A few weeks later, Biden's life was shattered by a tragic accident. His wife, Neilia, and their one-year-old daughter, Naomi, were killed in a car accident while out shopping for a Christmas tree. Their two young sons—Beau and Hunter—were also in the car, and they were critically injured. When Biden rushed to the hospital and heard the horrible news, he recalled that "I could not speak, only felt this hollow core grow in my chest, like I was going to be sucked inside a black hole."

Biden spent the next several weeks in his sons' hospital room as they slowly recovered from their injuries. He initially planned on giving up the senate seat he had just won so that he could devote all his time to his sons. But his sister and brother-in-law agreed to move to Wilmington to help him care for his boys. In addition, Senate Majority Leader Mike Mansfield offered him a number of prestigious senate committee assignments if he would agree to take the job on a six-month trial basis. Biden agreed after a great deal of soul-searching, and in January 1973 he took part in a swearing-in ceremony held in his sons' hospital room.

When Biden took office, every other U.S. senator lived in Washington DC or across the Potomac River in northern Virginia. Biden, however, knew that it would be easier for his sons to recover emotionally from the loss of their mother and little sister if they did not have to adjust to a new living environment. He decided to commute to work from Wilmington by Amtrak train. The 80-minute one-way trip made life a little more hectic, but he never regretted the decision. "Family has always been the beginning, the middle, and the end with me," he explained.

During his first term as senator, Biden did not go out of his way to make friends in Washington. He did his job, then took the train home while other Congressional leaders went out to expensive restaurants and fancy social events. "I think he was far more interested in his children than the social whirl," recalled Senator Patrick J. Leahy.

Biden decided to finish out his six-year term out of a sense of obligation to Delaware voters, but he doubted that he was going to seek re-election. Then, in 1976, he became involved in a romantic relationship with Jill Jacobs, a teacher in the Wilmington area. When they married one year later, Biden knew that Jill would be there for his sons if he decided to continue his political career in Washington. He decided to run for a second term in 1978, and he easily won re-election.

Biden campaigning in Chicago for the Democratic nomination for president, 1988. Biden, left, is shown with Chicago Mayor Harold Washington, Illinois Sen. Frank Demuzio, civil rights leader Jesse Jackson, and U.S. Sen. Paul Simon.

"A Happy Warrior"

During the late 1970s and 1980s Biden became a well-known figure in the U.S. Senate. Throughout this period he served as the top Democrat (either as chairman or ranking minority member) on the Senate Judiciary Committee, one of the most visible and important committees in Congress. He also compiled a voting record that won high praise from liberal groups and voters.

At the same time, though, Biden exhibited a strong independent streak. On the issue of abortion, for example, he believed that women should have the right to choose whether to end their pregnancies without interference from government authorities. But despite angry condemnation from liberal groups, he steadfastly opposed the use of federal money for any abortion services. "It's the only consistent position [to have] intellectually," he insisted. "If you say government should be out [of the process], government should be out."

Within Congress, most of Biden's fellow senators viewed him as a cheerful and friendly fellow who nonetheless enjoyed a spirited argument. "He's a happy warrior," said one colleague. "He loves the whole thing, but he'll punch you out [in a debate]." Another older senator who often worked with Biden freely acknowledged that "Joe gets worked up," but argued that his sharp tongue reflected his convictions. "Some people think he gets too candid sometimes, but that's a mark of his generation. Better his short fuse than no fuse at all." Biden was not universally admired, though. Some rivals and observers grumbled that he was a showboat and a know-it-all.

In early 1987 Biden decided to make a run at the biggest political job in the world: president of the United States. After formally announcing his candidacy for the 1988 Democratic presidential nomination on June 9, 1987, he began dividing his time between Washington DC and the campaign trail. Biden's bid for the presidency lasted less than four months, though. In September his campaign was rocked by accusations from journalists and political opponents that he had plagiarized speeches delivered by British politician Neil Kinnock. Biden insisted that he usually credited Kinnock in his speeches, but that he forgot to do so at a single campaign event. The controversy refused to go away, however, and he eventually realized that his presidential candidacy was doomed. Even after ending his campaign, though, Biden remained squarely in the public spotlight. Upon returning to Washington, he played a major role in defeating the nomination of conservative lawyer Robert Bork for the U.S. Supreme Court in the fall of 1987.

Rebuilding His Career

In early 1988 Biden's life took a frightening turn for the worse. He suffered a ruptured brain aneurysm—an abnormal swelling in a blood vessel that can cause fatal levels of internal bleeding when it bursts. After two surgeries and seven months of recovery, Biden was finally able to return to the Senate, but the experience changed him forever. Vowing to put the controversies of 1987 behind him, he rededicated himself to his work in the U.S. Senate. "I understood that a single moment of failure—even one so public and wounding as the end of my presidential campaign—could not determine my epitaph," he wrote in his autobiography. "I had faith in the ultimate fairness and reason of the American people, and I had faith that I could rebuild my reputation."

Over the next several years, Biden became one of the Senate's most authoritative and influential voices on foreign policy issues. He was recognized as an expert on the Middle East and Asia, and he played a significant role in convincing President Bill Clinton to use military air strikes to stop horrible human rights violations in Eastern Europe in 1999.

During this same period, Biden enjoyed the greatest legislative triumph of his senate career: the passage of the Violence Against Women Act

Biden worked tirelessly on behalf of the Violence against Women Act of 1994, which funded programs that helped women who had been victims of rape or abuse. He is shown here at a news conference with Sen. Barbara Boxer (at the podium). Behind them, from left, are Rep. Constance Morello, Rep, Pat Shroeder (behind Boxer), and Rep. Carolyn Maloney (far right).

(VAWA) of 1994. Before this law was passed, most communities had no shelters to house victims of abuse or rape, and police departments were frequently unfriendly—or at least poorly equipped—to handle reports from women who had been battered or raped. Biden was outraged by the situation, and he wrote and sponsored a bill that would fund the construction of shelters, educate police about violence against women, and enable cities to hire counselors and prosecutors dedicated to the issue. Other senators tried to kill VAWA because of its price tag, but Biden refused to give in. "You can sponsor a bill, but if you just sponsor a bill and let it sit there, that's nothing," said one activist who worked with Biden. "He shepherded [VAWA]. He made sure it happened. He assigned staff to it, gave them carte blanche to do what they needed, they spent days and nights on it."

Biden's tireless efforts helped get VAWA through both houses of Congress, and President Clinton signed the bill into law in 1994. It proved so successful in reducing violence against women—and so popular with voters—that

Biden with Barack Obama at the 2008 Democratic National Convention, where they were nominated as their party's candidates for president and vice president.

it was reauthorized in both 2000 and 2006 with support from Republicans and Democrats alike. "If I were to choose the single most important event leading to broad-based awareness and change regarding domestic and sexual violence against women," said one domestic violence activist, "it would be Senator Biden's Violence Against Women Act of 1994."

Becoming Obama's Running Mate

By the time Republican George W. Bush became president in 2001, Biden's career seemed almost fully recovered. He routinely cruised to victory at election time, claiming 60 percent or more of the vote in both 1990 and 1996. In addition, he regularly represented his party on national television shows like "Meet the Press" and "Face the Nation." This comeback did not surprise Alan Hoffman, who served as Biden's chief of staff for several years. "He has a deep conviction and pride in the work he does, so failure doesn't always bother him," said Hoffman. "He always bounces back. Always. It doesn't even surprise me anymore." As the decade wore on, he emerged as one of the most visible critics of the Bush administration. He expressed profound regret for supporting Bush's invasion of Iraq in 2003, and he challenged the president on a wide range of domestic and foreign policy issues.

In January 2007 Biden announced his intention to launch another campaign for the White House. But when the list of Democratic presidential candidates rapidly expanded to include high-profile politicians like Senator Hillary Clinton, former vice presidential candidate John Edwards, and Senator Barack Obama, Biden's candidacy was ignored by the national media. After several impressive debate performances failed to ignite interest in his campaign, Biden realized that he should drop out. He left the race in January 2008, then watched with great interest as Obama narrowly beat out Clinton for the Democratic nomination.

"I started my career fighting for civil rights," Biden remarked, "[and to make history] with a guy who has such incredible talent and who is also a breakthrough figure in multiple ways—I genuinely find that exciting. It's a new America."

During the summer of 2008, Biden's name repeatedly came up in discussions about possible vice presidential candidates for Obama. Many political observers thought that Biden's foreign policy experience and ability to attract working-class voters would help Obama deal with accusations that he was weak in those areas. One day, Biden received a call from Obama, who asked him whether he would be interested in the vice presidency. If so, he would have to undergo "vetting"—an intense investigation of all aspects of his private and professional life to check for unknown scandals. Biden recalled the conversation vividly: "Obama called to ask me whether or not I would be willing to be vetted—and he was very specific, he said,'I'm not fooling around, it's down to three or fewer people, I'm not asking you to jump into a mix of ten people—would you be willing?' And I said,'I have to think about it.'"

Biden's cautious response came from two concerns. First, he already had a position that gave him great satisfaction and influence. "It wasn't self-evident to me that being vice president would be a better job—you know what I mean?" he later told the *New Yorker.* Second, Biden wanted to make sure that he and Obama shared the same vision for the country's future, and that the vice president would play a meaningful role in an Obama administration. When further conversations with Obama reassured Biden, he agreed to be considered for the slot.

A few weeks later, Obama formally asked Biden to be his vice presidential running mate. Biden accepted, and on August 23, 2008, Obama an-

Inauguration Day—Surrounded by his family, Biden is sworn in as vice president by Supreme Court Justice John Paul Stevens on January 20, 2009.

nounced his selection to the world. Democrats reacted positively to the pick, and even some Republicans praised Obama's decision. "Biden is good-natured, serious, and truly qualified," stated Ed Rogers, who served as a member of the White House staff in the presidential administrations of Republicans Ronald Reagan and George H.W. Bush. "Everyone who cares about good government and serious politics can imagine him as president."

Other political observers were more critical of Biden's selection. The most vocal criticism came from supporters of Republican presidential candidate John McCain. They charged that Biden's background did not compensate for Obama's "inexperience." In addition, they ridiculed the Delaware senator for some of his past verbal blunders. But as election day approached, the Obama camp seemed happy with their choice. "Joe Biden's strength is he speaks his mind, and every once in a while it may not come out the right way—a speed bump," said Obama advisor David Axelrod. "But those things were minor, and frankly did not hurt us. When you take the few times when he may have said something that would make you kind of scratch your head and weigh it against the good he did us, it isn't even a close contest."

Becoming Vice President of the United States

Throughout the fall of 2008, there was non-stop campaigning by the two tickets—Barack Obama and Joe Biden for the Democrats and John McCain and Sarah Palin for the Republicans. Biden proved to be an energetic and enthusiastic campaigner for the Democratic ticket. He delivered a strong performance in the lone vice-presidential debate against Republican vice presidential candidate Sarah Palin, and he appeared at rallies all across the country to generate support for Obama's candidacy. Time and time again, he argued that Obama's policies provided the best antidote for the many domestic and international problems facing the nation.

“

"I'm genuinely optimistic [for the future]," Biden said in early 2009. "It's going to be rough until we climb of out of this.... But I think we've got a ladder long enough, and I think when we climb out of this hole ... [we will] climb onto a platform that's clearer, sturdier, better, more competitive for America, and put us in a position where we're able to do in the 21st century what we did in the 20th century. I really, genuinely believe that."

On election day, November 4, 2008, the American people made their choice. The Obama-Biden ticket easily defeated the McCain-Palin ticket. Obama and Biden claimed 53 percent of the popular vote (7 percent more than the Republicans) and 365 electoral votes (compared to 173 for McCain-Palin). These election results were truly historic, for they made Obama the first African-American president-elect in U.S. history.

Afterward, Biden expressed delight with the decisive victory, as well as gratitude to be part of such a historic event. "I started my career fighting for civil rights," he remarked, "[and to make history] with a guy who has such incredible talent and who is also a breakthrough figure in multiple ways—I genuinely find that exciting. It's a new America."

Biden observed that the Obama administration will face difficult challenges, from resolving unpopular wars in Iraq and Afghanistan to reviving a sick American economy. "This is the worst of times to come into office," he acknowledged. "The responsibilities, the burdens, the crises exceed anything—and I said it during the campaign and I believe it even more now—

that any president has faced since Franklin Roosevelt.... But the flip side of that is, if you're ever going to do this job, this is the time to do it. If you're a surgeon, do you want to do a tonsillectomy or a heart transplant?"

Despite these challenges, Biden's reputation as "a happy warrior" remains intact. "I'm genuinely optimistic [for the future]," he said in early 2009. "It's going to be rough until we climb of out of this.... But I think we've got a ladder long enough, and I think when we climb out of this hole ... [we will] climb onto a platform that's clearer, sturdier, better, more competitive for America, and put us in a position where we're able to do in the 21st century what we did in the 20th century. I really, genuinely believe that."

MARRIAGE AND FAMILY

Biden married Neilia Hunter in 1966. They had three children—Joseph "Beau," Robert "Hunter," and Naomi. Neilia and Naomi were killed in a car accident in December 1972. Beau grew up to become the state attorney general for Delaware, and in October 2008 he was deployed to Iraq as a captain in the Delaware National Guard. Hunter is an attorney.

Biden was a single father for five years, until he married educator Jill Jacobs on June 17, 1977. They had one daughter together, Ashley, who is a social worker.

During Biden's years as vice president, he and his wife will live in the official vice presidential residence in Washington DC. This 19th-century Victorian-style mansion with 33 rooms is located on the grounds of the U.S. Naval Observatory, next to the British embassy. This move brought Biden's 36-year-streak of Amtrak commuting to an end. But the Bidens intend to keep their home in Wilmington and use it as their retirement home.

HOBBIES AND OTHER INTERESTS

Biden enjoys reading about history and many other subjects. He served for many years as an adjunct professor at the Widener University School of Law in Wilmington, where he taught a seminar on constitutional law.

WRITINGS

Promises to Keep, 2007

SELECTED HONORS AND AWARDS

Congressional Leadership Award (National Center for Missing and Exploited Children): 2004

George Arents Pioneer Medal (Syracuse University): 2005
Best of Congress Award (*Working Mother* magazine): 2008

FURTHER READING

Books

Biden, Joe. *Promises to Keep,* 2007

Periodicals

Christian Science Monitor, Aug. 28, 2007, p.15
CQ Weekly, Dec. 30, 2000, p.98
Current Biography Yearbook, 1987
Esquire, Feb. 2009, p.78
Los Angeles Times, Aug. 27, 2008, p.A10
National Journal, July 16, 2005, p.2281
New York Times, Sep. 1, 2008, p.A14; Oct. 2, 2008, p.A1; Oct. 24, 2008, p.A17; Nov. 3, 2008, p.A18; Nov. 26, 2008, p. A14; Feb. 8, 2009, p.A6; Feb. 20, 2009, p.A15
New Yorker, Mar. 21, 2005, p.32; Oct. 20, 2008, p.48
Newsweek, Oct. 13, 2008, p.46
Time, Nov. 10, 2008, p.44
U.S. News & World Report, Sep. 21, 1987, p.24; Nov. 17, 2008, p.26
USA Today, Aug. 25, 2008, p.A1; Aug. 28, 2008, p.A4
Washington Post, Aug. 24, 2008, p.A1; Aug. 25, 2008, p.A17
Washingtonian, Dec. 1985
Weekly Standard, Jan. 5-Jan. 12, 2009, p.14

Online Articles

http://abcnews.go.com
(ABC World News, "Get to Know Joe Biden," Dec. 13, 2007)
http://www.esquire.com/features/joe-biden-biography-0209
(Esquire, "Joe Biden, Advisor in Chief," Jan. 22, 2009)
http://topics.nytimes.com
(New York Times, "Times Topics," multiple articles, various dates)
http://topics.newsweek.com/people/politics/obama-administration
(Newsweek, "Joe Biden," multiple articles, various dates)
http://pewforum.org/religion08/profile.php?CandidateID=9
(Pew Forum on Religion and Public Life, "Joe Biden Background," no date)
http://topics.time.com
(Time, "Time Topics," multiple articles, various dates)
http://projects.washingtonpost.com/2008-presidential-candidates/joe-biden
(Washington Post, "Joe Biden," no date)

ADDRESS

Vice President Joe Biden
The White House
1600 Pennsylvania Avenue NW
Washington, DC 20500

WORLD WIDE WEB SITES

http://www.barackobama.com
http://www.whitehouse.gov

Cynthia Breazeal 1967-

American Engineer and Professor of Robotics
Pioneering Designer of Socially Interactive Robots

BIRTH

Cynthia Breazeal (pronounced *bruh-ZILL*) was born on November 15, 1967, in Albuquerque, New Mexico. Her parents, Norman and Juliette Breazeal, were both scientists. Norman Breazeal worked in a research lab, using supercomputers to analyze computer systems, while Juliette Breazeal was a computer scientist. They encouraged Cynthia and her older brother, William, to explore sports and the arts as well as science.

> "*At age 10 Breazeal was thrilled by the movie* Star Wars, *especially the friendly robots R2-D2 and C-3PO. "They were real friends and had a lot of admirable qualities," she recalled. "I didn't think it was possible to actually build stuff like that so I wasn't thinking about it as a career—yet."*"

YOUTH

In 1971, the Breazeal family moved to Livermore, California, a city about 45 miles east of San Francisco. Young Cynthia showed an early interest in animals and at age seven announced she wanted to be a veterinarian. She was a good student until she started third grade at a new school. Her teacher didn't encourage her creativity, and some of the other students made fun of her because she was short and had Asian features. (Her mother is of Korean descent.) Her older brother helped her overcome the teasing by showing her how silly it was. Her parents encouraged her to stay interested in science by taking her to local attractions, like the Dinosaur National Monument and San Francisco's science museum.

Science and science fiction had always intrigued young Cynthia. In third grade she wrote a story inspired by the television series "Star Trek," and at age 10 she was thrilled by the movie *Star Wars,* especially the friendly robots R2-D2 and C-3PO. "They were real friends and had a lot of admirable qualities," she recalled. "I didn't think it was possible to actually build stuff like that so I wasn't thinking about it as a career—yet."

In fifth grade, a new teacher brought out the best in Breazeal. He challenged her to try her hardest and gave her pep talks to boost her confidence. By the time she started seventh grade, she was taking honors classes. She also played soccer and took modeling classes, something she credits with giving her good interview and public speaking skills. She joined the track team and learned to run the hurdles. By reading about good technique and constantly practicing, Breazeal was soon winning events. She even tried cheerleading in eighth grade, but decided she would rather participate than cheer from the sidelines. At the same time she was excelling in sports, her mother was making sure she also had plenty of academic opportunities. She took young Cynthia to Women in Science conferences at local research labs, exposing her to the many careers available in science.

Breazeal's interest in Star Wars, *especially the robots C-3PO and R2-D2, became critical to her career years later.*

Breazeal looked for a new challenge the summer before high school and decided to learn to play tennis. All that summer, she took lessons, practiced hard, and even videotaped her game to see where she could improve. Her hard work not only earned her a spot on her high school team, she became the number one player. She won many tournaments and briefly considered turning pro, but her main goal was to become a doctor or engineer. She knew she would have to work hard to achieve that goal. As a freshman, she got Bs in math; through studying, she raised her math grades to As by her junior year. All throughout her high school career, her parents encouraged her to aim high and do her best—and never apologize for doing well because she was a girl. By the time she finished high school, Breazeal was ranked seventh of 328 students and had earned a local award for outstanding "scholarship, sportsmanship, citizenship, and integrity."

EDUCATION

When Breazeal graduated from Granada High School in 1985, she knew she wanted to study engineering. She enrolled at the University of California, Santa Barbara, excited to prove herself in a male-dominated field. She studied extra problems to make sure she thoroughly understood subjects like physics. She got practical experience by taking an internship at Xerox, working in computer microchip design. Breazeal graduated in 1989 with high honors, receiving her Bachelor of Science degree (BS) in electrical and computer engineering. She had a new goal, to become an astronaut and to study robots like the ones used in NASA's robotic rover program.

Breazeal earned a fellowship to attend graduate school at the Massachusetts Institute of Technology (MIT), which she calls the country's best engineering school. It's an intensive program that requires years of study, and she spent 10 years there attending graduate school. She studied under Rodney Brooks, a leader in developing Artificial Intelligence (AI) and autonomous robots (robots that think and behave on their own). In 1993 Breazeal earned her Master of Science degree (MS) in electrical engineering and computer science, and in 2000 she earned her doctorate (PhD). By that time, she was already making her name as a pioneer of interactive robots.

CAREER HIGHLIGHTS

Building a Better Robot

While Breazeal was a graduate student at MIT, she began working at MIT's Mobile Robot (or "Mobot") Lab. She worked with Brooks on miniature machines that could be useful for planetary exploration. Brooks had observed that insects can easily deal with uneven, even difficult terrain, the same challenge that robots might face on Mars. He had his teams brainstorm small, six-legged designs for these "micro-rovers." Breazeal's work on the project included two robots named Attila and Hannibal. Each robot had six jointed legs, each of which could move up, down, back, forth, and also bend at the knee. The robots had sensors that could detect when their path was blocked. Breazeal not only helped design and assemble the robots, she wrote software so that the robots could analyze and respond to obstacles. If these robots were to go to Mars, they couldn't be easily repaired, so she also worked on computer programs that would allow the robots to work around faulty parts. This work became her master's thesis, a paper with original research that she was required to write as part of earning her master's degree.

Breazeal wondered if it was possible to design a robot to interact with people and learn the same way babies did. After all, "the human environment is a profoundly social environment, and these robots are going to have to be able to do things not just independently of people but work with people, communicate with people."

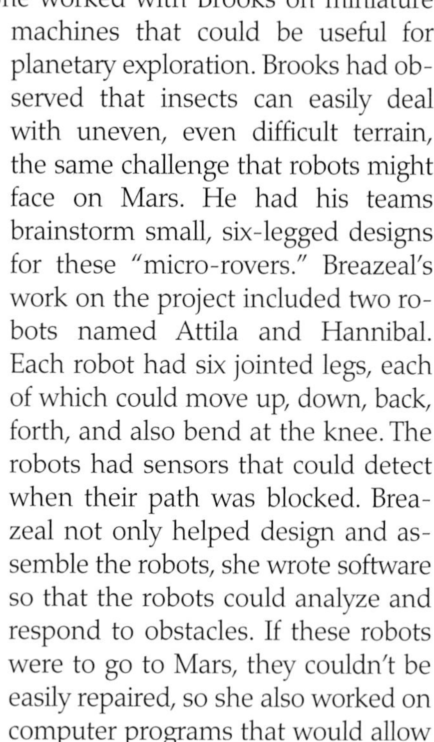

Breazeal also had opportunities to demonstrate her robots in public. Attila was part of a planetary rover display at the Smithsonian Air & Space Museum in Washington DC. While there, Breazeal met former Senator John Glenn, the first American astronaut to orbit the earth. She also took Hannibal to a Planetary Society conference held in Death Valley, Califor-

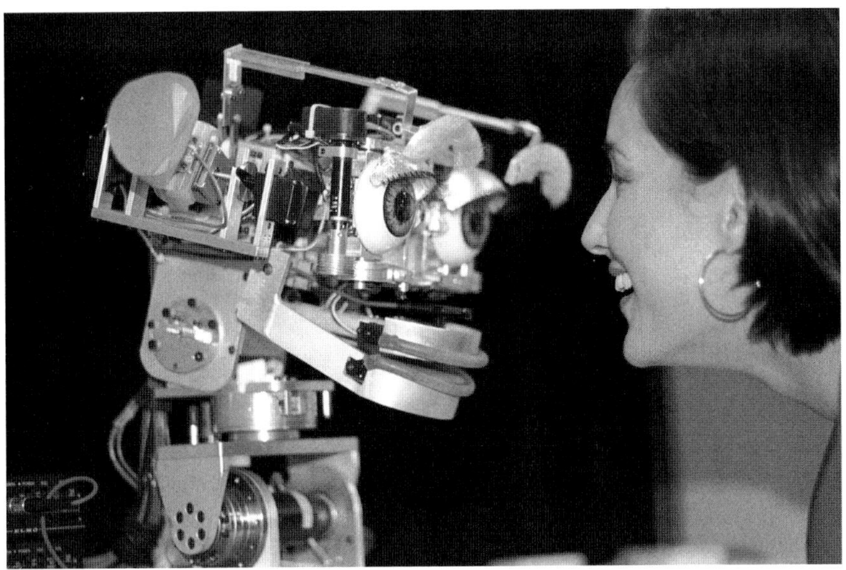

Breazeal reacting to her robot Kismet.

nia. There, in terrain similar to the Martian desert, she successfully showed her robot's capabilities. While she was eager to develop more complex robots, she was surprised when Brooks told his research group that they were going to skip reptile and mammal forms and start building humanoid robots.

Breazeal was excited by the challenge of creating a human-like robot. "So much of our engineered world, our cities and furniture, it's really constructed for our [shape], the fact that we walk, we have two arms, and so forth," she explained. She and the MIT team began working on a humanoid robot they named Cog. (A "cog" can refer to the tooth of a gear, but it is also an abbreviation for "cognition," or awareness.) They decided to focus on Cog's vision and hearing, so that it could respond more quickly to its environment. They created a six-foot-tall head and torso, with arms and hands that could perform tasks. Breazeal took a lead role in designing Cog's visual behavior system. She built complex visual sensors and wrote programs so that Cog could track objects it "saw" with its eyes. Eventually Cog was programmed to catch a ball, play with a Slinky, play a drum in time with music, and point at things.

It was a chance observation that led Breazeal in a new direction. One day she was taping her session with Cog and noticed that it appeared the robot was playing a turn-taking game with her. The game was only a quirk

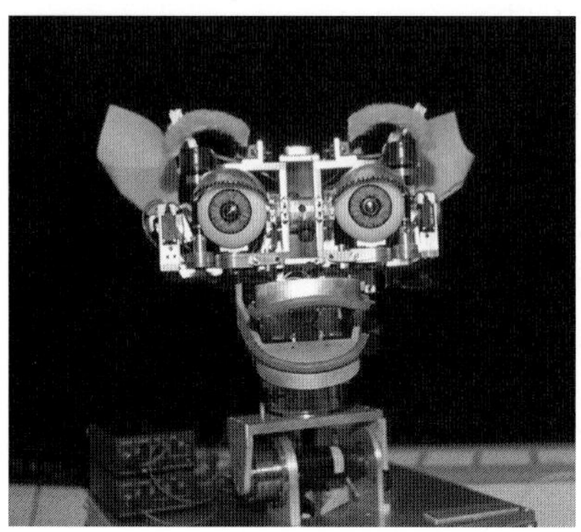

Kismet's various facial expressions seem to show different emotions, as it appears surprised (left) and downcast (right).

in the programming, but she began wondering: was it possible to design a robot to interact with people and learn the same way babies did? After all, "the human environment is a profoundly social environment, and these robots are going to have to be able to do things not just independently of people but work with people, communicate with people," she noted. Thinking that way, "suddenly the emotional intelligence was very, very important because people are going to try to interact with these robots not as tools but as other animate life-like things." When considering how to get people to interact with robots, "I began to get interested in the idea that infants are the simplest people, who eventually learn and grow to become adults," she explained. "I wanted people to be able to naturally fall into the mode of treating the robot as if it were an infant, to naturally help teach the robot as much as they could."

A New Kind of Robot

Before designing her new robot, Breazeal researched the field of developmental psychology, the study of how children's minds learn and eventually achieve adult performance. Because people focus on faces when they communicate, she decided to limit her robot to just an oversized head, mounted at face level. Although she gave it appealing, childlike eyes, she deliberately avoided giving it a baby's face; research shows that when simulating human appearance, "even the slightest mistake creeps us out." Breazeal's robot, which she named "Kismet," had fuzzy eyebrows, rubber lips, and flexible ears, but also visible metal parts. "It's a cute, appealing creature that's probably smarter than an animal," she explained. "You want to interact with it and try to teach it because it's fun."

In giving Kismet facial expressions, Breazeal decided to keep the robot's movements simple and recognizable, like cartoons. She studied psychology and film animation before limiting movement to the ears, eyebrows, eyelids, and lips. This could give Kismet enough flexibility to show recognizable "emotions." As Breazeal explained, "One of the aims of this project is to find a way for robots to interact with us in a more natural way. Using a face similar to our own is obviously an easy way of achieving that. Users don't need to learn anything new." To allow Kismet to recognize human faces, it had four color cameras, with visual sensors that could detect flesh tones and patterns of shading. To recognize vocal emotions, Kismet's auditory sensors could analyze the pitch and intensity of sounds. The robot couldn't understand or say words, but it could babble nonsense sounds, just as a baby does.

Breazeal and her team designed their robot "Kismet" to have fuzzy eyebrows, rubber lips, and flexible ears, but also visible metal parts. "It's a cute, appealing creature that's probably smarter than an animal," she explained. "You want to interact with it and try to teach it because it's fun."

Once she had designed Kismet's sensory systems (its "input"), Breazeal turned to programming its actions (its "output"). She decided to give the robot three "drives" (motivations) that would simulate infant behavior. One drive was the need for social stimulation: interaction with people. A second drive was for "play": the need to seek out brightly colored objects. The last drive was fatigue: a need to rest if it got too much interaction. When Kismet was started up, its drives were designed to be in a neutral state. The longer a drive went unsatisfied, the stronger it would get. If its need for social interaction went unanswered, for instance, Kismet was programmed to make noises and movements to gain human response—and learn through success which movements worked. "I'm building a robot that can leverage off the social structure that people already use to help each other learn," Breazeal stated. "If we can build a robot that can tap into that system, then we might not have to program in every piece of its behavior."

Still, there was a lot of computer programming involved in the Kismet project. To process sensory information and run its drive programs, Kismet had 15 separate computers connected into one parallel network. (A parallel network means computers each take individual steps of a program or calculation and perform them at the same time. It is much faster than calculating step by step, but requires sophisticated software to coordinate all the computers.) Breazeal supervised a whole team of students in building the robot. Some built hardware, assembling sensors and motors and networking computers together. Others worked on software, writing computer programs. Altogether it took Breazeal's team four years to build and test Kismet.

"We anthropomorphize [i.e., make human] all kinds of things, our pets, our cars, our computers.... People get angry at their cars for making them late for work, and of course they know that the car is just being a car, but it's natural for them to relate to something, to interact in a personal way."

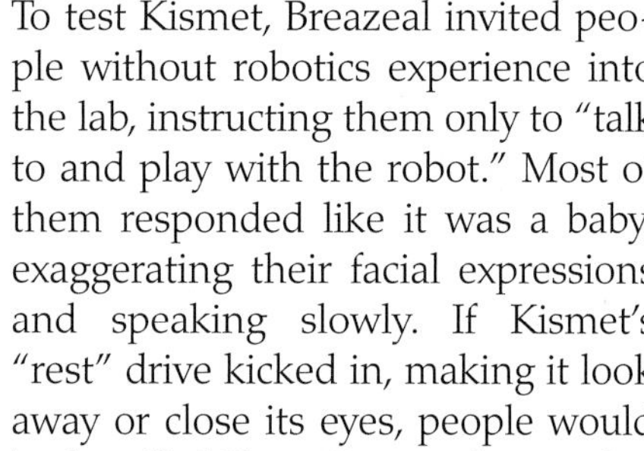

To test Kismet, Breazeal invited people without robotics experience into the lab, instructing them only to "talk to and play with the robot." Most of them responded like it was a baby, exaggerating their facial expressions and speaking slowly. If Kismet's "rest" drive kicked in, making it look away or close its eyes, people would back off. When Breazeal unveiled video of the MIT Media Lab's tests of Kismet, it surprised a lot of experts, who hadn't expected humans to be so accepting of a robot. It was no surprise to Breazeal, however. "We anthropomorphize [i.e., make human] all kinds of things, our pets, our cars, our computers.... People get angry at their cars for making them late for work, and of course they know that the car is just being a car, but it's natural for them to relate to something, to interact in a personal way." Breazeal assembled all her designs and test results for Kismet into her doctoral thesis. She received her PhD in 2000, and her thesis was published in 2002 as the book *Designing Social Robots.*

Working with the Movie Industry

With her thesis and her PhD finished and Kismet headed for retirement at the MIT Museum, Breazeal was considering what to do next when she was offered a unique opportunity. An executive from Warner Brothers movie studio had read about her work and called to ask if she would be willing to consult on one of its films. The film, called *A.I.: Artificial Intelligence,* followed the story of a highly advanced robot that is adopted by a family and then abandoned. It had all sorts of questions that intrigued her: Can a person love a robot? Can a robot love at all? Should robots

Breazeal's book Designing Sociable Robots *grew out of her PhD thesis.*

have rights? As a bonus, the film was being directed by Steven Spielberg, the man behind many of Breazeal's favorite science fiction movies, including *E.T.: The Extra-Terrestrial.* She accepted the offer and flew out to Hollywood.

As a consultant to the film, Breazeal mainly worked with journalists and discussed the current state of robotics, explaining how close modern robots were to the ones portrayed in the film. In April 2001 she helped host a press event for hundreds of reporters at MIT. She gave tours of the AI lab, demonstrated Kismet, and led a discussion titled "A.I. the Movie, A.I. the Reality, and A.I. the Future." It was a great chance to expose more people to her work and share her enthusiasm for robots. She was able to meet director Steven Spielberg to prepare him for media questions on the current state of robotics. She met him on the set of his next film, the science fiction thriller *Minority Report,* and also met the film's star, actor Tom Cruise. When *A.I.* debuted in the summer of 2001, Breazeal got a chance to walk the red carpet at the film's official premiere in New York. While her Hollywood experience was exciting, she was even more thrilled at the news that MIT was offering her a job at its Media Lab.

"Robots are not human, but humans aren't the only ones that have emotions," Breazeal claimed. "The question for robots is not, 'Will they ever have human emotions?' Dogs don't have human emotions, either, but we all agree they have genuine emotions. The question is, 'What are the emotions that are genuine for robots?'"

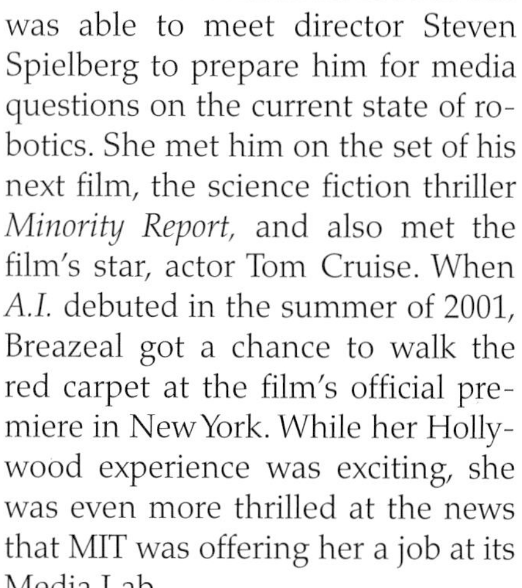

Becoming a Professor at MIT

Beginning in 2002, Breazeal became an associate professor of media arts and sciences at MIT; she also became director of the Media Lab's new Robotic Life Group (now called the Personal Robots Group). This group would focus on designing cooperative robots, building on the work Breazeal had already accomplished.

At the Media Lab, Breazeal began by challenging a group of her students to come up with a creative display for a top computer graphics conference. Her only rule was that their robot shouldn't imitate a real creature too closely. Her team came up with the idea of a robot that resembled a sea anemone, with tentacles instead of arms or legs. They built an artificial terrarium (including a waterfall and artificial plants) and programmed the robot to perform "chores" and then seek human interaction when it was finished. The terrarium also had "day" and "night" phases with interactive lighting features. When "Public Anemone" debuted at the conference in 2002, it was one of the most popular exhibits.

The robot's constantly changing behavior meant that people would see something different on each visit.

Breazeal's students created another unusual robotics display in 2003, for the National Design Triennial at New York's Cooper-Hewitt National Design Museum. Their display, "Cyberflor," involved lights, music, and robotic flowers that changed in response to human interaction. Some of the flowers responded to movement, some to body heat, and some to light. "The installation communicates my future vision of robot design," Breazeal noted. This robotic future "is intellectually intriguing and remains true to its technological heritage, but is able to touch us emotionally in the quality of interaction and their responsiveness to us—more like a dance, rather than pushing buttons."

Bringing Movie Magic to Robotics

Although Breazeal had enjoyed great success with Kismet, she wanted to take interactive robots to the next level. It would require a lot more time and materials, however; better motors for more realistic expressions, and better sensors and software for quicker response times. She also wanted her new robot to look more real. She recalled the high quality "robots" she had seen created for the film *A.I.*, although they were actually puppets run by remote control, not real robots. Still, she wondered whether Hollywood special effects designers might help her achieve her goal.

Breazeal used her Hollywood contacts to arrange a meeting with Stan Winston, whose Stan Winston Studios (SWS) produced the "robots" for *A.I.* In addition, the group had also won special effects Oscars for such movies as *Jurassic Park, Aliens,* and *Terminator 2: Judgment Day.* After touring the studio, she offered SWS a proposal: that her lab and SWS collaborate on an advanced sociable robot. MIT would share their state-of-the-art research on artificial intelligence, while SWS would provide design experience and financing.

The project began with SWS designing a character and building a puppet, just as it would for a movie. This puppet, however, included electrical motors that MIT could control with its computers and other technologies. Breazeal suggested that the design avoid humanoid or animal faces, in favor of something new. It should also be childlike, she said, so it would have broad appeal to people. Following these suggestions, SWS built a cute, furry creature with large brown eyes and long ears, with a large head and a big belly that could hide motors and sensory equipment. SWS nicknamed the robot Leonardo, after the great Italian artist and inventor Leonardo da Vinci.

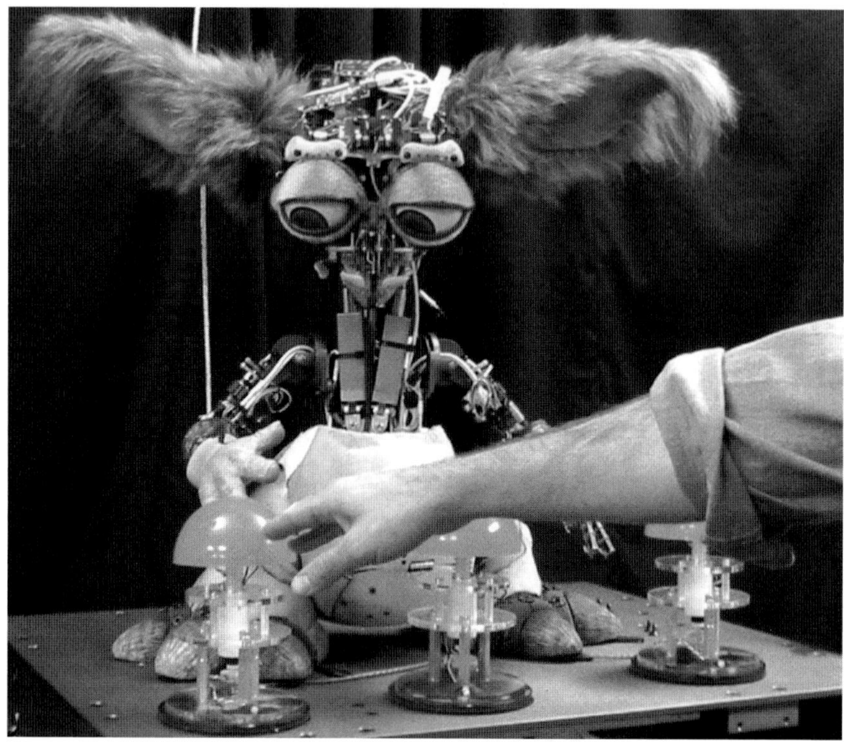

The robot Leonardo, named after the artist Leonardo da Vinci.

Leonardo not only had a more lifelike outer appearance, he had more motors and sensors underneath his "skin." His parts could move in 60 different directions, 30 of them in his face, including his ears. To transform Leo from puppet to robot, MIT installed sensors and software that drove him to look for and recognize people. Based on past experience, Leo would remember whether a person was friendly or not. Breazeal's team also programmed Leo to see the world from another person's point of view. He was able to understand the concept of "false belief," or the idea that another person can believe something different from you. For instance, Leo could witness someone put cookies into one box and potato chips in another box. If that person left the room and the contents of the boxes were switched, Leo understood that when the person returned, they would look in the wrong box for the cookies. He would then open the correct box to give the person the cookies. This is a cognitive skill that human children do not acquire until they are between three and four years old.

Leonardo was featured on the 2002 television program "Scientific American Frontiers," and thousands of people have watched videos of him on

YouTube. Although one critic has called Leo's behavior nothing more than "manufactured" or fake emotions, Breazeal believes that is the wrong standard to use in judging a robot's success. The goal is to make robot-human communication more natural, which happens with creations like Leo; judging robot emotions is a separate matter. "Robots are not human, but humans aren't the only ones that have emotions," the engineer claimed. "The question for robots is not, 'Will they ever have human emotions?' Dogs don't have human emotions, either, but we all agree they have genuine emotions. The question is, 'What are the emotions that are genuine for robots?'"

Exploring New Types of Robotics

Breazeal's Personal Robotics Group continues to explore ways that robots can interact with people. Simple robots include RoCo, a computer monitor that responds to its user and could improve posture and productivity, and the AUR, a robotic desk lamp that someday could be used in hospital operating rooms. More complex creations include the Huggable™, a teddy bear–shaped robot designed to be used in hospitals and schools. The Huggable has "sensate skin," which can measure temperature, force, and electrical fields. Breazeal supervises graduate students who are working on such projects as a robotic weight-loss coach and Nexi, a mobile manipulator robot with very expressive face and hands that can manipulate objects.

"I wouldn't say that having children has changed my perspective as much as broadened it and made my research and its application much more personal," Breazeal observed. "[Having children] has certainly influenced my work to pursue projects like the Huggable—to try to make a more direct connection between my academic life and helping real people."

In addition to her duties at MIT with the Personal Robots Group and as LG Career Development Chair in Media Arts and Sciences, Breazeal also works to inspire young people. She has been a judge at the FIRST Robotics Competition, a nationwide high school robotics competition. She has worked with the Boston Museum of Science on exhibits, including the very popular "Star Wars: Where Science Meets Imagination." That installation included a film of Breazeal having a discussion with the character C-3PO on how her group tries to give robots mobili-

Leonardo was designed to look cute and cuddly so it would be appealing to humans.

ty, perception, and understanding. As a working mother, she shows girls that a career in science doesn't mean giving up a family life; she feels this is important because "girls aren't discouraged [to become scientists], but they aren't encouraged either." In addition, being a mother has had an impact on her work. "I wouldn't say that having children has changed my perspective as much as broadened it and made my research and its application much more personal," she observed. "[Having children] has certainly influenced my work to pursue projects like the Huggable—to try to make a more direct connection between my academic life and helping real people."

Breazeal sees a bright future for sociable robots. While many of today's robots are only toys, she believes that soon they will become advanced enough to improve lives, and her designs work toward that goal. For instance, some researchers think sociable robots could be useful in caring for the sick or elderly. "In many ways I think about a blind person's relationship with a seeing eye dog," Breazeal said. The disabled and elderly "want to remain active and engaged, they want to feel self-sufficient and independent.... So we're interested in robots that are basically interacting as partners, rather than robots that are like slaves or tools." Perhaps someday she will build a robot, like her old favorite R2-D2, that can grow beyond the role of tool into something more. "To me, the ultimate milestone is a robot that can be your friend. To me, that's the ultimate in social intelligence."

MARRIAGE AND FAMILY

Breazeal first met Robert (Bobby) Blumofe in the early 1990s, when they were both graduate students at MIT. They were only friends at first, sharing an enjoyment of winter sports, but reconnected in 2000 through a mutual colleague. They married on June 7, 2003, and have three sons, Ryan, Nathan, and Caleb. They live in the Cambridge, Massachusetts, area, where Blumofe is an executive for Akamai Technologies, an Internet services company.

HOBBIES AND OTHER INTERESTS

Breazeal enjoys sports, particularly snowboarding, skiing, wind-surfing, and tennis. She still enjoys reading science fiction, which gives her inspiration as well as pleasure.

WRITINGS

Designing Social Robots, 2002
Biologically Inspired Intelligent Robots, 2003 (editor, with Yoseph Bar Cohen)
Star Wars: Where Science Meets Imagination, 2005 (contributor)

HONORS AND AWARDS

Young Investigator Award (Office of Naval Research): 2005
Robots at Play Prize (Robots at Play Festival, Denmark): 2006, for Huggable
International Robot Design Competition (IEEE Ro-Man): 2007, Gold Prize, for AUR

FURTHER READING

Books

Brown, Jordan D. *Robo World: The Story of Robot Designer Cynthia Breazeal,* 2005

Periodicals

Current Science, Jan. 21, 2000, p.8
Discover, Oct. 1999, p.66
New York Times, June 10, 2003, p.F3

New York Times Magazine, July 29, 2007, p.28
Sunday Times (London), Nov. 22, 1998, p.18
Time, Dec. 4, 2000, p.110
Times (London), Nov. 18, 1998, p.16
U.S. News & World Report, Apr. 23, 2001, p.45
Vector, Mar. 28, 2006
Washington Post, Sep. 17, 2000, p.A1

Online Articles

http://web.mit.edu/newsoffice/2001/kismet.html
(MIT News Office, "MIT Team Building Social Robot," Feb. 14, 2001)
http://www.pbs.org/wgbh/nova/sciencenow
(NOVA ScienceNOW, "Profile: Cynthia Breazeal," Nov. 21, 2006)
http://www.pbs.org/saf
(Scientific American Frontiers, "A Conversation with Cynthia Breazeal," Mar. 1, 2005)

ADDRESS

Cynthia Breazeal
Personal Robots Lab
MIT Media Lab
20 Ames Street, E15-468
Cambridge, MA 02139

WORLD WIDE WEB SITES

http://web.media.mit.edu/~cynthiab
http://www.iwaswondering.org/cynthia_homepage.html
http://robotic.media.mit.edu/index.html

Michael Cera 1988-

Canadian Actor

Star of *Superbad, Juno,* and *Nick & Norah's Infinite Playlist*

BIRTH

Michael Austin Cera was born on June 7, 1988, in the Canadian town of Brampton, Ontario. He is the son of Luigi and Linda Cera, both of whom worked for Xerox at the time of his birth. Michael is the second of three children and has an older sister named Jordan and a younger sister named Molly.

YOUTH

Cera grew up in Brampton, which is a suburb of Toronto. While still quite young, he began to display an offbeat sense of humor that made an impression on his parents. "He never connected with the over-the-top humor that usually made other kids laugh, making faces and stupid dances and things," said Linda Cera. "But if I'd knock my arm into the furniture and pretend I was hurt, that made him laugh." Overall, Cera's personality was more laid-back than outgoing, and his mother noted that "he wasn't ever the one hamming it up for attention."

"He never connected with the over-the-top humor that usually made other kids laugh, making faces and stupid dances and things," said Linda Cera. "But if I'd knock my arm into the furniture and pretend I was hurt, that made him laugh."

Though he may have been reserved in some ways, Cera became interested in acting at a very young age. He was initially inspired by the movie *Ghostbusters,* which he watched over and over when he was sick with the chicken pox at age three. Soon after, he had all of the film's dialog memorized and was especially enthralled with star Bill Murray, who has remained one of his idols. Around this time, he informed his parents of his future plans: he was going to be an actor.

EDUCATION

Responding to his interest, his parents enrolled him in drama classes, and he soon showed enough promise that he was advised to seek out an agent. Cera studied various approaches in honing his dramatic skills. One of them was improvisational acting, which he learned in classes with the Second City comedy troupe in Toronto. This approach involves making up dialog for characters on the spur of the moment rather than reciting lines from a script, and Cera later put this approach to use in some of his films. He also learned by immersing himself in his favorite television comedies, which included "Mr. Show" and "The Tom Green Show."

Meanwhile, there was general schoolwork to attend to. Initially, Cera was educated in Brampton-area public schools, including Heart Lake Secondary School. But as his career gained steam, he completed independent studies and worked with a tutor, and he eventually earned his diploma in that manner. His last full year in a regular school took place when he was in 10th grade—his initial year of high school. "I never got to have anyone below me in high school," he later explained. "I never got to be on top.... Maybe that's good. It shaped who I was. I wasn't ever able to look at people as beneath me."

Even while he was attending a regular school, Cera was somewhat of an outsider, though he sometimes deliberately chose to be "uncool" just for the fun of it. Reflecting on his experiences as a seventh grader, he recalled that "there was a day when my friend Chris and I decided we didn't care what people thought of us." To prove that point, he began wearing a pink bicycle helmet and unusual clothing to school. "I decided to start wearing the helmet and see if people thought I was an idiot," he said. "And then I was excited about people thinking I was an idiot." Cera's interest in uncomfortable circumstances has extended to more recent times as well. "I always kind of end up in situations where I don't know too many people," he explained, "and I'm not very social, and I feel, you know, extremely uncomfortable. But there's some secret pleasure I take in things like that, in things going horribly wrong."

CAREER HIGHLIGHTS

Cera's professional career began when he was nine years old. His first job was in a television commercial for Tim Hortons, a popular coffee-and-doughnuts chain that started in Canada and has since expanded into the United States. Another commercial for Pillsbury followed, but this success was short-lived. He was turned down for some 200 other roles in advertising before deciding to focus on dramatic roles. His first job in that field came in 1998, when he provided the voice of Little Gizmo in the Disney Channel animated program "Rolie Polie Olie," and he later undertook voice work for other cartoons. On-camera roles began in 1999 with his part in "I Was a Sixth-Grade Alien" on the Canadian YTV channel, and he also appeared in several made-for-television movies.

In 2000, Cera made the jump to the big screen, and his early film work included supporting roles in *Frequency, Steal This Movie,* and *Confessions of a Dangerous Mind*. During this period, he and his mother began spending time in the Los Angeles area so that he would have more opportunities to audition for roles. In the years since, he has regularly resided in California for certain periods, though the family home in Brampton continues to be his permanent home base.

In 2002, Cera was cast in "The Grubbs," a new Fox television series. Five episodes were produced, but the show proved to be his introduction to the uncertain nature of TV work. Advance screenings of the series received a very poor response, including an E! Online review that called it "the worst

Scenes from Cera's career: "Rolie Polie Olie," "Arrested Development," and "Clark and Michael."

sitcom ever produced." As a result, the network decided to cancel "The Grubbs" before it ever aired. Cera then landed a role doing the voice of Brother Bear on the cartoon series "The Berenstain Bears." After that, he was cast in another Fox series, "Arrested Development." Unlike his experience with "The Grubbs," his performance in this new series not only made it to the airwaves, it provided the launching pad for his later acting success.

"Arrested Development"

The new series was a situation comedy entitled "Arrested Development." When he read the script, Cera was excited by the mock-documentary style and by the offbeat storylines, which relay the comic adventures of a formerly wealthy family that has fallen on hard times. Cera auditioned for the role of George Michael Bluth—the 13-year-old son of the show's main protagonist—and was one of the first actors cast in the show. When "Arrested Development" hit the airwaves in 2003, his portrayal of the gawky George Michael, who develops a crush on his cousin, was one of the highlights that impressed critics.

In fact, reviewers liked almost everything about the program, particularly its quirky and sophisticated humor. In 2004, "Arrested Development" earned six Emmy Awards and a TV Land Award, and the cast was nominated for Screen Actors Guild awards in two consecutive years. Unfortunately, the official honors and critical praise did not translate into high ratings, and the show was cancelled in 2006, much to the disappointment of its small but devoted audience. Nonetheless, "Arrested Development" provided Cera with valuable acting experience, and his performance as George Michael gave him a much higher profile in the entertainment industry. Mitchell Hurwitz, the creator of "Arrested Development," was one of those who recognized that Cera was destined for further success. "He just has this uncanny maturity," Hurwitz explained in 2007, "and I think he's going to be a big part of this next generation of comic actors."

"Arrested Development" also proved important because it allowed Cera his first substantial opportunity to depict a confused adolescent character, and such roles have become the mainstay of his career to date. His George Michael Bluth character became famous for delivering a high-pitched laugh that indicates his uneasiness. In addition, Cera's work in "Arrested Development" and later projects demonstrated his skill in creating awkward silences that allow the viewer to experience some of the self-conscious embarrassment that is felt by the characters he plays.

Cera had the opportunity to explore dramatic disasters in greater detail when he collaborated with his friend Clark Duke on the Internet-only series "Clark and Michael." At that time, in 2005, Duke was enrolled in film school at Loyola Marymount University. The "Clark and Michael" show began as a project for his film-school studies and expanded into 10 episodes of about 10 minutes each. Utilizing the "mockumentary" approach, "Clark and Michael" relays the mishaps of two inept screenwriters who try to convince Hollywood executives to produce a script they have written. Cera and Duke wrote the screenplay as well as serving as the program's stars, and the episodes demonstrate the dry sense of humor that Cera frequently exhibits when not playing movie roles. The series was sold to CBS, and in 2007 it became one of the network's first scripted online video shows, available on the "Clark and Michael" web site.

Cera has had a hand in several other short comic video segments that have become popular on sites such as YouTube. He wrote and starred in "Impossible is the Opposite of Possible," an offbeat spoof of a real-life video resume, and had a role in an episode of "Drunk History." In addition, he was part of a short comedy piece related to the film *Knocked Up*, appearing as an actor who gets into a shouting match with the film's director, Judd Apatow, during a screen test. The mock audition was included as an extra feature on the DVD release of the movie.

Superbad

The *Knocked Up* comic segment proved to be just one of Cera's projects with Apatow. Their larger collaboration was the 2007 film *Superbad*, in which Cera delivered a breakout performance in his first leading role in a motion picture. The comedy follows two high school seniors, Evan and Seth—played by Cera and costar Jonah Hill—over the course of a very eventful 24-hour period shortly before graduation. Up to this point in their lives, the two have not enjoyed much success with the opposite sex, but they see an opportunity to change their status when a popular female classmate invites them to a party. The catch is, they need to supply alcohol for the underage party-goers, which launches the duo and their friend Fogell into a series of adventures that involve a fake ID, stolen liquor, and numerous run-ins with two less-than-upstanding police officers.

Produced by Apatow and written by Seth Rogen and Evan Goldberg, *Superbad* features many of the film elements often associated with Apatow's work, including raunchy situations, off-color humor, and lots of profane language. Most critics took the crudeness in stride, however, and appreciated the film's realistic portrayal of teen dialog and preoccupations. Moreover, Cera and his costars frequently received high marks for their honest

Christopher Mintz-Plasse (left), Jonah Hill (center), and Cera (right) in a scene from Superbad.

depiction of teen anxiety and vulnerability. Reviewer Claudia Puig, writing in *USA Today*, noted that "humiliation, fear, and occasional elation are the dominant emotions for these bumbling but oddly likable young men" and added that audiences would react to the movie with "side-splitting laughter, along with some powerful cringing." *Newsweek* reviewer Devin Gordon deemed Cera and Hill "a duo for the ages" and praised Cera as "a world-class sputterer. He delivers all his lines a split second faster than you expect, turning each joke into a sneak attack."

Debuting in August 2007, *Superbad* was the No. 1 film in the nation during its first two weeks of release and proved to be a summer favorite. Its popularity and high-profile promotion campaign gave Cera a great deal of exposure, including newspaper and magazine profiles and appearances on television talk shows. It was a sign of things to come: just one month after *Superbad* made him a star, his next film project debuted, and it proved to be even more popular.

Juno

Cera's next role was in the 2007 film *Juno.* In winning that role, he had the good fortune to be part of a small-budget independent film that ended up

Cera with Ellen Page, his co-star in Juno.

being one of the most talked about pictures of the year. The title character, played by Ellen Page, is a smart and sharp-tongued 16-year-old who gets pregnant and considers having an abortion before deciding to find someone to adopt the baby. Cera played Paulie Bleeker, the teenage father of the baby, though he and Juno are better described as friends than as lovers, and their relationship manages to survive the difficulties they find themselves in.

The movie drew a lot of attention for dealing with the hot-button topics of teen sex and abortion, but, as several reviewers noted, *Juno* focuses on the experiences of its characters rather than promoting a social message. "*Juno* is not really about the realities of teen pregnancy or of adoption," wrote David Heim in *Christian Century*. "It is a clever riff on teen lingo and a cheerful fantasy of how a sense of humor and a good friend can get you through almost anything." *New Yorker* writer David Denby was another critic who was very positive about the film, proclaiming it "a coming-of-age movie made with idiosyncratic charm and not a single false note." A surprise hit with filmgoers, *Juno* won acclaim at film festivals and then went on to do big business across the nation, racking up more than $143 million in domestic sales after being made for the relatively low sum of $7.5 million. The film received four Academy Award nominations, including consideration as Best Picture, and screenwriter Diablo Cody took home the Oscar for Best Original Screenplay.

Though Cera was not the principal character in *Juno*, he made a big impression. Todd McCarthy, writing in *Variety*, noted that "Cera's low-key modesty and reserve prove an effective counterbalance" to Page's more outgoing character. Similarly, *Maclean's* writer Brian D. Johnson asserted that "Cera, with his skinny legs in jogging shorts and his sincere puppy-dog charm, must be the most laid-back leading man/boy to ever make comedy romantic."

Such comments illustrate Cera's growing reputation as a celebrity heartthrob, despite the fact that he usually plays characters with somewhat "geeky" personalities. He had gotten his first taste of that kind of attention during his promotional work for *Superbad*. During an appearance at Comic Con International in San Diego, for instance, he was fawned over by a succession of young female fans proposing marriage. When questioned about his status as a "hottie," Cera responds with low-key bewilderment. "A sex symbol?" he said in disbelief at a 2008 press conference. "Like I symbolize sex?" He has also pointed out that he is not a conventionally handsome type. "If you stood me in line with all my ex-girlfriends and asked who's more attractive, it's always them." While typical movie-star perfection may not be his stock in trade, Cera's appeal is widespread, especially among teenage girls, and some observers see him as a new type of leading man. Noting the actor's "sad baby-seal cuteness and mastery of the uncomfortable pause," an *Entertainment Weekly* feature in June 2008 asserted that "Cera has made teenage awkwardness not just funny but cool."

*"*Juno *is not really about the realities of teen pregnancy or of adoption," wrote David Heim in* Christian Century. *"It is a clever riff on teen lingo and a cheerful fantasy of how a sense of humor and a good friend can get you through almost anything."*

Nick & Norah's Infinite Playlist

Cera's ability to play a romantic lead was put to a demanding test in *Nick & Nora's Infinite Playlist,* which debuted in October 2008. Once again cast as a high school senior, Cera plays Nick, an aspiring rock musician who falls for Norah, portrayed by Kat Dennings. Their romance is kindled during an evening when they travel through New York City with a small group of fellow teens on a quest to find a secret concert being staged by one of their favorite bands.

While *Nick & Norah's Infinite Playlist* did not repeat the blockbuster success of *Juno,* the film did receive mostly positive reviews. *Chicago Tribune* reviewer Michael Phillips was one of those who gave the film high marks and singled out Cera's perfomance: "The way he acts and reacts, he's especially astute at capturing a certain kind of young adult, perched on a fence between hesitant adolescence and premature middle age." David Ansen, writing in *Newsweek,* declared that "the movie has a genuine, unforced sweetness. Its

An example of the chemistry between Cera and his co-star, Kat Dennings, in Nick & Norah's Infinite Playlist.

charm is in the details, the attitude, the slowly building chemistry between Cera (a master of stone-faced irony) and the beguiling Dennings."

The rapport between the actors resulted partly from the film's production process. Director Peter Sollett brought the cast together before beginning the filming so that they could get comfortable with one another. "We all hung out before shooting, so we weren't total strangers," explained Cera. "We played poker, played PS3, watched movies, talked." There was also a sense of shared adventure once the cameras rolled, which largely came from the film's shooting locations. "We had some crazy nights filming the movie," noted Dennings. "Well, you know, middle of the night in New York City, drunk people throwing things, yelling at us, wanting us out of their places where they like to be." Cera's status as a rising celebrity also inspired some of the production disruptions, with vocal onlookers sometimes interrupting scenes by shouting "Hey, Superbad!" when they caught sight of the actor.

An Uncertain Star

As his fame has grown, Cera has become increasingly unhappy about all the attention he receives in public. "When you're in a movie that's really popular, it's a strange life change," he observed. "Literally overnight people recognize you on the street. Sometimes they're nice, sometimes they're not, and sometimes they lose track of how to treat other human beings." He also finds it difficult to interact with fans who assume they know what he's like because of his on-screen personas. "I'm not like these parts I play, you know. I mean, it's just acting. I do the work on the set, and then it's over."

Despite his misgivings, Cera is likely to receive a lot of attention for upcoming films, which include *The Year One, Youth in Revolt,* and *Scott Pilgrim vs. the World*. Once those projects are completed, he has suggested that he might focus on smaller parts to avoid some of the negative aspects of being a star. "I don't really want to be famous, and I'm kind of scared that might be happening," he admitted. "I guess I need to make sure that it's worth all that comes with it."

HOME AND FAMILY

Cera splits his time between an apartment in Los Angeles and his parents' home in Brampton.

HOBBIES AND OTHER INTERESTS

An amateur musician, Cera formed a band called The Long Goodbye with Clark Duke but doesn't expect that they will devote a lot of time to developing the act. "Now that people know me as an actor, I don't think they'd be able to get past that and listen to the music," he noted. In addition, Cera is said to be composing music for the upcoming film *Paper Hearts*, and he also writes short stories in his spare time.

SELECTED CREDITS

Television Programs

"Rolie Polie Olie," 1998 (voice of animated character)
"I Was a Sixth Grade Alien!," 1999-2001
What Katy Did, 1999 (TV movie)
Custody of the Heart, 2000 (TV movie)
My Louisiana Sky, 2001 (TV movie)
"The Grubbs," 2002
"The Berenstain Bears," 2003 (voice of animated character)
"Arrested Development," 2003-2006

Films

Frequency, 2000
Steal This Movie, 2000

Confessions of a Dangerous Mind, 2002
Juno, 2007
Superbad, 2007
Nick & Norah's Infinite Playlist, 2008

Internet Series

"Clark and Michael," 2006

HONORS AND AWARDS

Beaver Award (Canadian Comedy Foundation for Excellence): 2008, Best Film Actor, for *Superbad*

FURTHER READING

Periodicals

Entertainment Weekly, Aug. 17, 2007, p.20; Oct. 17, 2008, p.76
Globe and Mail, Oct. 3, 2008
Los Angeles Times, Sep. 7, 2008
New York, Aug. 6, 2007
New York Times, July 8, 2007; Sep. 28, 2008, p.11
Newsweek, Sep. 27, 2008
Times (United Kingdom), Oct. 4, 2008
USA Today, Aug. 17, 2007, p.D8

ADDRESS

Michael Cera
Paradigm Talent Agency
360 North Crescent Drive, North Building
Beverly Hills, CA 90210

Michael Cera
Thruline Entertainment
9250 Wilshire Blvd., Ground Floor
Beverly Hills, CA 90212

WORLD WIDE WEB SITES

http://www.clarkandmichael.com
http://www.foxsearchlight.com/juno
http://www.sonypictures.com/homevideo/superbad
http://www.sonypictures.com/movies/nickandnorah

Miranda Cosgrove 1993-

American Actress and Musician
Star of the Nickelodeon Series "iCarly"

BIRTH

Miranda Taylor Cosgrove was born on May 14, 1993, in Los Angeles, California. Her father, Tom Cosgrove, runs a dry-cleaning business, while her mother, Chris Cosgrove, is a homemaker who also takes an active role in her daughter's professional life. Miranda does not have any brothers or sisters.

YOUTH

Los Angeles has been Cosgrove's home throughout her life. That turned out to be a good thing for her entertainment career because much of the television and film production in the United States takes place in the L.A. area. In fact, she got her start in the business partly because she happened to be in the right Southern California restaurant at the right time. When she was just three years old, she was dining out with her parents and began to entertain herself by singing and dancing. Her performance caught the attention of a talent agent who was in the restaurant, and just like that, Cosgrove was discovered. "An agent just walked up to my mom and asked if I wanted to do modeling and stuff," Cosgrove explained. "My mom had never even thought about putting me in acting or anything." After mulling it over, her parents decided to let her take a shot at show business, and she entered the world of auditions and acting lessons.

"

Cosgrove has said that when she was three, "An agent just walked up to my mom and asked if I wanted to do modeling and stuff," Cosgrove explained. "My mom had never even thought about putting me in acting or anything."

"

EDUCATION

Cosgrove attended a regular school during her elementary years. Since completing the fifth grade, she has studied independently, as many child actors do, completing home-school and online courses and working with a private tutor. She plans to attend college and has expressed an interest in becoming a marine biologist.

CAREER HIGHLIGHTS

When Cosgrove first started working, she focused on television and print advertising and soon landed jobs in TV ads for Mello Yello and McDonald's. She continued with that type of work for several years before she began to think about an acting career. "I just kind of did commercials and modeling and stuff," she recalled. "And then when I was seven, I realized that I loved doing it, and that's when I started trying out for more theatrical things and actually roles and plays and stuff like that."

The year 2002 turned out to be a breakthrough for the young actress, who was then turning nine. She landed the role of Megan Parker in "Drake &

In this poster from School of Rock, *Cosgrove is shown to the immediate left of Jack Black, along with the other students that he molds into a band. She played Summer Hathaway, the band's manager.*

Josh," a Nickelodeon series that was being launched, and was also cast in the feature film *School of Rock*. With parts in two major projects, she suddenly found herself in the "big leagues" of acting. She began by working on the "Josh and Drake" pilot episode—a "test" show that allows the network to decide if it wants to approve the series. Once that was completed, she went to New York City to film *School of Rock*.

School of Rock

Much of the movie *School of Rock* takes place at a prep school, where Summer Hathaway (played by Cosgrove) is one of the students. Summer is a bit prissy, the student who always has the right answer and always has her homework done. But classtime changes quickly with the arrival of substitute teacher Dewey Finn, played by Jack Black. He immediately assesses the students' skills and forms the class into a rock-and-roll band. Working with Black was a lot of fun, according to Cosgrove. "The first week it was like, 'Oh, my God, that's Jack Black,' but two weeks later it was fine. He's really funny. Sometimes the director would say, 'Jack you can't make them laugh so much.'"

"

Working with Black was a lot of fun, according to Cosgrove. "The first week it was like, 'Oh, my God, that's Jack Black,' but two weeks later it was fine. He's really funny. Sometimes the director would say, 'Jack you can't make them laugh so much.'"

"

The role forced Cosgrove to take on some difficult acting challenges, especially when it came to singing. At one point in the movie, her character tries out as a vocalist for the band but is unable to carry a tune. She found that performing poorly—on purpose—wasn't easy. "I got a 45-minute lesson from Jim O'Rourke of Sonic Youth on how to sing badly," she said after filming was completed. "I've been taking singing lessons for about five years, so getting to sing badly was new. The director kept saying, 'Try to sing even worse, Miranda,' so it was weird."

Cosgrove has gone on to play other movie roles, but *School of Rock* remains her best-known work on the big screen. In addition to boosting her acting career, the movie introduced her to a lot of classic rock songs she wasn't familiar with and inspired her to study music more intensely. "After the movie I discovered Led Zeppelin and I've taken up the electric guitar," she explained, and she has continued to rock out in the years since.

"Drake & Josh"

After production concluded on *School of Rock,* Cosgrove returned to Los Angeles and began work on the first season of programs for "Drake & Josh." The show paired two high school students, Drake (played by Drake Bell) and Josh (played by Josh Peck), who have to adjust to living in the same house after Drake's mother marries Josh's father. Drake is the cool, guitar-playing slacker who draws Josh, his dorky, responsible stepbrother, into his shenanigans. The two forge a brotherly bond through their adventures. Cosgrove soon became well known to viewers as the mischievous younger sister Megan Parker, who is constantly scheming against her brother, Drake, and stepbrother, Josh, and pulling pranks on them. The series became one of the most popular live-action shows in the history of Nickelodeon and continued to air new episodes from 2004 through 2007.

> *"It's like a big family," Cosgrove said about working on "Drake and Josh." "We know each other so well, nothing is embarrassing anymore.... It's really comfortable, and it's really fun." She described Drake and Josh as "two of the funniest guys ever.... They make me laugh every day a million times."*

Cosgrove developed a close relationship with the other actors on the show and enjoyed the camaraderie they shared on the set. "It's like a big family," she noted shortly after the production wrapped up on the show's final season. "We know each other so well, nothing is embarrassing anymore.... It's really comfortable, and it's really fun." The stars of the show provided Cosgrove with valuable advice about handling the pressures of fame, and she described Drake and Josh as "two of the funniest guys ever.... They make me laugh every day a million times."

"Drake & Josh" also gave Cosgrove a chance to develop a strong partnership with Dan Schneider, the show's executive producer. Schneider has a long track record of creating popular shows for Nickelodeon, including "Zoey 101," "The Amanda Show," "Kenan & Kel," and "All That." Part of his recipe for success is to take one or more supporting actors who appear on one of his programs and create a new series in which they become the primary star. As "Drake & Josh" was ending its run in 2007, the producer began focusing on a new comedy, and in this case, he tailored it to be a showcase for Miranda Cosgrove.

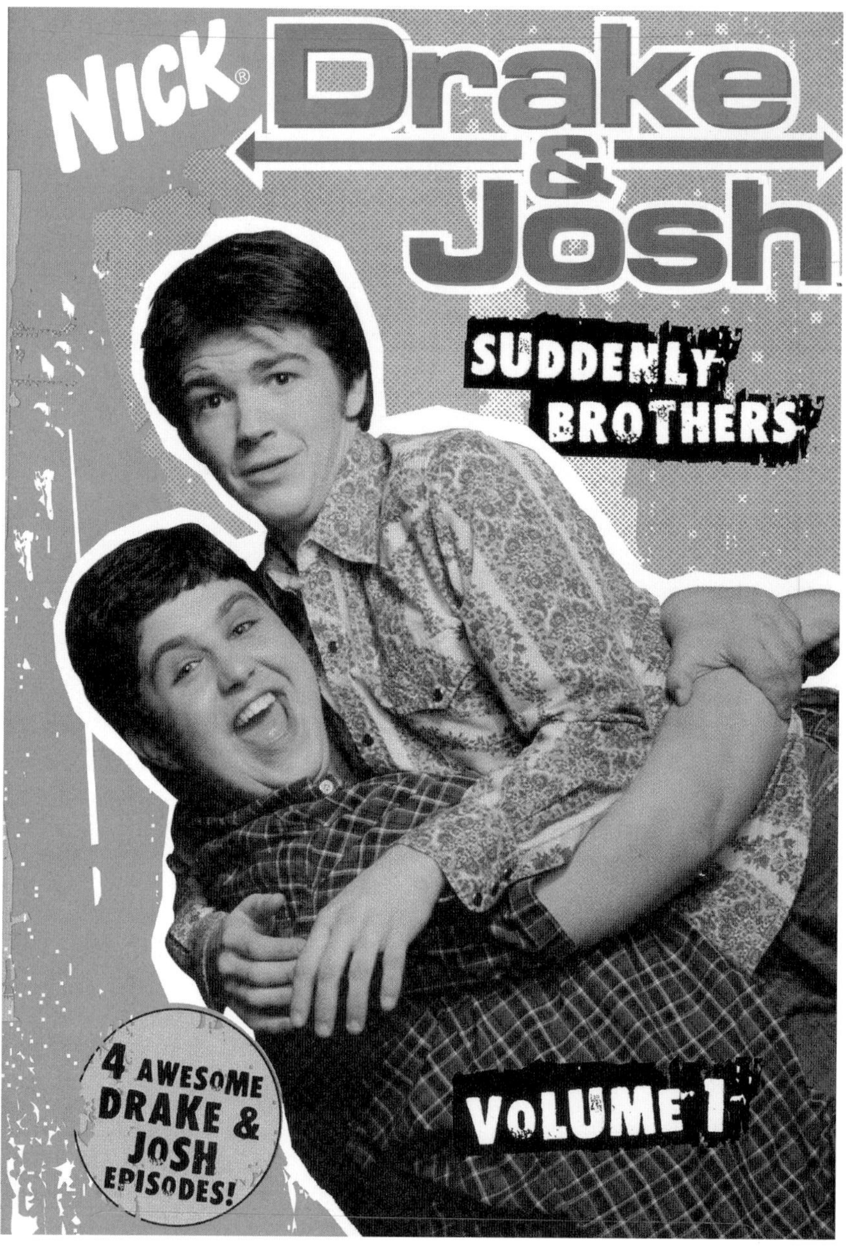

Cosgrove played younger sister Megan alongside Drake Bell (right) and Josh Peck on the hit Nickelodeon show "Drake and Josh."

"iCarly"

Schneider and his staff created the program "iCarly," and they set out to appeal to the widespread interest that young people have in the Internet. Cosgrove was given the role of Carly Shay, who hosts a webcast entertainment show with her friends. Viewers get to watch the kids' program and also share in Carly's adventures when she's away from the webcam.

The series has introduced a new idea for allowing the audience to get directly involved in the program. Viewers are invited to submit their own YouTube-style homemade videos, and the most entertaining segments are included as part of Carly's show. On occasion, the audience members who made the clips may be brought in as special guests. In addition, a number of the submitted videos are featured on the "iCarly" Internet site, which also includes blogs by the show's characters, photos, songs, and more.

"When I first heard about the idea, I thought it was so cool," Cosgrove said about "iCarly." "If I were home and watching TV, I'd want to send in a video."

Cosgrove was excited by "iCarly," and especially by the opportunities for audience participation. "When I first heard about the idea, I thought it was so cool," she said. "If I were home and watching TV, I'd want to send in a video." The viewer-submitted features include a wide range of material, including kids playing jokes on their parents and people with unusual "talents," such as the man who can squirt milk out of his eye sockets.

After debuting in September 2007, "iCarly" proved a hit with young viewers. By the summer of 2008, it had become the third highest rated show on TV for viewers in the 9-14 "'tween" age group. A special extended episode, "iCarly Saves TV," was the most-viewed entertainment show on cable TV when it aired in June 2008.

Having been part of two successful television shows, Cosgrove is often asked to compare her two characters—Carly and Megan from "Drake & Josh." "I think I'm more like Carly," she observed, "because she usually comes up with a plan, and I'm a little like that." Cosgrove also feels that "Carly is more like a real person [because she] is embarrassed and has problems with boys."

From Actress to Singer

Following the plan set by such other teen stars as Miley Cyrus and Hilary Duff, Cosgrove is seeking to prove herself as a musician as well as an ac-

Cosgrove in images from "iCarly": on the "iCarly" CD, with music from the show (top); with Sam (Janette McCurdy) and Freddy (Nathan Kress, center); and with Shane (James Maslow, bottom).

tress. She started out by recording "Leave It All to Me," the theme to "iCarly," and got a helping hand on that song from her former costar Drake Bell, who sings on the track. "I had never been in a studio or anything like that before, so I was really excited," Cosgrove said of the recording session for the theme song, and she later returned to cut three additional tracks. All four numbers were released in June 2008 on *iCarly: Music From and Inspired by the Hit TV Show,* which also includes 10 songs by other artists. The album was an immediate success, debuting at No. 1 on the Billboard Top Kid Audio album chart, and her single "Stay My Baby" has received significant airplay.

Cosgrove has enjoyed becoming a celebrity. "It's kind of nice sometimes when people recognize you and it's really cool, like, to be with your friends and people come up to [talk to] you."

”

Cosgrove plans to record a full-length album of material, including songs that she helped compose. "For my own CD I've been co-writing and getting really into it," she said. "It's still pop-rock fun music like the 'iCarly' soundtrack, but I think it's a little more mature. They're love songs and just fun songs about hanging out with your girlfriends."

With her entertainment success, Cosgrove is starting to get a better understanding of what it means to be famous. While there may be some drawbacks to being a celebrity, she claims that she still enjoys meeting her fans in person. "It's kind of nice sometimes when people recognize you and it's really cool, like, to be with your friends and people come up to [talk to] you." For now, she has few fears that the pressures of show business will cause her difficulties, noting that she has a lot of parental supervision to help her keep things in perspective. "My mom's always on set with me, and my dad comes by a lot," she said. "I don't really worry about it.... I don't have time to go crazy or anything."

HOME AND FAMILY

Cosgrove lives with her parents in Los Angeles.

HOBBIES AND OTHER INTERESTS

Typical teen activities play a big part in Cosgrove's daily life. "My room is never clean," she confessed. "I play Guitar Hero all the time and throw things around my room." An admitted "movie junkie," she often goes to films with her friends and spends a lot of time trading text messages and instant messages with others. She also makes time for her hobbies of fencing and horseback riding.

SELECTED CREDITS

Movies

School of Rock, 2003
Here Comes Peter Cottontail, 2005 (voice of animated character)
Yours, Mine & Ours, 2005
Keeping Up with the Steins, 2006
The Wild Stallion, 2006

TV Series

"Drake and Josh," 2004-2007
"iCarly," 2007-

Made-for-TV Movies

Drake and Josh Go Hollywood, 2006
Drake and Josh: Really Big Shrimp, 2007

RECORDINGS

iCarly: Music From and Inspired by the Hit TV Show, 2008 (selected songs)

FURTHER READING

Periodicals

Detroit Free Press, Sep. 20, 2007
Entertainment Weekly, July 20, 2007
GL (Girls' Life), Oct./Nov. 2008, p.50
New York Times, Sep. 7, 2007, p.E1
People, July 28, 2008, p.71
USA Today, Sep. 4, 2007, p.D10; June 13, 2008, p.E2
Washington Post, Nov. 6, 2007, p.C13

Online Articles

http://www.mtv.com/music/artists
(MTV, "Miranda Cosgrove Plans Solo Album after Conquering TV with 'iCarly'," July 24, 2008)
http://www.thestarscoop.com/2006dec
(The StarScoop, "Miranda Cosgrove," Dec. 2006)

ADDRESS

Miranda Cosgrove
Nickelodeon Studios
231 West Olive Ave.
Burbank, CA 91502

WORLD WIDE WEB SITES

http://www.icarly.com
http://www.myspace.com
http://nick.com/icarly

Lupe Fiasco 1982-

American Rap Artist and Entrepreneur
Grammy-Award Winning Creator of the Hit Records
Food & Liquor and *The Cool*
Founder of the Companies 1st & 15th (FNF) and
Righteous Kung-Fu

BIRTH

Lupe Fiasco was born Wasalu Muhammad Jaco on February 17, 1982, in Chicago, Illinois. His mother, Shirley, worked as a gourmet chef. His father, Gregory, worked as an operating plant engineer and also owned Army Surplus stores and a martial arts school. Fiasco has nine brothers and sisters, of which six are half brothers and sisters.

YOUTH

Fiasco, called Lu as a child, grew up on the west side of Chicago, Illinois. His family lived in an apartment in Chicago's Madison Terrace housing project. The neighborhood was rough, but Fiasco's parents worked hard to help their children thrive. "I grew up in the 'hood around prostitutes, drug dealers, killers, and gangbangers," he explained. "On the doorknob outside of our apartment, there was blood from some guy who got shot; but inside, there was National Geographic magazines and encyclopedias and a little library bookshelf situation. And we didn't have cable, so we didn't have the luxury of having our brains washed by MTV. We watched public television—cooking shows and stuff like that."

"I did martial arts." Fiasco recalled." If I had to fight, I could defend myself. But it also taught me how to see when a fight is coming and how to defuse it. I learned how to think. That's the most important thing my mother and father taught us."

Fiasco's parents exposed their children to a wide range of experiences, including the culture of Chicago's many different ethnic groups. He credits these early adventures as a major influence on his development as an artist. "My father was a real prolific African drummer, and can play anything from the djiembes [African drums] to the bagpipes. My mom is a gourmet chef that has traveled the world. We were always around different cultures. It is because of these artistic experiences there are no limitations to what I talk about on my records."

Fiasco's father had also been a member of the Black Panthers civil rights activist group and a former Army Green Beret. His father was also a martial arts master. Under his direction, Fiasco began practicing martial arts when he was only three years old. "My father told me to respect weapons," he recalled. "I learned to respect them so much that I never wanted one. I did martial arts. If I had to fight, I could defend myself. But it also taught me how to see when a fight is coming and how to defuse it. I learned how to think. That's the most important thing my mother and father taught us." By the time he was ten years old, Fiasco had already earned four black belts in martial arts and two in samurai swords.

Fiasco loves skateboarding, which was the subject of one of his first hit songs, "Kick Push."

When Fiasco was five years old, his parents divorced. After that, Fiasco lived with his mother, but his father continued to be a strong presence in his life. "After school, my father would come get us and take us out into the world—one day, we're listening to [rap group] N.W.A., the next day,

> *Fiasco and his family were devout Sunni Muslims. "We would go to different mosques around the city," he recalled. "Each mosque would be in a different community, so it would be a different ethnic group. It would be Pakistanis, it would be Indians, it would be Palestinians, or it would be Africans.... I got to see a lot of different people.... It's like we were almost traveling the world.... I got exposed to a lot of different cultures."*

we're listening to [Indian sitar player] Ravi Shankar, the next day, he's teaching us how to shoot an AK-47, the next day, we're at karate class, the next day, we're in Chinatown.... We experienced everything with my father because the things he was into were so vast." With this type of experience, Fiasco began developing his musical tastes even before he started school, becoming interested in jazz and classical music. By the time he was six years old, he loved listening to the music of Beethoven and Tchaikovsky, playing the same records over and over.

For Fiasco and his family members, these cultural explorations extended to their religious practice as devout Sunni Muslims. "We would go to different mosques around the city," he recalled. "Each mosque would be in a different community, so it would be a different ethnic group. It would be Pakistanis, it would be Indians, it would be Palestinians, or it would be Africans.... So I was always all over the city in different neighborhoods. I got to see a lot of different people.... It's like we were almost traveling the world.... I got exposed to a lot of different cultures."

Fiasco's mother has described him as "a great spirited child. Smart, a bit complex; he kind of was a loner, he didn't hang with a lot of people.... He always had the glasses, always had a book bag over his shoulder and some kind of a writing tablet. He loved to skateboard, too. You could hear those little raggedy wheels ... ka-kunk-ka-kunk-ka-kunk, all night long." Fiasco loved reading comics and any other kind of books. His childhood favorites were Dr. Seuss, the Berenstain Bears, the science fiction novels of Jules Verne and George Orwell, and the books of Mark Twain.

EDUCATION

When Fiasco was in the sixth grade, he went to live with his father in the south Chicago suburb of Harvey, Illinois, and attended school there. Science was his favorite subject, and he especially liked chemistry. He thought of pursuing a scientific career but abandoned that goal because his math skills were not good enough for advanced study in the sciences. In high school, Fiasco discovered a love of the theater, and he ran the lights and sound for most of the school's theatrical productions. He joined the chess club and was also a member of the school's Knowledge Bowl Decathlon Team. Fiasco graduated from Thornton Township High School in Harvey, Illinois.

CAREER HIGHLIGHTS

Becoming a Rapper

Fiasco first began rapping in eighth grade because he wanted to find a way to express himself through music. "I come from a literary background, and I loved to tell stories. I remember freestyling stories, not in rhyme, by just coming up with things when I was a kid on the bus. But I couldn't play an instrument, so I decided to take my storytelling mind and to apply it to rap, which seemed like a natural thing. So I practiced a lot and really tried to apply the techniques I'd learned from poetry—which, of course, is the predecessor of rap."

At first, Fiasco tried out stage names like Little Lu and Lu tha Underdog. But by the time he was in high school, his friends were calling him Lupe. Then he chose the name Fiasco from a track called "Firm Fiasco" by hip-hop supergroup The Firm. Although some people tried to talk him out of the name, he was committed to it. "I simply liked the way the word looked. You know how rappers always have names like MC Terrorist—like they're 'terrorizing' other rappers? I knew fiasco meant a great disaster or something like that, but I didn't realize that the person named Fiasco would be the disaster, and that you should be calling other MCs fiascos—not yourself. I was moving real fast at the time, and it kind of humbled me in a sense. It taught me like, 'Yo, stop rushing, or you're going to have some fiascos.' So I just kept it. It's like a scar, I guess, a reminder to not overthink or overrun anything ever again."

By the time he was 17 years old, Fiasco was thinking seriously about a career as a rapper. Although his parents didn't like the idea of their son pursuing a career as a hip-hop performer, his father allowed him to set up a recording and mixing studio in the basement. Fiasco scoured Chicago's flea markets and secondhand stores, where he bought the necessary equipment: an old mixing board and record player, a stack of old vinyl records, and mic stands. Working with a group of friends, Fiasco rigged the studio and began making demo tapes and remixes of songs by other artists.

Soon Fiasco had formed a rap group called Da Pak. Copying the style of California gangsta rappers like Spice 1 and Ice Cube, Da Pak began performing wherever they could. In 2000, when Fiasco was 19 years old, Da Pak signed a contract with Epic Records. But the success of the group was short-lived, and Da Pak disbanded after releasing their first single. "We had a song out about cocaine, guns, and women," he said, "and I would go to a record store and look at it and think, 'What are you doing?' I felt like a hypocrite. I was acting like this rapper who would never be judged, and I had to destroy that guy. Because what Lupe Fiasco says on this microphone is going to come back to Wasalu Jaco. When the music cuts off, you have to go home and live with what you say."

"

"We had a song out about cocaine, guns, and women," Fiasco said, "and I would go to a record store and look at it and think, 'What are you doing?' I felt like a hypocrite. I was acting like this rapper who would never be judged, and I had to destroy that guy. Because what Lupe Fiasco says on this microphone is going to come back to Wasalu Jaco. When the music cuts off, you have to go home and live with what you say."

"

In turning away from the violent images of gangsta rap, Fiasco found that he was more attracted to the lyricism of rappers like Nas and Jay-Z. Around this time, his mother gave him some recordings of 1960s poetry performance groups like the Watts Prophets, who were among the first to use spoken word with music in a format that would later evolve into rap.

The First Big Break

Fiasco was inspired and determined to build his career as a rapper. By 2001, he founded a music production company called 1st & 15th (also known as FNF), named after the traditional twice-monthly paycheck dates. He signed a recording contract with Arista records, but the deal fell through. However, the Arista deal wasn't a complete failure because it allowed Fiasco to meet Jay-Z, who was then the president of Def Jam Records. Jay-Z called Fiasco a "breath of fresh air" and said Fiasco reminded him of himself early in his career. In 2004, Jay-Z helped Fiasco get a new contract with Atlantic Records. Fiasco then began recording the tracks that would eventually become his first album.

While he worked on his new music, Fiasco released his critically acclaimed mixtape series *Fahrenheit 1/15* over the Internet. As word spread, his remix-

Fiasco's first album, Food & Liquor, *was nominated for four Grammy Awards and won one award.*

es were downloaded by people all over the world, quickly resulting in a global fanbase. His remix "Muhammad Walks," based on Kanye West's "Jesus Walks," became popular with Muslims all over the world.

Fiasco's big break came when his track "Conflict Diamonds," a remix of Kanye West's "Diamonds from Sierra Leone," caught West's attention. West was so impressed with the remix that he invited Fiasco to perform on his upcoming single "Touch the Sky." The success of Fiasco's contribution to "Touch the Sky" resulted in the early release of his first official solo single. Entitled "Kick Push," this skateboard-themed song was inspired by Fiasco's own childhood hobby and soon became a hit. "It's a skateboarding song. I used to skateboard when I was younger. I was really into it. I never really knew that skateboarding was so deep as a culture. It's just as deep as hip-hop." "Kick Push" was nominated for two 2007 Grammy Awards.

Food & Liquor

Fiasco's first full-length album, *Food & Liquor,* was released in 2006. The album's artwork shows him surrounded by a collection of various items, including a ninja doll, a Nintendo game console, and a copy of the Muslim holy book, the Koran (also spelled Qur'an). He explained the image on the cover like this. "All of that is out of my book bag. It's the stuff I carry around every day." The album's title also has a significant meaning for Fiasco. "The title reflects on me being Muslim and being from the streets. In Chicago, instead of having bodegas like in New York, the majority of the corner stores are called 'Food and Liquors.' The store is where everything is at, whether it be the wine-o hanging by the store, or us as kids going back and forth to the store to buy something. The 'Food' is the good part and the 'Liquors' is the bad part. I try to balance out both parts of me.... Food to me represents growth and progression. You eat food and you get strength. You need it to live. Liquor is not a necessity; it is a want. It destroys you. It breaks you down. I can see why it's prohibited in Islam.... I've always felt like liquor represents the bad, and food represents the good, and everyone is made up of a little of both."

"

"Without dipping his toes into violent imagery, wanton obscenity, or other hip-hop clichés," wrote one Rolling Stone *reviewer, "Fiasco reflects on the personal and the political, and reminds fans of everything hip-hop can be. It's full of surprising, creative moments."*

Food & Liquor received rave reviews, with some music critics even calling Fiasco "the savior of the genre." Fiasco was praised for his storytelling talent and his ability to present mature subject matter grounded in his Muslim faith. A *Rolling Stone* reviewer said, "Without dipping his toes into violent imagery, wanton obscenity, or other hip-hop clichés, Fiasco reflects on the personal and the political, and reminds fans of everything hip-hop can be. It's full of surprising, creative moments." His raps were called complex, thought-provoking, and playful, and the beats were praised as inventive. An *Interview* magazine critic said, "The album straddles hip-hop and rock, with songs that segue from funky blaxploitation grooves into grunge, cabaret, and swirling cinematic string arrangements."

Food & Liquor was widely considered one of the best hip-hop records of the year and received a total of four Grammy nominations. In 2007, *Food & Liquor* was nominated for Best Rap Album, and "Kick Push" won two nominations, for Best Rap Song and Best Rap Solo Performance. The following year, "Daydreamin'" was nominated for and won the Grammy Award for Best Urban/Alternative Performance. The album also received four BET Hip Hop Award nominations. It appeared on several Billboard music charts, ranking No. 8 on the Billboard 200 and taking the No. 2 spot on Billboard's Top R&B/Hip-Hop Albums chart.

The Cool

Fiasco's second album, *The Cool,* was released in 2007. The album's title is taken from a track on *Food & Liquor,* and several tracks on *The Cool* expand on the story presented in the original song. Here Fiasco introduces three distinct characters: Michael Young History, representing "My Cool Young History"; The Game, representing the damaging influences of greed, vice, and hustling; and The Streets, representing temptation and corruption. Fiasco explained the story told in these songs. "It's about how The Cool starts off as this little boy, he grows up without a father, he's raised by The Game, falls in love with The Streets, goes on to be this big-time hustler, gets killed, and comes back to life.... Digs his way out of his own grave, and goes back to his old neighborhood and gets robbed by these two kids, ironically with the same gun he was shot with."

The Cool was described as a dark examination of life's pleasures, but Fiasco was careful not to glamorize any aspect of the story. He believes that what people think is "cool" will ultimately dominate every choice they make, positive or negative. "I always put myself as a storyteller first. I talk about the same concepts as Young Jeezy, but I deglamorize it and put it on a cinematic level that leaves it open to interpretation. So in essence, the story is of all of us. The Cool, The Streets, and The Game—those characters represent all of us.... In high school I was a nerd, and I haven't changed. Nerds, those with or without glasses, are the coolest people on this planet. The stuff that they do and the things that they talk about and the outlook they have on life.... This is the theory that runs my existence as a rapper.... If you want to effect change in society, you have to make it cool to be uncool; you gotta make it hip to be square. Because it is the things that have been made hip that destroy us and that we will be blamed for.... I want the cool things to become uncool, and the world will be less destructive."

The Cool also includes some tracks that are not directly related to this story. In "Superstar," Fiasco raps about becoming famous and dealing with too much attention, including the lyrics "A fresh, cool young Lu, trying to cash his microphone check, 2, 1, 2, wanna believe my own hype, but it's too untrue, the world brought me to my knees." In "Hello Goodbye," he compares recording artists to slaves being owned by a music industry that promotes "the faith that being a slave is so great."

One *Rolling Stone* reviewer said that in *The Cool,* "bleak raps clash with the smoothed-out vibe of the music, maybe even more than they're supposed to, and some of the tracks fall short.... Fiasco speaks in the voice of the ultimate con man—a drug dealer, a slave trader, a politician, and a rapper.... It's a scary sound." However, other critics found plenty to praise in Fiasco's second album, including its soft, jazzy R&B feel and the tough lyrics that attacked hip-hop's materialistic culture. *Entertainment Weekly* credited Fiasco's mass appeal to his "versatile beats, melodic pop hooks, and articulate lyrics."

The Cool proved to be a big hit with fans and with critics. It received four Grammy nominations: the album was nominated for Best Rap Album; "Paris, Tokyo" was nominated for Best Rap Solo Performance; and "Superstar" (with Matthew Santos) was nominated for Best Rap Song and Best Rap/Sung Collaboration. The album also appeared on several Billboard music charts, ranking No. 14 on the Billboard 200 and No. 4 on the Top

R&B/Hip-Hop Albums. The track "Superstar" appeared on Billboard's Pop 100, Hot Rap Tracks, and Top 40 Mainstream.

Next Projects

After the release of *The Cool,* Fiasco formed a hip-hop supergroup known as CRS (Child Rebel Soldiers) with Kanye West and Pharrell. CRS released the single "Us Placers," and all three artists appeared on West's Glow in the Dark tour in 2008. In 2009, Fiasco was honored as one of the USA Network's Character Approved award winners. The award included a $10,000 donation to a charity chosen by each winner. Fiasco gave his donation to Action Against Hunger, an international network committed to helping malnourished children and families, saying, "I love to feed people, especially those in need." Fiasco was also nominated for a 2009 Urban Music Award, for Best Hip Hop Act.

"

"In high school I was a nerd, and I haven't changed," Fiasco declared. "Nerds, those with or without glasses, are the coolest people on this planet. The stuff that they do and the things that they talk about and the outlook they have on life.... This is the theory that runs my existence as a rapper."

Fiasco plans to release at least three more albums before retiring as a recording artist. When creating new music, he prefers to focus on quality over quantity. Fiasco described his musical style as "'simple complexity.' I'm a big jazz fan. You might have the same three instruments but the beats, the rhythms, and everything they're doing is really, really complex. So I always take that approach when I make rap records." His Muslim faith also influences the subject matter included in his raps. "[Islam] affects my music as far as the stuff I don't talk about. I don't degrade women in my records. I try not to use profanity in my records or put anything negative in my records. I always try to put a positive message or solution in my records," Fiasco pointed out. "What you put out into the world comes back to you. You actually change the world with what you do. I want to put some good in the world."

HOME AND FAMILY

Fiasco considers Chicago to be his full-time home, although he has no permanent place to live there. "I'm kind of … just living out of a suitcase.

Fiasco brings a lot of intensity to all his live performances.

I'm so busy.... I'm kind of a drifter. No place to really call home. I'd like to live in Paris. I'd like to see what Paris is talking about."

HOBBIES AND OTHER INTERESTS

When he is not rapping, Fiasco says he is usually writing. He would like to someday finish the novel he has been working on for years. "A lot of the stuff I want to say musically, it has a limit. You can't compress and process certain things into 16 bars, or a song. It needs to be in a book, or it needs to be in a dissertation, or a speech, or a movie."

Fiasco collects Japanese toys and robots, is fascinated by quantum mechanics and chaos theory, and enjoys reading the works of German philosopher Friedrich Nietzsche. He enjoys listening to all kinds of music, especially jazz. His favorite jazz recording is Robert Glasper's jazz piano album *G&B.* His favorite song is "Somebody to Love" by Queen, and he says that there are several Queen albums that he can sing word for word.

Fiasco also devotes much of his time to his various business ventures. In 2005, he founded Righteous Kung-Fu, a company that designs fashions, sneakers, toys, video games, comic books, and graphics for album covers and skateboard decks. He has endorsement contracts with Reebok and has designed logos for some Reebok shoes, including the "OG." Fiasco has sponsored a skateboard team and also has endorsements with skateboard outfitter DGK.

As a devout practicing Muslim, Fiasco does not drink alcohol, smoke, use drugs, or go to clubs or bars. He also doesn't skateboard any more, having given it up after a 2007 street-skating accident that he says might have killed him if he hadn't been wearing a helmet.

RECORDINGS

Food & Liquor, 2006
The Cool, 2007

HONORS AND AWARDS

AOL Music Award: 2006, Breaker Artist
Artist to Watch (*Rolling Stone*): 2006
MTV2 Freshest MC (MTV): 2006
Breakout Artist of the Year (*GQ*): 2007
Grammy Award: 2008, Best Urban/Alternative Performance, for "Daydreamin'"
Character Approved Award (USA Network): 2009

FURTHER READING

Periodicals

Billboard, July 15, 2002, p.24; Jan. 6, 2007, p.40; Dec. 1, 2007, p.30
Ebony, Dec. 2006, p.152
Entertainment Weekly, Oct. 27, 2006, p.72; Jan. 18, 2008, p.56
Interview, Mar. 2006, p.200
New York Times, May 15, 2008, p.1
Rolling Stone, Sep. 21, 2006, p.22

Online Articles

http://www.chicagomag.com
(Chicago Mag, "Word Star," Aug. 2007)
http://www.mtv.com/music/artists
(MTV, "Lupe Fiasco," undated)
http://www.rollingstone.com/artists
(Rolling Stone, "Lupe Fiasco Biography," undated)
http://soundslam.com
(Soundslam, "Hip to Be Square," undated)

http://www.vibe.com/news/online_exclusives/2006/08/lupe_fiasco_weirder_than_your_average/
(Vibe, "Lupe Fiasco: Weirder Than Your Average," Aug. 18, 2006)

ADDRESS

Lupe Fiasco
Atlantic Records
1290 Avenue of the Americas, 28th Floor
New York, NY 10104

WORLD WIDE WEB SITES

http://www.lupefiasco.com
http://www.atlanticrecords.com/lupefiasco/bio
http://www.usanetwork.com/characterapproved/honorees/fiasco
http://www.actionagainsthunger.org

James Harrison 1978-

American Professional Football Player with the Pittsburgh Steelers
NFL Most Valuable Defensive Player in 2008

BIRTH

James Harrison Jr. was born on May 4, 1978, in Akron, Ohio. His father, James Sr., worked as a chemical truck driver. His mother, Mildred, was the primary caregiver for James and his 13 siblings.

YOUTH AND EDUCATION

Harrison was the youngest child in his large family, and his brothers and sisters picked on him sometimes. But his mother was a strict disciplinarian who made sure that things never got too out of hand. "The only person allowed to raise their voice at home was Mildred," she said about herself. She also worked hard to make sure that her youngest son never felt ignored or forgotten. To the contrary, Harrison grew up knowing that coming home late or other forms of misbehavior would result in stern punishment.

"

When Harrison was young, his mother didn't want him to play football. "I didn't want my son getting hurt running around on that field." But he and his best friend, David Walker, finally convinced her to let him give it a try. "I had to go and help convince his mom to let him sign up," remembered Walker. "We went together and begged her."

"

Harrison loved football from an early age. His favorite National Football League (NFL) team was the Cleveland Browns, who played their home games only about 40 miles away from his hometown of Akron. He admits that he even used to cry when the Browns lost big playoff games. Harrison's own football career began over the objections of his mother, who recalled that "I didn't want my son getting hurt running around on that field." But he and his best friend from childhood, David Walker, finally convinced her to let him give it a try. "I had to go and help convince his mom to let him sign up," remembered Walker. "We went together and begged her."

From his earliest days of youth football, Harrison displayed uncommon strength and fearlessness on the field. He excelled at both linebacker and running back. By the time he entered high school, area coaches agreed that he was one of the most promising young players in Akron. Harrison attended two Akron-area high schools (Archbishop Hoban and Buchtel) as a freshman before ending up at Coventry High School in suburban Akron. He spent his last three years of high school at Coventry, from which he graduated in 1998.

Harrison was one of the best players in Coventry's history. His strength, speed, and intensity made him such a fearsome linebacker that college football scouts regularly sat in the stands to watch him play. His immaturity, though, nearly derailed his high school career at several different points.

Harrison (#16) at Kent State, making the tackle.

Harrison paid little attention to his grades or college entrance tests, and by his senior year he had become a disruptive presence on the football team. Early in his senior season, the Coventry staff suspended him for two games for challenging an assistant coach to a fight. Soon after his return to the lineup, he received a one-game suspension for making obscene gestures at opposing fans who were allegedly taunting him with racial insults. Harrison then found himself in court for firing a BB gun in the school locker room. He pleaded guilty to a minor charge and was able to return to school to finish out his senior year. But the incident—combined with his earlier suspensions—scared off major college football programs like Ohio State, Notre Dame, and Nebraska, which had shown interest in him earlier in the year.

CAREER HIGHLIGHTS

NCAA—Kent State Golden Flashes

When Harrison failed to obtain the football scholarship that he thought was coming his way, he decided to attend nearby Kent State University in Kent, Ohio. His parents agreed to pay for his freshman year. They hoped that if he made a strong showing in the classroom and on the football field, the school would take note and give him an athletic scholarship for his remaining years of school.

The football coaches for the Kent State Golden Flashes were happy to have such a talented athlete on their squad, but Harrison's poor study habits remained a big problem. He posted such terrible grades in his first semester that his mother nearly pulled him out of school once and for all. "When I got the first report card," she recalled, "I went up there with my brother and said, 'Get all his stuff and put it in the van. We're going home. I'm not paying for this.'" An alarmed Harrison was finally able to convince her to give him another chance. As he watched his mother drive away, though, he knew that he had to improve his grades.

"

Harrison's grades were so bad that his mother nearly pulled him out of college. "When I got the first report card," she recalled, "I went up there with my brother and said, 'Get all his stuff and put it in the van. We're going home. I'm not paying for this.'"

"

The Kent State coaching staff helped Harrison by arranging extra tutoring help. In addition, they began demanding more accountability and effort from him on the practice field. "The guy [Harrison] was playing behind wasn't even close to as good as he was," recalled Dean Pees, who served as head coach during Harrison's years at Kent State. "He knew it. I knew it. He also knew I wasn't going to change. I wasn't going to play him until he gave me what he had."

Harrison buckled down in all phases of school. He raised his grades to become a 3.0 student, and he treated practice more seriously. At the start of his senior season, he was even selected as a team captain. As the 2001 season progressed, Harrison took his game to a new level of excellence, earning first team All Mid-American Conference honors at linebacker. His ferocious play helped lift Kent State to its first winning season in 14 years. Harrison left Kent State in the spring of 2002 a few credits shy of earning a bachelor's degree in general studies.

NFL—Pittsburgh Steelers

Despite Harrison's breakout senior season at Kent State, no NFL team claimed him in the 2002 draft. Pro scouts appreciated his competitive nature and tackling abilities. But they worried that he was too short (about six feet tall) to play linebacker in the NFL, yet too light (about 240 pounds) to be successful on the defensive line.

Harrison felt intense disappointment at going undrafted. A few teams, though, did approach him with offers to attend their upcoming training camps as a free agent (a player who is not under a long-term contract with a team). After weighing his options, Harrison decided to bid for a spot on the roster of the Pittsburgh Steelers, one of the most successful and respected franchises in the NFL.

Harrison spent the next year and a half trying to make the Steelers' roster. He showed flashes of tremendous potential, but Head Coach Bill Cowher and the rest of the Pittsburgh coaching staff cut him from the roster on three different occasions. Harrison suggested that he had trouble convincing the team that NFL linebackers could come in all shapes and sizes. "People said I was too short, too slow, couldn't do this or that," he recalled.

Teammates from that time period, however, indicate that the staff grew tired of Harrison's stubborn nature and his difficulties mastering defensive coordinator Dick LeBeau's complex schemes. "He was a knucklehead that didn't know the plays," said fellow linebacker James Farrior. "We'd be in practice, in training camp, and he might not know what he was doing so he'd just stop and throw his hands up and tell [the coaches] to get him out of there. We thought the guy was crazy."

Getting cut for a fourth time almost convinced Harrison to give up on the NFL. "I didn't want to be that guy who [keeps trying] to get in for three or four years and then it never happens," he explained. "I felt like I would have given it an honest two years, it didn't work, so it just wasn't meant to be. I would have found a regular job."

After Harrison was cut for the third time in February 2004, the Baltimore Ravens picked him up. They promptly shipped him off to Germany to play for the Rhein Fire in NFL Europe, a "developmental" league for promising young players and coaches. Harrison disliked living and playing in Germany, however, and in June 2004 Baltimore cut him loose.

Getting One Last Chance

Harrison returned to Akron after being let go by the Ravens. He was not sure what to do with his life at this point. He loved football, but he later admitted that getting cut for a fourth time almost convinced him to give up on the NFL. "I didn't want to be that guy who [keeps trying] to get in for

Harrison hurdles over San Diego Chargers' LaDanian Tomlinson while making a 25-yard interception, San Diego, 2005.

three or four years and then it never happens," he explained. "I felt like I would have given it an honest two years, it didn't work, so it just wasn't meant to be. I would have found a regular job."

Harrison briefly thought about becoming a veterinarian. He then decided to follow in his father's footsteps and seek a commercial driver's license.

But at that point he received an unexpected telephone call from the Steelers. The team informed him that one of its veteran linebackers, Clark Haggans, had injured his hand in a freak weightlifting accident. The Steelers asked Harrison if he wanted to try to make the team one more time. He accepted the offer and headed off for training camp.

When Harrison arrived at camp, he signaled his determination to make the most of this final chance at an NFL career. Unlike other teammates who relaxed in front of the television after a grueling day of practice, Harrison spent hours each night studying his playbook. He also adopted a different attitude on the practice field. "The way I took coaching, the way I talked to coaches ... that was all different," he said. "I had to change all of that because it was basically the last hurrah."

Coaches and teammates alike took note of Harrison's improved attitude. He made the Steelers roster for the opening of the 2004 season, and as the season progressed he became one of the top players on Pittsburgh's special teams, handling punts and kickoffs. On November 5, 2004, he made his first NFL start at linebacker when one of Pittsburgh's regular starters had to serve a one-game suspension. Harrison had five solo tackles, including a quarterback sack, and played well for all four quarters. "From that time on," recalled Le Beau, "we thought we had a chance of having a really special player."

By the end of the 2004 regular season, Harrison had earned a measure of job security with the Steelers. "He's developed into quite a football player," explained Coach Cowher. "He's matured tremendously from two years ago when he came here. He's taken a very professional approach. He prepares. He's an integral part of our special teams and I think he's going to be a pretty good linebacker in this league." The Steelers, meanwhile, won 15 out of 16 regular season games and looked poised to claim the fifth Super Bowl championship in the team's history. Harrison and his teammates were tripped up, though, in the AFC Conference Championship by the eventual Super Bowl champion New England Patriots by a score of 41-27.

Earning Rewards through Patience and Hard Work

Harrison spent the next two seasons in Pittsburgh as a valuable but mostly anonymous role player. He excelled on special teams and in occasional linebacker duty throughout the 2005 campaign, which turned into a special one for the Steelers. The team clinched a playoff berth with an 11-win, 5-loss regular season, then ripped off three straight victories in the playoffs to claim a spot in Super Bowl XL (40). When Pittsburgh defeated the Seat-

Harrison sacks Ryan Fitzpatrick (#11) of the Cincinnati Bengals early in the 2008 season, with the Steelers on their way to a Super Bowl and Harrison on his way to Defensive Player of the Year.

tle Seahawks in the Super Bowl by a 21-10 score, Harrison earned his first Super Bowl ring.

The following year was a big disappointment for the Steelers. The team struggled to an 8-8 record due to injuries and bad breaks, and Cowher retired at the end of the season. Harrison, though, remained confident that the future remained bright for him in Pittsburgh. He respected the team's new head coach, Mike Tomlin, and at the end of the 2006 season the Steelers signed Harrison to a four-year, $6.5 million contract. Harrison knew that the generous contract reflected the team's strong belief that he was ready to become a starting linebacker.

This opportunity came in the 2007 season, when longtime starting linebacker Joey Porter left Pittsburgh to play for the Miami Dolphins. Harrison was placed in Porter's slot as a full-time starter, and he quickly proved that the Steelers had made the right choice. By the time the season was over, Harrison ranked second on the team in tackles (86) and first in quarterback sacks (8.5), and he had been elected to his first Pro Bowl. Moreover, he was credited with almost singlehandedly winning a Monday Night Football game against the Ravens in early November. Harrison racked up 3.5 quarterback sacks, forced three fumbles, and intercepted a pass before the night was through.

The Steelers posted a 10-6 record in 2007, which was good enough to get the team back in the playoffs. Pittsburgh lost in the first round, but NFL analysts predicted that the tough Steelers defense would make them a force to be reckoned with in 2008. And the Steelers coaches agreed that Harrison had become an important part of that squad. "To me, the story on James Harrison is a guy who never gave up on himself," said Le Beau. "[He] continued to work through the rejections, through the adversity, all the disappointments."

"To me, the story on James Harrison is a guy who never gave up on himself," said defensive coordinator Dick LeBeau. "[He] continued to work through the rejections, through the adversity, all the disappointments."

”

A Dominant Force

Harrison was excited about the Steelers' prospects for the 2008 season. Before training camp even began, though, he faced renewed questions about his maturity and temperament. In March 2008 Harrison was charged with simple assault and criminal mischief for allegedly slapping his girlfriend, Beth Tibbott. The charges were eventually dropped by Tibbott after Harrison took responsibility for the incident and agreed to attend anger-management classes.

Once the 2008 season began, Harrison put the controversy behind him and concentrated on football. By mid-season, NFL experts and opponents were referring to him as a one-man wrecking crew. Opposing quarterbacks and running backs described him as a dominant force, and Harrison's teammates were quick to agree. "He demands a lot of attention," said Farrior. "And when you've got a guy like that dominating and making every play, it just opens the door up for everybody else." By the end of the season, Harrison and his defensive teammates were known around the league as the main reason for the Steelers' 12-4 record. The Pittsburgh defense allowed the fewest yards and fewest points in the entire NFL.

— " —

Harrison was excited leading up to Super Bowl XLIII. "It means a little bit more to me [this time] because I am a starter instead of playing just on special teams," he said, comparing his experiences in 2009 with those in 2006. "I have matured. I handle situations a lot differently now than I would back then.... I have learned the game and taken time to study the game."

— " —

Harrison's importance to the Steelers was confirmed at the end of the regular season, when he was named the Associated Press Defensive Player of the Year. His coaches and teammates hailed the selection, which had never before gone to an undrafted player. "He's short, but in his case that's a real plus because he's got so much talent," explained Le Beau. "The offensive players are taller, and he's underneath them most of the time. Then, with his strength, he can use that to his advantage, and he's got enough speed that they have to honor that, too. He's got the combination of strength and speed, and that's what is unique about James. He never stops on any play, never gives up in any game." People from outside the organization praised Harrison as well. "He is an intense, serious guy with a great appreciation for football history," said former Dallas Cowboy great Troy Aikman. "[He is] consistently motivated to prove himself."

The AFC Central Division champion Steelers entered the 2008 playoffs with swaggering confidence. The team then rolled through the conference playoffs, defeating the San Diego Chargers 35-24 and the Ravens 23-14. The win over Baltimore earned Pittsburgh another trip to the Super Bowl—this time to face a high-scoring Arizona Cardinals team led by quarterback Kurt Warner and wide receiver Larry Fitzgerald.

Harrison (#92) runs for a 100-yard touchdown after intercepting the ball during the Pittsburgh Steelers-Arizona Cardinals Super Bowl game, 2009.

Leading up to the kickoff for Super Bowl XLIII (43) in February 2009, Harrison admitted that he was even more excited than he had been for Super Bowl XL in January 2006. "It means a little bit more to me [this time] because I am a starter instead of playing just on special teams," he explained. "I have matured. I handle situations a lot differently now than I would back then.… I have learned the game and taken time to study the game."

Spectacular Play Leads to Super Bowl Glory

The clash between Pittsburgh and Arizona was tight from the opening kickoff to the final gun, and it made for one of the greatest games in Super Bowl history. The Steelers seemed to have the momentum for most of the first half. But with 18 seconds to go in the half, they were only ahead 10-7 and the Cardinals were poised on Pittsburgh's one-yard line, ready to take the lead.

At that point, though, Harrison made an extraordinary play. Warner tried to hit Arizona receiver Anquan Boldin on a quick pass in the end zone for a touchdown, but Harrison stepped back into the passing lane and picked off the pass. The interception alone was a huge play, but Harrison was not satisfied with just killing the Cardinals drive. Clutching the football in his arms, he rumbled down the sidelines for a 100-yard touchdown return to give the Steelers a 17-7 lead at the half. "I wasn't able to see him around my linemen," Warner said after the game. "He made a great play, not just the interception but to get it in for the touchdown." Harrison's teammates were thrilled—but not all that surprised—at his heroics. "Those are the types of plays he has been making all year," said Steelers quarterback Ben Roethlisberger. "That's the reason why he was the Defensive Player of the Year."

As the second half unfolded, Arizona came storming back on the strength of Warner's arm and Fitzgerald's acrobatic catches. The Cardinals even took a 23-20 lead with less than three minutes to go in the game when Warner hooked up with Fitzgerald on a long touchdown pass. But Pittsburgh's offense responded. Roethlisberger guided the Steelers on an 88-yard game-winning drive. The drive was capped by a touchdown pass to receiver Santonio Holmes in the corner of the end zone in the final seconds of the game.

Afterwards, an exhausted but happy Pittsburgh team basked in the glow of their triumph. Harrison, meanwhile, took great satisfaction in the knowledge that his 100-yard interception return—the longest touchdown in Super Bowl history—had helped lift his team to the championship. "It was tiring," he admitted, "but it was all worth it."

HOME AND FAMILY

Harrison lives in the Pittsburgh area. He has a young son, James Harrison III, with Beth Tibbott. He and Tibbott no longer have a romantic relationship, but she lives close by and Harrison sees his son almost every day. "That's the greatest blessing God has given me," Harrison said. "I'm extremely happy and fortunate to have him."

HOBBIES AND OTHER INTERESTS

Harrison loves to watch classic cartoons like "The Flintstones" and "The Jetsons," as well as adult cartoons like "Family Guy." "That's my thing, man," he said. "I like cartoons. I'll watch just about any cartoon." His other off-the-field interests include fishing.

HONORS AND AWARDS

All-Conference First Team Defense (Mid-American Conference): 2001
NFL Pro Bowl selection: 2007, 2008
Team Most Valuable Player (Pittsburgh Steelers): 2007
NFL All-Pro Team: 2008
NFL Defensive Player of the Year (Associated Press): 2008
NFL Defensive Player of the Year (*Pro Football Weekly*): 2008

FURTHER READING

Periodicals

Akron Beacon Journal, Oct. 9, 2004; Feb. 10, 2008
Beaver County (PA) Times, Aug. 4, 2008
Boston Herald, Jan. 25, 2009
Kansas City Star, Jan. 30, 2009
Los Angeles Times, Jan. 31, 2009, p.D1
New York Times, Dec. 9, 2007, Sports, p.9; Jan. 6, 2009, Sports, p.10; Feb. 2, 2009, Sports, p.3
Pittsburgh Post-Gazette, Dec. 17, 2004; Dec. 27, 2004; Apr. 14, 2006
Sporting News, Dec. 22, 2008; Feb. 2, 2009, p.27
Sports Illustrated, 2009 Commemorative Issue, p.68; Feb. 11, 2009
USA Today, Dec. 1, 2008, p.C4

Online Articles

http://sports.espn.go.com
(ESPN, "Harrison Gives Steelers 'Scary' Presence," Jan. 29, 2009; "A Fascinating Super Bowl, from Start to Finish," Feb. 3, 2009)
http://www.sportingnews.com
(Sporting News, "Steelers' Harrison First Undrafted AP Defensive Player of the Year," Jan. 6, 2009)

ADDRESS

James Harrison
Pittsburgh Steelers
P.O. Box 6763
Pittsburgh, PA 15212

WORLD WIDE WEB SITES

http://www.nfl.com
http://www.steelers.com

Jimmie Johnson 1975-

American Professional Race Car Driver
Three-Time NASCAR Sprint Cup Champion

BIRTH

Jimmie Johnson was born on September 17, 1975, in El Cajon, California. Jimmie is his given name. "My father's best friend was unfortunately killed when they were teenagers racing motorcycles, and his name was Jimmie, and they spelled it with an IE," he explained. "So my dad said then when he had a son he would name him Jimmie and spell it with an IE." Jimmie's father, Gary Johnson, operated heavy machinery for a living. His mother, Cathy Johnson, drove a school bus. Jimmie has two younger brothers, Jarit and Jessie.

YOUTH

Johnson grew up in a double-wide mobile home in El Cajon, a working-class suburb of San Diego. He belonged to a close-knit family that enjoyed spending time in the outdoors, either camping or riding motorcycles. His grandparents owned a motorcycle shop, and he received a little 50cc bike for Christmas when he was four years old. "My parents didn't have the means to buy me anything but motorcycles," he noted. Jimmie started racing on his motorcycle at age five and won his first league championship at age eight.

"Johnson's father worked as a mechanic on a desert buggy race team, and his son enjoyed hanging out at these events. "He'd drag me to a lot of races, and I'd volunteer to work in the pits, scrape mud off the buggies," Jimmie recalled. "It gave me a chance to get into the pit area and meet other drivers and crew members.""

As he got older, Johnson often accompanied his father to off-road auto races. Gary Johnson worked as a mechanic on a desert buggy race team, and his son enjoyed hanging out at these events. "He'd drag me to a lot of races, and I'd volunteer to work in the pits, scrape mud off the buggies," Jimmie recalled. "It gave me a chance to get into the pit area and meet other drivers and crew members."

A polite, curious, and well-spoken young man, Johnson soon talked his way into the driver's seat of a racing buggy. Before he even got his driver's license, he started racing in the Mickey Thompson Stadium Racing Series, which took place on dirt courses set up inside baseball and football stadiums. He also drove buggies in desert races organized by the Short Course Off-Road Enthusiasts (SCORE). His strong performances earned him an opportunity to drive a Chevrolet in the Grand National Truck Series. Johnson won the first of three consecutive truck championships in 1992, at the age of 16.

Throughout his early racing career, Johnson never felt any pressure to win or even to compete. His father just encouraged him and his brothers to do their best. "If we got [done with a race] and we'd tried as hard as we could, he was fine," he remembered. "It didn't matter where we finished. That's something I've been extremely lucky about—that my parents took that approach with us."

Although Johnson showed a great deal of talent as a young racer, he still needed to mature as a driver. For a while, his desire to go fast made him reckless. He learned an important lesson in 1994, during the Baja 1000 endurance race across the Mexican desert. After 20 straight hours of driving, he fell asleep at the wheel and flipped his truck into a sand wash. Luckily, he suffered only minor injuries. But he had two days to sit and think about his mistake before his support crew finally rescued him. "Until that point, I was extremely aggressive, flipping trucks. I tore up a lot of equipment," Johnson acknowledged. "My career was at a critical point there. I was fast and aggressive but I wasn't winning because I was making a lot of mistakes. That low point of almost killing myself in a crash changed me as a driver."

EDUCATION

Johnson graduated from Granite Hills High School in El Cajon in 1993 with a solid B average. He played water polo and competed on the school's swim team.

CAREER HIGHLIGHTS

Becoming a Race Car Driver

After graduating from high school, Johnson worked for a construction company and for a company that made shock absorbers. But his true love was racing, and he hoped to find a way to turn it into a career. In 1996, at the age of 21, he decided to leave California to pursue his dream of becoming a professional racer. He moved across the country to Charlotte, North Carolina—the capital of NASCAR.

The National Association for Stock Car Auto Racing (NASCAR) was founded in 1948. The organization oversaw various racing leagues that had formed throughout the south and applied a common set of rules for tracks, cars, and drivers. One of the main rules of NASCAR was that the racing machines must be "stock cars," based on American-made models sold in automobile dealerships. Over time, though, the base vehicles were modified in many ways to increase performance and safety. As of 2008, NASCAR sanctioned around 1,500 events each year at 100 tracks across the country. Drivers compete in a series of 36 races over the course of the season, and they receive points for the order in which they finish a race. The driver with the most points at the end of the season wins the title.

A view of the action in the pit, during a pit stop in the Napa Auto Parts 500, 2002. Johnson went on to win the race.

NASCAR actually oversees several different levels of racing series. But when people talk about NASCAR, they are usually referring to the most popular NASCAR race series, the Sprint Cup series. (The name of this series has changed over the years: it was known as the Winston Cup until 2004 and the Nextel Cup through 2008, and it's now known as the Sprint Cup.) The Sprint Cup series starts with the Daytona 500 in February in Daytona Beach, Florida, and continues until the Ford 400 in November in Homestead, Florida; other big races include the Brickyard 400 at the Indianapolis Motor Speedway and the Coca-Cola 600 at Lowe's Motor Speedway near Charlotte, North Carolina.

When Johnson traveled to Charlotte, he was determined to become a NASCAR driver. Once he arrived, he set about making contacts among NASCAR crew members, drivers, and car owners in hopes of eventually working his way up to the Sprint Cup series. He hung around places frequented by racers, looking for opportunities to introduce himself, shake hands, and ask for advice. "I would go to places where I knew crew guys ate lunch and I'd sit there all through lunch just trying to meet people," he recalled.

Johnson's persistence paid off in 1997, when he was offered a chance to compete in the American Speed Association (ASA) AC Delco Challenge short-track series. Since he had always raced on dirt tracks, he initially struggled to adjust to pavement. In fact, he spun out 12 times in his first race. He learned quickly, though, and soon established himself as a talented young driver. During the 1998 season Johnson finished fourth in the ASA national championship point standings and earned Rookie of the Year honors. The following year he won two races and moved up to third in the point standings.

Johnson was a reckless driver when he was young, until he flipped his truck during a race in the Mexican desert and had to wait two days for someone to rescue him. "Until that point, I was extremely aggressive, flipping trucks. I tore up a lot of equipment," he acknowledged. "My career was at a critical point there. I was fast and aggressive but I wasn't winning because I was making a lot of mistakes. That low point of almost killing myself in a crash changed me as a driver."

Breaking into NASCAR

Johnson's strong performance in the ASA short-course series earned him an opportunity to compete in the Nationwide Series (formerly known as the Busch Grand National Series), which is considered the second tier of NASCAR racing behind the Sprint Cup. He started three Nationwide races in 1998 and five the following year, while also competing in the ASA series. In 2000 Johnson moved up to compete in the Nationwide Series on a full-time basis. He finished in the top 10 in six different events to end the season ranked 10th in the point standings. In 2001 Johnson won his first Nationwide Series race, at Chicagoland Speedway, on his way to an eighth-place finish in the point standings. He also made his first appearance in the prestigious Sprint Cup Series that October, qualifying 15th and finishing 39th at Lowe's Motor Speedway in Charlotte.

Around that time, Johnson learned that the corporate sponsor of his Nationwide Series car planned to end its relationship with NASCAR. With his ride in jeopardy, he decided to approach a fellow driver for advice. He knocked on the motor home of Jeff Gordon—another young driver from California who had already won three Winston Cup championships and would win a fourth that year—and asked him what his next career move should be. "I went to Jeff and said, 'Hey, do you have any advice?'" Johnson remembered. "He said, 'You're not gonna believe this, but we're interested in starting a fourth Winston Cup team in 2002, and we want you to possibly drive that car.' I was like, 'What did you say?' It was so amazing to go in looking for some advice and walk out of the back of that truck thinking I might have a shot at a Winston Cup ride."

"He impressed me," Jeff Gordon said about meeting Johnson. "He was the guy I wanted. We hit it off from the beginning. I knew that's why he'd fit so well. I knew it was going to be a team that was under the same roof as the 24 [Gordon's car] and that those people had to work really well together and the drivers had to work really close together."

After discussing the choice with Rick Hendrick, team owner of Hendrick Motorsports, Gordon made Johnson an offer to drive the team's fourth car, which he co-owned. Many NASCAR analysts and fans were shocked by the move. Since Gordon and Hendrick could have had their pick among the best racers available, they wondered why they chose a young, unknown, unproven driver like Johnson. "He impressed me," Gordon explained. "He was the guy I wanted. We hit it off from the beginning. I knew that's why he'd fit so well. I knew it was going to be a team that was under the same roof as the 24 [Gordon's car] and that those people had to work really well together and the drivers had to work really close together."

Joining the Hendrick Motorsports Team

When Johnson joined Hendrick Motorsports, he became part of one of the largest and most successful teams in NASCAR history. Hendrick's resources included 500 employees, a brand-new race shop with state-of-the-art technology, and a friendly, cooperative atmosphere among the race teams. "All four cars are an open book to one another from Daytona testing [prior to the start of the Cup season] all the way to the final laps at Homestead [the last race of the year]," said Steve Letarte, Gordon's crew chief. "We share air pressures during the race, pit strategies, setup information all weekend long."

Johnson's new car was the number 48 Chevrolet sponsored by Lowe's home improvement stores. "There were numbers to choose from, and 48

Johnson is shown here with Jeff Gordon, who helped him get his start in NASCAR and who is part owner of his car.

was one of them," he recalled. "I've had a lot of success through the years with the number 4 and the number 8, and it all fit in place with the 24 car and Jeff owning a part of the team I was driving."

Johnson soon proved that the team's confidence in him was well-founded. He burst onto the Winston Cup scene in 2002 by qualifying on the pole (in the first position) at the season-opening Daytona 500. He finished among the top 10 six times in his first 12 races in NASCAR's top series. He managed to win his first Winston Cup race—the NAPA Auto Parts 500 in Fontana, California—in just his 13th career start.

Johnson's strong early-season performance made him the first rookie driver ever to sit atop the Winston Cup point standings. (Drivers receive points based on their finish position in each race. The winning driver is awarded 182 points, and the number of points awarded drops gradually for each lower finish position. Competitors can also earn up to 10 bonus points per race: 5 for any driver who leads a lap; and 5 for the driver who leads the most laps.) Johnson ended his spectacular rookie season with three victories and a fifth-place finish in the point standings. "Rick was happy, Lowe's was thrilled, and I was breathing a little easier," Gordon recalled. "Having Jimmie perform so well eliminated a lot of worry."

Johnson was pleased with his instant success at NASCAR's highest level, although he was taken aback by the sudden increase in attention and demands on his time. "I'm used to sitting around, hanging with the guys, talking about setups, and now there are 200 people outside saying your name and trying to get autographs," he noted. "It really cuts into some of that downtime I was used to having."

"It was just a great year for the entire Lowe's team. We have a great relationship, great equipment, and great sponsors.... I'm so fortunate to have the crew that I do. They've made a sophomore finish second this year," Johnson said after the 2003 season. "If you look at history, it usually takes three, four, or five years to get the driver and the team into championship form. Maybe next year will be that special year for us."

Falling Just Short of a Title

Over the next three seasons, Johnson consistently ranked among the top Cup competitors. Each year, however, he fell just short of earning enough points to claim the championship. In 2003 Johnson posted three victories and 14 top-5 finishes, to end the season ranked second in the point standings. It was a remarkable performance for a second-year driver. "It was just a great year for the entire Lowe's team. We have a great relationship, great equipment, and great sponsors.... I'm so fortunate to have the crew that I do. They've made a sophomore finish second this year," he said afterward. "If you look at history, it usually takes three, four, or five years to get the driver and the team into championship form. Maybe next year will be that special year for us."

Prior to the start of the 2004 season, NASCAR changed the system that determined which driver earned the coveted Cup points title. Instead of simply adding up each driver's points at the end of the 36-race season, the organization instituted a 10-race playoff called the Chase for the Cup. Only the top 12 drivers in the point standings at the end of 26 races qualified to compete in the Chase. The 12 qualifiers had their points reset to 5,000, and they also received 10 additional points for each victory they had

Johnson and the 48 Chevrolet at Daytona in 2004.

registered during the season's first 26 races. During the 10-race Chase, points were awarded as usual. This system effectively wiped out any big point leads that a driver may have accumulated, making the end of the season more exciting for fans.

Johnson started out strong in 2004 and led the point standings by mid-season. But he hit a rough patch from August to October that dropped him all the way down to ninth place, 247 points behind the leader. "I didn't feel [the championship hopes] were over, but I'm a realist and I knew it was out of our control," he said. "We were going to need mistakes made by everybody ahead of us to catch up." Johnson launched an amazing come-back, winning four of the last six races of the year. Unfortunately, his eight victories and 14 top-5 finishes were not quite good enough to win the title. In the closest points race in Cup history, he finished second to Kurt Busch by eight points. "It showed me at the end of the year that you can't give up until the last lap," he noted.

The 2005 season proved to be a difficult one for Johnson. Although he led the point standings for half the year, he hit another rough patch in late summer that saw him drop to sixth place. During this period—for the first time in his Cup career—he was involved in a couple of on-track incidents that drew criticism from fellow drivers. "It makes me think harder about who I am, what I am, and the type of driver I am," he said of this experience. "I'm not going to let anybody's opinion change what I do or who I am." As in previous years, Johnson worked his way back up in the standings and entered the final race of the Chase in second place. Unfortunately, a blown tire knocked him out of the race early and dropped him to fifth in points for the season.

Although Johnson ended 2005 with a respectable four victories and 13 top-5 finishes, it was a low point in his career. He and his crew had failed to perform up to expectations, and they felt deeply disappointed. Johnson and his chief, Chad Knaus, took out their frustrations on each other. The situation became so bad that the team owner had to step in to offer some perspective. "I think we had so much built up on the early success that we had had and we were so frustrated with the fact we hadn't won, that we were fighting like cats and dogs," Johnson remembered. "Mr. Hendrick is a great people person, and can really relate to anybody in any situation. And we were acting like kids, so he sat us down like kids, and had a gallon of milk, some Mickey Mouse plates with cookies, … and said, 'All right, guys, if you are going to act like this, then I will treat you like this.' And, you know, we hashed out the issues that were bothering us, and then won every championship since."

Winning the Nextel Cup

As the 2006 Cup season approached, Johnson and his crew were prepared to do everything possible to claim the elusive championship. Just prior to the first race of the year—the fabled Daytona 500—crew chief Chad Knaus came under criticism for going too far in his efforts to win. A pre-race technical inspection revealed that some parts of Johnson's car had been modified in ways that were not allowed under NASCAR rules. The illegal modifications resulted in Knaus being suspended for the race. Johnson overcame this setback and won his first Daytona 500. "We play within a set of rules. Chad broke the rules. He's admitted that. We're serving our penalty," he said afterward. "We stepped up today and won the biggest race in our sport, and that is something I am so proud of."

Johnson continued to run well for much of the 2006 season, leading the point standings for 22 weeks. Following his usual pattern, however, he experienced a late-season slump in which he placed 10th or lower in nine straight races. He qualified for the Chase for the Cup, but his chances of claiming the title looked slim. "We're pretty far out, and it's going to be tough to make up the deficit that we have," he acknowledged. "But the way this Chase has started and the way every year the Chase has been that I've been a part of it, it's so unpredictable. Anything can happen."

Sure enough, Johnson came charging back into contention during the Chase. He soared up the standings over a six-race stretch, enabling him to reclaim the top position by the time the series entered the final race of the season in Homestead, Florida. He only needed to finish 12th or better in this event to capture his first Cup championship. Just 16 laps into the Homestead race, though, a spring broke off a competitor's car and flew through Johnson's window, hitting him in the nose. His crew managed to fix him up during the next pit stop, but he lost so much time that he dropped back to 40th place in the race. He moved steadily through the field over the next 60 laps, however, and finished ninth—well enough to claim his first Nextel Cup title by 56 points over Matt Kenseth. "It may take a while to sink in. I knew we had a great team. I knew all along we could do it," he declared. "I've won a lot of big, big events, and they're very special. But there's nothing like a championship. There's nothing like having that respect through the garage, in the media, with the fans, of being THE guy." Johnson ended the season with 5 victories and 13 top-5 finishes, and he was named Driver of the Year by NASCAR.

"

"It may take a while to sink in.," Johnson said about winning the Cup in 2006. "I knew we had a great team. I knew all along we could do it. I've won a lot of big, big events, and they're very special. But there's nothing like a championship. There's nothing like having that respect through the garage, in the media, with the fans, of being THE guy."

"

Winning Three Consecutive Championships

Johnson was not satisfied with one championship, however. As the 2007 season got underway, he expressed determination to defend his title. "To be a repeat champion puts you in the top of our sport," he stated. "I want

Johnson (#48) and Dale Earnhardt Jr. (#8) battle for position.

to be in that elite status of guys." Johnson looked unstoppable at the beginning of the year, posting four victories in the first 10 races. But then he entered a slump in which he went 14 races without a win. This dry spell coincided with Knaus serving another suspension from NASCAR for making illegal modifications to the fenders of the 48 car.

Once again, though, Johnson made a terrific comeback during the Chase. He won four races in a row at the end of the season to earn a second consecutive championship by 77 points over Gordon, his mentor and car owner. "He's been the best in the sport, and it means a lot to me to beat Jeff Gordon when he's on his game and as competitive as he was last year. I'm really proud of that," Johnson said afterward. "In some ways it's difficult because he's a great friend and I'd love to see him as a five-time champion. So I had mixed emotions, but it was just a great battle through the whole season."

Johnson thus became the first driver to repeat as Cup champion since Gordon achieved the feat in the 1997 and 1998 seasons. In addition, his 10 race wins marked the first time any driver had posted double-digit victories in a season since Gordon had done so in 1998. In recognition of his efforts, Johnson received NASCAR's Driver of the Year Award for the second time. "Winning back-to-back championships is something I'm very, very proud of," he stated. "The good thing, I feel, is that we're just hitting our stride. I think we have a lot of good years ahead of us, and we'll be fighting for more championships and certainly winning more races as years go by. Hopefully we can be a three-time champion in the near future."

Johnson started out slowly during the 2008 season, but he improved steadily and looked strong toward the end. He went on to dominate the Chase, winning three races and posting eight finishes in the top 10. By the time the series reached the final race at Homestead, Johnson held an almost-insurmountable lead of 141 points. Needing to finish only 36th to claim a third straight title, he raced conservatively and avoided trouble. Johnson ended the season with 7 wins and 15 top-5 finishes to earn the championship by 69 points over Carl Edwards. He thus tied the legendary Cale Yarborough—who won titles in 1976, 1977, and 1978—as the only drivers in NASCAR's 60-year history to "threepeat." He also won his third straight Driver of the Year Award. "It's been an amazing run. I've worked all my life to get here, but I never could have dreamed of winning three championships in a row," Johnson said afterward. "We'll enjoy it for a little while, then we'll start working on getting number four."

"It's been an amazing run. I've worked all my life to get here, but I never could have dreamed of winning three championships in a row," Johnson said afterward. "We'll enjoy it for a little while, then we'll start working on getting number four."

Building a Dynasty

Through the end of the 2008 season, Johnson's career statistics included 40 race wins (placing him third among active drivers), 101 finishes in the top 5, and 156 finishes in the top 10 in 255 Cup starts. Showing remarkable consistency, he ranked among the top 5 in the point standings at the end of every Cup season in his seven-year career. Johnson also showed an amazing ability to turn in his best performances in important races. Out of the 50 Chase races held since 2004, he won 14—8 more than any other driver. His success helped him earn $23 million in prize money and endorsements in 2008 alone. "I'm so far ahead of the goals and dreams I set that this is all icing on the cake," he noted.

Johnson always made sure to give Hendrick Motorsports, Chad Knaus, and his whole crew equal credit for the performance of the 48 Chevrolet.

"Chad is real aggressive and is not afraid to make the tough call and put a lot of pressure on everyone around him," said fellow driver Jeff Burton. "They're a team with swagger. They're willing to make that gamble of possibly giving up a fifth place for a win." "The way you win championships in the Chase era is to use the first 26 races to get ready for the last 10, and Jimmie and Chad do that better than anyone else," added NASCAR analyst Darrell Waltrip. "They have as much engineering support at Hendrick Motorsports as anyone in the sport. Heck, I don't see why they can't win a fourth straight championship next season."

"

Johnson's story demonstrates that an unknown driver might just have the ability to make it big in racing. "A lot of it is who you know," he said. "A lot of people are bashful about introducing themselves, writing letters, approaching people. It's a touchy thing to do. You can definitely wear out your welcome. But if you show that enthusiasm and determination and you have some talent, you're going to get a shot."

While Johnson has emerged as the top driver on the Hendrick Motorsports team, he has remained close friends with Jeff Gordon. "I don't think many people could handle that situation better than he and I do," Gordon acknowledged. "I am happy for him, he's happy for me, but we also know how bad we want it for ourselves and our teams." Gordon has found himself in the unlikely position of studying his teammate's car and driving style for clues about how to improve his own performance. "Every time he's blistering fast, I say, 'Put that setup in,' and then I'm absolutely terrible," Gordon noted. "I know what's under their car, and I always shake my head. I don't know how they make that work. But Jimmie's driving style is different enough that it does."

Despite his three consecutive Cup championships, Johnson is not as popular with NASCAR fans as a number of less accomplished drivers. Some fans seem to resent the way that he and his well-funded Hendrick Motorsports team have dominated the sport in recent years. Others seem to find him bland and boring compared to the colorful personalities exhibited by some other drivers. After all, Johnson does not make many controversial statements to reporters, and he generally avoids becoming involved in conflicts or feuds with other drivers. "He doesn't have Tony Stewart's

Johnson (front right) leading the pack at the start of this 2008 race—and leading the way to his third consecutive title.

flame-throwing personality, but he's not an introvert," said team owner Rick Hendrick. "He's got as many friends or more than any other driver. He's got friends he went to school with, friends he raced with, and movie-star friends, and when they come together, he's the same with all of them. He's a fun-loving guy who plays as hard as he races."

Johnson's many friends rush to defend him from critics who say he is dull. "He's probably one of the best guys in the world and one of the most talented guys in the garage," said longtime friend Casey Mears. "At the same time, he's probably more easy to approach and more human than most. Jimmie's just a good guy." Still, Johnson admits that he sometimes has trouble letting his true self show through to fans. "I can be freaking out inside, but then I open my mouth and I sound calm. I don't know where this device comes from," he explained. "It helps me in racing because you never want to lose your cool, but it's also probably kept people from getting to know the real me."

Thanks to his incredible success on the track, the man who once knocked hopefully on the door to Jeff Gordon's trailer now has other people approaching him for advice on breaking into NASCAR. His own story demonstrates that an unknown driver might just have the ability to make it big in racing. "A lot of it is who you know," he said. "A lot of people are bashful about introducing themselves, writing letters, approaching people.

It's a touchy thing to do. You can definitely wear out your welcome. But if you show that enthusiasm and determination and you have some talent, you're going to get a shot."

MARRIAGE AND FAMILY

Johnson met his future wife, model Chandra Janway, at a party in New York City in 2002. He proposed to her a year later while they were skiing at Beaver Creek, Colorado. They were married on December 11, 2004, on the tropical island of St. Barts in the Caribbean. They have a 12,000-square-foot house in Mooresville, North Carolina, as well as a loft apartment in the Chelsea neighborhood of Manhattan in New York City. "Having Chandi in my life allows me not to worry about things outside of racing when I walk through the gates each weekend," Johnson stated. "This sounds corny, but Chandi and I are teammates. We're in love, and she gives me total peace of mind."

Johnson also remains close to his family. In fact, his father drives his million-dollar motor home from track to track throughout the NASCAR race season and often serves as a spotter in the stands during races.

HOBBIES AND OTHER INTERESTS

In his spare time, Johnson enjoys watching football, playing golf, and going downhill skiing and snowboarding. He also spends a lot of time cruising around Lake Norman in his 35-foot Fountain powerboat. "I love to be out on the water, going fast!" he admitted.

Johnson is deeply committed to charity work. "Chandra and I have been very blessed," he noted. "We get to do what we enjoy in life, and that is something we don't take for granted. We have incredibly supportive friends and family, and we feel that I have the best fans in our sport. It is in that spirit of thankfulness that we launched the Jimmie Johnson Foundation in February 2006."

The foundation works primarily to help families and children in need. It brings critically ill fans to NASCAR races through the Make-a-Wish Foundation, builds homes for deserving families in El Cajon through Habitat for Humanity, and sponsors Jimmie Johnson's Victory Lanes bowling alley at Kyle Petty's Victory Junction Camp for children with serious illnesses or chronic medical conditions. Johnson finds it very gratifying to give something back. "I am consumed with competition and success. You start using those as benchmarks for happiness," he acknowledged. "[But] when you see someone fighting for their life, the fact that they're smiling and they're happy, it just re-racks your brain."

HONORS AND AWARDS

Rookie of the Year (American Speed Association): 1998
NASCAR Driver of the Year: 2006, 2007, 2008
NASCAR Nextel/Sprint Cup Championship: 2006, 2007, 2008

FURTHER READING

Books

LeMasters, Ron Jr. *Jimmie Johnson: A Desert Rat's Race to NASCAR Stardom,* 2004
Gitlin, Marty. *Jimmie Johnson: Racing Champ,* 2008

Periodicals

New York Times, Nov. 19, 2008, p.B15
Sports Illustrated, Dec. 1, 2002, p.70; Nov. 26, 2007, p.54; Nov. 24, 2008, p.30
Sports Illustrated for Kids, Nov. 1, 2005, p.53; Feb. 2008, p.28
USA Today, Sep. 12, 2007, p.C1; Nov. 15, 2007, p.C1; Oct. 15, 2008, p.C8; Nov. 12, 2008, p.C1

Online Article

http://signonsandiego.com
("See How Far Jimmie Johnson Has Come from El Cajon," *San Diego Union-Tribune,* Feb. 20, 2005)

ADDRESS

Jimmie Johnson
Jimmie Johnson Fan Club
4325 Papa Joe Hendrick Blvd.
Charlotte, NC 28262

WORLD WIDE WEB SITES

http://www.jimmiejohnson.com
http://www.hendrickmotorsports.com
http://www.lowesracing.com
http://www.nascar.com/drivers
http://www.jimmiejohnsonfoundation.org

Heidi Klum 1973-

German Supermodel
Host of the Hit Reality TV Show "Project Runway"

BIRTH

Heidi Klum (pronounced *kloom)* was born on June 1, 1973, in Bergisch Gladbach, Germany. Bergisch Gladbach is a small city located east of the Rhine River, about six miles from the larger city of Cologne. Klum's father, Gunther, worked as an executive at a cosmetics and perfume company, and her mother, Erna, was a hairdresser. Heidi has one older brother.

YOUTH

As a young girl growing up in Bergisch Gladbach, Klum's life was fairly ordinary. "I had a very normal childhood with my brother and my parents, who are still together," she recalled. "We were always very close and would talk to each other about what we did during the day." Klum took ballet and jazz dance classes and developed an interest in fashion design. She liked to spend time shopping and hanging out with her friends. Her memories of childhood include favorite foods, such as her mother's sauerkraut soup, her grandmother's potato dumplings, and sweets, especially black licorice and hazelnut ice cream.

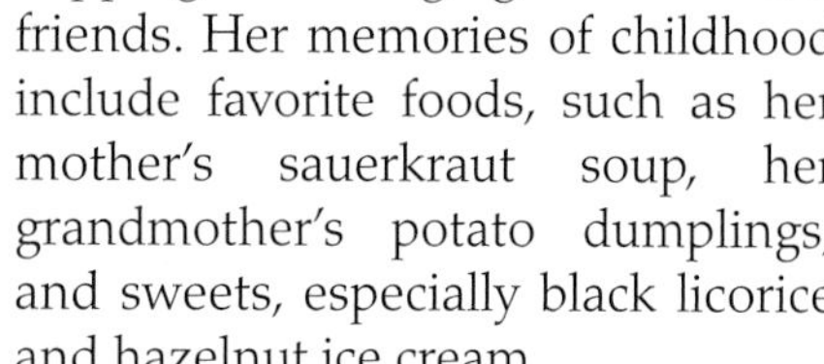

"My father was always early out of the house and coming home late," Klum recalled. "I saw that in order to make money—we didn't have a lot, but we did do things like go on holiday [vacation]—I understood it was because my father worked so hard."

Both of her parents worked, and Klum learned at a young age the value of working hard for what she wanted. "My father was always early out of the house and coming home late," she recalled. "I saw that in order to make money—we didn't have a lot, but we did do things like go on holiday [vacation]—I understood it was because my father worked so hard."

EDUCATION

Klum attended Integrierte Gesamtschule Paffrath (IGP) in Bergisch Gladbach. IGP is a German public school roughly equivalent to a U.S. middle and high school, where students are prepared to go on to a university. Art and math were her favorite subjects in school. Klum completed her studies in June 1992 and planned to enroll in a university in Dusseldorf, Germany, to study fashion design.

CAREER HIGHLIGHTS

Becoming a Model

Klum was interested in becoming a fashion designer and wanted to learn about the business side of the fashion industry. She never considered a career as a model until one day in the winter of 1991, when she happened to see a magazine ad for the Model 92 nationwide modeling contest in Germany. The contest was sponsored by *Petra* magazine and a New York mod-

Hair and make-up are a constant part of a model's work preparation.

eling agency. The winner would appear on national television in Germany and receive a $300,000 cash prize along with a three-year modeling contract. When her best friend Karin suggested that she enter the contest, Klum laughed at the idea.

But Karin continued to encourage Klum to enter, finally convincing her to send the application. Klum posed for a few photos wearing a bikini and mailed in her contest entry. Five months later, in the spring of 1992, she learned that she had been chosen for the final round of the competition. She went on to win the contest, beating 30,000 other contestants for the title of Model 92.

Abandoning her university plans, Klum used her contest prize winnings to begin modeling professionally when she was 19 years old. She knew that the choice to try modeling was a risk, but she was willing to take the chance. Klum started out with small jobs in Hamburg and Berlin, Germany, posing for a knitting magazine and modeling for women's clothing catalogs. She soon wanted more exciting modeling jobs and decided to leave Germany for the high-profile fashion runways of Paris, France and Milan, Italy.

Overcoming Rejection

During the early 1990s when Klum was beginning her modeling career, it was fashionable for runway models to be extremely thin and unsmiling. The most successful runway supermodels of that time, such as Kate Moss, were known as waifs. The word originally meant a child who was undernourished, frail, and homeless or lost. When used to describe a fashion model, a waif was an uncommonly thin woman who looked like a sad child. With her curvy figure and brilliant smile, Klum did not fit this image at all.

In Paris and Milan, Klum heard that she was too healthy-looking, too wholesome, and that her overall appearance was too American. She had a hard time finding work as a model. "In the beginning... I was being rejected all the time. When I started, Kate Moss was the hottest thing. It was not about being proud and upright with the smile glowing—a powerful woman. It was more about being a crushed, crumbled person in the corner, the beaten-down girl looking a little sad and tired."

In spite of this obstacle that seemed impossible to overcome, Klum was committed to building a career in modeling. She refused to give up. If she couldn't be a model in a runway fashion show, she was determined to find another kind of modeling work. "There were still other things out there for people who were normal-looking. You don't always have to go through the front door to get what you want.... When I figured out that editorial [magazine photos] and runway weren't really my thing because I am voluptuous and not this stick that you had to be at that time, I just found other ways to be a model."

Klum used her determination and self-confidence to push through the nearly constant rejection. Fashion designer Michael Kors told *In Style* magazine, "Fashion goes back and forth between the healthy bombshells and the waifs, and she came in to see me in Paris in the 90s during a sad-waif moment. In walked Heidi with glorious teeth and curves, and she was like, 'I know I'm not what's in right now, but I had to meet you.' That confidence struck me immediately."

Eventually, though, Klum became frustrated with the limited opportunities for her in the European fashion world. She asked her agency to transfer her to the U.S., and in the summer of 1993 she moved to Miami, Florida. After just a few months there, she moved again—this time to New York City.

In New York, Klum shared a rundown apartment with two other struggling German models. At first, adjusting to life in the U.S. while trying to land modeling jobs was extremely stressful. One of the other girls gave up and returned to Germany. Klum, however, was more determined than ever to succeed. "I was more ambitious, more business savvy. When everyone went out drinking, I went home.... You can't wait for things to come to you, especially in this business."

Klum went on hundreds of casting calls and was hired for many small jobs. Her first big success was appearing on the cover of *Self* magazine. During this time, most of her work still involved modeling for such catalogs as Newport News, Chadwick's, and J.C. Penney. While other models made catalogs their entire career, Klum never gave up her belief that there were bigger opportunities for her.

Klum's appearance on the cover of Sports Illustrated *magazine, shown here, was the big break she'd been working for.*

Breaking Through

Over the objections of her booking agent, Klum insisted on getting an appointment with the prestigious lingerie designer Victoria's Secret. Klum recalled, "My booker said I wasn't good enough and I said, 'It's great that you think that, but I want them to tell me that.'" Her confidence carried her through that first meeting, and in the end the Victoria's Secret executives loved her. Klum walked in her first Victoria's Secret runway show in 1997. She soon became one of the most recognizable Victoria's Secret Angels, and one of the company's top models.

This success lead to new opportunities for Klum, such as appearances on television talk shows, which in turn opened more doors for her. As a guest on a 1997 episode of "Late Night with David Letterman," she surprised everyone with her yodeling talent. An editor at *Sports Illustrated* magazine saw the show and thought that her charm would be a good fit for the magazine's swimsuit edition. Although Klum was not as well-known or as experienced as the models that *Sports Illustrated* usually hired, she landed the cover of the 1998 swimsuit edition. She later said of this milestone breakthrough, "Before that, no one connected my name with my face. From that day on, people could."

Klum soon became one of the fashion industry's highest-paid models. Her photos appeared on the covers of many major fashion magazines in the U.S. and Europe, including *Vogue, Marie Claire, Elle, GQ, Glamour,* and

Mademoiselle. As an established supermodel, Klum decided to use her growing celebrity status to branch out into acting. Appearing in movies and television shows seemed like a natural progression for her career.

In 1998, Klum made her acting debut with a recurring role in the television comedy series "Spin City." Appearances on many television shows in both the U.S. and Germany followed, with Klum acting for some roles and playing other parts as herself. In 2001, Klum's roles included an appearance on the popular cable television drama "Sex and the City" and a small part in the movie *Zoolander*. She appeared in guest roles in several TV series, was a guest on various television and radio talk shows, and was frequently seen in special programs about modeling and fashion.

"Project Runway"

In 2002, Klum was invited to collaborate on the development of a new reality television show called "Project Runway," envisioned as a competition for aspiring fashion designers. Klum was interested in the idea, but reluctant to participate at first. "I didn't think I was that good on camera," she later explained. She also wasn't sure of the level of involvement she would have if she became the host of "Project Runway." She said, "I didn't want to just show up and do the normal things I do when I am modeling." Klum decided to join the show once she was assured that she would be able to influence its direction. "I wanted to have some input into the show and have some ideas brought in. I liked the aspect of being more than just the host."

The "Project Runway" season begins with 16 contestants who are ready to compete. At the start of each episode, Klum and others present a design challenge to test the competitors' skills, creativity, and ability to perform under pressure. The designers are often asked to create high-style garments out of unusual materials or within unexpected restrictions. Some of the challenges have required the use of such odd materials as recycled items, edible foods, car parts, Hershey wrappers, apartment furnishings, plants and flowers, and other materials not traditionally used in clothing. Other challenges have involved designing for celebrities, including Tiki Barber, Victoria Beckham, Apolo Anton Ohno, Sarah Jessica Parker, Brooke Shields, and their own mothers. Still others have required creating a certain type of garment, like a prom dress, a wedding dress, a letter carrier uniform, or an outfit for a professional wrestler.

The contestants listen to the challenge, sketch some ideas, choose fabric and trim, sew the garments, select accessories, fit the models, and oversee the models' hair and makeup. They spend much of their time in the

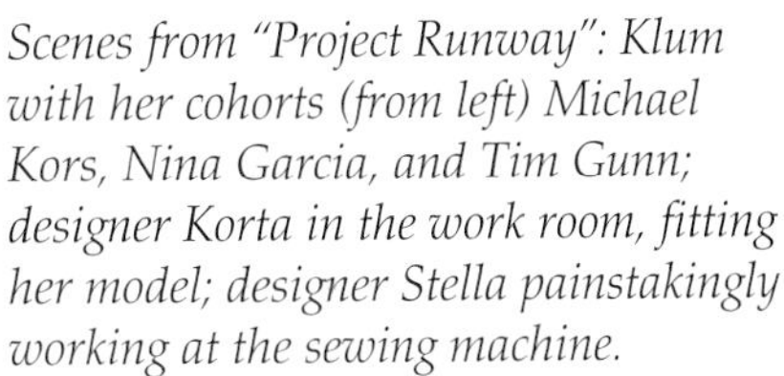

Scenes from "Project Runway": Klum with her cohorts (from left) Michael Kors, Nina Garcia, and Tim Gunn; designer Korta in the work room, fitting her model; designer Stella painstakingly working at the sewing machine.

work room, with frequent visits from mentor Tim Gunn, formerly the chair of fashion design at Parsons The New School for Design and now Chief Creative Officer at Liz Claiborne. At the end of each episode, the designers mount a runway show with their creations, and a team of judges—including Klum, fashion designer Michael Kors, and fashion magazine editor Nina Garcia—judge their work and select a contestant to eliminate. The final few contestants have a chance to show their designs during the prestigious New York Fashion Week. The ultimate winner receives a cash award, a chance to start his or her own fashion line, and other prizes.

"

Klum was reluctant to join "Project Runway" until she was assured that she would be able to influence its direction. "I didn't want to just show up and do the normal things I do when I am modeling," she explained. "I wanted to have some input into the show and have some ideas brought in. I liked the aspect of being more than just the host."

"

In addition to showcasing the work of new designers, each episode also features the squabbles, arguments, catty comments, personal dramas, and conflicting personalities of the competitors. Almost from the beginning, fans discussed and debated each episode's challenges, the judges' comments, contestants' behavior, the quality of work, and elimination decisions on Internet blogs and forums. Klum has admitted to being surprised by the show's success, saying, "I thought that people would like 'Project Runway,' but I didn't think they would get so obsessed!"

Perhaps Klum's most well-known contribution to "Project Runway" is her signature send-off for each week's eliminated contestant. She explained how the German phrase "auf Wiedersehen" was chosen for this purpose. "We were filming the first show and still didn't have the line to say goodbye to people. We were brainstorming, people were shouting, nothing was working, and then I got it.... I came up with it because it means 'I'll see you again.' It's meant to be a nice way to say goodbye, and it's not mean because that's just not who I am."

"Project Runway" debuted on the Bravo cable network in December 2004, and the show was an immediate success. It became one of Bravo's most popular shows in its first year, with more than two million viewers each week. Quickly gaining a cult-like following, the show was praised by both fans and critics as a standout reality TV series. The success of "Project Runway" was attributed to its outrageous design challenges, and it also gained credibility with a process for judging and eliminating contestants that was seen as fair and sensible. The first five seasons of "Project Runway" were each nominated for at least one Emmy award. In 2008, Klum received an Emmy nomination for Outstanding Host for a Reality or Reality-Competition Program.

Many fans were disappointed in 2009, when the series was temporarily halted due to a lawsuit. The show's producers wanted to move "Project Runway" from Bravo to the Lifetime TV network, and Bravo sued to stop the move. Season six had already been filmed, but everyone involved was sworn to secrecy until the episodes could appear on TV. The lawsuit was eventually settled, "Project Runway" moved to Lifetime, and season six aired in summer and fall 2009.

Klum has mentioned several episodes as some of her favorite moments. Her favorite designer challenge was the very first one, when contestants were given $50 to buy materials from a grocery store to make their garments. "That set the tone [for the competition] and that showed people out there, 'Wow, they think beyond the garbage bag.'" Another of her favorite challenges was in the second season, when the designers had to make new garments using only the clothes they were wearing at that moment.

A Full Career

Along with her duties as host and executive producer of "Project Runway," Klum finds time to work on many other projects. Her television appearances have included an episode of the popular crime drama "CSI: Miami" (2003) and the comedy series "How I Met Your Mother" (2007). Klum also had a part in the movie *Ella Enchanted* (2004), and a brief appearance as herself in *The Devil Wears Prada* (2006). In 2004, she published *Heidi Klum's Body of Knowledge: 8 Rules of Model Behavior,* a book that she describes as being "about trying different things and not being afraid of getting pushed back sometimes. It's about being creative to get ahead." In 2006, Klum created the reality television show "Germany's Next Topmodel," a competition based on "America's Next Top Model" which she hosts and produces for German television.

Klum continues to model in runway shows and magazines, primarily for Victoria's Secret, and has expanded her business ventures to include her

Klum works the runway in this Victoria's Secret fashion show.

own collections of perfume, swimsuits, Jordache jeans, Birkenstock sandals, fat-free candy, jewelry, skin care products, and more. Klum is very particular about endorsements and insists on being involved in product development. She said, "I need to have complete control over how something is going to look if my name is going to be attached to it."

Although she works hard to maintain control over her public image, Klum has a more relaxed attitude about her physical appearance. "I don't want to be wondering about how skinny I am, wondering what I'm going to eat because I don't want to gain and I want to look hot and young, always and forever.... You see so many people going out for plastic surgery.... I'm not going to do that. I want to get older and I'm going to have wrinkles. Beauty comes from the inside.... I drink lots of water and sleep! For me, sleep is holy, otherwise I don't feel fit and I don't look as good."

"I don't want to be wondering about how skinny I am, wondering what I'm going to eat because I don't want to gain and I want to look hot and young, always and forever.... You see so many people going out for plastic surgery.... I'm not going to do that. I want to get older and I'm going to have wrinkles. Beauty comes from the inside."

MARRIAGE AND FAMILY

Klum married stylist Ric Pipino on September 6, 1997. They divorced in 2003.

Klum and singer Seal (Sealhenry Samuel) were married on May 10, 2005, in Costa Careyes, Mexico. Seal and Klum first met in the lobby of the Mercer Hotel in New York City when a mutual friend introduced them. At the time, Klum was five weeks pregnant with her first child, conceived with ex-boyfriend Flavio Briatore, an Italian Formula One racing executive. "I was not looking for anybody," Klum later confided. "[Seal] was just there. He walked in the door.... He looked good. I was like, 'Wow.'"

The couple were engaged one year later. Seal proposed to Klum on top of a glacier in the Canadian Rockies. "He took me by helicopter. He had an igloo built there ... rose petals, candies. Very, very romantic! There was food and champagne, and then the helicopter left. It was a little scary, too, because you're so cut off from the world. No trees, nothing.... But I was ecstatic. I loved it. It was wonderful."

Klum has three children. Her daughter with Briatore, Leni, was born in 2004, followed by her two children with Seal, Henry (born in 2005) and Johan (born in 2006). The family divides their time between homes in Los Angeles, California, Costa Careyes, Mexico, New York City, and Bergisch Gladbach, Germany.

Reflecting on the challenges of balancing her celebrity status, her career, and family, Klum said, "I have a normal life and I have this glamorous life, but to me it's two different things. It's not like I'm this glamour diva who hands everything over and I just sit on my throne at home. When we're at home, we're cooking and doing things with the kids, driving them to school. We do the things that everyone has to do.... I never thought I would walk down the street and be followed by paparazzi, married to Seal, who I listened to when I was still in Germany. I never dreamed of this life because I didn't know there was a life like this."

HOBBIES AND OTHER INTERESTS

Klum enjoys spending time with her family and friends, playing tennis, ballet and jazz dancing, traveling, skiing, snowboarding, going to flea markets, and painting. She remains close to her parents and visits Germany often. She is also affiliated with charitable organizations, including the American Red Cross and the Elizabeth Glazer Pediatric AIDS Foundation.

SELECTED CREDITS

Writing

Heidi Klum's Body of Knowledge: 8 Rules of Model Behavior (To Help You Take Off on the Runway of Life), 2004

Television Appearances

"Spin City," 1998-99
"Project Runway," 2004- (creator and host)

Movie Appearances

Blow Dry, 2001
Ella Enchanted, 2004
The Life and Death of Peter Sellers, 2004

HONORS AND AWARDS

50 Most Beautiful People (*People* magazine): 2001
Style Icon of the Year (*Us* magazine): 2008

FURTHER READING

Periodicals

Entertainment Weekly, July 11, 2008, p.36
Forbes, June 30, 2008, p.96
Harper's Bazaar, May 2006, p.204
In Style, June 2006, p.274
Marie Claire, June 2008, p.78
People, May 14, 2001, p.140; Dec. 13, 2004, p.54; Mar. 28, 3005, p.73; May 9, 2005, p.156; July 24, 2006, p.102
Redbook, Feb. 2005, p.90; July 2008, p.112
Us, Apr. 28, 2008, p.66
USA Today, Dec. 3, 2007, p.D3

ADDRESS

Heidi Klum
"Project Runway"
Lifetime Television
2049 Century Park East, Suite 840
Los Angeles, CA 90067

WORLD WIDE WEB SITES

http://www.heidiklum.com
http://www.bravotv.com/project-runway
http://www.mylifetime.com

Courtesy, Deutsche Grammophon

Lang Lang 1982-

Chinese Classical Pianist
First Chinese Performer Nominated for a Grammy Award

BIRTH

Lang Lang (pronounced *Long Long)* was born June 14, 1982, in Shenyang, a large industrial city in western China. His mother, Zhou Xiulan, worked as a telephone operator. His father, Lang Guoren, was a police officer. Lang Lang is their only child.

YOUTH

Lang Lang's parents wanted him to be a pianist even before he was born. Their own dreams of careers in the performing arts ended during China's Cultural Revolution (1966-1976), a period in Chinese history known for repression and persecution by the government. Chairman Mao Zedong led a political campaign to revolutionize Chinese society. In the process, thousands of people were killed and millions were imprisoned or exiled. Cultural works that criticized Mao or his policies were forbidden, and many artists, musicians, and intellectuals were forced to give up their work and to do manual labor instead.

Before that point, Lang Lang's father played the erhu, an ancient stringed instrument sometimes called the Chinese violin. He had been the concertmaster (primary violinist and assistant to the orchestra's conductor) for a traditional Chinese orchestra in Shenyang. His mother had enjoyed singing and dancing and had hoped to become a concert singer. After the Cultural Revolution ended and people were once again free to study the arts, Lang Lang's parents became determined that their child would achieve the goals that they had been forced to abandon.

When Lang Lang's mother was pregnant with him, she listened to classical music as much as she could, hoping that her baby would be born with a love of music. When Lang Lang was just a year old, his father started teaching him the musical scale. Lang Lang could read music before he could read letters or words. Every day, a local radio station played two hours of classical music by such European composers as Ludwig von Beethoven, Johannes Brahms, Frederic Chopin, and many others. Lang Lang's parents played this music for him when he was a baby, hoping to encourage his interest in it. When he was about two years old, his parents bought him an old upright piano that cost about half of the money they earned in one year. The piano took up most of one room in their small apartment.

Beginning to Play Piano

As a young child, Lang Lang liked to watch cartoons on television. When he was about three years old, he saw a "Tom and Jerry" cartoon in which Tom the cat played the piano while being teased and tormented by Jerry the mouse. The piano music happened to be a piece by the famous Hungarian composer Franz Liszt, and Lang Lang later described this as his first memorable exposure to western classical music. Seeing this cartoon motivated Lang Lang to learn how to play the piano himself. Lang Lang said, "'Tom and Jerry,' of all things, opened my eyes. I thought, 'I want to be like that cat!'" Lang Lang immediately began taking piano lessons and soon proved to be a musical prodigy—a child with exceptional talent.

Lang Lang's father expected his young son to become the best pianist in China. Even at age three or four, Lang Lang was expected to practice his piano lessons for several hours each day. One day, his father was angry at him for playing games instead of practicing the piano, and he threw all of Lang Lang's favorite transformer toys out the window. When Lang Lang ran outside, he found that most of his toys had broken when they fell from the apartment window. As an adult, he was able to be philosophical about the pressure placed on him at such a young age. "Once you become a pianist, you need to give up part of your childhood," he acknowledged. "I was always jealous of other people when they would go to the park and I would be practicing."

"Once you become a pianist, you need to give up part of your childhood," Lang Lang acknowledged. "I was always jealous of other people when they would go to the park and I would be practicing."

In 1987, when Lang Lang was five years old, he gave his first public recital in the Shenyang Piano Competition. The contest was for piano students under the age of ten. "Right away, I really liked to perform.... Even then I wanted to be a world-class pianist. The piano felt very connected to me, and giving recitals, I felt totally relaxed, no nerves at all. I loved being on stage." Lang Lang won the competition, beating nearly 500 other young piano students.

EDUCATION

When he was seven years old, Lang Lang enrolled in the Shenyang Conservatory of Music, where he continued to study piano in addition to the usual school subjects. His favorite classes were literature, history, and geography. Meanwhile, his father created a schedule for Lang Lang that included a minimum of six hours of piano practice at home each day.

By the time Lang Lang was eight years old, his talent as a pianist had developed so much that he could learn nothing more from his teachers in Shenyang. To continue developing his talent, Lang Lang would have to find more experienced teachers. "Shenyang was a nice place to begin study, but not a good place to develop," he recalled. "My parents decided I should go to a more cultured place: Beijing. I could see a lot of great pianists play there, ... attend master classes with some of them, and also hear better orchestras and good conductors." His parents made the difficult decision to have Lang Lang study in Beijing, with the goal of being accepted to the Beijing Central Music Conservatory.

In his autobiography Playing with Flying Keys, *Lang Lang describes some of the challenges he faced while growing up.*

Leaving Home

In 1991, when Lang Lang was eight years old, he and his father moved to Beijing. His mother stayed behind in Shenyang, keeping her job there and sending money to support her husband and young son. Shenyang was a 12-hour train ride from Beijing, which meant that Lang Lang would not be able to see his mother very often. The decision was hard on the family. His mother later said, "At the time, Lang Lang was very small. It was very hard to say goodbye to him. I can never forget. His mouth was quivering, and then he and I both started up. He cried and I cried. But for his work, for the piano that he loves so much, I let him go."

In Beijing, Lang Lang and his father lived together in a tiny one-room apartment. It was only 100 square feet in size—the piano took up most of the space in the apartment. Also, it had no heat and no bathroom. The apartment building provided just one bathroom for each floor, and Lang Lang and his father shared the bathroom with three other families. The Beijing winters were long, cold, and damp, and Lang Lang often wore all of the clothes he owned, all at once, to try to stay warm. The apartment building was also infested with mice, and he would often wake up in the morning to find his music books chewed to pieces. His father worried that mice would bite Lang Lang's hands, preventing him from playing the piano.

To prepare for his audition with the Beijing Central Music Conservatory, Lang Lang practiced for many hours each day, much to the annoyance of his new neighbors. The apartment walls were thin, and neighbors would bang on the walls or shout to complain when he played the piano too late at night. His father insisted that Lang Lang practice until 11:00 at night and start again very early in the morning. Finally, the neighbors called the police, who negotiated a compromise on the number of hours that Lang Lang would play the piano.

Beijing was a much larger, busier, and more populated city than Shenyang. Lang Lang attended school and continued piano lessons, but he had no friends. His northern Chinese accent branded him as an outsider and made it difficult to communicate with people in Beijing. His intense schedule of piano practice and schoolwork left him with almost no time for himself. Lang Lang struggled with loneliness and missed his mother terribly.

Despite his dedication to practicing, even Lang Lang's piano lessons were going badly. His new teacher was mean, and she eventually dismissed Lang Lang as her student. This was the worst possible thing that could have happened. "It was a very difficult time. I was trying hard, but my lessons were going badly, and just before I was supposed to audition for the top music school in the country, the Central Conservatory, my teacher kicked me out of her studio. She told me that I wasn't meant to be a pianist, and that was devastating."

Quitting—and Starting Again

Lang Lang's father became enraged, convinced that his son's failure had shamed the family. He went so far as to demand that eight-year-old Lang Lang kill himself in shame. Horrified by his father's words, Lang Lang instead decided to stop playing the piano. Even after his father apologized and begged Lang Lang to begin playing again, he refused. He didn't speak to his father or touch a piano for four months.

Finally, Lang Lang's anger at his father faded and he did start playing the piano again. "At my school, the music teacher asked me why I wasn't playing anymore. I started crying and said, 'My teacher told me that I had no talent.' The schoolteacher put this Mozart sonata on the piano and said, 'Come on, play the slow movement.' So I did, and as I performed I suddenly realized how much I loved the instrument. Playing ... brought me hope again."

Lang Lang began studying with a new teacher and resumed preparations for his audition with the Beijing Central Conservatory. Of the 3,000 students who would audition for a place in the Conservatory's fifth grade, only 12 would be accepted. The pressure was the most intense he had ever experienced. Lang Lang wrote about the experience in his autobiography, *Playing with Flying Keys*, recalling how nervous he had been waiting in the audition line for half the day. When his turn finally came, he recalled, "As I adjusted the piano bench and positioned my fingers on the keys, however, a great calm washed over me.... My mind cleared. I began to play and nothing distracted me." After two rounds of auditions, Lang Lang was ranked number one.

When he was nine years old, Lang Lang began studying at the Beijing Central Music Conservatory. There he played on a grand piano for the first time. "For so many years, I had only played on upright pianos. The grand piano was like a new world. A whole new world of sound!" Lang Lang's focus on being the number one pianist in China intensified and soon expanded to include the goal of being number one in the world. He began entering as many competitions as he could.

A Winning Streak

Lang Lang's emphasis on competitions was soon rewarded. In 1993, he won first prize at the Fifth Xing Hai Cup Piano Competition in Beijing. In

Lang Lang at the piano. © Photo: J. Henry Fair/Deutsche Grammophon.

1994, when he was 12 years old, Lang Lang took first prize and a special award for outstanding artistic performance at the Fourth International Young Pianists Competition in Germany. Lang Lang then went on to win the 1995 Tchaikovsky International Young Pianists Competition in Japan.

Later in 1995, Lang Lang performed Chopin's "24 Etudes" at the Beijing Concert Hall. The "24 Etudes" are difficult, complicated, and challenging pieces for even the most skilled pianists. In the classical music world, the successful performance of the "24 Etudes" demonstrates a complete mastery of the piano. Lang Lang performed the "24 Etudes" to great critical acclaim when he was only 13 years old. This success led to his 1996 appearance as a soloist in the first concert of the China National Symphony.

Leaving China

By the mid-1990s, Lang Lang was receiving invitations to study at music conservatories all over the world. After sending a video of one of his concert performances, he was invited to audition in person for enrollment in the prestigious Curtis Institute of Music in Philadelphia, Pennsylvania. After two rounds of auditions, he was granted admission to the Curtis Institute, which included full tuition, housing, meals, and living expenses. In 1997, when Lang Lang was 15 years old, he and his father moved from China to live in Philadelphia.

In his autobiography, Lang Lang wrote in detail about how difficult it was to leave his mother again and move to the United States, a world away from his home in China. But he knew it was a necessary move if he was to develop his talent any further. "Western classical music in China is usually like Chinese food in the West—familiar but not quite the real thing," he observed. "A lot of musicians here [in China] don't do much beyond play the notes themselves.... The sound is nice enough, but there is none of that intensity. That is what I had to come to the West to learn."

Lang Lang and his father were given a large apartment to live in, which was very different from their home in Beijing. Most notably, this apartment had heat and its own bathroom. Lang Lang was amazed by all the new privileges he had. The Curtis Institute provided him with a Steinway grand piano in his apartment. The school also hired a private tutor to teach him English.

Lang Lang was also surprised when his new American piano teacher told him that he would not be entering any more competitions. In China, that had been the way for music students to advance their careers. But in the U.S., Lang Lang was instructed to focus on achieving his own personal best. His teachers told him to focus on his own work, and not to compare himself to others. When he was ready, they said, the right opportunity would come.

CAREER HIGHLIGHTS

A Big Break

Lang Lang's first big professional opportunity came in 1999 when he was 17 years old. He was called as a last-minute substitute soloist for a concert with the Chicago Symphony Orchestra at the Ravinia Music Festival. The scheduled pianist had fallen ill and was unable to perform. Lang Lang said, "Before this concert, one day my friend and I were in a bookstore and saw an ad for Ravinia. I said to my friend, if I play in this kind of concert, I will be world famous."

The performance was a great success. The *Chicago Tribune* called Lang Lang the "biggest, most exciting keyboard talent encountered in many years." For his part, Lang Lang said, "I wasn't actually nervous ... but it was so exciting and so surprising. This was my first time playing with such a world-famous symphony, especially in a gala concert." Lang Lang later told the *New Yorker* that he imagined Michael Jordan's slam dunk as he struck his first resounding chords and Tiger Woods's golf swing while he played the octaves. After the concert, world-famous violinist Isaac Stern invited Lang Lang to play a private recital for the musicians.

Lang Lang released his first recording, which included two live concerts at Tanglewood, when he was just 19.

After this debut, Lang Lang was invited to perform concerts all over the world. He decided to combine his studies at the Curtis Institute with concert tours. During 2001, he toured Europe, performed at the prestigious Carnegie Hall in New York City, and returned to China for the first time in four years as part of a tour with the Phildelphia Orchestra. Lang Lang also released his first recording in 2001, *Haydn, Rachmaninoff, Brahms, Tchaikovsky, Balarkirev,* which included two concerts he performed in Tanglewood, Massachusetts. In 2002, Lang Lang completed his formal studies at the Curtis Institute and became an official Steinway artist, agreeing to perform exclusively on pianos made by Steinway & Sons.

Lang Lang's early professional performances were a success with audiences but received mixed reviews from critics. One writer for the *New York Times* said, "Virtuoso fireworks are only a part of the story; and rather than being merely flashy, they reveal a deep underlying power." The *Chicago Tribune* praised his first recording for "stupendous pianism" and the "seemingly effortless way he has of enlisting the piano's full resources to realize the music beyond the printed page." However, a writer for the *American Record Guide* called Lang Lang's playing "superficially impressive" and "exhausting to listen to."

> *"I practice now much more in my head than at the piano. The best thing to do is close your eyes and visualize the score of what you're working on. You can do a lot of work that way, deciding on the direction of a phrase, the articulation, and other things.... Music without that kind of attention is nothing. If you play without it, you're getting some of the feeling, but you don't really understand what the piece is about."*

Life on the Road

Since 2002, Lang Lang has spent most of his time touring, giving concerts and teaching master classes all over the world. He averages 125 performances each year. "I love the audience because I love the tension there ... because it seems like a lot of people watching, I mean, the creation of this wonderful work. And then you are at the same time the interpreter. It's like building a bridge to their heart."

Even with such a grueling travel and performance schedule, Lang Lang still manages to practice at least four or five hours a day. But his piano practice now is very different from when he was a young boy. "I practice now much more in my head than at the piano. The best thing to do is close your eyes and visualize the score of what you're working on. You can do a lot of work that way, deciding on the direction of a phrase, the articulation, and other things. So by the time you get to the piano, you've already made a lot of progress.... I spend a lot of my practice time going over the score, noticing where the harmony changes, where the orchestration shifts, and so on. So when I begin to practice the piano part, I've already done a lot of work on the piece.... So music without that kind of attention is nothing. If you play without it, you're getting some of the feeling, but you don't really understand what the piece is about. That's what practice time is for; it's to reach an understanding of the piece."

Lang Lang also uses his time away from the piano to study the history, literature, and culture of the historical period in which music was composed. "You must do a lot of research to connect the music with its time, and to our own," he observed. "Reading literature of the time helps you to understand what people were thinking during that time. So when you play a piece, you understand its entire history better, and when you play, it's more real to you. When you read a book, it tells you what's going on. But when you play music, it becomes real life.... Every time I play, I try to see the images. For example, I see something. I can see [a] beautiful forest and everything's green."

Inspiring Young People

Lang Lang's phenomenal success at such a young age has inspired a generation of young musicians around the world. In China, the "Lang Lang Effect" refers to the growing number of children studying piano because of him. His popularity with children resulted in the creation of five "Lang Lang Steinway" pianos, designed especially for early music education. In 2004, he became an International Goodwill Ambassador to the United Nations Children's Fund (UNICEF). In this role, Lang Lang raises awareness of the needs and rights of children throughout the world. "Music is like a language, it's like a universal language, it has the connection to the people and also the feeling from your soul, from your heart. I think the best way to reach children is to play them music, this really opens their ears and their minds." In 2008, the Lang Lang International Music Foundation was created to further inspire and educate young musicians. Another way to inspire kids might be through his appearance in the "Second Life" video game, where he became the first classical artist ever to perform an exclusive concert in this digital world.

Also in 2008, Lang Lang published his autobiography, *Journey of a Thousand Miles: My Story,* along with a version for young readers titled *Playing with Flying Keys*. In these books, he describes the life of dedication that led to his success as a pianist, including details about the stress and pressure placed on him by his strict and demanding father. Readers may be surprised by the trials and difficulties that young Lang Lang endured under his father's high expectations. *Booklist* called his story "suspenseful and engrossing." *Kirkus Reviews* praised the book as "a true rags-to-riches story told with fervor and variety," while *Children's Bookwatch* called it a "dynamic, moving story."

Lang Lang played with five-year-old Li Muzi at the opening ceremonies of the 2008 Olympics in Beijing.

Over the past few years, Lang Lang has achieved world renown. He has been featured on countless television programs and in newspapers and magazines—in the United States, in China, and in other countries, too. A documentary film, *Dragon Songs* (2006), followed him on a concert tour of China. In addition, he has been invited to perform for events broadcast around the world, including the opening ceremony of the 2008 Summer Olympics in Beijing. There Lang Lang performed for a stadium audience of 90,000 and for billions of television viewers worldwide.

In 2008, Lang Lang became the first Chinese performer to be nominated for a Grammy Award, for Best Instrumental Soloist Performance with Orchestra. That experience led to his most recent musical venture. At the Grammy Awards ceremony, he played a six-minute version of George Gershwin's "Rhapsody in Blue" with Herbie Hancock, a legendary jazz pianist, composer, and band leader. After that night, they decided to perform a series of concerts that would feature music from different traditions, including jazz pieces, classical pieces, and even Chinese folk songs. In 2009 they performed at musical venues around the United States. Their goal was "to bring new audiences to classical and jazz," Lang Lang explained, "because, especially in the U.S. … you don't have [much music instruction] in the public school system. But sometimes for classical or jazz, people do need to have some kind of a basic lesson before they start." It's an unexpected departure for the young musician, and it has left many fans wondering what Lang Lang might do next.

HOME AND FAMILY

When he is not touring, Lang Lang divides his time between homes in New York City and Beijing. He lives and travels with his father. Although his mother's primary home is in China, she often also travels with Lang Lang.

At his solo concerts, Lang Lang often invites his father to perform encores with him. For these encores, he and his father play traditional Chinese compositions. "I want to continue my family tradition, that we love playing together and performing for people," he commented. "Secondly, I love to promote Chinese culture and its musical instruments. Thirdly, my father was the principal for the erhu section in an excellent Chinese orchestra. He sacrificed his own career that he didn't play for ten years for my sake. Being able to perform in major concert halls in the world must have been in his dream. It is the least that I could do to help him fulfill that dream."

HOBBIES AND OTHER INTERESTS

Lang Lang is an avid fan of NBA basketball. His favorite team is the Philadelphia 76ers, and he also follows the career of Chinese basketball star Yao Ming. Lang Lang still enjoys watching cartoons when he can, along with movies and sports, including soccer and ping-pong. He is fascinated with any kind of technology gadget. Lang Lang admires professional golfer Tiger Woods and has said that Woods is a role model for living with fame and running the business of being a performer. Lang Lang is also a fan of jazz and hip-hop music. His favorite pop artists include Christina Aguilera, Beyoncé, and Alicia Keys.

SELECTED RECORDINGS

Haydn, Rachmaninoff, Brahms, Tchaikovsky, Balarkirev, 2001
Rachmaninoff: Piano Concerto No. 3, Scriabin Etudes, 2002
Tchaikovsky, Mendelssohn: First Piano Concertos, 2003
The Banquet Soundtrack, 2006
Dragon Songs, 2006
Memory, 2006
Beethoven Piano Concertos 1+4, 2007
The Painted Veil Soundtrack, 2007
The Magic of Lang Lang, 2008
Chopin: The Piano Concertos, 2009

HONORS AND AWARDS

Leonard Bernstein Award (Schleswig-Holstein Music Festival): 2002
President's Merit Award (Recording Academy): 2007

FURTHER READING

Books

Lang Lang, and David Ritz. *Journey of a Thousand Miles: My Story*, 2008
Lang Lang, and Michael French. *Lang Lang: Playing with Flying Keys*, 2008

Periodicals

American Music Teacher, Mar. 2008, p.22
Baltimore Sun, Apr. 15, 2001, p.9
Christian Science Monitor, Feb. 7, 2008, p.1
Current Biography Yearbook, 2003
Keyboard, Nov. 1, 2003, p.32
New York Times, Sep. 2, 2003, p.E1
New Yorker, Apr. 2, 2007, p.86; Aug. 4, 2008, p.52
People, Sep. 29, 2003, p.42; Nov. 19, 2008
Time, Nov. 17, 2001, p.137
U.S. News & World Report, June 11, 2001, p.66
Washington Post, Apr. 15, 2001, p.G1

Online Articles

http://www.cbsnews.com
(CBS News: 60 Minutes, "Lang Lang: Piano Prodigy," Jan. 9, 2005)
http://www2.deutschegrammophon.com/artist
(Deutsche Grammophon, "Lang Lang Biography," June 2008)
http://www.unicef.org/people
(UNICEF, "UNICEF People: Lang Lang," undated)

ADDRESS

Lang Lang
Lang Lang International Music Foundation
146 West 57th Street, Suite 36D
New York, NY 10019

WORLD WIDE WEB SITES

http://www.langlang.com
http://www.thelanglangfoundation.org

Leona Lewis 1985-

British Singer

Performer of the Hit Songs "Bleeding Love" and "Better in Time"

BIRTH

Leona Louise Lewis was born on April 3, 1985, in the Islington section of north London, England. She is of mixed ancestry, with a Guyanese father and a mother of Welsh, Italian, and Irish descent. Her father, Joe Lewis, is a youth corrections officer and a former DJ, and her mother, Maria Lewis, is a social worker who has also taught ballet. Leona has two siblings—a younger brother, Kyle, and an older half-brother, Bradley.

YOUTH AND EDUCATION

Lewis had a working-class upbringing. When she was five years old her family moved to Hackney, a multicultural neighborhood in East London. She has warm memories of those years and the support she received from her parents, who eagerly fostered her natural gifts. Her talent and passion were obvious from the beginning. "I remember singing into my hairbrush," Lewis recalled, "and every chance I could I'd be doing a show or performing in the front room for my family."

"I remember singing into my hairbrush," Lewis recalled, "and every chance I could I'd be doing a show or performing in the front room for my family."

When Lewis was six, she attended the Sylvia Young Theatre School to learn about singing and acting. The school fees were high, and her parents had to work multiple jobs to make ends meet. When Lewis was nine she advanced to the prestigious Italia Conti Academy and also began private voice lessons. By this point, however, the school fees became unaffordable and she had to transfer to a local public school. For the next two years she struggled to enjoy herself, complaining that the new school stifled her creativity.

Another door opened for Lewis when she was accepted at the BRIT School of Performing Arts and Technology, a renowned state-funded institution. For the next three years, she studied piano and guitars and soaked up knowledge about the entertainment field. She also began regularly hanging out with performers and musicians. Additional information about Lewis's school years is unavailable, and it's unclear whether she graduated or left school before finishing her degree.

FIRST JOBS

Near the end of her time at the BRIT School, Lewis began seeking out a recording contract. A demo that she recorded when she was 15 years old secured her an audition with Sony Records, although the label declined to sign her. For several more years she persistently promoted herself by recording more demos and sending them to labels. Booking studio time was expensive, however, so she worked a series of part-time jobs: as a cashier at the Gap, a waitress at Pizza Hut, and a receptionist for a mortgage adviser.

Lewis with Ray Quinn, another finalist from "The X Factor."

Lewis also found work as a performer, playing gigs at clubs in London. In addition, when she was 18 she secured a part in *The Lion King* musical at Disneyland in Paris, France. The idea of living that far from home did not appeal to her, however, so she turned down the job.

CAREER HIGHLIGHTS

"The X Factor"

After so many years of studying music and performing without a record deal, Lewis was discouraged. At one point, she considered putting her dreams on hold to go to college and pursue a career in social work. But in 2006, her boyfriend persuaded her to audition for "The X Factor." The British television series pits singers against each other in a closely followed competition. The winner usually receives a recording contract negotiated by Simon Cowell, the show's creator and one of its judges/mentors.

Lewis passed the audition and proceeded to stun the judges as well as millions of viewers each week. Her extensive vocal range was on full display with her renditions of such popular standards as "All By Myself," "Over the Rainbow" (in the style of one of her favorite singers, Eva Cassidy), and "I Will Always Love You," made popular by another of her idols, Whitney

Houston. Lewis advanced to the finals, which aired live on December 6, 2006, and attracted 13 million viewers. With a stellar performance of "A Moment Like This," Lewis clinched the title, winning a record deal worth 1 million pounds (roughly $1.5 million).

Along with winning the prize, Lewis received a serious endorsement from the finale's guest judge, Gary Barlow of the popular vocal group Take That. "This girl is probably 50 times better than any other contestant you have ever had," Barlow told Cowell, "so you have a big responsibility to make the right record with her." As a judge, Cowell is notoriously difficult to impress, but he agreed with Barlow, proclaiming Lewis "one of the best singers we've had in this country for 20 years."

While her popularity was still high after her victory on "The X Factor," Lewis released a studio recording of "A Moment Like This" a few weeks later on Cowell's BMG label. The single set a Guinness World Record for single-week sales by tallying 50,000 downloads in 30 minutes.

Launching a Singing Career

Cowell and Lewis were careful about the next big step. They decided to assemble a whole team of industry experts. High on their list of collaborators was legendary music executive and producer Clive Davis, credited with discovering Whitney Houston and helping to launch the careers of Alicia Keys and Kelly Clarkson. (For more information on these performers, see the following issues of *Biography Today*: for Houston, see *Biography Today,* Sep. 1994; for Clarkson, see *Biography Today,* Jan. 2003; for Keys, see *Biography Today,* Jan. 2007.)

Cowell knew how to spark Davis's interest. "You might have the next Whitney Houston on your hands," he told the CEO. Assured of Lewis's potential, Davis began a plan to break her into the U.S. market. He scheduled a showcase for her in February 2007 at the Hilton Hotel in Los Angeles, where Lewis performed before a room full of record label executives and songwriters. Not long after, Davis and Cowell collaborated to form a joint label, J Records/Syco Music, that would feature her as its first artist. Lewis signed a five-album contract worth $9.7 million.

Lewis and the record company executives soon assembled a superstar squad of producers and songwriters, including Akon, Ne-Yo, Dallas Austin, and Max Martin. As Lewis went to work on her CD, she wanted to ensure that her debut was a serious artistic statement and that it accurately represented her. "I wanted to make an album that was totally me," she said. "Each song is about something that either I've gone through or that someone around me has gone through." As a result of her deliberate pace, along with a bout of tonsillitis that briefly sidelined her voice, the highly anticipated album took several months to record. Fans began wondering if the album would ever be released.

In November 2007, Lewis's debut album finally reached the record stores. *Spirit* was released in the United Kingdom, with an American version scheduled for a later release. The album features "Bleeding Love," a catchy, soulful number with a heavy R&B beat, as well as ballads, cover songs, and two tracks that Lewis co-wrote, "Here I Am" and "Whatever It Takes."

Record sales proved that *Spirit* was worth the wait. "Bleeding Love" was that year's biggest-selling week-one single, moving over 200,000 copies in just seven days. The album performed even better, selling over 375,000 copies in its first week, which made it the United Kingdom's fastest-selling debut album of all time. Although the album was not yet released in the United States, critics couldn't help noticing the buzz *Spirit* had caused. "Lately she's been earning justified comparisons to Celine Dion, Whitney Houston, and yes, Mariah Carey," reported Nicholas Fonseca in *Entertainment Weekly*. "So divas, watch out." (For more information on Dion, see *Biography Today,* Sep. 1997; for more information on Carey, see *Biography Today,* Apr. 1996.)

Simon Cowell is notoriously difficult to impress, but he called Lewis "one of the best singers we've had in this country for 20 years."

Breaking Out in the U.S.

Team Leona Lewis pulled no punches when it began promoting the U.S. version of *Spirit*. By spring 2008, she had been featured on the cover of *Harper's Bazaar UK,* and *Entertainment Weekly* had listed her among the "8 to Watch in 2008."

Davis scheduled Lewis to sing at his pre-Grammy Awards party, which according to some reports is a bigger celebration than the Grammys. After giving a stirring performance of "Burning Love," she had the pleasure of mixing with the stars in attendance, many of whom were her childhood idols. "I nearly spontaneously combusted because everyone on my iPod was there!" she exclaimed. "Carrie Underwood, Alicia Keys, and I met Whitney Houston—that was crazy."

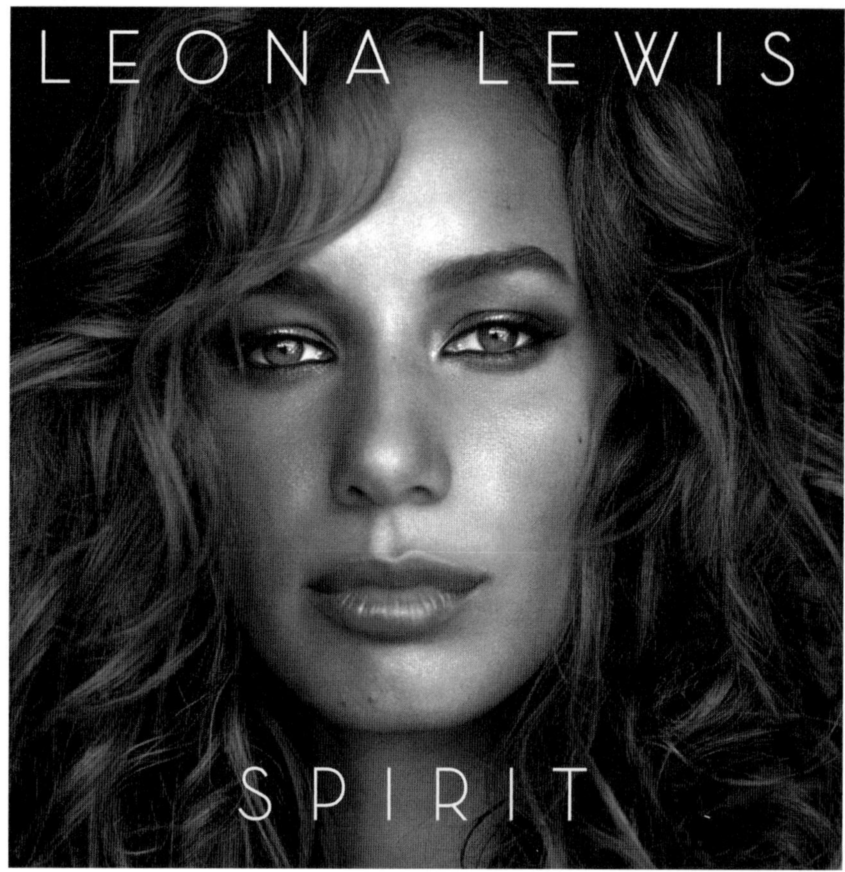

Lewis's debut CD, Spirit, *was a big success in the UK and in the U.S.*

The U.S. version of "Bleeding Love" hit stores on March 18, 2008. A day before its release, Lewis appeared with Oprah Winfrey on her popular daytime talk show. Lewis's performance of "Bleeding Love" received a standing ovation. In the days leading up to the release of *Spirit* on April 8, she endured an exhausting string of photo shoots, interviews, and performances. Grabbing the most attention were her appearances on "Good Morning America," "The Tonight Show with Jay Leno," and "Jimmy Kimmel Live!"

As in Great Britain, *Spirit* made a big splash in the U.S. market. It took the top spot on the *Billboard* album chart, selling 205,000 copies. The "Bleeding Love" single sold even better. Lewis became the first British female solo artist to scale the top of the Hot 100 singles chart in more than 21 years.

"Bleeding Love" eventually became iTunes' top-selling single of the year. Her second single, "Better in Time," also reached the *Billboard* Pop 100 chart, peaking at the No. 4 spot.

The critical reaction to *Spirit* was also positive. Writing in *Essence,* Kiera Mayo said that "Leona Lewis is a stunning vocal powerhouse" and has "the pitch and range of Mariah Carey, topped with the powerful pop appeal of Christina Aguilera." In the magazine *Interview,* Matt Diehl wrote, "Lewis's strength is her powerful voice: as showstopping as Whitney Houston's, as wrenchingly human as that of Lewis's favorite, Eva Cassidy."

In the wake of her accomplishments in the first half of 2008, Lewis received special honors during the rest of the year. In June she was invited to perform in London at the 90th birthday celebration of Nelson Mandela, a Nobel Peace Prize winner and the first black South African president. She also had the rare opportunity of rocking out with Jimmy Page, the legendary guitarist of Led Zeppelin, at the closing ceremonies of the 2008 Summer Olympics in Beijing, China. In December 2008, she was asked to join Beyoncé, Jay-Z, and other stars to commemorate the inauguration of U.S. president Barack Obama in January.

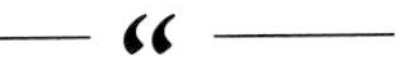

While singing at a pre-Grammy Awards party, Lewis had the pleasure of mixing with the stars in attendance, many of whom were her childhood idols. "I nearly spontaneously combusted because everyone on my iPod was there!" she exclaimed. "Carrie Underwood, Alicia Keys, and I met Whitney Houston—that was crazy."

”

Future Plans

With a promise of a long career before her, Lewis said she has no plans to stop producing music. She told *Glamour* magazine in October 2008 that she was thinking about beefing up her style by doing "rockier stuff." She also began to explore acting opportunities.

HOME AND FAMILY

Lewis maintains strong ties to her old neighborhood and her family. She still lives near her parents and her brothers in the Hackney section of London. She and her boyfriend, Lou Al-Chamaa, have been friends since

childhood—they met when she was 10 years old, and they lived on the same street. When she's home she likes spending time with Al-Chamaa and another family member, a rottweiler named Rome.

MAJOR INFLUENCES

As a child growing up in the 1990s, Lewis enjoyed listening to pop music and R&B. There were several female divas who first inspired her to sing, including Whitney Houston, Christina Aguilera, and Eva Cassidy. By listening to the records her dad spun as a DJ, she also grew familiar with stars from past generations, artists like Stevie Wonder, Michael Jackson, and Minnie Riperton, a soul singer who like Lewis was known for her multi-octave voice.

HOBBIES AND OTHER INTERESTS

Away from the spotlight, Lewis's life is low-key. Occasionally, she will spend a night dancing in clubs, but she has no interest in hard partying (to her, alcohol "tastes like hairspray"). A night at home relaxing with friends or having a nice meal is just as appealing for her. To stay fit, she swims and rides horses, a hobby that she learned from her mother.

Lewis's passion for social causes has led her to participate in various fund-raisers. She recorded the ballad "Footprints in the Sand" to help support the organization Sport Relief, which also coordinated her February 2008 trip to South Africa. She also joined 14 other female singers to record "Just Stand Up," a song that was released in September 2008 to benefit Stand Up to Cancer, an organization that raises funds for cancer research. That same month, the vocal group performed the song live during the Stand Up to Cancer telethon, which aired on major networks all over the world.

Lewis is also an animal activist and a vegan (someone who doesn't eat meat or use any products derived from animals). She announced in 2008 that she wants to develop an apparel line that promotes the humane treatment of animals. "I would love to promote an affordable line of non-leather bags and shoes," she said. "I'm trying to find the right companies to work with, sourcing different things and talking to creative teams."

SELECTED CREDITS

Television

"The X Factor," 2006

Recordings

Spirit, 2006 (UK release); 2007 (U.S. release)

HONORS AND AWARDS

MTV Asia Awards: 2008, Breakthrough Artist
World Music Awards: 2008, Best Pop Female and Best New Act

FURTHER READING

Periodicals

Billboard, Oct. 6, 2007; Dec. 1, 2007; Jan. 26, 2008; July 19, 2008; Aug. 16, 2008
Daily Telegraph, Oct. 18, 2007
Entertainment Weekly, Nov. 30, 2007; Dec. 14, 2007; Apr. 11, 2008; July 25, 2008
Glamour, Oct. 2008
Houston Chronicle, Apr. 20, 2008
Independent, Mar. 28, 2008
Interview, Mar. 2008
Observer, Dec. 17, 2006; Mar. 30, 2008
People Weekly, Apr. 28, 2008
Sunday Mail, Oct. 21, 2007
Times (London), Dec. 18, 2006; Nov. 15, 2007; Mar. 8, 2008; Mar. 27, 2008; Oct. 18, 2008; Nov. 1, 2008
US Weekly, Apr. 7, 2008

Online Articles

http://www.thisislondon.co.uk
(Evening Standard, "X Factor SuperStar: Leona Lewis on Fame, Fear of Failure and the Pressures of Being Simon Cowell's Biggest Hope," Oct. 21, 2007; "British Idol Leona Lewis Tops the U.S. Charts … But Still Can't Afford to Buy a House in London," Mar. 27, 2008)
http://www.rollingstone.com
(Rolling Stone, "Leona Lewis: British R&B Diva Wins Over Simon Cowell," Apr. 3, 2008)
http://www.seventeen.com
(Seventeen, "Fun Stuff, When I was 17: Leona Lewis," May 5, 2008)

ADDRESS

Leona Lewis
J Records
1540 Broadway, Suite 9W
New York, NY 10036

WORLD WIDE WEB SITES

http://www.leonalewismusic.co.uk
http://www.jrecords.com
http://www.xfactor.itv.com

Nastia Liukin 1989-

Russian-Born American Gymnast
2008 Olympic All-Around Champion

BIRTH

Anastasia "Nastia" Valeryevna Liukin was born in Moscow, Russia, on October 30, 1989. She is the daughter of Valeri and Anna Kochneva Liukin, who moved from Russia to the United States in 1992. Both of Nastia's parents were gymnasts. Valeri Liukin represented the Soviet Union in the 1988 Olympic Games in Seoul, Korea. He won two gold and two silver medals in that competition. Anna Liukin was a rhythmic gymnast on the Soviet team. She won a gold medal at the world championships in 1987. Nastia Liukin has said that her parents' success has motivated her to achieve high goals in her sport. "That's a real inspiration.... To have parents be such great gymnasts, you look up to them and think it might actually be possible for you."

"

Liukin was passionate about gymnastics from the beginning. "I never wanted to take my leotard off," she recalled. "I wanted to sleep in it all the time. [My parents] would try to come in when I was asleep and take it off. If I woke up, I was hysterically crying because I wanted to keep it on. I'm sure that's when they thought I really loved it, and gymnastics would probably be a big part of my life."

"

YOUTH

Liukin was two years old when her parents emigrated from Russia. Though they knew little English, the Liukins moved to the United States hoping to earn a living teaching gymnastics. They worked briefly in New Orleans, Louisiana, before moving to Texas to open their own gymnastics training center with partner and former teammate Yevgeny Marchenko. "We were dreaming big," Valeri Liukin told *USA Today*. "This country, we really believed, was the country of opportunity."

Her parents launched their business, the World Olympic Gymnastics Academy (WOGA), in a former supermarket in Plano, Texas. They could not afford a babysitter for her, so Liukin often accompanied them to work. She played nearby in the gym while her parents taught gymnastics skills to groups of students. Valeri and Anna Liukin did not want a career as a competitive gymnast for their daughter because they knew firsthand the sacrifices, injuries, and pressures involved in being an elite athlete. But they soon noticed that Nastia seemed to have a natural ability for the sport. Her father said in *Sports Illustrated* that his students "would struggle to learn skills, but Nastia just watched and, with no help, did them perfectly." He recalled in the *Atlanta Journal-Constitution,* "When she started rolling around, I was like, 'Oh gosh, she was doing so well! ... She could do some leg lifts 10 times and other girls were [straining].... She's incredibly flexible. We started thinking, 'God gives you that. I don't think we have a right to take it away.'"

In addition to her obvious natural talent, Liukin was passionate about the sport from the very beginning. "I never wanted to take my leotard off," she recalled. "I wanted to sleep in it all the time. [My parents] would try to come in when I was asleep and take it off. If I woke up, I was hysterically crying because I wanted to keep it on. I'm sure that's when they thought I really loved it, and gymnastics would probably be a big part of my life."

EDUCATION

Liukin attended public school until fifth grade. After that she was privately educated at Spring Creek Academy in Plano. The school offered a flexible program that allowed her to train seven hours per day, attending classes in between her morning and afternoon workouts. She completed high school in 2007 and plans to study business at Southern Methodist University in Dallas, Texas.

WOMEN'S GYMNASTICS

Gymnastics has a well-defined path for those who become competitive. Gymnasts are classified by skill level, from Level 1 to Level 10. Top gymnasts who advance beyond Level 10 reach the elite level and compete in national and international meets. The elite level is further divided into junior and senior divisions based upon age. Gymnasts become eligible to compete at the senior level when they reach the age of 15.

Women's gymnastics competitions include a variety of events. In a typical meet, competitors perform routines on four different apparatus: the balance beam, vault, uneven bars, and floor exercise. Judges award scores for each routine based on its degree of difficulty and the gymnast's performance. Competitors can earn medals in individual events by achieving the highest score on a given apparatus. The gymnast who achieves the highest total score for her performance on all four apparatus receives the prestigious title of all-around champion. In addition, the team that earns the highest total score wins a team medal. So in gymnastics there are actually three concurrent competitions: the individual champion on each apparatus; the all-around champion—the individual gymnast with the highest combined score on all four apparatus; and the team champion—the team with the highest combined score in all events.

CAREER HIGHLIGHTS

Competing as a Junior

Liukin began training seriously when she was very young. Initially she was coached by Marchenko, but eventually her father took over as her coach. She made her national debut at age 12 in the U.S. national championships in August 2002, competing at the junior level. She placed sixth in the competition, after injuring an elbow in a fall from the uneven bars during her first apparatus. Even though she did not win a medal, people immediately recognized her special talent. She combined the grace and elegance of her mother's rhythmic gymnastics with her father's acrobatic skills, physical power, and determination. The following year Liukin won four of the five gold medals awarded at the junior level at the 2003 U.S. national championships in Milwaukee, Wisconsin. She took first place in the all-around competition, the uneven bars, the balance beam, and the floor exercise. And, according to Jessica Steyers in *International Gymnast,* she "outclassed the field in terms of style, expression, and difficulty."

“

At the 2003 U.S. national championships, according to commentator Jessica Steyers, Liukin "outclassed the field in terms of style, expression, and difficulty."

By the time of the 2004 U.S. national championships, Liukin had undergone a growth spurt of five inches. Growing that much in one year means that a gymnast has to make important adjustments in order to continue performing at the same skill level with a taller, heavier body. Liukin worked hard to overcome the changes and focused on making herself stronger. One of her workouts included running with an automobile tire tied to a rope around her waist. She won the U.S. junior title again in 2004. One benefit of the growth spurt, however, was the long, lean figure that contributed to the expressiveness and beauty of her routines.

Liukin was too young to qualify for the 2004 Olympic Games in Athens, Greece. In order to compete in the Olympics, athletes must turn 16 years old in the Olympic year, and she was one year too young. Most observers in the sport believed that if age had not been a factor, she would have made the U.S. team. Martha Karolyi, the U.S. women's team coordinator, said at the time in the *Atlanta Journal-Constitution,* "We see a great future for her. Her perfect techniques and very exquisite style, which very few gymnasts have, differentiate the big group of gymnasts doing the same skill." Her father put things in perspective, "Her time is coming [but] it's not there yet," he told the *Houston Chronicle*. "She wasn't physically ready, and she could get hurt. That's the main point—not winning or losing, but ending her career as a healthy and happy person."

Liukin on the uneven bars during the 2004 U.S. Gymnastics Championships, where she won the junior title.

U.S. National Champion

In August 2005, Liukin won one of the most important titles in U.S. women's gymnastics, when she narrowly defeated Chellsie Memmel for the U.S. senior women's all-around title at the 2005 U.S. national championships. She scored 9.8 out of a possible 10 in the final round of competition on vault, 9.766 on uneven bars, and 9.8 on the balance beam to become the U.S. senior champion. A report in the *New York Times* raved about her routines on the balance beam and the bars. "A dazzling routine on the balance beam.... She did a side somersault—twisting a quarter-turn while flipping—as easily as if she were on flat ground. She whipped off her backflips as casually as most people do cartwheels," the reporter observed. "Liukin does one of the toughest bar routines in the world, yet she makes it look effortless. She flitted from bar to bar as if weightless, and her handstands were so straight it was as if an invisible cable were pulling her taut from above." Although Liukin beat Memmel for the U.S. crown, she lost the world all-around championship to her by one-thousandth of a point (0.001) a few months later, at the 2005 world championships in Melbourne, Australia. However, Liukin finished the world championships with event titles in balance beam and uneven bars and a silver medal in the floor exercise competition.

In 2006 a new scoring system went into effect for gymnastics competitions worldwide. The revised system used combined marks from two judging panels—one focused on difficulty and one focused on execution. A score of 10 would no longer be a winning score. Impressive marks would fall between 16 and 17. In order to score well under the new system, Liukin worked at increasing the difficulty in her routines and prepared for the world championships in the fall. Just before the world competition, however, she injured an ankle while practicing her tumbling. She still took part in the 2006 world championships in Aarhus, Denmark, but she was limited to competing in only one event—the uneven bars. Uneven bars routines make few demands on ankles, so her injury had little impact on her performance. She placed second in the event to Beth Tweddle of Great Britain, and the U.S. women won silver in the team competition behind China.

Overcoming Injury and Doubt

Upon returning from Europe, Liukin underwent ankle surgery to remove bone chips in late 2006. Her recovery took several months, during which time she could not compete. Preparing for her return to all-around competition, she began training on the uneven bars and the balance beam, the two events that would put the least demand on her ankle. In spring 2007, as Liukin began her comeback, her ankle began to swell after each workout and her future as an all-around competitor began to look questionable. She returned to international competition in July 2007 at the Pan American Games in Rio de Janeiro, Brazil. Unable to compete in vault or floor exercise, she did earn silver medals in both beam and uneven bars.

> *"Liukin does one of the toughest bar routines in the world, yet she makes it look effortless," a* New York Times *reporter observed. "She flitted from bar to bar as if weightless, and her handstands were so straight it was as if an invisible cable were pulling her taut from above."*

The following month Liukin competed in all events at the 2007 U.S. national championships in San Jose, California. She fell on her final tumbling pass during her floor exercise and scored only 13.75 for the routine. A bad landing on her vault resulted in a score of only 13.5. Undaunted, she presented what Kate Hairopoulos in the *Dallas Morning News* called "two world-class routines," winning a gold medal on uneven bars and a silver medal on balance beam. The national crown went to Shawn Johnson of Iowa; the second-place finisher was Shayla Worley of Florida; Liukin was third. After the meet, Liukin said, "It was definitely not the best meet I've ever had, possibly one of the worst.... It's OK. The low points do make you stronger."

Liukin scored 9.8 during this routine on the balance beam at the 2005 U.S. national championships, where she won the senior women's all-around title.

Liukin headed to Stuttgart, Germany, with the U.S. national team in September to compete in the 2007 world championships. She won gold on the balance beam, silver on the uneven bars, and gold in the team competition. Returning home to Texas she said, "It has been a long, tough year. I'm pretty sure the whole world has seen me through my ups and downs. This year was definitely a down until worlds—finishing on such a high note. It sets you in a good spot for the next year." As of 2007 Liukin had won nine world championship medals, tying Shannon Miller's record for the most world medals awarded to an American gymnast.

As the Olympic year 2008 began, observers in gymnastics wondered if Liukin would be able to overcome her previous injuries and the pressure of performing at the top of the sport. She and the smaller, more muscular Johnson battled for the top all-around position on the U.S. women's team in June 2008, with Johnson taking the national championship by one point (127.50 to 126.50) over two days of competition in Boston, Massachusetts. A few weeks later, Johnson placed first again at the Olympic team trials in Philadelphia, Pennsylvania. The rivalry seemed to inspire both gymnasts to peak performances. As Johnson told the *Washington Post*, "It really keeps both of us working so hard.... We kind of just push each other to the next level."

———— " ————

"It has been a long, tough year," Liukin said about her injury-prone period that began in 2006. "I'm pretty sure the whole world has seen me through my ups and downs. This year was definitely a down until worlds—finishing on such a high note. It sets you in a good spot for the next year."

Olympic All-Around Champion

In August 2008 Liukin and Johnson traveled to the Olympic Games in Beijing, China, along with teammates Chellsie Memmel, Samantha Peszek, Alicia Sacramone, and Bridget Sloan. Liukin had an outstanding Olympics, earning five medals: one gold, in the all-around; three silvers, in the team competition, the uneven bars, and the balance beam; and one bronze, in the floor exercise. Earning those medals tied her with Mary Lou Retton and Shannon Miller for winning the most Olympic medals in a single competition by an American gymnast. Liukin's silver medal on uneven bars was the subject of some controversy, however, because her score was exactly the same as He Kexin, the Chinese gymnast who was awarded the gold. Olympic rules do not allow for co-champions, so when two athletes have the same score, a complicated tie-breaking system goes into effect. Though He and Liukin each scored 16.725 for their bar routines, Liukin

Liukin earned a silver medal on the balance beam at the 2008 Olympics. Her stellar performance on the apparatus earned her the gold in the all-around, making her the women's gymnastics Olympic all-around champion.

wound up second. She did not dwell on the disappointment. "That's the rules," she said, "and you have to play by them."

Liukin won the most coveted prize in women's gymnastics when she outscored Johnson (63.325 to 62.725) and competitors from around the world to become the women's gymnastics Olympic all-around champion. The 18-year-old was only the third American woman to accomplish this feat. Mary Lou Retton won all-around gold at the Olympic Games in Los Angeles in 1984, and Liukin's friend Carly Patterson won all-around gold in the 2004 Olympic Games in Athens, Greece.

It was an especially gratifying victory for Liukin because her father and coach had come in second in the all-around competition at the Seoul Olympics in 1988, losing the gold medal by five-thousandths of a point (0.005). Nastia Liukin's determination and intensity helped her remain focused during each of the four events that comprise the all-around competition. "I knew I needed to hit my connections and get my start values as high as I could. I wasn't thinking whether I would make it or not, I was thinking how I was going to make it." Her father had difficulty putting into words the satisfaction he felt at his daugh-

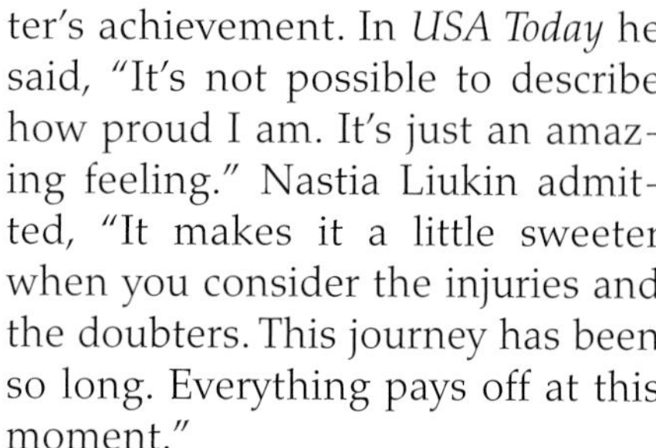

ter's achievement. In *USA Today* he said, "It's not possible to describe how proud I am. It's just an amazing feeling." Nastia Liukin admitted, "It makes it a little sweeter when you consider the injuries and the doubters. This journey has been so long. Everything pays off at this moment."

NBC analyst Tim Daggett said that Liukin's performance was "as close to flawless as you can possibly be" in her routines. According to his NBC colleague Elfie Schlegel, a former gymnast herself, "When I think about this team, I immediately think about Nastia and Shawn. What Nastia Liukin did, she epitomized the sport as it should be." The combination of balletic artistry and technical skill that characterizes Liukin's routines reminds many in the sport of the classic style of gymnastics practiced by many Russian and Eastern European athletes in a bygone era. "Nastia is in a class of her own," Schlegel said. "That beauty, that combination of what she has is so special. I think there are going to be a greater number of people … [who] will remember Nastia Liukin as a great Olympic champion."

> "
>
> *"Nastia is in a class of her own," said former gymnast Elfie Schlegel. "That beauty, that combination of what she has is so special. I think there are going to be a greater number of people … that will remember Nastia Liukin as a great Olympic champion."*
>
> "

Following the Olympics, Liukin toured the United States performing gymnastics exhibitions with other standouts from the Beijing Olympics during the fall of 2008. After her great showing at the Olympics, she had no plans to retire from the sport. As her father told the *Dallas Morning News*, "That's what she wants. She doesn't do it for the medals. That's what she is, a gymnast. She loves it."

HOME AND FAMILY

An only child, Liukin lives in Parker, Texas, with her parents.

MAJOR INFLUENCES

In addition to her parents, Liukin has cited the influence and inspiration of several other athletes: her former training partner, Carly Patterson, the 2004 women's Olympic all-around champion; the great Russian gymnasts

Lilia Podkapayeva and Svetlana Khorkina; swimmer Amanda Beard; and tennis star Maria Sharapova.

HOBBIES AND OTHER INTERESTS

Liukin's hobbies include beach volleyball and acting. In 2005 she had a small role in the movie *Stick It.* She loves the color pink and was wearing a pink leotard when she won the women's all-around competition at the Beijing Olympics.

HONORS AND AWARDS

U.S. Gymnastics Junior Championships: 2003, five gold medals (all-around, balance beam, floor exercise, uneven bars, vault); 2004, four gold medals (all-around, balance beam, floor exercise, uneven bars)

U.S. Gymnastics Senior Championships: 2005, three gold medals (all-around, balance beam, uneven bars); 2006, three gold medals (all-around, balance beam, uneven bars); 2007, one gold medal (uneven bars), one silver medal (balance beam), and one bronze medal (all-around); 2008, two gold medals (balance beam, uneven bars) and one silver medal (all-around)

World Championships: 2005, two gold medals (balance beam, uneven bars) and two silver medals (all-around, floor exercise); 2006, two silver medals (team, uneven bars); 2007, two gold medals (team, balance beam) and one silver medal (uneven bars)

International Gymnastics Hall of Fame: 2005, gymnast of the year

USA Gymnastics: 2005, athlete of the year; 2006, co-athlete of the year (with Chellsie Memmel); 2008, sportswoman of the year

American Cup: 2006, champion; 2008, champion

Pan American Games: 2007, one gold medal (team) and two silver medals (balance beam, uneven bars)

Olympic Games: 2008, one gold medal (all-around), three silver medals (balance beam, team, uneven bars), and one bronze (floor exercise)

FURTHER READING

Periodicals

Atlanta Journal-Constitution, Feb. 28, 2005, p.C1

Boston Herald, June 8, 2008

Dallas Morning News, June 22, 2003; Aug. 16, 2006; Aug. 19, 2007; June 21, 2008; Aug. 16, 2008

Fort Worth Star-Telegram, Aug. 8, 2008

Houston Chronicle, Aug. 11, 2005, p.3

International Gymnast, Nov. 2002, p.40; Mar. 2003, p.32; May 2003, p.32; Aug.-Sep. 2003, p.16; Aug.-Sep. 2004, p.30; Jan.-Feb. 2006, p.42; June 2008, p.12
Los Angeles Times, Sep. 4, 2007, p.D2
New York Times, Aug. 14, 2005, p.8; June 23, 2008, p.D7; Aug. 16, 2008, p.D3; Aug. 19, 2008, p.D4
Newsweek, Dec. 25, 2006, p.75
Orange County Register, Aug. 19, 2007
Philadelphia Daily News, June 22, 2008
Seattle Times, Nov. 27, 2005, p.C10
Sports Illustrated, Aug. 22, 2005; Sep. 4, 2006; June 30, 2008, p.64
USA Today, June 4, 2004; Feb. 25, 2005, p.C8; Aug. 11, 2005, p.C3; June 1, 2007, p.C2; June 16, 2008, p.C6; June 23, 2008, p.C1; July 21, 2008, p.C12; Aug. 11, 2008, p.D5; Aug. 12, 2008, p.D3; Aug. 14, 2008, p.D4; Aug. 15, 2008, p.C10; Aug. 18, 2008, p.D9; Aug. 19, 2008, p.D5; Aug. 20, 2008, p.A1
Washington Post, Aug. 17, 2007; June 21, 2008; June 23, 2008; Aug. 19, 2008, p.A1

ADDRESS

Nastia Liukin
World Olympic Gymnastics Academy
1937 West Parker Road
Plano, TX 75023

WORLD WIDE WEB SITES

http://www.nastialiukin.com/
http://www2.usa-gymnastics.org/bios
http://www.myspace.com
http://www.nbcolympics.com/athletes
http://www.woga.net/

Demi Lovato 1992-

American Singer and Actress
Star of *Camp Rock,* "Sonny With a Chance," and *Princess Protection Program*

BIRTH

Demi Lovato was born Demetria Devonne Lovato on August 20, 1992, in Dallas, Texas. Her parents, Patrick and Dianna, are divorced. Dianna, a former professional cheerleader and country singer, is currently married to Eddie De La Garza, a car dealership manager who is Lovato's stepfather and co-manager. Lovato has two siblings—an older sister, Dallas, and a younger sister, Madison. Lovato is of Hispanic, Irish, and Italian descent.

Lovato appeared on "Barney and Friends" as Barney's friend Angela.

YOUTH AND EDUCATION

Lovato learned a great deal about show business from her mother. Before having children, Dianna was a professional cheerleader for the Dallas Cowboys and then a country-western singer. She once opened a show at Six Flags for country stars Reba McEntire and George Strait, an achievement Lovato has proudly recounted in interviews.

Lovato's parents divorced in 1994, when Demi was about two. After the divorce her father moved to New Mexico, and since then he has had little contact with her. Her mother soon remarried, and Demi's stepfather helped raise her from an early age. Eddie and Dianna helped cultivate Lovato's interest in singing and acting. An early experience in a kindergarten talent show introduced her to the spotlight. She dared to sing a difficult number, "My Heart Will Go On" by Celine Dion, and forgot the words. Still, she was so thrilled to perform that she eagerly hoped for more opportunities like that one.

Dianna began arranging auditions for the aspiring young star. When she was six years old, Lovato was selected to join a cast of young actors on

"Barney and Friends," a children's show featuring a friendly purple dinosaur. Lovato appeared as Barney's friend Angela for two seasons. That's when she became good friends with one of her co-stars, Selena Gomez, who remembered the moment like this: "It was scorching hot, July. We were in line with 1,400 kids and we happened to be standing right next to each other. She had a little bow in her hair, and she turned around and she looked at me and said, "Do you want to color?' … After that we had a couple of callbacks, and I saw her from the other side of the room and it was kind of a movie moment. We still joke about it. We were inseparable after doing two seasons together, and our moms are best friends now." (For more information on Gomez, see *Biography Today,* Sep. 2008.)

Lovato struggled to cope with being bullied by her classmates. The bullying became so intense that she asked her mother to be home schooled. "I asked to leave public school," she revealed. "I was kind of bullied. I had a hate wall in the bathroom, and everyone signed a petition that said 'We all hate Demi Lovato.'"

Dealing with Bullying

Lovato was only seven when she started playing the piano. Taking encouragement from her mother, she also started to write songs. She naturally wasn't ready for the challenges of songwriting at such a young age. However, after a few years she realized that writing songs was a great way to express her pain and other feelings. While Lovato was attending middle school in Texas, she began having problems with bullies.

Lovato struggled to cope with being bullied by her classmates. The bullying became so intense that she asked her mother to be home schooled. "I asked to leave public school," she revealed. "I was kind of bullied. I had a hate wall in the bathroom, and everyone signed a petition that said 'We all hate Demi Lovato.'" She didn't understand why her classmates were attacking her like that. "They would text me and say, 'We're going to make your life a living hell.' I remember asking them, 'What did I do?' and no one could answer…. [One day] some of the girls were threatening to beat me up. They chased me into a bathroom upstairs. I hid. I was crying, and I called my mom, and I said, 'You need to take me out of school. I hate my life here.'" Her mother picked her up, and since then she has been home schooled. Since that difficult time, songwriting has served as a great outlet for her. "I've written probably around like 200, 300 songs," she said. "It's kind of like therapy for me. It is what I do in my spare time and I can't live without it."

Being home schooled suited Lovato. It allowed her to avoid the bullies, and she now had a schedule that let her audition for several television shows. Although she secured a small role on an episode of the TV drama "Prison Break," steady parts were hard to come by, and she became frustrated. "After hundreds of auditions and nothing, you're sitting home and wondering, 'What am I doing?'" she remembered.

CAREER HIGHLIGHTS

Breaking into Disney

When a Disney Channel talent search came to Dallas, Lovato agreed to try out. This time, the network was looking for actors for "As the Bell Rings," a TV series set to air in 2007 as five-minute segments between regular programs. Lovato was very nervous during the audition. "Even though the show was only, like five minutes, it was the Disney Channel!" she recalled. "I thought it was the coolest thing." But she was able to keep enough composure to land the part. "When I got the part, I actually cried," she admitted. "I thought, 'I'm not going to be able to do this—I'm not funny! I'm never going to be able to work for the Disney Channel, because they're based on comedy."

With the exposure from "As the Bell Rings," Lovato and her family were hoping for a big break. The perfect opportunity came when Disney announced openings for parts on an upcoming TV show. The series would star the wildly popular Jonas Brothers. By that point the rock trio—composed of Joe, Kevin, and Nick—had already achieved platinum album sales. (For more information on the Jonas Brothers, see *Biography Today,* Jan. 2008.) Lovato didn't land a regular role on "Jonas Brothers: Living the Dream," but her audition made a strong enough impression to ensure more auditions.

The Disney network next asked Lovato to audition for a part in the soon-to-be-filmed *Camp Rock,* a TV musical to feature the Jonas Brothers. She arrived at the audition prepared only to showcase her acting skills, but one executive at the meeting, Disney Channel Worldwide president Gary Marsh, asked to hear her singing voice. She obliged by launching into "Ain't No Other Man" by Christina Aguilera. "Our jaws just dropped," remembered Hollywood Records senior vice president and general manager Bob Cavallo. Lovato won the part in *Camp Rock,* plus Disney also signed her to Hollywood Records, the music label famous for breaking the Jonas Brothers, Hillary Duff, and Miley Cyrus. (For more information on Cyrus, see *Biography Today,* Sep. 2007; for Duff, see *Biography Today,* Sep. 2002.)

Camp Rock

In August 2007, Lovato began filming *Camp Rock* at a location in Canada, outside Toronto, Ontario. The movie was full of singing and dancing, much like the 2006 Disney blockbuster *High School Musical.* Lovato played Mitchie Torres, who like herself is a singer-songwriter. She hopes to shine at the rock camp but feels held back by her humble background. Her male counterpart is Shane Gray (played by Joe Jonas), a rock star who is forced to work as a camp instructor to clean up his ailing public image. Mitchie attends the camp at a discounted price and on the condition that she work in the camp's kitchen, where her mother is the head cook. She soon makes the mistake of lying about her background in hopes of fitting in with the popular kids.

Lovato performs in several of the musical's numbers, one of which is a stirring duet with Joe Jonas called "This Is Me." The song is about Mitchie's realization that she needs to drop her false façade and be herself. Gary Marsh saw a strong connection between the character and Lovato. "She was going through this same evolution as a human being at the same time as the character," he said. "When she sings 'This Is Me' in the end, this is just not Mitchie, this is Demi telling the world 'This is me.' This was literally her journey coming forward."

"When I got the part, I actually cried," Lovato said about auditioning for "As the Bell Rings." "I thought, 'I'm not going to be able to do this—I'm not funny! I'm never going to be able to work for the Disney Channel, because they're based on comedy."

The filming schedule was taxing for the actors, but Lovato took it in stride. One scene, which featured the final dance number "We Rock," took three long days to shoot. For Lovato, the challenge was keeping up a presentable appearance on camera. "I got my hair blown dry six times in one day," she remembered. "You're dancing so much, and you just don't want to glisten like that on camera!"

Camp Rock was a hit when it first aired in June 2008. Shown on several networks, including Disney and ABC, the movie reached 69.5 million viewers worldwide. The soundtrack CD to the film, released the same month, was a success as well, debuting on the *Billboard* Top 200 at No. 3. The single for "This Is Me" claimed the No. 2 spot on the Hot Digital Songs chart.

Scenes from Camp Rock, *including Lovato with the Jonas Brothers at the movie premier.*

The "Burning Up" Tour

While *Camp Rock* was introducing millions of viewers and listeners to Lovato, concert promoters were planning a nationwide tour for her with the Jonas Brothers. The "Burning Up" tour, featuring Lovato as a special guest, made perfect sense because the two acts shared a similar fan base. In addition, Lovato and the brothers had also become good friends and likely would make good tour mates. Before hitting the road, Lovato and the brothers collaborated in the studio to record her debut album. In the world of teen pop music, records are typically manufactured by seasoned professionals, with the young stars doing little behind-the-scenes work. These young musicians, however, proved to be the exception, handling the songwriting and recording duties themselves. Lovato wrote or co-wrote all but two of the songs, and the brothers co-wrote or co-produced a good chunk of the album.

The final dance number in Camp Rock *took three long days to shoot. For Lovato, the challenge was keeping up a presentable appearance on camera. "I got my hair blown dry six times in one day," she remembered. "You're dancing so much, and you just don't want to glisten like that on camera!"*

If there was any doubt that Lovato had made it, thousands of screaming fans attending the sold-out "Burning Up" tour served as proof. Running from July to September, the tour hit 56 cities in the United States and Canada. Lovato's show debuted songs from her upcoming album and exhibited her talents as a multi-instrumentalist.

Lovato hardly expected to celebrate her sweet 16 in a strange city and in the middle of a rock tour, but that is where she found herself on August 20. It was difficult being away from most of her family, although she still enjoyed the company of her stepfather, who traveled with her as her co-manager. Concertgoers, of course, were eager to wish her a happy 16th birthday. "Everyone was singing happy birthday to me—and by everyone, I mean 20,000 people at my concert," Lovato recalled. It was clearly a turning point for the teen star. "That was the moment when I said, 'Wow, my life is not the same, but it's even better.'"

Lovato's first album, titled *Don't Forget,* was the commercial hit that she had hoped for. It debuted at No. 2 on the *Billboard* Top 200, selling almost 90,000 copies in the first week of the album's release. It was also the most downloaded album on iTunes. *Don't Forget* scored well with critics and fans alike. Writing in *Entertainment Weekly,* Leah Greenblatt said that Lovato's album, "while full of catchy choruses, abandons the usual tinkly teen-pop tropes for meaty guitars and percussion; the raucous lead single "Get Back" is more Benatar than Backstreet." Newspaper reviewer Christopher Tessmer wrote, "While Lovato's 11 tracks are polished and hungry for mainstream radio, you can hear the raw emotion and vocal talent in every song."

"

"People have definitely said they weren't expecting the album to be as rock as it is," Lovato said about her debut album, Don't Forget. *"They were expecting the butterfly pop stuff."*

"

Several critics noted that Lovato distinguished herself from other teen stars because she wrote much of her own material. They also noted their surprise that Lovato rocked harder than other starlets did. "People have definitely said they weren't expecting the album to be as rock as it is," she explained. "They were expecting the butterfly pop stuff."

"Sonny With a Chance"

As the album hit the stores, Lovato began preparing for the next major venture: her own Disney sitcom. In "Sonny With a Chance," she stars as Sonny Munroe, a girl from Wisconsin who wins a nationwide search to be the next star of the sketch-comedy show "So Random!" Sonny faces many challenges adapting to the Hollywood lifestyle, including repeated clashes with fellow "So Random!" star Tawni (Tiffany Thornton) and an ongoing rivalry with the cast of "MacKenzie Falls," a soap opera that shoots on the next stage.

Those familiar with Lovato's career so far could identify the similarities between her and Sonny. Lovato's success also required her to move to Hollywood with her family. Such a transition made the sitcom character a natural fit for her. "She's faced with all these obstacles she has to go through to adapt to the Hollywood lifestyle," Lovato said. "My life kind of mirrors it."

Even after her successful turn in *Camp Rock,* Lovato found starring in a TV show—particularly a comedy—a daunting task. Since early childhood, she has considered acting a greater challenge than singing or playing music. But on the set of "Sonny With a Chance" she found the confidence she

Lovato (Sonny, right) with co-star Tiffany Thornton (Tawni) in a scene from the first episode of "Sonny With a Chance."

needed. "I've really let loose and totally had fun with it," she said. Her comfort on camera certainly contributed to the show's success. The first airing of "Sonny With a Chance" drew 4.1 million viewers and proved to be a huge hit with young teens.

Princess Protection Program

In 2009, Lovato appeared in the Disney TV movie *Princess Protection Program.* She was lucky to be able to co-star with her longtime real-life best friend, Selena Gomez, now appearing as the star of the hit comedy TV series "Wizards of Waverly Place." The two had a lot of fun making the movie. They filmed in Costa Rica, where they had sleepovers most nights at their hotel. "We don't really think of it as work," Lovato said.

In the movie, an evil dictator overtakes the tiny country of Costa Luna. The princess Rosalinda Marie Montoya Fiore (played by Lovato) was soon to become the country's ruler. She is rescued by an agent of the secret international agency Princess Protection Program. The agent takes the princess to a PPP base where she is given a new identity, Rosie Gonzalez, then takes her home to live with his family in rural Louisiana. His daughter Carter (played by Gomez) is shocked to learn that she will have to share her bed-

Lovato (Rosie) with her best friend, Selena Gomez (Carter), in a scene from Princess Protection Program.

room with Rosie, who is posing as Carter's cousin. Even worse, Rosie will be enrolling at Carter's school. Despite some conflict at the beginning, the two learn to help each other.

Lovato was able to continue to build her singing career with this movie also. Two of her songs were included in the movie: "One and the Same," a duet with Gomez, and "Two Worlds Collide," a cut from her debut album.

Lovato hopes that her successes so far mark the beginning of a long career that combines both singing and acting. "I plan on doing this for the rest of my life," she said. For upcoming musical projects, she plans a follow-up album, which she predicted would be more soulful and bluesy than her debut, and a subsequent tour. For upcoming acting projects, fans of *Camp Rock* were happy to hear news that Disney is preparing a sequel, for which Lovato, the Jonas Brothers, and the rest of the cast plan to reprise their roles. Production for the sequel will begin in 2009.

HOME AND FAMILY

Lovato enjoys a close bond with her family. While her parents are very protective of their daughter—a necessity for virtually any young superstar—Lovato does not consider them overbearing. She sees her mother as a best friend, and the time on the road spent with her stepfather has drawn them a lot closer. "We have a lot of trust in each other," she said of both her parents.

HOBBIES AND OTHER INTERESTS

Lovato's experiences with bullying have inspired her to advocate for other vulnerable children and teens. In October 2008 Love Our Children USA announced that she, the singer JoJo, and several other stars would participate in the STOMP Out Bullying awareness campaign. Lovato signed up to appear in commercials and on posters. She hoped her contribution would help those girls her age and younger who were not as fortunate as she was to find a solution. "I want to help with bullying because there are girls who can't just up and home-school and focus on their career," she said.

SELECTED CREDITS

Television

"Barney and Friends," 2004
"As the Bell Rings," 2007
Camp Rock, 2008
"Jonas Brothers: Living the Dream," 2008
Princess Protection Program, 2009
"Sonny With a Chance," 2009

Recordings

Don't Forget, 2008

Films

Jonas Brothers: The 3D Concert Experience, 2009

FURTHER READING

Periodicals

Boston Globe, Sep. 23, 2008
Entertainment Weekly, June 6, 2008, p.41; Oct. 3, 2008, p.44; Nov. 21, 2008, p.84; Jan. 23, 2009, p.38
Girls' Life, June/July 2008, p.86; Feb./Mar. 2009, p.44
Houston Chronicle, June 20, 2008, p.2
Orlando Sentinel, Feb. 7, 2009
People, Apr. 13, 2009, p.121; July 2009 (Special Edition, multiple articles)
Scholastic Choices, Apr.-May 2009, p.3
Scholastic Scope, Jan. 19, 2009, p.13

USA Today, Jan. 1, 2009; Feb. 3, 2009, p.D8
Washington Post, June 21, 2008

Online Articles

http://www.mtv.com
(MTV, "Demi Lovato Calls on Jonas Brothers for Help with Debut LP, Onstage Tumble," Aug. 28, 2008; "Demi Lovato Says She Relates to Her 'Sonny With a Chance' Character," Jan. 23, 2009; "Demi Lovato Looking to Have 'John Mayerish' Songs on New Album," Jan. 27, 2009; "Demi Lovato: 'I Feel Bad for Miley!'" Feb. 2, 2009; "Demi Lovato Wants to Be 'Funnier' in 'Camp Rock' Sequel," Feb. 27, 2009)
http://www.reuters.com
(Reuters, "'Camp Rock' Sets the Stage for Newcomer Demi Lovato," June 15, 2008)
http://www.tvweek.com
(TV Week, "'Sonny' Lights Up Sunday for Disney Channel," Feb. 10, 2009)
http://www.usmagazine.com
(Us Magazine, "Demi Lovato: I Was Bullied!" Oct. 1, 2008)
http://variety.com/youthimpactreport
(Variety, "Youth Impact Report," Oct. 3, 2008)

ADDRESS

Demi Lovato
Hollywood Records, Inc.
500 South Buena Vista Street
Burbank, CA 91521

WORLD WIDE WEB SITES

http://www.demilovato.com
http://tv.disney.go.com/disneychannel/originalmovies/camprock
http://tv.disney.go.com/disneychannel/sonnywithachance
http://tv.disney.go.com/disneychannel/originalmovies/princessprotection program

Jef Mallett 1962-

American Cartoonist
Creator of the Comic Strip "Frazz"

BIRTH

Jeffrey Alan Mallett was born on February 28, 1962, in Howell, Michigan. His parents are Gordon Mallett, a retired music teacher, and Janet Mallett, a violinist and church organist who performs for various orchestras. A middle child, Jef has an older sister, Martha, and two younger siblings, Sarah and Edward.

Mallett created "Birchbark," his first comic strip, during high school.

YOUTH

Mallett was three years old when his family moved across Michigan to Big Rapids, a small city in the west-central region of the state. Not long after settling into his new home, Mallett showed an early interest in cartoons. By reading comics he learned how to read, as well as how to draw.

By the time Mallett turned 10 he had become determined to create comic art. He wrote to the National Cartoonists Society and requested a brochure that described how to be a cartoonist. As he continued to follow the comics and teach himself techniques, he soon learned that being a cartoonist demanded the skills of a good storyteller as well as a good artist. "I thought,'Well, I'd better learn to write,'" he remembered, "and by god that was fun too, I really loved writing."

Mallett soon took advantage of opportunities to present his cartoons to others, distributing his comic strips around school and publishing them in his church's bulletin. He increasingly became more comfortable with promoting himself and his cartoons. (Already drawn to the limelight, he had earlier dropped the second "f" from his first name so that it stood out a bit more.)

A break came in high school, when he was paid $5 a week to write a daily comic strip for *The Pioneer*, the newspaper in Big Rapids. The strip, a series called "Birchbark," followed a French-Canadian adventurer and his Native American guide and ran for two to three years. Looking back, Mallett considered doing "Birchbark" a good introduction to the world of comics.

EDUCATION

Mallett graduated from Big Rapids High School in 1980. He decided to remain near home and enroll in Ferris State College (now known as Ferris State University) to receive training as a paramedic. After a year, he decided to shift his focus and transferred to Butterworth Hospital School of Nursing in Grand Rapids. Around that time, he also joined the staff of the local newspaper, the *Grand Rapids Press,* as a writer and illustrator. Confident that he could support himself working for a paper, he decided he did not need a fallback career and dropped out of nursing school.

Becoming a Cartoonist

A span of 20 years bridged the publication of "Birchbark" and the debut of "Frazz," the comic strip that put Jef Mallett on the map. In a biographical comment on the National Cartoonist Society web site, he states that he "got distracted" during those two decades. That may be the case, but his newspaper years were still productive ones. He worked at the *Grand Rapids Press* from 1981 to 1987 as a writer and illustrator. In 1987 he moved to the *Flint Journal* and added "columnist" to his list of responsibilities. Two years later, he moved to Lansing, Michigan, the state capital, to work for the Booth Newspapers' central branch. There he served as art director and editorial cartoonist.

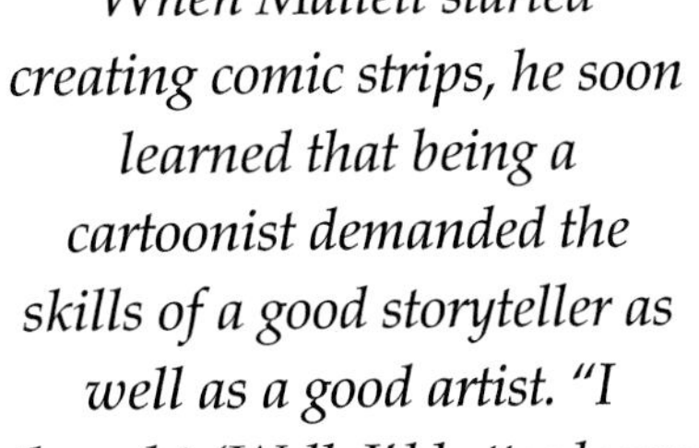

When Mallett started creating comic strips, he soon learned that being a cartoonist demanded the skills of a good storyteller as well as a good artist. "I thought, 'Well, I'd better learn to write,'" he remembered, "and by god that was fun too, I really loved writing."

In his new job, Mallett was assigned a number of positions: art director, graphic artist, photo editor, editorial cartoonist, and copy editor. Composing editorial cartoons—illustrations with a political and social message—was rewarding for Mallett, who had always enjoyed discussing philosophy and ideas. Also, as a copy editor—someone who ensures that newspaper articles read well and are free of grammatical errors—he could further sharpen his writing skills. He remembers his experiences in Lansing fondly. "It was actually really great because it was a small office, so you learned to do a little bit of everything," he said.

CAREER HIGHLIGHTS

Launching Out on His Own

By 1996, Mallett was publishing a couple of editorial cartoons a week for Booth Newspapers. That year he also introduced himself to a new audi-

Frazz enjoying a moment with students.
FRAZZ: © Jef Mallett/Dist. by United Feature Syndicate, Inc.

ence by publishing an illustrated children's book titled *Dangerous Dan*. The story followed a mischievous young daydreamer whose creativity cannot be contained. With his imagination, little Dan transforms his notebook into a flying carpet and his backyard into a jungle.

Mallett promoted *Dangerous Dan* by touring elementary schools, reading his book at student assemblies. The readings proved to be a great opportunity. Not only did Mallett get to interact with children, but he also stumbled upon an idea for a new character. During the assemblies, Mallett couldn't help noticing that the huge task of calming down students for his presentation often fell to the school janitor, who succeeded because he had a special connection with the students. "That's when I noticed that the janitor was 'the man,'" Mallett said. "He's the guy that all the kids looked up to." The idea for a popular elementary school custodian named Edwin Frazier ("Frazz") was born.

Mallett began working out the essential details of Frazz and his world. From the onset, he decided that Frazz was the kind of guy who liked his job, even though janitorial work is unglamorous and even though he has other career options. Frazz is also a songwriter who penned a few hit songs that continue to pay him royalties. "He likes it," Mallett explained of Frazz's situation. "He's not there because he has to be."

According to Mallett, "Basically, I just try and make [Frazz] me, only me if I was a lot cooler than I am."

Along with deciding that Frazz is content as an elementary school janitor, Mallett gave his character other passions to round out his personality. It is no coincidence Frazz's interests—literature, philosophy, cycling, running—are also Mallett's. It was a matter of the artist following the conventional wisdom of "write what you know." According to Mallett, "Basically, I just try and make him me, only me if I was a lot cooler than I am."

Frazz Discovers Friends—and Readers

Mallett's imagination continued to fill out the details of Frazz's world at Bryson Elementary. More characters took form and began interacting with the janitor, and a few became regulars. There is Mr. Burke, Frazz's best friend, an engaging teacher who often riffs with the janitor about big concepts while they play one-on-one basketball or cruise the bike trails. There is also Caulfield, a bright and clever third-grader named after Holden Caulfield of *The Catcher in the Rye*, who talks with Frazz to relieve his boredom. Caulfield's antics often land him in detention with his teacher, the stern Mrs. Olsen. (The punishment is bearable because it at least gives the third grader the opportunity to discuss books with Frazz.) Another major character is Miss Plainwell, the attractive first-grade teacher who has caught Frazz's eye.

In April 2001, Mallett landed a deal with United Feature Syndicate, a large company that sells comics to newspapers throughout the country and the world. He began producing daily strips while keeping his job with Booth

FRAZZ: © Jef Mallett/Dist. by United Feature Syndicate, Inc.

Newspapers. "I played it safe (in terms of security, if not health and sanity)," Mallett joked.

After a year juggling the daily strip and his newspaper job, Mallett resigned from his full-time position. By that time, "Frazz" had been introduced to 50 newspapers, which is not a huge number compared to established strips, which through syndicates can reach as many as 2,000 newspapers. Nonetheless, "Frazz" had backing from many believers, including Meegan Holland, Lansing bureau chief for Booth Newspapers. "Jef is one of those few people who can translate a concept into a few clever words and fun pictures," she told the *Lansing State Journal*. Like Holland, fans appreciated the subtle humorous style that became the strip's defining trait.

Readers immediately took note that in the world of "Frazz," kids like Caulfield and his peers expressed plenty of insight. Mallett has said that their maturity was a central part of his original vision. "There's an assumption that kids are somehow inferior to adults, and that's just plain wrong," he remarked. "They leave adults in the dust when it comes to figuring things out."

Young readers were not the only ones affected by the comic strip's fresh perspective on kids. Gene Weingarten, a *Washington Post* columnist and a friend of Mallett's, had a similar reaction. "It's the best cartoon I've ever seen at living in two worlds at the same time," he said to the *Lansing State Journal.* "It absolutely appeals to kids and it absolutely appeals to adults. His characters are existing in a kids' milieu, but it does not patronize kids who are reading it."

Expanding into a Major Market

As Mallett worked to introduce "Frazz" to more newspapers, it helped that the strip had fans in the newspaper business. Friends like Weingarten did

FRAZZ: © Jef Mallett/Dist. by United Feature Syndicate, Inc.

their part to help promote the comic strip and expand its audience. By 2005, the *Washington Post* had added "Frazz" to its comics page, as had other major papers like the *Chicago Tribune* and the *Los Angeles Times*. In total, 150 newspapers were carrying Mallett's strip.

Of course, Mallett was happy for more readers to find his work. It was more gratifying to learn that people were not only reading "Frazz" but also talking about its heady ideas. Another *Washington Post* columnist, Michael Cavna, began writing about the strips. He devoted some of the entries on his blog, "Comic Riffs," to exploring various concepts and cultural references in Mallett's strips. That type of response was not a surprise for Mallett, since he believed attentive readers like Cavna were out there. "You don't get dumb people reading the newspapers. You get the smarter people, the college graduates, the movers and shakers," he said.

Some readers also appreciated the values that Mallett promoted through his characters, as well as the racial and cultural diversity of Bryson Elementary. In 2003, the Religion Communicators Council bestowed him the Wilbur Award for "excellence in the communication of religious values." More recognition came in 2004 from the National Cartoonists Society, which listed "Frazz" as a finalist in the Best Comic Strip of the Year category. The following year, Mallett received the Wilbur Award again.

"Frazz" had earned a place among other nationally read comics, and so in 2005 Mallett published the first collection of cartoons, *Live from Bryson Elementary*. Over the next three years, two more collections were published: *99% Perspiration* (2006) and *Frazz 3.1416* (2008). The books' titles were examples once again of the clever allusions Mallett's readers had come to expect: "99% Perspiration" refers to a quote by Thomas Edison ("Genius is 1% inspiration and 99% perspiration") and the numbers "3.1416" are the first five digits of pi (the famous numerical ratio used in math).

Comic strip collections offer Mallett's fans more opportunities to enjoy the strip.

Other Works

Regularly cranking out editorial cartoons and comic strips can be demanding, but Mallett still has been able to take on other projects as an illustrator. During his early newspaper days, he developed a working relationship with *Detroit Free Press* columnist Mitch Albom, best known for his best-selling memoir *Tuesdays with Morrie*. Mallett illustrated two of the columnist's collected writings—*Live Albom II* (1990) and *Live Albom IV* (1995). Over the years, Mallett has also been a regular guest on the nationally syndicated morning radio program "The Bob and Tom Show" and has been recruited twice to do cover art for that duo's sketch comedy albums.

Mallett has also found work that directly related to his two favorite hobbies, cycling and competing in triathlons (endurance races that combine swimming, cycling, and running). He illustrated *Roadie: The Misunderstood World of a Bike Racer* (2008) by Jamie Smith, an insider's guide on the life of the cyclist fanatic. Other steady gigs that Mallett has landed for sports periodicals include writing a column for *Inside Triathlon* magazine and publishing one-panel cartoons for the bicycle racing periodical *VeloNews*.

After illustrating a book on cycling, it seemed fitting that Mallett would embark on a guide about triathlons as well. Drawing from his training as a journalist, Mallett decided to take on the dual role of writer/illustrator. With a working title of *Trizophrenia: Inside the Minds of a Triathlete*, the book is scheduled to be released in fall 2009 by Velo Press, which also published *Roadie*. *Trizophrenia* is "about the way triathletes train, think, and live," said Mallett. "It's sort of like *Roadie* and yet very different."

MARRIAGE AND FAMILY

Mallett lives with his wife, Patty, in a modest ranch home in Lansing. They have been married since 1988. She plays a pivotal role in the production of "Frazz" as the official "letterer," the person who draws the comic strip's text. As a professional communications manager, Patty has the right skills for crafting the strip's dialogue. Jef has been vocal about his gratitude for his wife's contribution to "Frazz." "[Her] normal handwriting is better than just about anybody's careful lettering.... [She is] one of the best copy editor/proofreaders I know," he said.

Luckily for Jef, Patty enjoys cycling as well. He calls riding tandem with her his "top cycling priority." Both also work together to help stray pets at the Capital Area Humane Society.

MAJOR INFLUENCES

Frazz the janitor exhibits much in common with the Calvin of the legendary strip "Calvin and Hobbes," even though Frazz is a few decades older. Both characters regularly discuss philosophy and use difficult words that often send readers reaching for their dictionaries. In fact, the similarities between the two were so striking for some comic strip followers that they helped fan rumors that the true creator of "Frazz" was not Jef Mallett, but "Calvin and Hobbes" creator Bill Watterson. Internet chatter helped spread the rumors about the strip's false authorship. Mallett, who considers Watterson a huge influence, has made an effort to put the rumor to rest, declaring he is not Watterson, nor is he trying to replace "Calvin and

Cycling and triathlons are Mallett's two favorite sports—and Frazz's, as well.
FRAZZ: © Jef Mallett/Dist. by United Feature Syndicate, Inc.

Hobbes" with his cartoon. "You might as well try to replace or copy the Mona Lisa," Mallett said in praise of the older strip.

Along with modeling his work on elements of established strips like "Calvin and Hobbes," Mallett looks for inspiration from great storytellers, like 20th-century novelist John Steinbeck and contemporary novelist Richard Russo. He also has said that he learns a lot reading humor writer Bill Bryson and considers him among his favorites. As a mark of his respect, Mallett even named the elementary school in "Frazz" after Bryson.

HOBBIES AND OTHER INTERESTS

Mallett's pursuits outside of work are by no means ordinary. Among his former pastimes, he has flown hang gliders and airplanes. In recent years, however, he has focused more on competing in cycling races and triathlons. He has been running competitively since he was a teenager, and he has also been a cycling aficionado for nearly just as long. By adding swimming to that repertoire, he entered the world of Olympic-distance triathlons (competitions that involve swimming 0.9 miles, cycling 25 miles, and running 6.2 miles).

Of his two favorite sports—cycling and triathlon—Mallett devotes more attention to triathlons since the balanced nature of the sport does not demand cycling very long distances, which he says can be dangerous. Being in top physical condition, which is essential for competing in triathlons, has a practical value for Mallett: "I'm not as efficient with the job or the family if I'm not in shape." Along with the physical benefits, Mallett enjoys the bragging rights of frequently taking first place in his age group.

Impressed by Mallett's fitness record, in 2006 television producers of the reality adventure show "Nevada Passage" invited him to compete on a two-person team against 18 other athletes. The one-hour feature show, which is syndicated on national networks, stages outdoor competitions like cycling and auto racing in various locales throughout the country. Mallett and his teammate, a freelance writer from New York, did not win the competition, but they had the distinction of appearing on a show that draws 2 million annual viewers.

As if completing a regular triathlon wasn't a great enough feat, in November 2008 Mallett reached his long-held dream of finishing the ultimate endurance test, the Ironman triathlon (a longer race that involves a 2.4-mile swim, a 112-mile bike, and a 26.2-mile run). He loved the experience and looks forward to participating in more Ironmans in the years ahead.

SELECTED WRITINGS

"Frazz"

Frazz: Live from Bryson Elementary, 2005
99 Percent Perspiration, 2006
Frazz 3.1416, 2008

Other Works

Live Albom II, 1990 (by Mitch Albom, illustrated by Mallett)
Live Albom IV, 1995 (by Mitch Albom, illustrated by Mallett)
Dangerous Dan, 1996
Roadie: The Misunderstood World of a Bike Racer, 2008 (by Jamie Smith, illustrated by Jef Mallett)

HONORS AND AWARDS

Wilbur Award (Religion Communicators Council): 2003, 2005, Editorial Cartoons/Comics category
Best Comic Strip of the Year Finalist (National Cartoonists Society): 2004, for "Frazz"

FURTHER READING

Periodicals

Albany Times Union, Mar. 3, 2004
Grand Rapids Press, May 9, 2006
Lansing State Journal, May 12, 2004; Jan. 27, 2005; Dec. 18, 2007
News & Observer, Nov. 24, 2006
San Antonio Express-News, Oct. 11, 2008

Online Articles

http://www.capitalgainsmedia.com
(Capital Gains, "The Frazz with Jef Mallett, Cartooning Genius," Jan. 16, 2008)
http://www.ncs-glc.com/GLC/jef_mallett/jefmallett.html
The GLyph, "'... The janitor was always the coolest guy ...': A Chat with Jef Mallett," Apr. 7, 2005)
http://www.suite101.com
(Suite101, "2003 NEA Holiday Comics Special, by Jef Mallett, Creator of Frazz," Dec. 23, 2003)
http://www.velonews.com
(Velo News, "Author Jamie Smith and Illustrator Jef Mallett Launch Book at Kinetic Systems," Apr. 1, 2008; "Q&A: Cartoonist Jef Mallett on 'Frazz,'" May 23, 2004)
http://voices.washingtonpost.com
(Washington Post, "The Morning Line:'Frazz' & the Evolution of a Comic Mystery," Aug. 8, 2008)

ADDRESS

Jef Mallett
United Feature Syndicate
200 Madison Avenue
New York, NY 10016

WORLD WIDE WEB SITES

http://www.comics.com/comics/frazz
http://www.unitedfeatures.com

Warith Deen Mohammed 1933-2008

American Religious Leader
Former Head of the Nation of Islam and the American Society of Muslims

BIRTH

Warith Deen Mohammed was born on October 30, 1933, in Hamtramck, Michigan, the son of religious leader Elijah Poole Muhammad and Clara Evans Muhammad. His birth name was Wallace Delaney Muhammad, but in 1978 he adopted different first and middle names and an altered spelling of his last name. In addition, he is sometimes referred to as W. Deen Mohammed and W. D. Mohammed. He

Mohammed was greatly influenced by his father, Elijah Muhammad.

was the seventh of eight children, with older siblings named Emmanuel, Ethel, Lottie, Nathaniel, Herbert, and Elijah Jr., and a younger brother named Akbar.

YOUTH

Mohammed's childhood—and, indeed, his entire life—was strongly influenced by his father's work in building the Nation of Islam, an African-American religious group. An understanding of Elijah Muhammad and of the movement that he led is essential to understanding the events and ideas that would shape his son.

Originally known as Elijah Poole, the elder Muhammad had grown up in Georgia and later settled in Detroit with his wife, Clara, and their growing family. In 1930, he became a devotee of charismatic leader Wallace Dodd Fard and Fard's newly formed Nation of Islam religious sect. By the time Warith Deen Mohammed was born in 1933, his father had adopted the name Elijah Muhammad and had become the group's chief minister. Fard, who was also known as W. D. Farad Muhammad, mysteriously disappeared in 1934, and Elijah Muhammad claimed leadership of the movement. Soon after, he moved his family to Chicago, where a second Nation of Islam group had been established.

Expanding on the ideas of Fard, Elijah Muhammad refined the religious principles that became the basis of the Nation of Islam, some of which are very controversial. Appealing exclusively to blacks, the group maintains that African Americans are the original and chosen people of Allah (God) while whites are an inferior race of "devils" that was created by a black scientist 6,000 years ago. Rather than seeking peaceful coexistence between the races, the Nation of Islam has been a proponent of black separatism—the idea that African Americans should form their own separate nation. In addition, the group has proclaimed that whites will one day be vanquished by Allah, and blacks will be liberated from oppression. In terms of theology, the religion proclaims that Fard was Allah in human form and that Elijah Muhammad was his divine messenger.

The Nation of Islam's name and some of its practices are derived from the traditional Islamic faith, but there are also important differences between the two groups. Most importantly, followers of traditional Islam do not proclaim superiority for any race. They believe that the prophet Muhammad founded Islam in the seventh century and was the final prophet of Allah. Therefore, the Nation of Islam tenet that Elijah Muhammad is a divine messenger is unacceptable to traditional Muslims. Though the members of the Nation of Islam sometimes refer to themselves as "Black Muslims," followers of mainstream Islam generally do not recognize them as being part of the Muslim faith.

A Turbulent Childhood

Warith Mohammed, who was then going by the name of Wallace, grew up amid the turmoil and the threats that surrounded his father. After Elijah Muhammad took over the Nation of Islam in 1934, he faced harassment from law enforcement agencies, but his most serious opposition came from other followers of Fard, who disputed his leadership. Internal struggles marked by violence continued to be part of the Nation of Islam for decades, and Elijah Muhammad came to rely on a militaristic security force known as the Fruit of Islam to help maintain his hold on power.

> *Mohammed began to have doubts about his father's religious message when he was still a child. "I had common sense," he later explained, "and my common sense told me this was ridiculous, the idea that God is a God that wants one people to dominate others."*

In the mid-1930s, Elijah Muhammad feared that his life was in danger and chose to depart Chicago, leaving his wife and children behind. He spent the next seven years living in other U.S. cities, and during World War II, he served three years in prison for evading the draft—mandatory service in the U.S. military. During this period, Warith Mohammed saw his father only on rare occasions, and he came to view the religious leader as an all-powerful figure whom he both respected and feared.

Warith and his siblings were primarily raised by their mother, Clara, and grew up as part of the Nation of Islam community in Chicago. But even as a young child, Warith Mohammed was no ordinary member of the Nation: he was considered the "chosen son." It was said that Wallace Dodd Fard had predicted that Elijah Muhammad's seventh child would become a great leader. From the time of his birth, Warith, the seventh born, was looked to as the eventual successor to his father, and his special status was indicated by his birth name, Wallace—after Wallace Fard.

EDUCATION

Mohammed attended a school operated by the Nation of Islam in Chicago. In addition, his father wanted him to learn about the traditional Muslim faith, so he attended religious schools taught by Islamic immigrants, and he learned Arabic with a tutor. The language studies allowed him to read the Koran (also spelled Qur'an), the religious scripture of Islam, in the language in which it was originally composed, and this proved to be an important turning point in his life. He found nothing in the Koran to support the racially based beliefs being promoted by the Nation of Islam. By age 12, he was beginning to have doubts about his father's religious message. "I had common sense," he later explained, "and my common sense told me this was ridiculous, the idea that God is a God that wants one people to dominate others."

Despite his growing skepticism, Mohammed remained deeply involved in the movement, and he joined with other young people in the Junior Fruit of Islam youth group, an experience that he later recalled as one of the happiest of his childhood. Mohammed also undertook studies in some non-religious institutions as an adult. He enrolled in college classes at Woodrow Wilson Junior College and Loop College in Chicago but did not attain a degree. According to some sources, he also studied at the University of El-Azhar in Cairo, Egypt.

CAREER HIGHLIGHTS

By the time Warith Mohammed reached his late teenage years, the Nation of Islam was emerging from its early struggles. Elijah Muhammad had consolidated his power, and the group's membership was growing steadily. The Nation enjoyed its strongest support in poor urban neighborhoods, and its appeal was related to the difficult conditions that existed there. Leaders of the movement made a point of reaching out to those who had struggled with poverty, criminal activity, substance abuse, and other problems. The religion's message of black empowerment and self-affirmation was a welcome sign of hope for many of these individuals, and the Nation's strict code of behavior offered a means of ordering their lives. Members agreed to abstain from tobacco, alcohol, and drugs, to follow specific moral guidelines, and to adopt a modest, neatly groomed appearance. Economic issues also played a part in the group's appeal. The Nation promoted the creation of black-owned businesses and launched several enterprises of its own, including the *Muhammad Speaks* newspa-

A meeting of the Nation of Islam in the early 1960s in Olympia Stadium, Detroit.

per that became prominent in black communities across the country. These ventures ultimately brought great wealth to Elijah Muhammad and members of his family and inner circle.

When he was around the age of 17, Warith Mohammed began preaching in Nation's places of worship, which are known as temples or mosques. At this point, he still supported the movement his father had built, though the influence of the traditional Islamic concepts he had learned in his studies was already evident. In his first sermon, he complained that "we give more attention to the Devil than to Allah," suggesting that the congregation should put more emphasis on their own faith rather than the racial injustices they may have experienced. In some ways, Mohammed seemed ill suited to his role as a religious leader. A shy person who spoke with a lisp, he had little of the fiery charisma and eloquent speech possessed by many preachers, but he balanced these shortcomings with his deep spiritual knowledge and quiet intensity.

After serving as a minister in the Chicago temple, Mohammed was appointed as the head of the Nation of Islam community in Philadelphia in 1958, when he was 25 years old. There, he introduced the membership to readings from the Koran and other elements of traditional Muslim worship. Two years later, his ministerial career came to a temporary halt after he was convicted of draft evasion. Like his father and many other Black Muslims, Mohammed had refused to serve in the United States military, believing it to be against his religious convictions. For 14 months, between late 1961 and February 1963, Mohammed was an inmate at the Sandstone Federal Correctional Institution in Minnesota.

Doubts, Dissent, and Malcolm X

During his time in prison, Mohammed spent a great deal of time reflecting on his beliefs and on the doubts he had long held about his father's religious message. It was during this period that he came to a life-changing conclusion that he later summed up in these simple words: "Elijah Muhammad was not a prophet." In other words, he accepted the Muslim belief that the final prophet of Allah was Muhammad in the seventh century. In so doing, he converted to the traditional Islamic faith. As a result, he resolved that he would no longer preach about the divinity of Elijah Muhammad and Wallace Dodd Fard, but he did not yet publicly disavow these basic beliefs that were the foundation of the Nation of Islam. Upon his release from prison, he resumed his duties at the temple in Philadelphia.

Warith Mohammed was not the only Black Muslim to have doubts about Elijah Muhammad. Another was Malcolm X, who had joined the movement in the early 1950s and soon became one of the Nation's senior leaders. His electrifying speeches drew many converts to the religion and made him one of the most vocal proponents for African-American rights in the nation. Malcolm X's beliefs underwent a change in the early 1960s and, like Warith Mohammed, he moved toward conventional Islam. His new outlook was partly caused by his loss of faith in Elijah Muhammad after he learned that the leader had fathered numerous children outside his marriage and that he and members of his family had misused the Nation's income to enrich themselves.

Warith Mohammed was also upset at his father's behavior, and he and Malcolm X became closer during this time. In 1964, Mohammed began to

Malcolm X in the early 1960s, about when he began to question the Nation of Islam.

publicly challenge his father's teachings and leadership. His actions, along with those of Malcolm X, fueled a growing division within the Nation of Islam. In response, Elijah Muhammad temporarily suspended both men from the movement. Shortly thereafter, Malcolm X formally left the Nation of Islam, and the group's leaders viewed this as an unforgivable betrayal. Several violent clashes took place between supporters of Malcolm X and Elijah Muhammad, and numerous public threats were made against Malcolm.

On February 21, 1965, Malcolm X was assassinated while speaking before an audience in Harlem, a section of New York City. The gunmen were three members of the Nation of Islam. Elijah Muhammad denied responsibility for the killing and was never directly linked to the assassins. Nonetheless, many believe that he ordered the shooting. Even if he was not directly involved, his criticism of Malcolm X certainly encouraged extremists to target the former Nation leader.

For Warith Mohammed, the assassination of Malcolm X was a reminder of the dangers that he was facing in deviating from his father's teachings, and the events seemed to convince him to temporarily give up his rebellious position. Less than a week after the assassination, Warith appeared before the Nation of Islam's national convention and publicly asked for forgiveness for questioning Elijah Muhammad. "I judged my father when I should have let God do it," he stated. Years later, he would claim that he rejoined the Nation in the "interest of using my influence to keep them from going to more extremes," but many observers believe he did so because he feared that his own life was on the line.

The Return of the Chosen Son

While no longer in open rebellion against his father's teachings, Warith Mohammed still refused to be completely obedient to Elijah Muhammad. As a result, he was excommunicated, or banished, from the Nation on several different occasions between the mid-1960s and mid-1970s. Each time, he was later reinstated, but his refusal to publicly affirm his father as a prophet meant that he was not allowed to hold a paid position with the movement. He and his family subsisted on the small income he earned from welding, painting, and working other jobs. Meanwhile, he faced ongoing harassment and threats from those who were unhappy with his views.

While Warith Mohammed and Elijah Muhammad were often at odds, the two still maintained a bond with one another. "When he put me out of the Nation, he did it in a way to make me feel that he wished he didn't have to do it," Warith explained. "I had no bad feelings for him." In addition, Warith continued to be viewed by many as the so-called chosen son, and that status may have been part of the reason that he was able to challenge his father in certain ways. "Because they said I was a special person, that freed me up to criticize, to question things," Mohammed noted.

Elijah Muhammad's growing tolerance of his son's views became clear in 1974, when Warith Mohammed was given permission to resume preaching in Nation of Islam mosques. Moreover, Warith was allowed to proclaim his mainstream Islamic teachings, which did not uphold the divinity of his father and Fard. With this development, Warith was recognized as a lead-

Mohammed greets followers at Saviours' Day services in Chicago on February 26, 1975, the day after the death of his father.

ing candidate to succeed Elijah Muhammad. The question of who would next head the movement was becoming increasingly urgent at this point because Elijah Muhammad—then in his mid-70s—was in poor health. On February 25, 1975, he passed away. The following day, Warith Mohammed was recognized as the new supreme minister of the Nation of Islam.

Reforming a Religious Movement

Almost immediately, Mohammed began to make important changes to the religious group his father had built. To help heal the wounds caused by past disputes in the organization, he disbanded the Fruit of Islam security force and renamed the New York City mosque in honor of Malcolm X. He relaxed the strict dress code that had been in place for decades, and he sold many of the Nation's businesses to pay overdue taxes and settle other debts. While Elijah Muhammad had ruled over a highly centralized organization, Warith Mohammed began to allow local mosques more control over their own affairs, and he no longer required them to contribute money to the organization's headquarters. Ultimately, the religious movement he headed became a loosely connected association of mosques that looked to Mohammed for guidance but were not held to strict rules. Around 1977, he decided to signify the group's new direction by renaming it the World Community of Al-Islam in the West, and it was at this point that he changed his own name to Warith Deen Mohammed. The religious organization later took on a succession of other titles, the best known being the Muslim American Society.

> *When Mohammed became the supreme minister of the Nation of Islam, he abandoned some of the group's core beliefs, including the Nation's teachings about the evils of white people. "It's time for us to stop calling white folks the devil," he proclaimed, "because there's some black devils, too."*

Some of the most startling changes for members had to do with the religious beliefs that had been the core of the Nation of Islam's theology. Mohammed publicly renounced his father as a prophet and began to lead the movement's members toward the principles of Sunni Islam. He urged followers to pray five times each day, to learn Arabic, and to study the Koran. Perhaps most strikingly, the Nation of Islam teachings about the evils of whites were abandoned, and the movement even began accepting nonblacks as members. "It's time for us to stop calling white folks the devil," Mohammed proclaimed, "because there's some black devils, too."

In the span of a few years, Mohammed overhauled a religious group that had been in existence for more than four decades. Given the scope of the changes he introduced, he ran the risk that many members would abandon the movement. He also faced the possibility that his reforms would spark violent battles between rival factions, as had happened previously in the Nation's history. For several years, he was able to keep the movement unified, but in the late 1970s, a figure stepped forward to oppose his reforms.

Louis Farrakhan and the "New" Nation of Islam

In the years before Elijah Muhammad's death, Warith Mohammed had been just one of several people who were considered as possible successors. Another was Louis Farrakhan, the head of the Nation of Islam's Harlem mosque in New York City and the movement's national spokesperson. When Warith Mohammed became supreme minister in 1975, Farrakhan initially pledged his support, but his loyalty was short-lived. In 1978, Farrakhan began reviving the original race-based teachings of the Nation of Islam, and he formally broke away from Mohammed's movement the following year to start his own religious group. Farrakhan called his organization the Nation of Islam, and the revival of the old name was fitting. In essence, Farrakhan's group continued the original spiritual beliefs that had been established by Elijah Muhammad. Farrakhan maintained that Wallace Dodd Fard was Allah in human form, that Elijah Muhammad was a prophet, and that whites were an evil, inferior race.

Farrakhan and Mohammed were now rivals, and the two men would engage in a war of words for more than 20 years. Their conflict never escalated beyond verbal attacks, however. Unlike previous divisions in the movement, this clash did not lead to violence and killings, and the lack of bloodshed was another testament to the new direction Mohammed was forging. He refused to use force to strengthen his hold on power.

With the division between Mohammed and Farrakhan, the movement's members were forced to choose which leader and beliefs they would follow. Judged on this account, Mohammed's organization proved more popular, as it is believed to have a much larger membership than Farrakhan's Nation of Islam does. A study by the Council on American-Islamic Relations in the early 2000s found that two-thirds of the mosques in the United States that were predominantly African American were affiliated with Mohammed's organization, with the remainder divided between the Nation of Islam and several other organizations. The exact number of people that belong to these groups is unknown, however, and estimates vary considerably. The total membership of Mohammed's association in the mid-2000s has been estimated by some sources to be as small as 50,000 while others put it at around two million.

In terms of public perception, however, Farrakhan emerged as the better known leader. This was largely the result of his teachings about black supremacy and his statements against the Jewish people, both of which drew a great deal of media attention. In 1995, he played a leading role in the Million Man March in Washington DC, which drew together blacks from all across the country, though not all of them endorsed Farrakhan's controversial ideas. Mohammed condemned the Million Man March as a moneymaking scheme by Farrakhan, and he continually criticized the divisive and confrontational stance of his rival. "Farrakhan is working from a position of anger, and I'm working from a position of peace," he asserted in the mid-1990s. In another interview, he characterized Farrakhan's teachings as negative influences that have "taken our people further and further into darkness."

Mohammed in 1992, with a portrait of his father.

A Voice of Moderation

The division between Mohammed and Farrakhan reflected a larger debate among African Americans: the degree to which they should focus on the legacy of racial injustice experienced by blacks in the United States. In Mohammed's view, African Americans were enjoying new opportunities by the turn of the 21st century, and he felt it was time to give up what he regarded as "an emotional rage directed at the past." This was part of the reason that he opposed Farrakhan's continuation of his father's teachings. "The Nation was designed to attract poor and hopeless blacks to come to something created for nobody but them," he noted in 2001. "But we live in new realities now.... Blacks are being encouraged to aspire to the highest positions in America now. Everything is open to us. There is very little place for the extreme idea of the Nation of Islam in America today."

Not surprisingly, this message was better received by African Americans who had achieved a certain degree of financial security, while more militant views, such as those expressed by Farrakhan, proved more popular with blacks who suffered hardship. Consequently, the followers of Mohammed's Islamic association, on the whole, have tended to belong to the middle class, while Farrakhan's Nation of Islam has enjoyed its strongest support in poor inner-city areas—the same locations that had been the stronghold of the Nation under Elijah Muhammad.

In keeping with his moderate views, Warith Mohammed also voiced strong support for the existing political values and institutions of the United States—a striking contrast with his father's belief that blacks should have a nation unto themselves. Mohammed believed this acceptance was justified because of the tremendous social changes that had taken place in the country since the mid-1900s, stating that "we should love America passionately now that America has changed so drastically within a relatively short time." The same man who once refused to serve in the armed forces did away with the anti-military tenets of the old Nation of Islam, and the U.S. flag was prominently displayed in the mosques of his organization.

Mohammed's patriotic views defied the stereotypical image of Muslims as being anti-American, and his stance helped demonstrate that Islam includes a wide range of people with differing views. In the wake of the terrorist attacks on September 11, 2001, he strongly supported the U.S. military invasion of Afghanistan, stating that "the government should go wherever there is oppression of human beings and show them the way. My only regret is that I'm not the president. I would like to take the Army there myself." In addition, he used many of his post-9/11 interviews to fight against the perception that Muslims approved of violent extremism. "Terrorism has no place in Islam," he said, "just as it has no place in Christianity or Judaism."

A World Leader

During his decades of leadership, Mohammed began receiving greater recognition from political leaders and from religious authorities from other faiths. In 1992, he became the first Muslim leader to deliver a prayer and invocation before the U.S. Senate. "It felt for the first time that I was going to be free in America," he said of that event. "It was a sign of being accepted." In addition, he was invited to take part in the 1993 and 1997 inaugurations of President Clinton as a representative of America's Muslim citizens.

An increasingly prominent figure on the world stage, Mohammed frequently met with officials from other faiths. In 1996, he led a delegation of Muslims to Rome to consult with Pope John Paul II, and he made a second appearance at the Vatican in 1999. He also became the first Muslim to address the general assembly of the National Council of Churches. Mohammed received great respect from the worldwide Muslim community as well, and he enjoyed an especially close relationship with the government of Saudi Arabia. Their ties reached back to the late 1970s, and for a number of years Mohammed's religious movement received financial support from the Saudis. This funding ended in the mid-1990s, according to Mohammed, because he refused to support the Saudi's position on certain international issues.

Mohammed made use of his contacts in the Muslim world to create new business opportunities for the members of his association. A partnership was formed with several Islamic nations that allowed members of the Muslim American Society to purchase international goods at a discount for resale in the United States. This was part of his organization's ongoing efforts to assist in the creation of black-owned businesses. The most prominent of these endeavors was the Collective Purchasing Conference, later known as CPC/Comtrust, which allowed small investors to pool their resources to improve their buying power.

Reaching Out to a Rival

Public speeches were a common part of Warith Mohammed's life, but the appearance he made at the McCormick Center in Chicago on February 26, 1999, stood apart from the rest. On that day, he spoke at the annual Saviours' Day gathering of the Nation of Islam—the group headed by his longtime rival Louis Farrakhan. Mohammed's appearance at the event signified an attempt at mending the 21-year old division between his Muslim American Society and Farrakhan's followers, and in his speech he endorsed unity and brotherhood among all Muslims. The following year, the reconciliation went a step farther. Farrakhan and Mohammed publicly embraced at the 2000 Saviours' Day event, and Farrakhan stated that "we will be together as a family.... Not for evil, but for love—not hatred, but in good."

This development came about as Farrakhan's group moved closer to the mainstream Islamic practices and beliefs that Mohammed had adopted years before. Farrakhan's health was also reportedly a motivating factor, as his battle with prostate cancer in the late 1990s had convinced him to promote unity. Mohammed welcomed the improved relations and later remarked that "it is very clear to me that Minister Farrakhan and the Nation of Islam are very serious in embracing the love and peace message of Islam and putting the harsh rhetoric behind." In the years that followed, the two groups have generally been on good terms with one another, but there has been little progress toward officially unifying into one organization. At times in the 2000s, Mohammed and Farrakhan even resumed their criticisms of one another, though their attacks were less frequent and less antagonistic than in decades past.

Mohammed embraces Louis Farrakhan at the Nation of Islam Saviours' Day gathering, 2000.

Final Years

In September 2003, as he approached his 70th birthday, Warith Mohammed resigned as the head of the American Society of Muslims, a move that was partly inspired by his wish to reduce his responsibilities. "When I told the imams [Muslim religious leaders] about my resignation," he noted, "a big burden went off my back." In addition, he confessed that his decision to step down came partly out of the frustration that he felt toward some of the local imams who were part of the association. "I have tried over the last 10 to 12 years to encourage them to get more religious education, but I have made no progress. They want their followers to just obey them, but not to question them or right their wrongs."

Even though he gave up his official position, Mohammed still served as an influential religious authority for many African-American Muslims. He remained a prominent public figure as well, delivering sermons, speeches, and interviews, and he also devoted himself to Mosque Cares, a charity organization he had founded. His busy schedule continued through the final weeks of his life, and when he passed away at his home in Markham, Illinois, on September 9, 2008, the loss took many of his followers by surprise. His death at age 74 was attributed to heart disease and complications from diabetes. Some 8,000 of his friends and followers attended his funeral.

At the time of Mohammed's passing, many people commented on the surprising transition that he was able to achieve in convincing thousands of African Americans to accept Sunni Muslim beliefs. "I don't think people understand the tremendous change that occurred when he made that move," noted Lawrence Mamiya, a professor of religion at Vassar College, who was quoted in the *Chicago Tribune*. "He moved people from that concept of black nationalism into universal consciousness of the faith." Abdullah El-Amin, the head of Muslim Center in Detroit, echoed that idea in the *Detroit Free Press*, stating that Mohammed "was a reviver of the religion.... He brought a whole lot of people to the correct worship of Islam."

Others focused on Mohammed's role as a mediator who reached out to other faiths. Quoted in the *New Journal and Guide*, Imam Muhammad Asadi of Virginia voiced the opinion that "W. D. Mohammed's legacy as a human being was to bring humanity together and use truth and understanding to build bridges." The ideal of finding common spiritual ground with others was a continuing priority for Mohammed, particularly in the later decades of his life. When asked to sum up his goals in a 2001 interview, Mohammed did so by linking his faith to other major religions. "My dream is the same as (the dreams of) faithful and loving Jewish, Christian, and Buddhist leaders," he affirmed. "Our dream is the dream of scripture.... We want to see human society be the best it can possibly be."

HOME AND FAMILY

The details of Warith Mohammed's family life are not well known. At the time of his death, he was married to Khadija Mohammed, and he had been wed three times previously and had married one of his wives on two separate occasions. Some sources indicate that he had nine children while others cite eight, and he had five stepchildren. He was a longtime resident of the Chicago area, living his final years in the suburb of Markham. He also had a second residence in Little Rock, Arkansas.

In his later years Mohammed served as an influential religious leader and spoke at many different types of gatherings, including this lecture at the University of Arkansas Clinton School of Public Service in Little Rock, Arkansas.

SELECTED WRITINGS

The Man and the Woman in Islam, 1976
The Teachings of W. D. Muhammad, 1976
Prayer and Al-Islam, 1982
Religion on the Line, 1983
Imam W. Deen Muhammad Speaks from Harlem, N.Y., 1984
An African American Genesis, 1986
Al-Islam Unity and Leadership, 1991
Islam's Climate for Business Success, 1995
The Champion We have in Common: The Dynamic African American Soul, 2002

HONORS AND AWARDS

100 Most Influential African Americans in the World (*Ebony* magazine): 2000 and 2001
Ghandi King Ikeda Award for Peace (Morehouse College): 2002

Hall of Honor Inductee (Martin Luther King Jr. International Chapel): 2002
Honorary Doctorate of Humane Letters (Sojourner-Douglass College): 2003
Outstanding Leadership Award (Council on American-Islamic Relations): 2005

FURTHER READING

Books

Blake, John. *Children of the Movement,* 2004
Britannica Biographies, 2008
Evanzz, Karl. *The Judas Factor: The Plot to Kill Malcolm X,* 1992
Who's Who among African Americans, 2008

Periodicals

Chicago Tribune, Sep. 10, 2008
Current Biography Yearbook, 2004
Detroit Free Press, Sep. 10, 2008
Islamic Horizons, July/Aug. 2005
Los Angeles Times, May 15, 1999, p.2; July 8, 2000, p.2
Middle East, Sept. 2001, p.19
Tampa Tribune, Feb. 16, 1997, p.1
Washington Post, Sep. 10, 2008, p.B7
Wilson Quarterly, Autumn 2005, p.16

Online Articles

http://www.csmonitor.com/2002/0214/p03s01-ussc.htm
(Christian Science Monitor, "America's Black Muslims Close a Rift," Feb. 14, 2002)
http://www.pbs.org/thisfarbyfaith
(PBS, This Far by Faith, "Warith Deen Mohammed," 2003)

WORLD WIDE WEB SITE

http://www.ar-razzaq.org/MosqueCares

Walter Dean Myers 1937-

American Writer of Books for Children and Young Adults

Author of More Than 80 Books, Including the Award-Winning Novels *Fallen Angels, Scorpions,* and *Monster*

BIRTH

Walter Dean Myers was born Walter Milton Myers on August 12, 1937, in Martinsburg, West Virginia. His parents, George Ambrose and Mary (Green) Myers, lived about 10 miles from the plantation where their ancestors had once been held in slavery. The family lived in extreme poverty, and Myers's parents struggled to provide the basic necessities for their chil-

A photo of Harlem in 1949, when Myers was 12 years old.

dren. In addition to two older half-sisters from his father's first marriage, Myers had two older sisters, one older brother, and one younger sister.

When Myers was two years old, his mother died in childbirth, and his father was unable to care for the large family on his own. He arranged for his two oldest daughters to go and live with their mother, Florence Dean, a factory worker, and her husband, Herbert Julius Dean, a shipping clerk. When the Deans came to take the two girls home, they decided to adopt Walter too. He was three years old when he went to live with the Deans. The adoption was informal but permanent, and the Deans became, in every way, his "real" parents. Later in life, Myers changed his middle name to Dean to honor them.

YOUTH

Myers grew up in New York City's Harlem neighborhood, a section of the borough of Manhattan with a long history as a center of African-American culture. There he was surrounded by a vibrant, thriving community that would provide the inspiration for many of his books. Myers described these early years in his autobiography *Bad Boy: A Memoir* (2001), recalling that "[Harlem was] a magical place, alive with music that spilled into the busy streets ... full of colors and smells." On the sidewalk near his home, he sometimes danced to the music blaring from apartment windows. People passing by would give him pennies, which he used to buy candy or popsicles at the corner grocery store.

Life at home was often just as lively. Myers's adoptive father and grandfather were both storytellers, and they entertained him with stories from the Old Testament of the Bible as well as long and fanciful tales of monsters and other imaginary creatures. Although his adoptive mother could not read very well herself, she was able to teach Myers to read before he started school. She read aloud the stories in *True Romance* magazines, showing him the printed words as she spoke them, and soon he was able to read stories to her. This was the beginning of Myers's lifelong appreciation for good stories and his love of reading.

"[Harlem was] a magical place, alive with music that spilled into the busy streets ... full of colors and smells."

”

EDUCATION

In *Bad Boy: A Memoir,* Myers writes in detail about the problems he had in school. The trouble began almost as soon as he started first grade. "I was a good student, but a speech impediment was causing problems," he remembered. He stuttered when he spoke, and he was teased by his classmates because of this. He was big for his age, and he often fought back by kicking or hitting other students, sometimes even lashing out at teachers. Myers quickly gained a reputation as a problem student and was in trouble at school so often that he was nearly expelled.

Because he had trouble getting along with the other students, Myers increasingly took refuge in books. His first favorite books were *Tom Sawyer, Huckleberry Finn, Little Men, The Three Musketeers,* and *Robin Hood.* Myers began reading anything he could find, including a growing collection of comic books discarded by a neighbor. One day when he was 10 years old, a teacher saw him reading a comic book. "She grabbed my comic book and tore it up. I was really upset, but then she brought in a pile of books from her own library. That was the best thing that ever happened to me." One of those books became his new favorite, a collection of Norwegian folk tales titled *East o' the Sun, West o' the Moon.*

Discovering a Love of Writing

That same teacher also encouraged Myers to try writing. "She thought that if I wrote something, I would use words I could pronounce." She gave the whole class writing assignments and almost always praised his work, choosing to read his poems aloud to the class. After that, he recalled, "I began writing little poems. I began to write short stories, too.... Writing, for me, was a natural extension of my love for reading and books." At the end of the school year, a poem Myers wrote about his adoptive mother was chosen to appear on the front page of the school's magazine.

"I liked to look at pictures of writers, and none of the writers whom I was studying in school had any relation to anything I knew as being real. They were all, as far as I knew, dead. Those who weren't dead were probably English, which meant about the same thing to me."

As he progressed through school, Myers continued to win praise for his writing. But despite the growing number of hours he spent reading or writing his own stories, he did not yet realize that he could have a career as a writer. His adoptive parents did not encourage what they saw as his hobby. "I was from a family of laborers and the idea of writing stories or essays was far removed from their experience," he pointed out. "Writing had no practical value for a black child."

Myers also recalled that at that time—the early 1950s—he was not aware of any books written by or about African Americans. In everything that he read, he found no characters like himself, his family, or his friends. "I liked to look at pictures of writers, and none of the writers whom I was studying in school had any relation to anything I knew as being real. They were all, as far as I knew, dead. Those who weren't dead were probably English, which meant about the same thing to me."

Leaving School

Throughout elementary school, Myers was a very good student who was ranked at the top of his class. When he was in the sixth grade, he had been placed into a special class for the brightest students and had also been honored as that year's Outstanding Boy. But he also continued to struggle with stuttering and being teased by the other students. He was often punished for fighting or otherwise causing trouble in and out of class. By the time Myers was a teenager attending Stuyvesant High School, his stuttering problem was seriously interfering with his schoolwork. He was frustrated, his grades were slipping, and he began skipping school frequently.

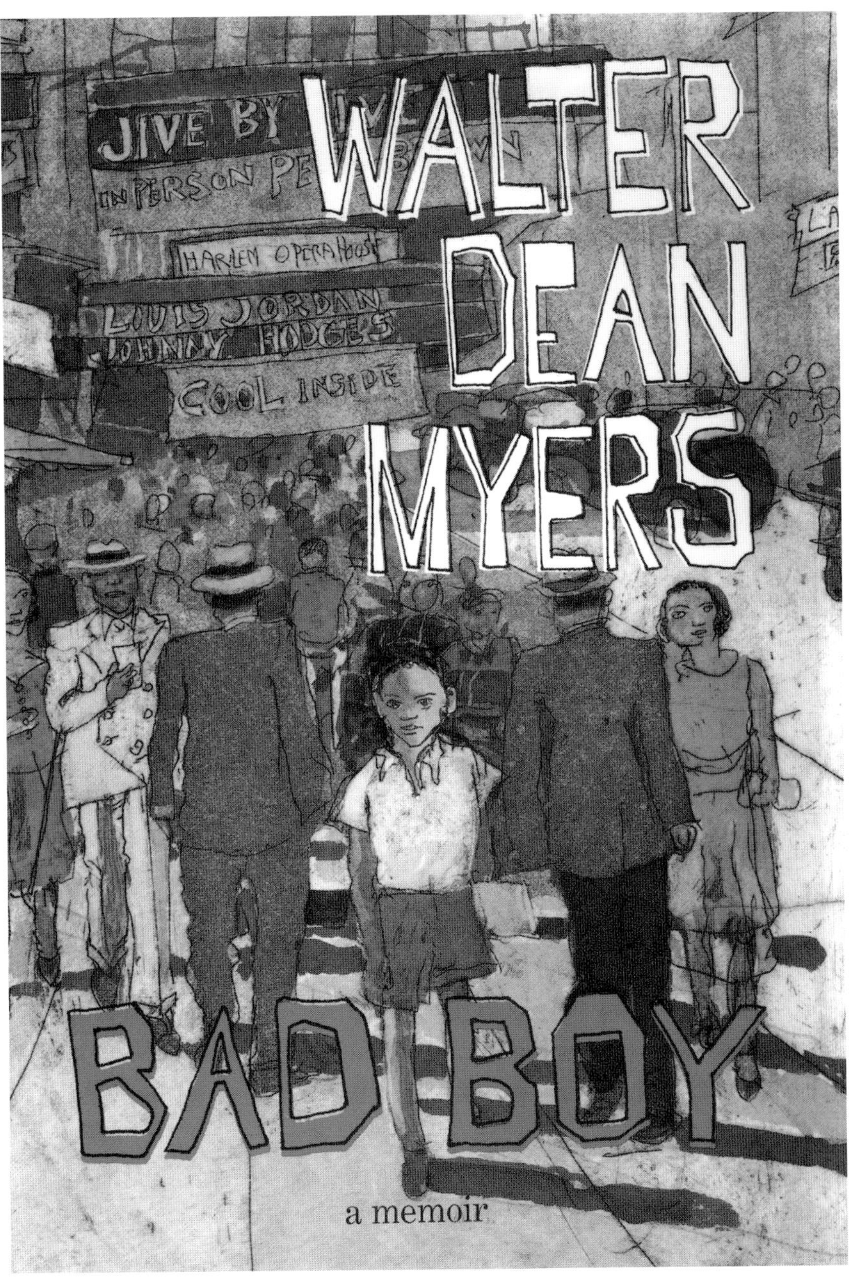

In his memoir Bad Boy, *Myers told stories about his experiences growing up—about his early childhood, his years in school, how he got started as a writer, and more.*

There was also pressure from teachers, school counselors, and others who wanted Myers to go to college or choose a career. As he wrote in his autobiography, "I didn't see anybody talking about being a poet, or a short-story writer, as a career. Nor did I see anybody defining a real man as somebody who paid a lot of attention to books." Around the same time, Myers was also becoming aware of the ways in which his world was shaped by racism. "When I thought of the major careers, I thought of whites, not blacks.... My definition of a black man was, except for the rare instance, a man without an outstanding career.... These definitions were reinforced everywhere I looked."

"

As Myers grew older, he became aware of the ways in which his world was shaped by racism. "When I thought of the major careers, I thought of whites, not blacks.... My definition of a black man was, except for the rare instance, a man without an outstanding career.... These definitions were reinforced everywhere I looked."

"

Myers's growing realization of the few options open to him left him feeling lost, with no direction for his future. Instead of attending classes, he spent his days exploring New York City, most often settling down under a tree in Central Park to read his books undisturbed. He read three or four books each week and continued writing volumes of his own stories and poems. With no real interest in finishing high school, and no idea how to pursue the kind of work he wanted, Myers still needed to find an occupation. He decided on a whim to join the Army, enlisting in 1954 on his 17th birthday. The U.S. was not at war during his three years of Army service. He was stationed at various Army posts in the U.S., including a stint at a military base in the Arctic Circle, the most northern part of the Northern Hemisphere. Myers attended the Army's radio repair school, but says that he spent most of his time in the Army playing basketball. In his autobiography, he described his years in the Army as "numbing ... years of nongrowing."

BECOMING A WRITER

First Jobs

After leaving the Army in 1957, Myers worked a series of odd jobs. He worked in a factory, loaded trucks on a shipping dock, took a job with the

U.S. Postal Service, worked as a messenger, and did construction work. Myers has said of this difficult time, "Few of the jobs were worth mentioning. Leaving school seemed less like a good idea." He had stopped writing during his years in the Army, but he soon started again. "I didn't need to get published, or to make money from my writing; I just needed to be able to think of myself as a person with brains as well as a body," he recalled. "Once I began writing again, I couldn't stop. I produced poems, short stories, articles, even ideas for advertising campaigns."

Although he never graduated from high school, Myers also enrolled in college during this time on the G.I. Bill, a special government program that helps military veterans earn university degrees. He attended the State College of the City University of New York, earning a Bachelor of Arts (BA) degree. Myers also began to work with a speech therapist to control his stuttering. He was finally able to overcome the problem with an interesting technique that he had read about. Myers found that if he spoke with a southern accent, he did not stutter at all. In this way, he was finally able to put his speech difficulties behind him.

Getting Published

Around this time, Myers was working as a supervisor for the New York State Department of Labor. He was writing every night, and he began submitting his poetry and stories to literary magazines in the hope that his work would be published. Through seemingly endless rejections, Myers never stopped writing. "I would save my rejection slips, and every six months or so I would put them into a neat pile to check my progress. Then I would throw away the pile and start a new one." Some of his poems were eventually published, followed by a few of his stories. He wasn't making much money, but he felt he had become successful enough to begin thinking of himself, finally, as a writer.

CAREER HIGHLIGHTS

Over the course of his career, Myers has written and published more than 80 books for children and young adults, spanning a wide variety of subjects and formats and often focusing on inner-city life. A full-time writer since 1977, he is best-known for his award-winning novels featuring young urban African-American characters, including *The Young Landlords* (1979), *Fallen Angels* (1988), *Scorpions* (1988), *Slam!* (1998), *Monster* (1999), and many more. Myers has also written fairy tales, folk tales, ghost stories, adventure sagas, mysteries, science fiction, and fantasy. His books have covered many different subjects, including friendship, sports, music, school, slavery, the U.S. Civil War, Prohibition (a time when alcoholic beverages were illegal in the U.S.), the American western frontier, the civil rights movement, and life in America's inner cities. Myers has also tackled such difficult and controversial subjects as drug abuse, gangs, crime, violence, suicide, teen pregnancy, gambling, parental neglect, child abuse, and war.

In addition to his many popular works of fiction, Myers has published a number of nonfiction books. He has written on a variety of topics, including blacks' struggle for freedom from the days of slavery through the 1940s and 1950s; the discovery and exploration of the frozen continent of Antarctica; the 1797 naval vessel the *USS Constitution,* also known as Old Ironsides; and the Harlem Hellfighters, a popular name for the 369th Infantry Regiment, an all-black military unit that fought in World War I. Myers has also written a number of nonfiction books about important historical figures. He has written two biographies of civil rights leader Malcolm X. *Malcolm X: By Any Means Necessary* (1993) puts Malcolm's life in historical context for young adult readers and was named a Coretta Scott King Honor book. *Malcolm X: A Fire Burning Brightly* (2000) presents an illustrated life story for younger readers. Myers has also written an account of important events in the civil rights movement, *Now Is Your Time!: The African American Struggle for Freedom* (1991), which won a Coretta Scott King Award. He has also written biographies of many significant African Americans, including Dr. Martin Luther King Jr. and Muhammad Ali.

"

Myers strives to create for African-American children "literature that includes them and the way they live, that celebrates their life and their person. It upholds and gives special place to their humanity."

Myers has also published books of poetry for children and young adults using a variety of engaging techniques. Some of these collections of poems around a single theme are written for younger readers, but they can be enjoyed by any age. His picture book *Harlem: A Poem* (1997) was illustrated by his son Christopher and won several major book awards. He also worked with his son on *Jazz* (2006), a picture book that combines Myers's poetry and his son Christopher's illustrations. These father-son pairings were praised for the connections between the poetry and the artistry, what Bill Ott described in *Booklist* as "an absolutely airtight melding of words

Brown Angels combines Myers's poetry with old photos of African Americans.

and pictures." He has published several collections of his poems illustrated with antique photos of African Americans, such as the book *Brown Angels: An Album of Pictures and Verse* (1993). These books arose out of Myers's hobby of collecting old photos of African Americans. When he would bring these old photos to classroom speaking engagements, the students would be enthralled by the old photos. So he created these books to help give young readers a more complete sense of African-American history. "Kids know that 'Black is beautiful' slogan from the 1970s, but unless they see the images, they don't believe it." His illustrated volumes of poetry have been praised by critics as "visually striking" and "haunting."

Today, Myers is considered one of the preeminent contemporary writers for young adults. Along with a handful of other writers, he is credited with helping to change the image of African Americans in young adult literature. While his many different works have won critical praise and admiration, he is perhaps best known for his novels for young adults, both lighter stories for younger readers and deeper, more challenging novels for older teens.

Finding His Voice

One common theme that recurs throughout Myers's diverse writing is the growth and personal development of young African Americans. Regardless of his subject or the format of his writing, Myers strives to create for African-American children "literature that includes them and the way they live, that celebrates their life and their person. It upholds and gives special place to their humanity." In an autobiographical essay, Myers wrote, "I realized how few resources are available for black youngsters to open the world to them. I feel the need to show them the possibilities that exist for them that were never revealed to me as a youngster, possibilities that did not even exist for me then." He later said, "I have only one point of view. There should be lots of books about the African-American experience."

"

"I realized how few resources are available for black youngsters to open the world to them. I feel the need to show them the possibilities that exist for them that were never revealed to me as a youngster, possibilities that did not even exist for me then." He later said, "I have only one point of view. There should be lots of books about the African-American experience."

"

When Myers was just beginning to have his work published, he was not yet using his own life experiences as possible subject matter. It took another African-American author's work to help him find his true voice as a writer. In his autobiography, Myers described the critical turning point in his writing, the discovery that would change his life. It was the short story "Sonny's Blues," written by James Baldwin. "It was a beautifully written story, but, more important, it was a story about the black urban experience," Myers recalled. "Baldwin, in writing and publishing that story, gave me permission to write about my own experiences."

Where Does the Day Go?

Myers was inspired by the work of James Baldwin and others he met through the Harlem Writer's Guild, a creative organization that had been formed in 1950 to bring together African-American writers and help pro-

mote their work. With a new outlook on his writing, he decided to enter a contest sponsored by the Council on Interracial Books for Children in 1968. He won the contest, and his entry became his first published book. The children's picture book *Where Does the Day Go* (1969) tells the story of a multicultural group of children who discuss their ideas about night and day with a sensitive and wise African-American father. Critics praised the book for its positive portrayal of diverse ethnicities.

Not yet able to support himself with his writing, Myers continued to work in a variety of jobs while writing in his spare time. By 1970, he was working as a book editor for the New York City publishing company Bobbs-Merrill. Part of his job was helping to decide which books would be published. In the process, he learned about the publishing industry and the business side of being a writer. The insider's knowledge Myers gained in this position would prove invaluable to his future career.

Myers followed the success of *Where Does the Day Go?* with two more picture books. *The Dancers* (1972) was praised for its positive portrayal of a strong father-son relationship and the friendship between an African-American boy and a white girl. However, his book *The Dragon Takes a Wife* (1972) caused a stir for its modern retelling of a traditional fairy tale.

The story featured a streetwise African-American fairy named Mabel Mae Jones, who spoke in the common slang Myers had grown up hearing in Harlem. "There had never been a black fairy before," he commented. "Especially a black fairy that sort of had jive talk." Some parents thought the character stereotyped African Americans, but Myers thought it was an honest portrayal of voices that would be familiar to African-American children.

Fast Sam, Cool Clyde & Stuff

Before long, Myers hired a literary agent to help him publish his short stories. He recalled, "My agent thought that I could write a novel for teenagers because much of my short fiction was about young, inner city males. She gave one of my short stories to an editor, touting it as a potential novel. The editor said that she had read the 'first chapter' and asked me how the rest of it went. The book turned out to be *Fast Sam, Cool Clyde & Stuff,* which is really a book of related short stories."

"I cut out pictures of my characters and my wife puts them into a collage, which goes on the wall above the computer. When I walk into that room, I see the characters, and I just get very close to them."

Published in 1975, *Fast Sam, Cool Clyde & Stuff* tells the story of a boy growing up in Harlem with his adventurous friends. Myers's first attempt at a novel earned praise from critics and was named a Coretta Scott King Honor Book and an American Library Association Notable Children's Book. *School Library Journal* called the book "alternately funny and sad, but always very natural and appealing." Myers said the book "changed my life because I had no real education, and I needed something to validate myself. I needed to find value, and publishing gave me that value." The success gave Myers the courage to try becoming a full-time writer when he was laid off from his position at Bobbs-Merrill in 1977.

Two years later Myers published *The Young Landlords* (1979), the story of a group of African-American teenagers in New York City who become the owners and managers of a run-down apartment building. Myers won a Coretta Scott King Award for this comedic novel, called "zany" by the *New York Times Book Review* and a "slick and easy-going adventure" by *School Library Journal.* Myers won another Coretta Scott King Award in 1984 for the publication of *Motown & Didi: A Love Story*. This novel for young adults tells the story of two young people who want to escape their dangerous, difficult lives in Harlem. They come together to rely on each other's strength as they struggle to make their dreams come true. The *Horn Book* praised Myers for "suggesting there is good to be found and choices to be made on even the toughest streets."

Fallen Angels

In 1988, Myers published his groundbreaking young adult novel *Fallen Angels*. The book tells the story of a Harlem teenager who volunteers for U.S. military service during the Vietnam War. The story was inspired by Myers's own life experiences. "My thinking about war has changed over the years. As a 17-year-old, having seen all of the John Wayne movies, I eagerly joined the Army. When my brother, who followed me into the Army, was killed in Vietnam, it was a rude awakening. War had suddenly become personal. I needed to write about it in a way that countered the romantic ideas. *Fallen Angels* was the result."

"My thinking about war has changed over the years. As a 17-year-old, having seen all of the John Wayne movies, I eagerly joined the Army. When my brother, who followed me into the Army, was killed in Vietnam, it was a rude awakening. War had suddenly become personal. I needed to write about it in a way that countered the romantic ideas. Fallen Angels *was the result."*

Fallen Angels created some controversy when it was first published. Some critics objected to the depictions of violence and the language used in the book, calling the subject matter inappropriate for young adult readers. But others praised the book for its accuracy and genuine tone. *Fallen Angels* received a Coretta Scott King Award and was named among the American Library Association's Best Books for Young Adults. One *Kirkus Reviews* critic said, "Myers masterfully recreates the combat zone … its crushing tension and the distortion of values brought on by the relentless proximity of death." The *New York Times Book Review* called *Fallen Angels* "a candid young adult novel that engages the Vietnam experience squarely. It deals with violence and death as well as compassion and love, with deception and hypocrisy as well as honesty and virtue. It is a tale that is as thought-provoking as it is entertaining, touching, and, on occasion, humorous."

In Fallen Angels, *Myers dealt with the reality of war.*

Along with drawing complaints from some book reviewers, *Fallen Angels* also became one of Myers's most-challenged books. Concerned parents requested that the book be removed from school libraries in Virginia, Texas, and elsewhere. Due to objections over the book's "strong content," it has been banned and removed from school libraries in Indiana, Kansas, Mississippi, and Ohio. Despite the uproar, *Fallen Angels* has had significant impact on readers over the years. As the author recalled, "Since *Fallen Angels* was published, many women have thanked me for helping them understand why their husbands were so reticent to speak about their wartime experiences, and I have had hundreds of letters from young people who, for the first time, had some idea of what their fathers had gone through."

Scorpions

Myers's next novel, *Scorpions,* was published in 1988, the same year as *Fallen Angels*. This young adult novel tells the story of a seventh grade student who feels pressured to take over his brother's leadership role in a gang after his brother is sent to prison. Myers once again takes on controversial subject matter, writing about gang violence, guns, and drugs. "I was writing here about a scene I know only too well, about a family like so many I grew up with—low-income families, headed by a single parent, a hard-working woman who leaves her young children every morning and carries around with her all day long a fear that they may go wrong." The book was well-received and recognized as "a realistic look at a boy who wants to do the right thing but gets caught up in the culture of violence." *Scorpions* was named an American Library Association Best Book for Young Adults and a Newbery Honor Book.

"

In Scorpions, *according to Myers, "I was writing here about a scene I know only too well, about a family like so many I grew up with—low-income families, headed by a single parent, a hard-working woman who leaves her young children every morning and carries around with her all day long a fear that they may go wrong."*

"

In 1992, Myers published *Somewhere in the Darkness,* a story of a 14-year-old boy on the run with his gravely ill, escaped-convict father. *Kirkus Reviews* called the story "thought-provoking, rich in insight and detail," while *School Library Journal* observes that "readers will find this universal journey of self-discovery gratifying." *BookList* said that in *Somewhere in the Darkness,* "Myers has never written better." The novel was named a Newbery Honor Book. He followed that up with *Slam!* (1996), a coming-of-age

The moving novel Monster *was acclaimed by critics and won many awards for literary excellence.*

story about 17-year-old Greg, known as "Slam" for his unparalleled talent in basketball. The story unfolds as Slam transfers to a new school where African Americans are in the minority. Slam must deal with new challenges as well as conflicts that strain old friendships. The *Horn Book* observed that "readers will appreciate *Slam!* for the honesty with which Myers portrays the dreams of one Harlem teenager." Critics appreciated it too, giving it Coretta Scott King Award.

Monster

In 1999, Myers published *Monster*, the tale of 16-year-old Steve, accused of murder because of his role as the lookout during a robbery in which a murder is committed. The story unfolds in the form of diary entries and the notes for a screenplay being written by Steve during his trial. Readers piece together information as the trial progresses and must form their own conclusions about Steve's guilt or innocence. Myers wrote *Monster* to convey the idea that "the other side of the 'war on crime' is the huge number of young people caught up in the juvenile justice system.... More and more teenagers like Stephen are being tried as adults. Everyone writes and talks about stopping crime, I thought I needed to write about it from the teenagers' point of view."

Monster was published at a time when American society was developing a growing concern about rising crime among young people. Consequently, the book received a tremendous amount of attention. One *Booklist* reviewer praised Myers for combining "an innovative format, complex moral issues, and an intriguingly sympathetic but flawed protagonist." *School Library Journal* said that readers of the book "will find themselves feeling both sympathy and repugnance" for Steve, calling the story "compelling and disturbing." *Monster* received the first Michael L. Printz Award for literary excellence and was named both a National Book Award Finalist and a Coretta Scott King Honor Book. *Monster* has also been added to the New York Public Schools' required reading curriculum.

Street Love

In *Street Love* (2006), Myers focused on the family of a woman who has been sent to prison. Her daughter Junice is determined not to follow in her drug-addicted mother's footsteps and fights to keep the family together in her mother's absence. Then Junice falls in love with high-achiever Damien, who has plans to escape the neighborhood by going to college and making a better life for himself. The two characters must struggle to overcome their very different life experiences, in a world that sees them as completely wrong for each other. Myers combines poetry and prose to tell their story, using a free-verse writing style that flows with the casual, conversational rhythms of the teenagers in his own neighborhood.

Street Love was a hit with readers and critics alike. One TeenReads.com contributor wrote, "Myers's talent for turning words on end to spin phrase after powerful phrase is truly amazing." A reviewer for *Kliatt* called *Street Love* a "deeply felt, poignant story … told in deft strokes, with memorable language and some rap cadences." Myers explained, "I want my books to be bridges between the reality of urban life and the ideal. The only way that my inner city characters can be truly humanized is for me to bridge the gaps both in language and understanding. This is what I have tried to do in this book."

"

Myers wrote **Monster** *to convey the idea that "the other side of the 'war on crime' is the huge number of young people caught up in the juvenile justice system.... More and more teenagers like Stephen are being tried as adults. Everyone writes and talks about stopping crime, I thought I needed to write about it from the teenagers' point of view."*

"

Sunrise Over Fallujah

In 2008, Myers again addressed the topic of war with the publication of *Sunrise Over Fallujah,* a companion to his earlier book *Fallen Angels.* Birdy, the main character in this young adult novel, is the nephew of the main character in *Fallen Angels.* After the terrorist attacks of 9/11, Birdy joins the U.S. military against his father's wishes, but with noble intentions. He wants to help end terrorism and spread democracy. Once Birdy is overseas, however, he begins to see the complexity of the situation in Iraq and questions whether his service is making a difference. In a letter to his uncle back home, Birdy writes, "I used to be mad with you when you wouldn't talk about Vietnam. I thought you were being selfish, in a way. Now I understand how light the words seem." One critic for the *New York Times Book Review* called *Sunrise Over Fallujah* "astonishing," while *School Library Journal* praised Myers's "precise, believable dialogue."

Of *Sunrise Over Fallujah,* Myers said, "Writing about war is a daunting task. There is the need to honor the brave men and women who have stepped up to defend our country. There is also the grim reality of what they will face. War is a difficult thing to talk about for those who are involved in it, and for them to explain to others.... The quiet conversations in bookstores with people who had read [*Fallen Angels*] a decade earlier, made me want to shoulder the responsibility of again writing about America at war."

In Sunrise Over Fallujah, *Myers revisited the topic of war, which he had also addressed in* Fallen Angels.

Winning Awards and Critical Acclaim

Myers has been called one of the best writers of children's and young adult fiction in the country, and many of his books have been honored with generous critical acclaim. Critics have recognized his writing for its genuine depiction of the lives of young people growing up in American cities. According to the *Dictionary of Literary Biography*, "Myers captures the essence of the developing experiences of youth." A reviewer for *Book Report* stated, "Many feel that Myers understands the problems of young African Americans better than any other author." As the author said of his own work, "One of the things that brings young people to books is seeing something they recognize in their own lives.... I feel that I have a kinship with many teenagers and young people that I write about, and I try to reflect that in my books."

In addition, Myers and his books have been honored with prestigious national literary awards. He has received the ALAN Award, the Margaret A. Edwards Award, the Virginia Hamilton Literary Award, the Michael L. Printz Award, several Coretta Scott King Awards, multiple Newbery Honors and Boston Globe-Horn Book Honors, and he as been a two-time National Book Award finalist. Several of his many books have been recognized by the American Library Association as Notable Children's Books, with more being named among the Best Books for Young Adults. Myers attributes his success to hard work and a love for what he does. "I so love writing. It is not something that I am doing just for a living, this is something that I love to do."

The Writing Process

As such a prolific writer, Myers has developed a process that keeps him focused on his many projects. To begin, he is constantly gathering ideas for new books, mostly from his own life experiences and sometimes from historical events or artifacts such as old photos and letters. He explained, "My best ideas come as I lie in bed in the mornings after a good night's sleep.... I think my own teen years were so troublesome that I'm constantly exploring them."

"One of the things that brings young people to books is seeing something they recognize in their own lives.... I feel that I have a kinship with many teenagers and young people that I write about, and I try to reflect that in my books."

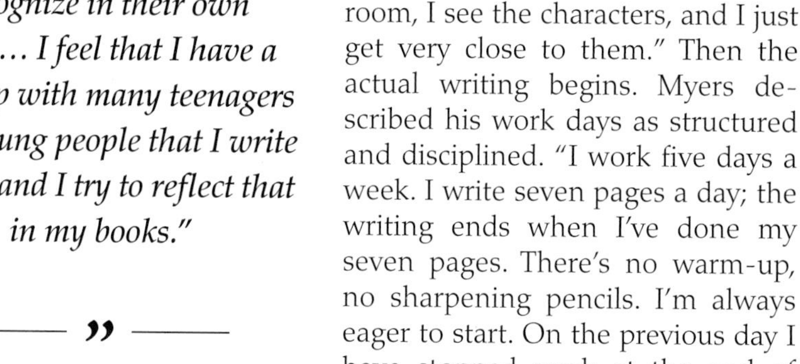

Once he has an idea in mind, the next step is to visualize the characters and settings for the story. "I cut out pictures of my characters and my wife puts them into a collage, which goes on the wall above the computer. When I walk into that room, I see the characters, and I just get very close to them." Then the actual writing begins. Myers described his work days as structured and disciplined. "I work five days a week. I write seven pages a day; the writing ends when I've done my seven pages. There's no warm-up, no sharpening pencils. I'm always eager to start. On the previous day I have stopped work at the end of seven pages, often in the middle of an idea, or a scene. The idea/scene has been on my mind since my last session and needs to be released onto the paper.... My advice to young writers is to read as much good literature as they can so they will experience the best uses of language and the most sensitive storytelling, and then train themselves to write on a regular basis.... Writers don't fail because they don't write well, they fail because they don't produce."

MARRIAGE AND FAMILY

Myers met his first wife, Joyce Smith, when they were both working for the U.S. Postal Service. They had two children, a daughter Karen, born in 1961, and a son Michael Dean, born in 1963. The marriage ended in divorce in 1970. Myers married Constance Brendel on June 19, 1973. They have one son, Christopher, born in 1974, who has illustrated many of Myers's books. The Myerses live in Jersey City, New Jersey.

Myers meeting with his readers on a visit to Detroit.

HOBBIES AND OTHER INTERESTS

For fun, Myers sometimes writes short stories or plays that he doesn't plan to publish. "My major hobby, writing, is also my job." He also enjoys doing crossword puzzles and is a self-taught flute player.

SELECTED WRITINGS

Fiction

Where Does the Day Go? 1969 (as Walter M. Myers)
The Dancers, 1972
The Dragon Takes a Wife, 1972
Fast Sam, Cool Clyde & Stuff, 1975
It Ain't All for Nothin', 1978
The Young Landlords, 1979
The Black Pearl and the Ghost: or, One Mystery After Another, 1980
The Golden Serpent, 1980
Hoops, 1981
The Legend of Tarik, 1981
Won't Know Till I Get There, 1982
The Nicholas Factor, 1983
Tales of a Dead King, 1983

Motown and Didi: A Love Story, 1984
The Outside Shot, 1984
Sweet Illusions, 1986
Crystal, 1987
Shadow of the Red Moon, 1987
Fallen Angels, 1988
Me, Mop, and the Moondance Kid, 1988
Scorpions, 1988
The Mouse Rap, 1990
Mop, Moondance, and the Nagasaki Knights, 1992
The Righteous Revenge of Artemis Bonner, 1992
Somewhere in the Darkness, 1992
The Glory Field, 1994
Slam!, 1996
Smiffy Blue: Ace Crime Detective: The Case of the Missing Ruby and Other Stories, 1996
Monster, 1999
145th Street: Short Stories, 2000
Patrol, 2001
Handbook for Boys, 2002
Three Swords for Granada, 2002
The Dream Bearer, 2003
Shooter, 2004
Autobiography of My Dead Brother, 2005
Street Love, 2006
Harlem Summer, 2007
What They Found: Love on 145th Street, 2007
Game, 2008
Sunrise Over Fallujah, 2008

Nonfiction

Now Is Your Time!: The African-American Struggle for Freedom, 1991
A Place Called Heartbreak: A Story of Vietnam, 1992
Young Martin's Promise, 1992
Malcolm X: By Any Means Necessary, 1993
Toussaint L'Ouverture: The Fight for Haiti's Freedom, 1996
Amistad: *A Long Road to Freedom*, 1998
At Her Majesty's Request: An African Princess in Victorian England, 1999
Malcolm X: A Fire Burning Brightly, 2000
Bad Boy: A Memoir, 2001
The Greatest: Muhammad Ali, 2001
I've Seen the Promised Land: The Life of Dr. Martin Luther King, Jr., 2003
Antarctica: Journeys to the South Pole, 2004

USS Constellation, 2004
The Harlem Hellfighters: When Pride Met Courage, 2006

Poetry

Brown Angels: An Album of Pictures and Verse, 1993
Remember Us Well: An Album of Pictures and Verse, 1993
Glorious Angels: A Celebration of Children, 1995
Harlem: A Poem, 1997
Angel to Angel: A Mother's Gift of Love, 1998
blues journey, 2001
Here in Harlem: Poems in Many Voices, 2004
Voices from Harlem, 2004
Jazz, 2006

SELECTED HONORS AND AWARDS

Council on Interracial Books for Children Award: 1968, for *Where Does the Day Go?*

Book of the Year designations (Child Study Association of America): 1972, for *The Dancers*

Notable Children's Books list (American Library Association): 1975, for *Fast Sam, Cool Clyde & Stuff*; 1978, for *It Ain't All for Nothin'*; 1979, for *The Young Landlords*; 1981, for *The Legend of Tarik*; 1988 (two awards), for *Me, Mop, and the Moondance Kid* and *Scorpions*; 1993 (two awards), for *Somewhere in the Darkness* and *Brown Angels: An Album of Pictures and Verse*; 1994, for *Malcolm X: By Any Means Necessary*; 1997, for *Toussaint L'Ouverture: The Fight for Haiti's Freedom*

Best Books for Young Adults (American Library Association): 1978, for *It Ain't All for Nothin'*; 1979, for *The Young Landlords*; 1981, for *The Legend of Tarik*; 1982, for *Hoops*; 1988 (two awards), for *Fallen Angels* and *Scorpions*; 1990, for *The Mouse Rap*; 1992, for *Now Is Your Time!: The African-American Struggle for Freedom*; 1993, for *Somewhere in the Darkness*; 1998, for *Harlem: A Poem*; 1994, for *Malcolm X: By Any Means Necessary*; 1995, for *The Glory Field*; 1997, for *Slam!*; 2000 (two awards), for *Monster* and *145th Street: Short Stories*

Coretta Scott King Book Award (American Library Association): 1980, for *The Young Landlords*; 1985, for *Motown and Didi: A Love Story*; 1989, for *Fallen Angels*; 1992, for *Now Is Your Time!: The African-American Struggle for Freedom*; 1997, for *Slam!*

National Endowment for the Arts Grant: 1982, 1989

Parents' Choice Award for Literature: 1982, for *Won't Know Till I Get There*; 1984, for *The Outside Shot*; 1988, for *Fallen Angels*

Myers worked with his son Christopher to celebrate the community of Harlem in this award-winning illustrated poetry collection.

Best Book of the Year (School Library Journal): 1988, for *Fallen Angels*; 1997, for *Malcolm X: A Fire Burning Brightly*

BookList Young Adult Editors' Choice (American Library Association): 1988, for *Fallen Angels*

MacDowell Fellowship: 1988

Boston Globe/Horn Book Award: 1992, for *Somewhere in the Darkness;* 1997, for *Harlem: A Poem*
ALAN Award (National Council of English Teachers): 1994, for outstanding contributions to literature
Margaret A. Edwards Award (American Library Association Young Adult Library Services Association): 1994 (4 awards), for *Hoops, Motown and Didi: A Love Story, Fallen Angels,* and *Scorpions*
Virginia Hamilton Literary Award: 1999
Michael L. Printz Award for Young Adult Literature (American Library Association): 2000, for *Monster*
Jane Addams Peace Award, 2003, for *Patrol*
Odyssey Award (American Library Association Association for Library Service to Children and Young Adult Library Services Association): 2008, for *Jazz*

FURTHER READING

Books

Bishop, Rudine S. *Presenting Walter Dean Myers,* 1990
Myers, Walter Dean. *Bad Boy: A Memoir,* 2001
Sickels, Amy. *Who Wrote That: Walter Dean Myers,* 2008
Silvey, Anita. *Children's Books and Their Creators,* 1995

Periodicals

Black Issues Book Review, Nov./Dec. 2005, p.39
Book Report, Sep.-Oct. 2001, p.42
Booklist, Feb. 15, 2000, p.1101
Current Events, Apr. 2, 2007, p.6
Jet, Apr. 28, 2008
New York Times, May 22, 1994, p.NJ1
Publisher's Weekly, July 20, 1992, p.217; Mar. 22, 1999, p.45
Reading Today, Oct.-Nov. 2007, p.40
Washington Post, Dec. 9, 1989, p.C1
Washington Post Book World, May 13, 2001, p.3
World Literature Today, May/June 2007, p.63
Writing, Feb./Mar. 2004, p.10
USA Today, Apr. 24, 2008, p.D7

Online Articles

http://www.bookpage.com/0102bp/walter_dean_myers.html (BookPage, "In the Ring with Walter Dean Myers," Feb. 2001)

http://www.harpercollins.com/author/browse.aspx
(Harper Collins, "Author: Walter Dean Myers," undated)
http://www.kidsreads.com/authors/authors.asp
(Kidsreads, "Author: Walter Dean Myers," undated)
http://content.scholastic.com/browse/contributor.jsp?id=3437
(Scholastic, "Walter Dean Myers Biography," undated)
http://www.teenreads.com/authors/index.asp
(Teenreads, "Author Profile: Walter Dean Myers," undated)

ADDRESS

Walter Dean Myers
HarperCollins Children's Books
1350 Avenue of the Americas
New York NY 10019

WORLD WIDE WEB SITE

http://www.walterdeanmyers.net

Michelle Obama 1964-

American Lawyer and Administrator
First Lady of the United States

BIRTH

Michelle Obama was born Michelle LaVaughan Robinson on January 17, 1964, in Chicago, Illinois. She was the second child of Fraser Robinson III, a Chicago city pump operator, and Marian (Shields) Robinson, a homemaker and secretary. Her older brother, Craig Robinson, is her only sibling; he gave up a high-paying career as an investment banker to start a new career as a basketball coach. In 2008 he became head coach of the Oregon State University Beavers.

YOUTH

Obama grew up on the South Side of Chicago, where her family shared the top floor of her great-aunt's bungalow. They didn't have a lot of money, but they made the most of what they had: the family used paneling to split their apartment's living room into separate bedrooms for Michelle and her brother Craig. Obama learned the value of hard work from the example of her parents. Her mother stayed home with the kids until they entered high school, then took a job as a secretary. Fraser Robinson had been diagnosed with multiple sclerosis, a disease that attacks the nerves, before he was even 30 years old. Nevertheless, he went to work every day, even if he had to get up earlier or use a walker to get there on time. Inspired by her parents, young Michelle learned to read before kindergarten, studied hard in school, and skipped the second grade. In sixth grade she took science classes at a local college, hoping she might become a pediatrician some day. She spent many hours practicing the piano and writing stories, but she described herself as "just a typical South Side little black girl. Not a whole lot of money. Going to the circus once a year was a big deal. Getting pizza on Friday was a treat. Summers were long and fun."

"

Obama once described herself as "just a typical South Side little black girl. Not a whole lot of money. Going to the circus once a year was a big deal. Getting pizza on Friday was a treat. Summers were long and fun."

"

Obama attended Chicago public schools and earned a place into the Whitney M. Young Magnet School for gifted and talented students. She had to travel three hours by bus and train each day, but she was determined to make the most of the opportunity. She was class treasurer and participated in choir, talent shows, and school plays. Although she was athletic and enjoyed competing against her brother, she avoided organized sports because she wanted to avoid the stereotypes that can come with being a tall woman (she is 5′11″). She studied hard, earned all A's, and won a place in the National Honor Society. When her brother earned a basketball scholarship to an Ivy League university, she told herself she could succeed there too. After all, she remembered, "My mother always taught me to work hard to achieve my dreams and to never let anyone tell me that I couldn't do something."

EDUCATION

Obama graduated from Whitney M.Young Magnet School in 1981 and followed her brother Craig to Princeton University, a prestigious Ivy League school in New Jersey. At a school where less than one percent of the students were African American, she sometimes felt like an outsider—her freshman roommate's mother even requested that her daughter be moved. Obama got involved with the Third World Center, an academic and cultural group that supported minority students, and ran a day care they sponsored that included afterschool tutoring. She majored in sociology with a minor in African-American studies and produced a senior thesis examining how the Princeton experience had affected black graduates. She earned her Bachelor of Arts (BA) degree cum laude with departmental honors in 1985. She decided to attend law school and earned a spot at Harvard Law School, another Ivy League institution. There she worked in the Harvard Legal Aid Bureau, assisting low-income tenants with housing cases. She earned her Juris Doctor or Doctor of Law (JD) degree in 1988.

CAREER HIGHLIGHTS

Beginning Her Career in Law

After graduating from Harvard in 1988, Obama took a job with the prestigious Chicago law firm of Sidley & Austin. She served as an associate attorney and specialized in copyright and trademark cases, disputes over who owns rights to ideas. She didn't find the work very interesting, she later noted. "I didn't see a whole lot of people who were just thrilled to be there. I met people who thought this was a good life. But were people waking up just bounding out of bed to get to work? No." Still, with many student loans to pay off, her job at the law firm provided a good paycheck. As she later admitted, "the idea of making more money than both your parents combined ever made is one you don't walk away from."

At Sidley & Austin she first met Barack Obama when she was assigned to advise him during his summer internship there in 1988. At first, she resisted his invitations to go out, thinking it wouldn't be appropriate because of their work relationship. Besides, "I was more focused on my plan," she said. "I had made this proclamation to my mother the summer I met Barack,'I'm not worrying about dating … I'm going to focus on me." His persistence, and her co-workers' reassurance that they did not disapprove, eventually led to their first date. Michelle soon realized that, although they had grown up in very different environments, she and Barack shared many of the same values: hard work, respect for others, and a commitment to telling the truth. One day she was watching him speak to a group of

Michelle and Barack Obama on their wedding day, October 1992.

church women. "He was able to articulate a vision that resonated with people, that was real," she remembered. "And right then and there, I decided this guy was special. The authenticity you see is real, and that's why I fell in love with him." A friendly game of one-on-one basketball with her brother secured her family's approval, and they eventually got engaged.

In 1991, Michelle Obama suffered two losses that caused her to reassess her life. First, her father died unexpectedly of complications from multiple sclerosis. Only a few months later, a close college friend died of cancer at the age of 25. "It made me realize that I could die tomorrow," she recalled. "I had to ask myself, 'Is this how I want to spend my time?' I knew I would never feel a sense of passion or joy about the law." She decided to leave her law firm and take a pay cut to work as a public servant. In 1991 she became an assistant in the office of Chicago Mayor Richard M. Daley. "I needed to consider what I really cared about, which was work that had a community-based feel, using my education to benefit others," she said. It meant "a temporary financial setback, but in the end, when you're living your dream, the economic stability comes."

Obama decided to leave the law firm to work in public service. "I needed to consider what I really cared about, which was work that had a community-based feel, using my education to benefit others," she said. It meant "a temporary financial setback, but in the end, when you're living your dream, the economic stability comes."

"

Much of Obama's job in the mayor's office involved helping develop programs for the community, especially lower-income residents like the people she grew up with. She contributed to programs intended to decrease infant mortality, provide afterschool activities for kids, and promote immunization through mobile health facilities. In 1992, she became an assistant commissioner of planning and development for the city of Chicago. She earned a reputation as a troubleshooter who could work with different people to resolve problems quickly.

That same year, in 1992, she married Barack Obama. They held their wedding reception at a cultural center that had once excluded African Americans from their facilities. They went on to have two daughters, Malia and Natasha (Sasha).

Working with the Community

At the suggestion of her husband, Michelle Obama changed jobs again in 1993. He was on the board of Public Allies, an AmeriCorps program that

Obama worked in a variety of positions that combined law, administration, community advocacy, and service to others. At the University of Chicago, shown here, she worked as associate dean of student services & director of the university community service center. Credit: University of Chicago.

prepares youth for public service. The program was starting a Chicago chapter, and Barack Obama suggested that his wife serve as executive director. (He left the board after she was hired to avoid any potential conflicts of interest.) It meant another pay cut, but Michelle Obama had become frustrated by the slow pace of city bureaucracy. The new job "sounded risky and just out there," she later said. "But for some reason it spoke to me. This was the first time I said,'This is what I say I care about. Right here. And I will have to run it.'"

As someone who had grown up on Chicago's South Side but gone on to the Ivy League, Obama had a unique perspective. "We had people who had just graduated high school taking internships alongside people who had just graduated from Harvard," she noted. "I learned that you can go to the best school in the country and still not realize what you can do to help the community." She would later call her job at Public Allies "by far the best thing I've done in my professional career. It was the first thing that was mine, and I was responsible for every aspect of it." After three years of working 60-hour weeks, Obama had established a strong program.

Obama questioned her husband's involvement in politics. "But each and every time I confronted that doubt in my own mind," she recalled, "I started thinking beyond myself.... I started thinking about the type of person that I want to see in politics. And that always turned out to be a guy like Barack."

In 1996 Obama brought her experience working with youth to the University of Chicago, taking a position as associate dean of student services and director of the university community service center. She helped the university develop a community service program that tried to get students involved in the local area. That same year, her husband ran for the Illinois State Senate. Michelle Obama wasn't thrilled with the idea and told her husband, "I married you because you're cute and you're smart, but this is the dumbest thing you could have ever asked me to do." She has said that she was cynical about politics and wondered whether it was really the best use of her husband's time. "But each and every time I confronted that doubt in my own mind," she recalled, "I started thinking beyond myself.... I started thinking about the type of person that I want to see in politics. And that always turned out to be a guy like Barack." He won that election and was re-elected in 1998, the same year their first child was born. In 2000 he made his first bid for national office. He ran in the Democratic primary for a seat in the U.S. House of Representatives, but lost in the primary. He returned to the Illinois Senate in 2002.

Michelle Obama has spoken frequently of challenges she faced as a working mom. "Every other month [since] I've had children I've struggled with the notion of 'Am I being a good parent? Can I stay home? Should I stay home? How do I balance it all?'" she admitted. "I have gone back and forth every year about whether I should work." When interviewing for a job at the University of Chicago Hospitals in 2002, for example, she hadn't been able to find a babysitter for her new baby daughter, so she brought her along in a stroller. Although she wanted to be home for her girls, she enjoyed the sense of independence and self-worth that come from a job well done. "Work is rewarding," she stated. "I love losing myself in a set of problems that have nothing to do with my husband and children. Once you've tasted that, it's hard to walk away."

Still, with her husband often away in the State Senate or campaigning, Obama was left to manage the household and kids by herself much of the time. She felt resentful, until she finally came to terms with the demands of her husband's political career and accepted that help didn't have to come from him. "I spent a lot of time expecting my husband to fix things, but then I came to realize that he was there in the ways he could be," she observed. Instead, she asked herself, "How do I structure my world so that it works for me and I'm not trying to get him to be what I think he should be?" She got help from friends, from neighbors, and especially from her mother. She is not shy about sharing these early difficulties with people. "I think every couple struggles with these issues," she said. "People don't tell you how much kids change things.... If we can talk about it, we can help each other."

Becoming a Political Asset

In 2002, Obama took a job with the University of Chicago Medical Center as executive director of community affairs. The University of Chicago and its affiliated hospitals are considered among the best in the country, but many local residents feel shut out. "I grew up five minutes from the university and never once went on campus," she stated. "All the buildings have their backs to the community. The university didn't think kids like me existed, and I certainly didn't want anything to do with that place." Obama began several programs that reached out to poorer neighborhoods near the hospital. As a result, the number of hospital employees serving in community clinics increased five times, and the number of volunteers coming in from the community multiplied four times. In addition, she also contributed to the hospital's efforts to improve staff diversity, helping to recruit minority doctors to the hospital.

Meanwhile, Barack Obama's political career was taking off. But when he was elected to the U.S. Senate in 2004, the Obamas decided that Michelle and the girls would stay in Chicago. "I have a big village here," she commented at the time, referring to the adage that it takes a village to raise a child. "Unless it was absolutely necessary, we felt it would just be good to stay close to our base. It's proven to be a smart move, and he's come to understand the wisdom of my plan." Because he arranged his schedule to be home Thursday through Sunday, the family often saw him more often than when he was serving and campaigning as a state senator. Later that year Barack Obama began to develop a broader national profile when he gave a keynote speech at the Democratic National Convention that was widely praised. His book *Dreams from My Father* hit the bestseller list, bringing the family extra financial security, and people began talking of a possible presidential run in the future.

"Every other month [since] I've had children I've struggled with the notion of 'Am I being a good parent? Can I stay home? Should I stay home? How do I balance it all?'" Obama acknowledged. "I have gone back and forth every year about whether I should work." But she also said that "Work is rewarding. I love losing myself in a set of problems that have nothing to do with my husband and children. Once you've tasted that, it's hard to walk away."

In the meantime, Michelle Obama was promoted to vice-president of community and external affairs at the University of Chicago Medical Center in 2005, a promotion that also brought her a six-figure salary. Her new responsibilities included working on a contracting system that would encourage the hiring of more women- and minority-owned businesses. Obama also started a program to get local residents to use health clinics instead of emergency rooms. She felt this was important because, according to medical studies, poor residents who wait to go to the emergency room for medical treatment often become sicker than those who have access to primary care clinics. Obama created mobile units to bring medical services for children into poorer neighborhoods and increased volunteer participation in programs. She earned praise from community leaders for her management style. She didn't just try to make things easier for the hospital, but showed real concern for the public's needs as well. In 2005, she and her family also moved into a $1.6 million home on Chicago's South Side. "I'm in the community where I grew up, where I live, and it feels like it's all coming full circle," she said.

At the same time, Barack Obama was getting more political support for a possible presidential run. In 2006 he published another bestselling book, *The Audacity of Hope,* and the following year he announced his candidacy to become president. By now he had earned his wife's full support. "Barack is special, and I'm willing to share him…. I'm willing to share the girls," she said. "If we can have better schools and health care and help moms who are struggling and get back on track internationally, then all this? Big deal. I can handle it."

MALIA AND SASHA OBAMA

Malia Obama was born on July 4, 1998, in Chicago, Illinois. She is the more serious of the Obama girls; her mom calls her "focused." She attends Sidwell Friends School and plays soccer and tennis. She also has taken dance, drama, and piano lessons. She enjoys photography and could be seen taking pictures during the Inauguration. She lists ice cream as her favorite food, and enjoyed reading the Harry Potter series together with her dad. She has some allergies, which is why her family was careful in choosing a pet dog for the family. Malia says she would like to become an actress when she grows up, but she plans to get a good education in case it doesn't work out.

Natasha Obama was born on June 10, 2001, in Chicago, Illinois. She's known as Sasha. During the 2008 campaign, she often could be seen waving to crowds; her mom calls her a ham. She attends Sidwell Friends School and joined the basketball team so she could share the sport with her father. She has also taken gymnastics, tap dance, tennis, and piano lessons. Sasha is a big fan of the Jonas Brothers and Hannah Montana, and she would like to be a singer or dancer when she grows up.

Until their father was elected president, the Obama girls spent most of their time in Chicago, going to school and spending time with friends. When school was out, they might accompany their parents on a campaign trip; otherwise, they kept to their daily routine with their mother or grandmother. They had to leave all their friends and activities behind when the Obamas moved from Chicago to Washington DC. They moved into the White House on January 21, 2009, the day their father was inaugurated. They had a sleepover that night, with a scavenger hunt to help introduce them to their new home. As a bonus, their favorite band, the Jonas Brothers, stopped by for a visit.

Living in the White House has many other benefits. It has its own swimming pool, bowling alley, tennis and basketball courts, and movie theater. The girls got to redecorate their rooms, and they made room for Bo, the new dog they were promised during the campaign. Best of all, because they now live in the same building as their dad's office, they get to have dinner together as a family every night. Despite all these bonuses, the Obama girls still have to do chores. They set and clear the dinner table, make their own beds, do homework, practice the piano, and clean up their play areas. Bedtime is at 8:30, unless they want an extra half hour to read, and they have to get themselves up and ready for school. As their mom explained: "I want the kids to be treated like children, not little princesses."

As the campaign got underway, Michelle Obama reduced her work hours at the University of Chicago to help her husband campaign. She made speaking appearances by herself—usually without notes—and often drew crowds in the thousands. Although she traveled all over the country, she always tried to be home for her daughters' bedtime. "You've got to make trade-offs in life," she said. "I'm okay with that. I've come to realize I am sacrificing one set of things in my life for something else potentially really positive." In the end, she noted, "the little sacrifice we have to make is nothing compared to the possibility of what we could do if this catches on." Of course, she added, she couldn't have done any of it without the help of her mother, who retired from her secretarial job to watch the two girls.

> *"In our generation, we were just taught that if you know who you are, then what somebody calls you is just so irrelevant.... If I wilted every time someone in my life mischaracterized me or called me a bad name, I would have never finished Princeton, would have never gone to Harvard, and wouldn't be sitting here with [Barack Obama]," she said. "My view on this stuff is I'm just trying to be myself, trying to be as authentic as I can be," she said. "I can't pretend to be somebody else."*

The Road to the White House

Michelle Obama's style on the campaign trail was forthright, down-to-earth, and sometimes controversial. In February 2008, she was speaking of the number of new voters getting involved in the political process when she said, "For the first time in my adult life, I am proud of my country." She said her words were taken out of context—she had always been proud of America, but not of a political system that once denied rights to some citizens. But critics still questioned her patriotism and tried to stereotype her as an angry black woman. Obama didn't let the criticism bother her, a lesson she says she learned as a girl. "In our generation, we were just taught that if you know who you are, then what somebody calls you is just so irrelevant.... If I wilted every time someone in my life mischaracterized me or called me a bad name, I would have never finished Princeton, would have never gone to Harvard, and wouldn't be sitting here with [Barack Obama]." She kept going on the campaign trail, making appearances on national television and dealing with any con-

President Barack Obama and First Lady Michelle Obama wave to the crowd as they make their way down Pennsylvania Avenue during the 2009 presidential inaugural parade in Washington DC, January 2009.

"

"The truth is, I'm not supposed to be here, standing here," Obama said. "I'm a statistical oddity. Black girl, brought up on the South Side of Chicago. Was I supposed to go to Princeton? No.... They said maybe Harvard Law was too much for me to reach for. But I went, I did fine....

"

troversy head-on. "My view on this stuff is I'm just trying to be myself, trying to be as authentic as I can be," she said. "I can't pretend to be somebody else." Many people were charmed by her style and confidence, and as the public got to know her better, her approval ratings went up.

In August 2008, Michelle Obama spoke at the Democratic National Convention, where her husband would be officially nominated as the Democratic candidate for president. She gave a heartfelt speech, sharing the story of her life and her belief "that each of us—no matter what our age or background or walk of life—each of us has something to contribute to the life of this nation." On November 4, 2008, Barack Obama was elected president, becoming the first African American to achieve the office. For Michelle Obama, it wasn't just her husband's historic victory that made the campaign worthwhile. "It has been a blessing for us to have this opportunity to spend this year traveling the country," she noted. "We've been in almost every state in this nation—in people's homes, in their kitchens, in their community centers—and just having the opportunity to be reminded of how decent the American people are and how our values are so closely linked, that gives me hope."

As the Obamas got ready to move into the White House, Michelle Obama said that her primary focus was on making the transition easy for her daughters. She resigned her position at the University of Chicago Medical Center and invited her mother, Marian Robinson, to join them in Washington. She started looking for new schools for the girls in Washington. She was eager to make a home for her family in the White House, but she also wanted to make it more open to the public. "We feel privileged, and we feel a responsibility to make it feel like the people's house," she said. "We have the good fortune to sleep here, but this house belongs to America."

First Lady of the United States

Barack Obama was sworn in as the 44th president in January 2009. As he became president, Michelle Obama became first lady. This is a position with no set duties; each president's wife has molded the role to fit her concerns. Traditionally, first ladies have one or two issues they plan to promote, and Obama said she wanted to bring attention to work-family issues (especially for military families) and increasing public service among young people.

The new First Lady quickly made good on her promises to begin working for the American people. She spent time volunteering, putting together care packages for members of the military. She made visits to cabinet-level agencies to familiarize herself with Washington politics and say thank you. She also dropped in on local schools, church groups, and community centers, including some time volunteering at a soup kitchen. "[Washington DC] is our community now," she said. "It's our home." As for opening the White House, she hosted tours of the White House kitchens for local cuisine students, sponsored a "bring your child to work" day, and offered a "girls' night in" with movies for secretaries and staff alike. She invited the media to watch as she established an organic kitchen garden, complete with beehive, and had a play set installed on the White House lawn. She had come into the White House with the highest favorability ratings of any incoming first lady since 1980, at 46%; after three months, her approval ratings were up to 76%, including 60% of Republicans.

The first lady has also found a new role as fashion icon, which she has found surprising. Obama is tall and fit and enjoys looking her best, but she didn't expect people to pay that much attention to her clothing. While she does enjoy occasional designer outfits, her fashion choices are often practical, and many of her outfits have come from retail chains like J. Crew. "First and foremost, I wear what I love," she explained. "That's what women have to focus on: what makes them happy and what makes them feel comfortable and beautiful. If I can have any impact, I want women to feel good about themselves and have fun with fashion." She charmed the European press during a spring 2009 visit, although that may have had less to do with her fashion sense and more with the genuine warmth and emotion she displayed when talking with underprivileged students in London.

"I know that all I can do is be the best me that I can. And live life with some gusto. Giving back is a big part of that. How am I going to share this experience with the American people? I'm always thinking about that."

The first lady can take on a lot of different roles, as shown here: working with children to create a White House garden; speaking to elected leaders and others about important issues; and advocating for education while visiting a local bilingual school.

For Michelle Obama, life in the White House has been more than she ever dreamed. Best of all, she said, "We have dinner as a family together every night, and Barack, when he's not traveling, tucks the girls in. We haven't had that kind of time together for [years], so that explains a lot [of] why we all feel so good in this space." She is happy to be a partner in her husband's political career, and he supports her in return. "He's my biggest cheerleader, as a mother, as a wife and as a career person," she said. "He is always telling me how great I'm doing. That helps keep you going when you realize that you have someone who appreciates all the hard work that you are doing." As for finding her new role challenging, she said, "I have very full days. When we're done, I can structure a more formal career if that's where I choose to go."

Right now, Obama is satisfied to serve the country as a first lady and as a role model. "The truth is, I'm not supposed to be here, standing here," she said. "I'm a statistical oddity. Black girl, brought up on the South Side of Chicago. Was I supposed to go to Princeton? No.... They said maybe Harvard Law was too much for me to reach for. But I went, I did fine." In the end, she remarked, "I know that all I can do is be the best me that I can. And live life with some gusto. Giving back is a big part of that. How am I going to share this experience with the American people? I'm always thinking about that."

MARRIAGE AND FAMILY

Robinson married Barack Obama on October 18, 1992. Their first daughter, Malia Ann, was born July 4, 1998; their second daughter, Natasha (nicknamed Sasha), was born on June 10, 2001. After moving into the White House in 2009, the family added a pet, a Portuguese water dog called Bo, to the family. They still maintain a home in Chicago's Hyde Park neighborhood and plan to return there after President Obama's time in office is over.

HOBBIES AND OTHER INTERESTS

As a working mom, Obama has little free time to indulge in hobbies. She makes room in her schedule to work out at least four times a week; she says that fitness "has become even more important as I've had children, because I'm also thinking about how I'm modeling health to my daughters." Otherwise, she enjoys spending time with her family and friends, especially watching movies and playing board games together.

HONORS AND AWARDS

Woman of the Year (*Essence magazine*): 2008

Books

Brophy, David Bergen. *Michelle Obama: Meet the First Lady,* 2009 (young adult)
Colbert, David. *Michelle Obama: An American Story,* 2009 (young adult)

Periodicals

Chicago Magazine, Feb. 2009, p.50
Chicago Sun-Times, Sep. 1, 2004; Apr. 22, 2007; July 9, 2008
Chicago Tribune, Feb. 26, 2009
Current Biography Yearbook, 2008
Daily Princetonian, Dec. 7, 2005
Ebony, Mar. 2006, p.58; Feb. 2007, p.52; Sep. 2008, p.72
Essence, Sep. 2007, p.200; Sep. 2008, p.150; Jan. 2009
Good Housekeeping, Nov. 2008, p.144
Maclean's, Apr. 20, 2009, p.24
People, June 18, 2007, p.118; July 23, 2008; Aug. 4, 2008, p.50; Feb. 2, 2009, p.69; Mar. 9, 2009, p.112
New York, Mar. 23, 2009, p.26
New York Times, Aug. 26, 2007, p.A1; Jan. 20, 2009, p.A1; Feb. 8. 2009, p.A18
New Yorker, May 31, 2004; Mar. 10, 2008, p.88
Newsweek, Jan. 29. 2007, p.40; Feb. 25, 2008, p.26
O, the Oprah Magazine, Sep. 2005, p.22; Nov. 2007, p.286; Apr. 2009, p.140
U.S. News & World Report, Feb. 11, 2008, p. 14
Us Weekly, Nov. 24, 2008, p.46
USA Today, July 5, 2008
Vogue, Sep. 2007, p.774; Mar. 2009, p.428
Washington Post, May 11, 2007, p.A1

Online Articles

http://abcnews.go.com/GMA/Vote2008/story?id=5643969&page=1
(ABC News, "Who Is Michelle Obama," Aug. 25, 2008)
http://www.ebonyjet.com/ebony/articles/index.aspx?id=8650
(Ebony, "The Real Michelle Obama," Aug. 6, 2008)
http://www.essence.com/news_entertainment/news/articles/michelleobama besidebarack
(Essence, "Michelle Obama, Beside Barack," Nov. 5, 2008)
http://topics.nytimes.com/top/reference/timestopics/people/o/michelle_obama/index.html
(New York Times, "Times Topics," multiple articles, various dates)
http://topics.newsweek.com/people/politics/obama-administration/
(Newsweek, "Michelle Obama," multiple articles, various dates)

http://www.pbs.org/newshour/bb/politics/jan-june09/firstlady_03-12.html (PBS, "Michelle Obama Works to Define Agenda as First Lady," Mar. 21, 2009)
http://www.time.com/time/politics/article/0,8599,1900067,00.html (Time, "The Meaning of Michelle," May 21, 2009)

ADDRESS

Michelle Obama
The White House
1600 Pennsylvania Ave. NW
Washington, D.C. 20500

WORLD WIDE WEB SITES

http://www.whitehouse.gov
http://www.barackobama.com/about/michelle_obama

Omarion 1984-

American Singer and Actor
Creator of the Solo Records *O* and *21*, and *Face Off* (with Bow Wow)

BIRTH

Omari Ishmael Grandberry, who later adopted the professional name Omarion, was born on November 12, 1984, in Inglewood, California. He is the son of Leslie Burrell and Trent Grandberry. His parents were both teenagers at the time of his birth and did not stay together. Remaining with his mother, who worked as a hairstylist, Omarion was raised in the Los Angeles area. He has five siblings, three from his mother's side of the family and two from his father's side. Growing up, he was closest to his younger brother O'Ryan, who has also established a career in the music business.

YOUTH

Omarion's mother was still in school when he was born, so his grandmother, or "Nana," played a big part in raising him. His aunts and great-grandmother also pitched in to baby-sit and help out in other ways. Omarion notes in his autobiography, *O*, that "we were actually a really, really close family," adding that "I couldn't have been raised in a more loving and supportive household." He accompanied his great-grandmother to church, although he later confessed that he wasn't very interested in the religious message while young. But he did enjoy hearing the choir and singing along on sacred hymns. His mother encouraged him to think about a career in entertainment. He got his first taste of the business when he appeared in local theater productions and television commercials for McDonald's and Kellogg's Corn Pops cereal. He later tried his hand at being a rapper, working with a crew called the Wild Kingdom.

"Everybody was carrying weapons," Omarion said about his teen years in Los Angeles. "Every other person was on the corner slinging dope.... Everybody seemed to be angry."

Omarion's father, Trent Grandberry, didn't play a large role in raising his son. Trent began serving time in prison shortly after his son was born, and the two didn't spend time together until later in Omarion's childhood, when they developed a friendly relationship. Though he didn't have a strong male role model within his family, Omarion got some helpful guidance from others. One such mentor was his boxing coach at the local recreation center, who talked with him about responsible behavior and developing self-confidence.

Less positive influences were entering Omarion's life by the time he reached his teenage years, however. The area of Los Angeles where he lived was a violent place, filled with gang activity and other dangers. "Everybody was carrying weapons," he recalled. "Every other person was on the corner slinging dope.... Everybody seemed to be angry." Partly for self-protection, he fell in with a group of kids in his neighborhood that became known as the Under Age Criminals (UAC), which evolved into a gang. Despite their name, the UAC didn't get involved in criminal activity, but there were plenty of fights. Grandberry and his friends considered arming themselves with guns for more serious gang-banger showdowns.

Fortunately, he had retained his interest in music, which ended up providing a way out of the UAC. Through high school classes, he had the opportunity to study voice and piano and to learn the basics of recording. When he came to realize that he could have an impact on others through his abilities as a singer, he began to focus his energy there rather than spending time with the gang. "My decision to step back from the Under Age Criminal vortex when I did changed my life," he wrote. "I could've really hurt someone out there—and I could've gotten hurt."

"It was like a transforming moment," Omarion claimed about his first impromptu performance with B2K. "I felt a flood of positive energy swamping me.... A new door had opened, and I was now looking into the future. I liked what I was seeing."

EDUCATION

Attending public schools in Inglewood and Los Angeles, Omarion found his elementary school to be an encouraging place that had a positive influence on him. He was less enthusiastic about his junior high and high school, but he generally kept up with his assignments and earned average grades. He spent most of his high school years at Alexander Hamilton High School in Los Angeles. During his senior year, as his career took off, he studied with a tutor.

CAREER HIGHLIGHTS

On December 31, 1999, shortly after he turned 15, Omarion accompanied his aunt to a New Year's Eve party. It proved to be an exciting night, partly because it marked the arrival of the year 2000 and the new millennium, but more importantly because it marked the starting point of his professional music career.

The party that night took place at the home of entertainment manager Chris Stokes, and it was there that Omarion was introduced to a group of three other young men—Dreux "Lil' Fizz" Frederic, De Mario "Raz-B" Thornton, and Jarell "J-Boog" Houston. The three had been trying to form a musical group but lacked a lead singer. Stokes thought Omarion might

B2K's first CD came out in 2001.

be the person to fill the opening and so encouraged all four to try some dance steps together in front of the partygoers. "It was like a transforming moment," Omarion recalled of their impromptu performance. "I felt a flood of positive energy swamping me.... A new door had opened, and I was now looking into the future. I liked what I was seeing." Under the supervision of Stokes, the four young men began serious rehearsals two days later, and their manager named the act in honor of the occasion when they first came together: B2K—the Boys of the New Millennium.

Though the group got its start in the early days of 2000, it took two years of hard work before it found success. During that time, the members spent countless hours honing their singing and dancing at the rehearsal studio of Stokes's management company, The Ultimate Group. Omarion found the process very challenging. "Let me tell you, it's hard to get in sync with three other people," he explained about their dance choreography. "Add singing and harmony to the mix, and that's a lot of precision to master." The four members became very good friends as they improved their skills. Omarion has revealed that he does not like to spend time by himself, and he took comfort in being part of a group of performers. In fact, B2K became a sort of second family for him. "We were like a band of brothers," he explained. "Unimaginably tight." The young musicians received valuable advice from the members of IMX—another act managed by Stokes—which had already scored a number of hit songs. Omarion formed an especially close bond with IMX member Marques Houston. In fact, the two sometimes claim to be brothers, though they are not biologically related.

It took two years of hard work before B2K found success, with countless hours spent at the rehearsal studio honing their singing and dancing. "Let me tell you, it's hard to get in sync with three other people," Omarion said about their dance choreography. "Add singing and harmony to the mix, and that's a lot of precision to master."

Once it had refined its act, B2K sought a record deal. The group was turned down by many companies, but its fortunes turned when it landed an audition with Epic. After seeing the boys perform just one number, label executives offered a recording deal, and B2K soon headed into the studio to begin work on its first sessions.

Teen Sensations

In September 2001, the band's debut single, "Uh Huh," was released. It wasn't an immediate smash, but by the end of the year it began to receive heavy airplay. It went on to be the best-selling rhythm-and-blues song of 2002. "Uh Huh" was followed by the successful singles "Gots Ta Be" and

Omarion appeared in the movie You Got Served *along with the other members of B2K.*

"Why I Love You," all of which were part of the band's first album, *B2K*. More hits were included on a second full-length 2002 release, *Pandemonium*, including the song "Bump, Bump, Bump," which went all the way to No. 1 on the pop charts. The band members' popularity was fueled by their image as teen heartthrobs, and they put a lot of effort into presenting a style that would appeal to young music fans, particularly females. "We worked out a lot and stayed in shape," Omarion wrote in his autobiography. "We were throwing out the young, hip, sexy vibe, and it was working."

B2K hit the road to promote its music as soon as the first single was released, visiting radio stations and record stores and later launching its full-scale "Scream" concert tours. The band members heard a lot of screaming. By the spring of 2002, B2K had become one of the hottest "boy bands" in the industry, with throngs of enthusiastic fans flocking to its appearances. "The fans, especially the girls, were getting more and more intense with every show," Omarion recalled. On several occasions, riots broke out within crowds intent on seeing the group, and the members narrowly escaped from some terrifying incidents where crazed mobs threatened to overwhelm them.

Looking to expand into new territory, B2K and its manager, Stokes, began to consider film projects. In the summer of 2003, they began production on *You Got Served*, which Stokes wrote and directed. The film tells the story of a street-dance crew in Los Angeles and included roles for all of the group members. Initially, Omarion was going to take a supporting part while Jarell "J-Boog" Houston would play one of the leads. Before the cameras rolled, however, Stokes decided Omarion was the best choice for one of the costar roles, with the other lead going to Marques Houston. For Omarion, his promotion to leading man fit well with his long-term career plans to be an all-around entertainer who mixes acting with music. When released in early 2004, *You Got Served* received mixed reviews but did well in theaters.

The Breakup

B2K was at the height of its popularity in the final months of 2003, headlining the "Scream Tour III" and looking forward to the release of the film. "We were one of the hottest acts in pop music," Omarion said of that period. "We had it all." The group's time in the spotlight came to a sudden end, however. Tensions within the organization had been brewing for months, and matters came to a head at the end of the year. The final B2K show took place on December 28, 2003. Shortly thereafter, Lil' Fizz, Raz-B, and J-Boog went public with their complaints about Chris Stokes, and they also had unkind things to say about Omarion. Though the act had two concerts scheduled in early 2004, Omarion ended up playing them as a solo act. B2K was no more.

The reasons for the split have been debated by those involved. In their statements, Lil' Fizz, Raz-B, and J-Boog put most of the blame on Stokes, claiming that he failed to pay them for their work on "Scream Tour III." In addition, Raz-B initially claimed that he had been sexually molested by the B2K manager, but he later retracted his statement and publicly apologized to Stokes. Omarion, who has remained with Stokes's management company, defended his manager and said that there was no wrongdoing. Initially, he felt that the breakup came about because the members wanted to pursue their own professional interests. "It's not about me leaving or them leaving," he said in 2004. "It's about us growing up and wanting to do our own thing." He later attributed the band's demise to "inner turmoil," and "personal issues" without offering many specific details. In addition, he has noted that the other members of the band may have resented the increasing attention he had been receiving, particularly since he had taken one of the central roles in *You Got Served*.

"

"It's not about me leaving or them leaving," Omarion stressed about the breakup of B2K. "It's about us growing up and wanting to do our own thing."

Whatever the cause, the end of B2K had a lasting effect on Omarion, and his relations with the other members of the group have been stormy ever since. At times, Omarion has seemed upbeat about his former band mates, and he declared in 2007 that "our friendship is back." But a year later, he expressed dismay about the disrespect the others were showing him. Meanwhile, Lil' Fizz, Raz-B, and J-Boog have continued to accuse Stokes of improprieties.

Solo Stardom

Following the B2K split, Omarion set about establishing himself as a solo artist. His debut album, *O*, was released in February 2005, a little more than a year after the breakup. It shot to No. 1 on the Billboard 200 album chart, a feat that B2K had never achieved. Most critics were positive about the album, and many echoed the thoughts of *People* reviewer Chuck Arnold, who remarked that "Omarion stands strong on his own." The singer saw his debut as a way to separate himself from the "boy band"

Omarion's recent work includes O *and* Face Off, *his joint CD with Bow Wow.*

image of B2K and to present himself as a grownup artist. "Before we would talk about love, but we were only 16," he noted. "Now I can talk more about spending some real quality time with a young lady, and people can really feel what I'm saying."

Maturity was also the theme of his second solo project, *21*—a reference to Omarion's age during the period when the album was written and recorded. Again, he hit No. 1 on the album chart and earned favorable comparisons to such artists as Justin Timberlake, Michael Jackson, and Stevie Wonder. In keeping with the idea of greater responsibility, Omarion served as the executive producer of *21* and took a more assertive role in its production than he had on previous albums. Nonetheless, he still sought help from a variety of talented producers, including Timbaland, who oversaw "Ice Box," one of the album's hit tracks. Their initial collaboration led to further discussions, and in August 2008 it was announced that Omarion was leaving his previous record company to sign with Timbaland's Moseley Music Group.

———— " ————

Omarion frequently attributes his success to God and is thankful for the success he has enjoyed. "I am a very fortunate person to be doing what I'm doing. I feel I was put on this earth to entertain, and that's what I will continue to do."

———— " ————

Omarion has also established a productive partnership with rapper and longtime friend Bow Wow. In 2005 the duo scored a hit single with "Let Me Hold You," and in 2007 they released the album *Face Off.* This project continued Omarion's move toward adult-oriented subjects, with some of the tracks offering a steamier and more explicit take on relationships than had been found on his previous recordings. *Face Off* pleased most reviewers and has enjoyed respectable sales, but the album did not sell as well as Omarion's two solo efforts.

Multimedia Performer

Continuing to pursue a dual career as an actor and musician, Omarion has had parts in a number of motion pictures since *You Got Served.* After a supporting role in 2004 in the animated movie *Fat Albert,* he returned as a leading man in two films that were released in 2007. In *Feel the Noise,* he played Rob, an aspiring New York City rapper who gets on the wrong side of a local thug and is forced to flee to Puerto Rico. There, he launches a career as a performer in reggaeton—a type of music that blends hip-hop

Omarion had a starring role in the 2007 film Feel the Noise.

with Jamaican and Latin styles. The role gave Omarion another chance to showcase his dance and music skills on the big screen. Unfortunately his dramatic performance received mixed reviews, with *Variety* critic Joe Leydon calling him "charisma-challenged." He also starred in the "slasher"-style horror film *Somebody Help Me,* which tells the story of a group of friends who encounter deadly mayhem during a weekend trip. For this project, Omarion once again worked under the direction of Chris Stokes and shared top billing with Marques Houston, as he had in *You Got Served.*

For the future, Omarion's plans include additional projects that allow him to develop all of his talents. "I want to be doing more of what I'm doing now," he said. "More records. More live performances. More movies. More and better." He also hopes to become involved in other endeavors, including producing other artists and perhaps developing other types of businesses. A self-described "spiritual dude," Omarion frequently attributes his success to God and is thankful for the success he has enjoyed. "I am a very fortunate person to be doing what I'm doing. I feel I was put on this earth to entertain, and that's what I will continue to do."

HOME AND FAMILY

Omarion has lived in the Los Angeles area for most of his life. He has stated that he "wouldn't mind getting married early" but vows that he won't do so until he finds the person that is right for him.

HOBBIES AND OTHER INTERESTS

In his spare time, Omarion enjoys playing basketball, football, and videogames, and he also watches a lot of movies.

SELECTED CREDITS

Recordings with B2K

B2K, 2001
Santa Hooked Me Up, 2002
Pandemonium, 2002

Recordings as Omarion

O, 2005
21, 2006
Face Off, 2007 (with Bow Wow)

Movies

You Got Served, 2004

Fat Albert, 2004
Feel the Noise, 2007
Somebody Help Me, 2007

FURTHER READING

Books

Grandberry, Omari. *O*, 2005

Periodicals

Current Biography Yearbook, 2008
Houston Chronicle, Oct. 5, 2007, p.1; Dec. 11, 2007, p.1
Jet, Jan. 26, 2004, p.56; May 9, 2005, p.56; Jan. 14, 2008, p.63
Newark (NJ) Star Ledger, May 15, 2007, p.F9
Teen People, Aug. 2002, p.134; Apr. 1, 2004, p.73
Washington Post, Dec. 29, 2006, p.T6

Online Articles

http://www.mtv.com
(MTV, "Omarion Opens Up About New Boss Timbaland—And Why It Was Time to Cut Off His Hair," Aug. 20, 2008

ADDRESS

Omarion
c/o The Ultimate Group
848 La Cienega Blvd., Suite 201
West Hollywood, CA 90069

WORLD WIDE WEB SITES

http://www.omariononline.com
http://www.myspace.com

Suze Orman 1951-

American Financial Advisor and Television Commentator
Bestselling Author and Host of CNBC's "The Suze Orman Show"

BIRTH

Suze (pronounced "Suzie," short for Susan) Orman was born on June 5, 1951, in Chicago, Illinois. She was the youngest of three children of Morry Orman, a store owner and businessman, and Ann Orman, a legal secretary. They raised Suze and her two older brothers on the south side of Chicago, where the family ran a chicken take-out shop.

YOUTH

Orman's parents had emigrated from Russia, and they struggled at times to make ends meet. "The shame, fear, and anger I felt growing up … as poor little Suze Orman from the south side of Chicago, daughter of a chicken plucker, defined me well into adulthood," she remembered in her book *The Courage to Be Rich.* "No matter how well I did or how much money I made, I never felt good enough, smart enough, attractive enough." Her self-esteem was further weakened during elementary school, where she struggled with reading because of a speech problem. When a teacher decided to seat her class by their scores on a reading exam, "my three best friends [were] in the first three seats of the first row, while I was banished to the last seat in the sixth row," Orman recalled. "If I always secretly felt dumb, it was now officially confirmed for everyone to see."

"The shame, fear, and anger I felt growing up … as poor little Suze Orman from the south side of Chicago, daughter of a chicken plucker, defined me well into adulthood. No matter how well I did or how much money I made, I never felt good enough, smart enough, attractive enough."

To make matters worse, her parents suffered a series of financial setbacks that affected the entire family. When Orman was 13, a fire destroyed the chicken take-out shop her family owned. She watched as her father ran back into the burning building to save the cash register, which held all the family's earnings. "When he threw the register on the ground, the skin on his arms and chest came with it," she recalled. "That was when I learned that money is obviously more important than life itself." The family couldn't afford insurance, so they had to rebuild from scratch. Morry Orman recovered from his burns and opened a deli in downtown Chicago, but then was sued by a woman paralyzed at a boarding house he owned with his father. To help make ends meet, Ann Orman took a full-time job as a legal secretary, which was unusual for a mother at the time. To help out, Suze and her brothers often worked in the family store or at odd jobs.

Although Orman worried about measuring up to her classmates, it didn't slow her down in high school. She was very involved in school activities, joining a dozen clubs and serving on several school committees. There were no organized sports for girls, so she and her many friends often let off steam by playing "hide-and-seek tag" at Chicago's famous Museum of Science and Industry. Because she felt she wasn't as smart as her fellow students, she didn't try to get top grades; still, she planned to attend college after she finished high school.

EDUCATION

After graduating from Chicago's South Shore High School in 1969, Orman enrolled at the University of Illinois. Although she hoped to become a brain surgeon, a guidance counselor discouraged her because of her average grades and test scores. Instead, she majored in social work. She worked her way through college and shared a house with a couple of friends, one of whom was future comedy superstar John Belushi. Orman was scheduled to graduate in 1973, but she failed to complete a foreign language requirement and left school to travel around the country. Several years later, she completed the needed courses at a school in California and received her bachelor's degree from the University of Illinois in 1976.

CAREER HIGHLIGHTS

A Rocky Road to Success

After leaving school in 1973, Orman borrowed enough money from her brother to buy a van. She and three friends drove across the country and ended up in California. In Berkeley, she got a job cutting and clearing dead trees and lived in her van for a few months. Eventually she settled down and found a job as a waitress at the Buttercup Bakery. Orman worked there for nearly seven years, until she decided she wanted to open her own restaurant. She had little savings of her own to start a business, however, and her parents couldn't afford to help her out. It was her regular customers at the Buttercup who ended up lending her the seed money to start her own business.

Orman's customers were able to lend her $50,000. But that wasn't enough to start a business from scratch, so one customer recommended she take the money to invest with a stockbroker at the local Merrill Lynch office. Knowing little about financial markets, Orman trusted the broker there to handle her money properly. "I did exactly what he asked, never thinking that it was stupid or dangerous for me to sign blank papers," she recalled. Instead of putting her money in something conservative, like a money market account, the broker put it into a high-risk investment. For the first couple of weeks the gamble paid off and Orman made a lot of money. Then the markets changed, and after three months she had lost everything.

Despite the financial difficulties she faced early in life, Orman went on to become a respected expert on financial issues.

Orman knew she couldn't make enough money to pay back her loans on her waitress's salary of $400 a month. She had been studying the stock market and figured she couldn't do any worse than her first advisor. She walked into Merrill Lynch and asked for a job interview. Although she didn't know how to dress for business and had no financial experience, they gave her a job. During her first days there, Orman felt like she had in school—like she wasn't smart enough to belong—but she studied hard to take her stockbroker's exam. During her studies, she discovered that the broker who had lost her money had broken the rules. Although she thought it might jeopardize her job, she decided to sue the Merrill Lynch office where she was working.

Orman didn't know that Merrill Lynch couldn't fire someone who was suing them, so she kept her job despite the lawsuit. During the months it took to litigate the case, Orman earned her stockbroker's qualifications and became one of her office's top sellers. Merrill Lynch ended up settling the lawsuit out of court, giving her enough money to pay back her friends at the Buttercup. In the meantime, she was earning a six-figure salary, partly by taking on unconventional clients, like low- and middle-income waitresses and truck drivers. She remained at Merrill Lynch until 1983, when she traveled to India and Nepal to study meditation and explore spirituality. When she returned to California, she took a job with Prudential Bache Securities, eventually becoming vice-president of investments. In 1987 she went into business for herself, creating the Suze Orman Financial Group and working as a Certified Financial Planner.

Learning Lessons from Loss

Orman had won many clients with her bubbly personality and personal service, and she planned on taking them with her into her new business. She had barely set up shop when an assistant stole all her records, both paper files and computer programs. Orman tried to keep the business going, but she was forced to resort to credit card debt to maintain appearances. Soon she owed almost $250,000 and had reached the limits of her credit; she also became depressed. She sued her assistant for $500,000, but was only awarded $6,000 in damages. She couldn't even collect the money after the woman declared bankruptcy. Despite these troubles, Orman found a valuable lesson in the experience. She decided to forgive the woman and claimed responsibility for her part in the dispute. "I apologized to that woman," she explained. "I needed to learn the lesson that money can't buy happiness. Even with my spiritual quest, I thought I was better than people because I had money."

Orman learned the importance of living within one's means: "We're all so busy worrying about impressing people we don't know or like, that we're not saving money."

With a new attitude toward money and lots of hard work, Orman rebuilt her business. Within three years she had repaid her debts and was once again on the path to success. She felt the need to share the lessons she had learned and began "telling everyone I knew what had happened to me," she explained. "The more I opened up, the happier I felt." In 1995 she published *You've Earned It, Don't Lose It,* a book based on her experiences and a retirement seminar she had developed. *You've Earned It, Don't Lose It* was geared towards lower- and middle-income people who can't afford to lose any of their hard-earned savings. It stressed protecting money, rather than trying to grow it. Orman opened each chapter with a story of a financial mistake, then showed how the mistake could have been prevented. She covered a broad range of important financial subjects: insurance, wills and inheritances, retirement issues, and legal and medical troubles that can affect a person's finances.

You've Earned it, Don't Lose It *was Orman's first published book.*

Orman worked hard with her publisher to promote the book and eventually convinced QVC, a television shopping channel, to give her time to sell it. In that first segment, aired October 1995, she sold all 2,500 copies they had in stock. Three months later, on Super Bowl Sunday, she sold 10,000 copies in just 12 minutes. Eventually, Orman sold over 700,000 copies of *You've Earned It, Don't Lose It.* She also became a featured vendor on QVC, hosting the channel's "Financial Freedom Hour" beginning in 1996.

To help sales of her first book, Orman toured the country to sign copies in different cities. During one of those signings she met a producer from a local Public Broadcasting System (PBS) television station. The producer suggested she appear during the station's next pledge drive to sell her book and help the station raise money. When Orman published her second book, *The 9 Steps to Financial Freedom* (1997), she created a TV program of the same title to be broadcast on PBS stations nationwide. Orman toured 21 stations around the country and helped the network raise more than $2.3 million, their most successful fundraiser to that point.

Orman's career in broadcasting really took off after she began appearing on "The Oprah Winfrey Show." She first appeared as a guest in January 1998. After several more visits to the show, *The 9 Steps to Financial Freedom* topped the *New York Times* list of best-selling nonfiction. In the book, Orman again used real-life stories to illustrate how people let their feelings about money get in the way of using it wisely. She emphasized dealing with your emotional responses to money as part of a sound financial plan. "Money will not set you free," she explained. "It's your control over your thoughts and fears about money that will set you free." *The 9 Steps* became her biggest-selling book, with over 3.1 million copies in print.

Becoming a Media Superstar

Orman also reached the top of the best-seller list with her next book, *The Courage to Be Rich* (1999), which sold 1.2 million copies. She wrote the book, she said, after seeing many of her friends get divorced over money issues. "A lot of them were treating their money the exact same way they treated their relationship: in essence, they weren't quite honest. So I started to realize that the way we related to people was the exact same way we related to money." Again, she used real-life examples to show ways to deal with marriage, divorce, and death without letting money issues complicate things. Her 2001 book *The Road to Wealth* was another chart-topper, selling more than 660,000 copies. It was designed as a one-stop reference for all kinds of financial questions. The book was so successful that Orman brought out an updated version in 2008.

Even as she conquered the best-seller charts, Orman was finding more ways to reach an audience. She continued as a regular guest on "The Oprah Winfrey Show" and also made appearances on NBC's "Today" morning show and the news network CNN. She also brought out a DVD

Many of Orman's popular books were made into DVDs also, expanding her reach.

to accompany each new book, and soon Orman was answering questions on her own radio show. Then "The Suze Orman Show" debuted on cable financial network CNBC in March 2002. The "Can I Afford It?" segment became very popular, as viewers called in to ask whether they could afford various items—from designer jeans to luxury cars. After listening to their financial information, Orman would shout, "Approved!" or "Denied!"

Orman continued hitting the best-seller charts with finance books that offered advice for different times and different groups. The 2003 book *The Laws of Money, The Lessons of Life* was written after the terrorist attacks on 9/11 ended the economic boom of the 1990s. It focused on how to deal with difficult financial times and offered the advice to "look at what you have, not at what you had." *The Money Book for the Young, Fabulous, & Broke,* published in 2005, focused on money issues important to people in their 20s: car payments, taxes, student loans, and how to save and invest money. Orman suggested the most important thing for young people is to establish and maintain good credit, because people with good credit pay less interest. She also suggested young workers focus on jobs that provide the best chance for advancement, rather than the best salary. She stressed the importance of living within one's means: "We're all so busy worrying about impressing people we don't know or like, that we're not saving money."

Orman tailored her advice to women in the 2007 book *Women & Money: Owning the Power to Control Your Destiny.* She encouraged women to save for their own future rather than spend their money solely on others. Although women might have the reputation of being thrifty, "they save and then they give it to their best friends, who need it," Orman commented. "They give it to their children, who need it. They give it all away once they've saved it." She added, "I want to change women from savers to investors." To further the cause of educating women about finances, in 2008 she become a consultant to Avon, the in-home cosmetics company that employs almost half a million women in the U.S. alone.

In 2009 Orman published a new book, *Suze Orman's 2009 Action Plan.* Given the stock market freefall, the credit crunch, the drop in the housing market and the many home foreclosures, and the steep rise in unemployment, Orman felt the need to publish timely information that's relevant to today's economic conditions. *Suze Orman's 2009 Action Plan* is a one-time book targeted to help people deal with the recent economic crisis and take advantage of new laws and tax breaks that have been passed in response to the crisis. It helps readers develop action plans for dealing with such issues as the credit market, saving and spending, real estate, and paying for college. The book is for sale in stores and other locations, but it was also offered as a free download from oprah.com when it was first published.

In addition to selling millions of books and DVDs, Orman has also created financial kits and sold them through her web site. Various kits show people how to check and fix their credit, develop a will or trust, buy necessary insurance, and avoid identity theft. She is also a very popular public speaker who has lectured to many groups around the country, including a 2005 tour with hip-hop mogul Russell Simmons to promote financial planning for urban youth. Orman has won numerous awards for her work, including two Emmys for her television show. In 2008, *Time* magazine named her one of the 100 most influential people in the world. Orman has become so famous that she even inspired several skits on the comedy program "Saturday Night Live." She has said that she doesn't mind being the subject of a spoof: "One of those times I was in the audience," she recalled. "By all means, if they ever ask me [to appear on the show], it would be one of the greatest honors of my life."

———— " ————

Orman makes financial advice entertaining, which helps everyday people understand important issues. According to critic Henry Goldblatt, "Her boisterous delivery is so compelling that it doesn't matter if she's spouting off about variable life insurance or reciting [Russian literature]. She's just a blast to be around."

———— " ————

Response to Her Work

Orman has had her share of critics. Some have called her advice too conservative and one-size-fits-all. Others have faulted her endorsement of certain financial products. Orman has responded that she only promotes products she believes in and doesn't receive any money for her recommendations. (She earns enough from her own businesses; observers estimate she is worth around $25 million.) To critics who call her advice overly simplistic, she has said, "get out there and talk to people like I do. The truth is, they haven't got any money. Who has money to invest anymore? Invest what?" Others have faulted her emphasis on emotional issues, but Orman noted that "even though I'm the last person to say money will buy happiness—because it won't—I'll be the first to say the lack of money will make you miserable." She believes that in dealing with financial issues, the

Orman has become so famous that she was even a subject of parody on "Saturday Night Live," including this skit featuring Kristen Wiig.

focus should be on "people first, then money, then things." Her ability to make financial advice entertaining helps everyday people understand important issues. As critic Henry Goldblatt wrote in *Entertainment Weekly*, "Her boisterous delivery is so compelling that it doesn't matter if she's spouting off about variable life insurance or reciting [Russian literature]. She's just a blast to be around."

Many would argue that Orman's advice is appealing because it is full of common sense: avoid credit card debt; contribute as much as possible to a 401(k) retirement savings account to get matching funds from your employer; and use any extra money to pay off auto loans and other debts before putting it into investments. She also advocates spending within one's means and warns against hiding money from a spouse. Finally, she stresses the importance of learning everything possible about your loans and investments—never just sign an empty form and trust your finances to someone else. While this advice has been common for years, she has an ability to describe it in terms a non-expert can understand.

Orman's enthusiasm and communication skills are a great part of her success. She takes a subject many people find boring or confusing and relates it to everyday experiences. She encourages people to separate feelings of shame and guilt from how they handle money. "The time has come for each and every one of us when our self-worth has to mean more than our net worth," she declared. Most important, she noted, is for people to take charge of their own finances. "Power doesn't come from relying on someone else to handle your money. It is created when you—and only you—take the initiative to learn about your money and to make sure that you have what you need."

"Power doesn't come from relying on someone else to handle your money. It is created when you—and only you—take the initiative to learn about your money and to make sure that you have what you need."

HOME AND FAMILY

Even after becoming a best-selling author, Orman kept the small house in Oakland Hills, California, that she bought when she was waitress. Later she moved to Pacific Heights, in the San Francisco area. She has also purchased a small apartment (only 900 square feet) in New York City and a home in Florida, which is her official residence. She also owns a home in South Africa, where she has expanded her consulting business. All four of her homes are completely paid off, with no debt attached to them.

In 2007, Orman came out as a lesbian, acknowledging her long-time partner, Kathy "K.T." Travis, a marketing executive who now works for Orman's company. She hopes that someday they can be legally married. "It's killing me that upon my death, K.T. is going to lose 50 percent of everything I have to [pay] estate taxes, or vice versa."

HOBBIES AND OTHER INTERESTS

Orman takes time from her busy schedule to practice Siddha yoga meditation. She also spends considerable time and money on behalf of charity. She devoted a chapter on charitable giving to *The Courage to Be Rich* and believes by sending money into the world, you won't feel poor and "your demeanor will be instead expansive and open, ready to receive." She donates around one-quarter of her income to charity, especially religious, environmental, and women's groups. The National Multiple Sclerosis Society gave her their first MS Spirit Award in 2006 for her support of the organization.

Orman also donates her services to worthy groups. She participated in "Military Saves" week by giving speeches and free copies of her books to military families. During the financial crisis of 2008, she donated her to time to create public service announcements for the Federal Deposit Insurance Corporation (FDIC), assuring people their money was safe in banks.

WRITING AND TELEVISION CREDITS

Books

You've Earned It, Don't Lose It, 1995, revised edition, 1999 (with Linda Mead)
The 9 Steps to Financial Freedom, 1997
Suze Orman's Financial Guidebook, 1998
The Courage to Be Rich, 1999
The Road to Wealth, 2001; revised edition, 2008
The Laws of Money, the Lessons of Life, 2003
The Money Book for the Young, Fabulous & Broke, 2005
Women & Money: Owning the Power to Control Your Destiny, 2007
Suze Orman's 2009 Action Plan: Keeping Your Money Safe and Sound, 2009

Television

"Financial Freedom Hour," 1996-
"The 9 Steps to Financial Freedom," 1997
"The Courage to Be Rich," 1999
"The Road to Wealth," 2001
"The Suze Orman Show," 2002-
"Suze Orman: The Laws of Money, the Lessons of Life," 2003
"Suze Orman: for the Young, Fabulous & Broke," 2005
"Women & Money: Owning the Power to Control Your Destiny," 2007
Also makes regular appearances on "The Oprah Winfrey Show," "Larry King Live," "The View," and "Today."

HONORS AND AWARDS

Books for a Better Life Award (National Multiple Sclerosis Society): 1999, Motivational Award, for *The Courage to Be Rich;* 2003, Hall of Fame induction
Luminaries Award (TJFR Group News): 2002, for lifetime achievement in business journalism
Crossing Borders Award (Feminist Press): 2003
Gracie Allen Award (American Women in Radio & Television): 2003, for Outstanding National/Network/Syndication Talk Show; 2005, for Individual Achievement Award as Outstanding Program Host; 2006, for Individual Achievement Award as Outstanding Program Host; 2007, for

Outstanding Talk Show; 2008, for Outstanding Talk Show, all for "The Suze Orman Show"
Daytime Emmy Awards (National Academy of Television Arts and Sciences): 2004, for Outstanding Service Show Host, for "Suze Orman: The Lessons of Money, The Lessons of Life;" 2006, for Outstanding Service Show Host, for "Suze Orman: For the Young, Fabulous & Broke"
Multiple Sclerosis Spirit Award (National Multiple Sclerosis Society): 2006
Amelia Earhart Award (Crittenton Women's Union): 2008
CableFAX Program Award (CableFAX magazine): 2008, for Best Show or Series in Talk Show/Commentary, for "The Suze Orman Show"
National Equality Award (Human Rights Campaign): 2008

FURTHER READING

Books

Orman, Suze. *The Courage to Be Rich,* 1999

Periodicals

American Prospect, Dec. 2007, p.35
Biography, Apr. 2001, p.62
Current Biography Yearbook, 2003
Entertainment Weekly, Sep. 12, 2008, p.125
Fortune, June 16, 2003, p.82
Kiplinger's Personal Finance Magazine, Nov. 1998, p.96
Minneapolis Star-Tribune, Aug. 3, 2001, p.E1
New York Times, Mar. 18, 2007, p.BU7
New York Times Magazine, Feb. 25, 2007, p.L19
People, May 17, 1999, p.153
Publishers Weekly, Feb. 24, 2003, p.41
Sales & Marketing Management, Aug. 1999, p.120
San Francisco Chronicle, Oct. 25, 2008, p.C1
Self, Dec. 1997, p.114
USA Today, Mar. 21, 2005, p.B6; Mar. 19, 2007, p.B9
Wall Street Journal, Oct. 17, 2008, p.B4

Online Articles

http://www.chicagomag.com/Chicago-Magazine/February-2007/Before-They-Were-Famous
(Chicago Magazine, "Before They Were Famous," Feb. 2007)
http://www.oprah.com/article/omagazine/suze_orman
(O, The Oprah Magazine, "Suze Orman: Personal Finance Expert," undated)

http://www.oprah.com/tows
(Oprah Winfrey Show, multiple articles, various dates)
http:www.time.com
(Time, "The 2008 Time 100: The World's Most Influential People," undated)

ADDRESS

Suze Orman
"The Suze Orman Show"
CNBC
900 Sylvan Avenue
Englewood Cliffs, NJ 07632

WORLD WIDE WEB SITES

http://www.suzeorman.com
http://www.cnbc.com

Kenny Ortega 1950-

American Director and Choreographer
Director and Choreographer of the *High School Musical* Films

BIRTH

Kenny Ortega was born Kenneth John Ortega on April 18, 1950, in Palo Alto, California. His parents were of Cuban and Spanish descent; his father worked in a factory, while his mother was a waitress. They raised their family, which included Kenny's sister and brother, in a small tract house in Redwood City, California. They divorced when Kenny was 12. Although he found their split difficult to deal with, "I gotta say they were both there for me and for my [siblings]."

YOUTH

Although Ortega's family was not wealthy, they were supportive and close-knit. His family instilled in him a love of song and dance from a young age. "My grandmother was singing flamenco and banging her heels into the vinyl kitchen floor from the time I could walk," he recalled. His parents also loved to dance. "My earliest memories are of my mom and dad swing dancing and mambo dancing in the living room. They were World War II kids and met on a dance floor." When he watched them dance, "That was love. He was so handsome and she was so beautiful. She'd laugh and they threw all caution to the wind. I thought, that's the best part of life, right there." Ortega was only four when his mother took him to watch two cousins participate in a dance class. "I couldn't sit still, so the teacher came over and offered me a scholarship."

"

"My earliest memories are of my mom and dad swing dancing and mambo dancing in the living room. They were World War II kids and met on a dance floor." When he watched them dance, "That was love. He was so handsome and she was so beautiful. She'd laugh and they threw all caution to the wind. I thought, that's the best part of life, right there."

"

By the time he was 13, Ortega had become a member of theater companies in the San Francisco area. At age 14, he appeared in a production of the musical *Oliver!* with Tony-nominated actress Georgia Brown. By 16 he was auditioning for productions in Los Angeles and getting to work with Broadway choreographers. He performed in high school productions as well, finding the stage a great way to make friends and fit in. "Dancing saved me from getting beat up and from being paralyzed at home. I was known as a lover, not a fighter," he said. He added that "I always felt closest to making dances, even though that wasn't all I could do. You see, when I was a kid I was the gang's mascot; I arranged the parties, invited the girls—they came to our parties because I could dirty dance." Those skills would later prove important to his career.

EDUCATION

Ortega graduated in 1968 from Sequoia High School in Redwood, California. He briefly attended Cañada College, a local community college. There

Ortega appeared in the groundbreaking rock musical Hair *in the late 1960s.*

he studied theater arts and dance while still performing in San Francisco area productions. He left his studies behind when he received an opportunity to join the cast of a national tour.

FIRST JOBS

Ortega was 18 when he got his first big role, appearing in the stage musical *Hair.* He played the part of George Berger, a hippie, in the San Francisco production. *Hair* was a groundbreaking rock musical, the first with a racially integrated cast. It was also a social commentary on the times, controversial for its depiction of antiwar themes, nudity, sex, and drug use. After two years, Ortega left the San Francisco cast to play the same role in the national touring company of *Hair.* While on tour in the South—where some communities attempted to ban the musical—Ortega found himself in trouble when someone planted illegal drugs in his dressing room. "I was facing 25 years in prison because somebody didn't like politically what we represented: change," he remembered. "I thought my life and my career were over." Luckily, the lawyer for the production company was able to resolve the situation, and Ortega was able to continue touring with the company.

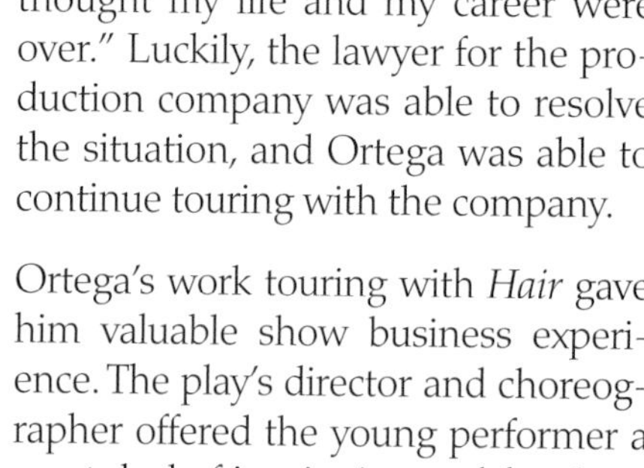

"Hair *was all about breaking from convention and setting new boundaries," Ortega recalled. "It was this experience that shaped my thinking, enlightened me, and gave me a process I have used to conduct my life from that time forward."*

Ortega's work touring with *Hair* gave him valuable show business experience. The play's director and choreographer offered the young performer a great deal of inspiration and freedom. The cast was instructed to "live" their roles, not "act" them, and Ortega learned to listen to "one's inner voice." Choreographer Julie Arenal gave him a set of movements to learn, but she encouraged him to express himself within each dance. "*Hair* was all about breaking from convention and setting new boundaries," Ortega recalled. "It was this experience that shaped my thinking, enlightened me, and gave me a process I have used to conduct my life from that time forward."

CAREER HIGHLIGHTS

From Rock Stars to Dance Legends

After touring with the national company of *Hair* for nearly three years, Ortega returned to California. He didn't want to go back to working in traditional musicals; instead, "I wanted something bigger." He met up with the Tubes, a rock band from San Francisco that aspired to turn their concerts into theatrical spectacles. They hired Ortega to help design and choreograph their stage show, which included seven musicians, eight dancers, and several television monitors. The group was notorious for complex numbers like "Rock and Roll Hospital," in which the lead singer sported a

Ortega in his role as film director.

chain saw, and "White Punks on Dope," which poked fun at rock and roll excess. By the mid-1970s, the Tubes were gaining international attention for their entertaining concerts, as well as their music. All in all, Ortega directed and performed in five of the group's world tours.

Ortega's work with the Tubes brought him to the attention of the wider music world. Singer-entertainer Cher approached him after a Tubes performance and asked him to help choreograph her next television special. That led to work with Toni Basil, a singer, dancer, and choreographer. (Although Basil is best known for her catchy 1982 song "Mickey," she has worked most frequently as a choreographer, producing shows for such superstars as David Bowie, Bette Midler, and Tina Turner.) Ortega worked with Basil on a dance production that brought together everything from classical ballet to hip-hop, an experience he said "added another dimension to my development as a choreographer." Basil also hired him to assist on choreography for the 1979 film *The Rose,* starring Bette Midler.

"

Ortega started working on choreography for live stage shows. "People's live performances needed to be more than someone standing on stage with a band behind them. Everybody wanted this connection. I started to bring my theatrical background into the world of popular music."

"

In addition to her work in *The Rose* and other films, Midler was well known as a singer and live performer, and eventually Ortega worked with her on her stage show. This led to a new career working with some of the biggest names in music: Michael Jackson, Elton John, Barbra Streisand, Diana Ross, Gloria Estefan, and others. He helped produce TV variety shows, like the American Music Awards. "People's live performances needed to be more than someone standing on stage with a band behind them," he explained. "Everybody wanted this connection. I started to bring my theatrical background into the world of popular music."

Ortega still had an ambition to work in the movies, however. When Basil couldn't accept the job of choreographing a new movie musical starring singer Olivia Newton-John, she suggested Ortega for the job. Although he had no formal choreography or film training, Ortega jumped at the chance to work on the 1980 film *Xanadu.* He discovered that Hollywood dancing legend Gene Kelly was considering appearing in the movie, and after meeting Ortega, Kelly signed on to the project.

Working with Kelly was one of the defining experiences of Ortega's career. Gene Kelly is considered one of the greatest dancers and choreographers in the history of American film, starring in such classics as *Singin' in the Rain* and *An American in Paris.* In addition to acting and dancing, according to Ortega, "Kelly was a master at filming dance. He didn't just choreograph a dance; he conceived it with the camera in mind.... He insisted that I direct his on-screen dance and took that opportunity to teach me what he knew." The star tutored Ortega on camera angles and motion; Kelly even invited the young choreographer to his house to explain details of his old films. "He gave me this incredible education. He said he believed in me and chose me to pass on his knowledge. It's one of the most significant relationships that I've ever had." To this day, Ortega uses a director's viewfinder that Kelly gave him.

"Kelly was a master at filming dance," Ortega declared about working with screen legend Gene Kelly. "He didn't just choreograph a dance; he conceived it with the camera in mind.... He insisted that I direct his on-screen dance and took that opportunity to teach me what he knew."

Although Ortega had a great experience working with Kelly, *Xanadu* was a flop at the box office. Interestingly, it has since become a cult favorite, inspiring a Broadway musical. Still, *Xanadu* gave Ortega valuable movie experience.

Making It in the Movies

Ortega's experience on *Xanadu* helped him get choreography jobs in a string of later films. He worked several times with powerhouse producer-writer-director John Hughes, who made some of the most popular comedies of the 1980s. Ortega choreographed sequences in *St. Elmo's Fire* (1985), *Ferris Bueller's Day Off* (1986), and *Pretty in Pink* (1986). "The whole time I was thinking, 'I'm working with John Hughes. Suck it up, Kenny, you're learning here,'" the choreographer recalled. "I just felt like the luckiest guy in the world. It was my responsibility to know how blessed I was and to take advantage of it." Hughes gave Ortega his first chance to direct, making him a second-unit director for the parade sequence in *Ferris Bueller,* and encouraged him to join the Directors Guild of America.

Ortega had his greatest success to date with his work choreographing the 1987 film *Dirty Dancing.* This sleeper hit told the story of a girl spending a summer at a Catskills resort in the early 1960s. Frances, also known as

Ortega's choreography for Dirty Dancing *was based on the sexy moves he developed as a teenager.*

"Baby," is a guest at the resort and is bored with the upper-class boys and their obsession with superficial things. Eager to discover the wider world, Baby watches the workers at the resort indulging in an exciting, sensual style of dance. Unbeknownst to her parents, she learns this "dirty dancing" from the staff instructor and falls in love. The film was a surprise success at the box office, much of it due to the passionate dance routines Ortega designed. "I drew much of [the dance] from my own high school experience," he later revealed. "I remember having all this sexual tension bottled up inside of me that couldn't wait to explode on the dance floor." *Dirty Dancing* made over $63 million at the box office and became a cult hit still popular today.

Ortega continued developing his skills as a filmmaker in the new field of music video. In the early 1980s he began to direct, producing videos for popular acts like the Pointer Sisters, Supertramp, Gladys Knight, Billy Squier, Gloria Estefan, and his old colleagues the Tubes. He also choreographed videos for some of the biggest stars of the 1980s: Billy Joel, Elton John, Cher, and Madonna, whom he put in a Hollywood-style song-and-dance number for her 1985 video "Material Girl." For the 1988 movie *Salsa,* he served as associate producer as well as choreographer, allowing him more control over how the dance sequences were edited. He got more experience directing with a couple of short-lived TV shows, "Dirty Dancing" (1988) and "Hull High" (1990).

In 1992 Ortega finally got the chance to fulfill a long-time dream: directing a feature film musical. The Disney production *Newsies* was an old-fashioned movie musical set in New York City at the beginning of the 1900s. The story followed a group of newsboys who go on strike against an increase in newspaper prices. Critics called the film old-fashioned, and it fared poorly with audiences, earning only $2.8 million at the box office. Still, it gave Ortega the experience to keep directing. He oversaw the 1993 Disney comedy *Hocus Pocus* with Bette Midler and Sarah Jessica Parker, and in the 1990s and 2000s he got steady work in television, directing episodes of several popular TV series, including "Chicago Hope," "Ally McBeal," and "Gilmore Girls."

"

Dirty Dancing *was a surprise success at the box office, much of it due to the passionate dance routines Ortega designed. "I drew much of [the dance] from my own high school experience," he later revealed.*

"

Ortega's varied background gave him the skills needed for another kind of show: the sports spectacular. He choreographed the halftime show for Super Bowl XXX in 1996, creating a show that involved audience cards, pyrotechnics, special effects, and a helicopter that took headliner Diana Ross off the field at the end of the show. Later that year he worked on the Summer Olympic Games held in Atlanta. He and Judy Chabola choreographed both the opening and closing ceremonies, with each show lasting 90 minutes and involving thousands of performers. He won an American Choreography Award for the production, and also earned a job staging the opening ceremonies for the 2002 Winter Olympic Games held in Salt Lake City. For that event, which involved a portable ice rink, fiber optics, projection screen, and thousands of performers, Ortega earned two Emmy Awards: for Outstanding Choreography and Outstanding Directing.

High School Musical

In 2006, the Disney Channel asked Ortega to helm an original film for its TV network. The story of *High School Musical* was simple: after sharing a musical moment during summer vacation, teens Troy and Gabriella think they will never meet again. When Gabriella transfers to Troy's high school, they have to break away from their cliques to make music together again. Set in high school and interspersed with song and dance numbers, the movie brought elements of old-school musical theater to a new audience, set to a fun and funky beat. A *Variety* reviewer said the film "makes a convincing case for the return of the musical" and called Ortega "a master of the group dance." The film earned numerous awards, including an Outstanding Choreography Emmy and a Director's Guild Award for Ortega.

Ortega felt strongly about the film's message: "Listen to your voice and have the courage to let it come out no matter what sort of pressures there are. Don't suppress it, don't bury it, don't hide it." Forced to choose between sports and musicals while in high school, Ortega himself found the pressures the kids face in *High School Musical* unfair: "You should be able to have options! You should be able to let all of them blend and balance in your life." The movie's uplifting message and exciting song-and-dance numbers made it an instant hit. It drew more than 170 million fans in over 100 countries and spawned a best-selling soundtrack, DVD, stage show, and ice show (which Ortega directed and produced). The film appealed to a wide audience, the director explained: "My grown-up friends are telling me they're enjoying it, too, as they watch it as a family. It's a real thrill knowing we've created family entertainment. It's bringing families together."

"

Ortega felt strongly about the message of High School Musical: *"Listen to your voice and have the courage to let it come out no matter what sort of pressures there are. Don't suppress it, don't bury it, don't hide it."*

"

After directing another Disney Channel musical, *Cheetah Girls 2,* Ortega reunited with the *High School Musical* cast for a sequel. When *High School Musical 2* aired in August 2007, it became the most-watched basic cable telecast of all time, with 17.2 million viewers for its initial showing. (Since many families held viewing parties, the actual number of viewers was most likely even higher.) It was the most-watched program on television—broadcast and cable—of the entire summer season. A *Variety* reviewer noted that the sequel "actually surpasses the first movie in sheer energy and verve." Ortega attributed the films' success to their hopeful attitude: "I think [kids are] saying they'd like high school to be more like [the films] than perhaps the way it really is. They'd like things to lighten up, to be safer, to have more hope at the center. To be more fun."

Ortega's success continued with his work as stage director for the Miley Cyrus/Hannah Montana "Best of Both Worlds" tour in 2007. The sold-out tour not only produced highly in-demand tickets but also a record-

With High School Musical, *Ortega helped revive the musical genre.*

setting 3-D movie that hit No. 1 in early 2008. In the meantime, Ortega was busy working on a new installment of the HSM franchise, this one to debut in theaters. With a bigger budget and a bigger screen, Ortega declared, "There [are] more scale and details in *High School Musical 3,* but it's still our world—young people wishing and aspiring." Fans apparently agreed. *High School Musical 3: Senior Year* debuted in October 2008 at No. 1, with $42 million at the box office for opening weekend alone. This shattered the previous record for the highest-grossing musical debut, the $27.7 million set by *Mamma Mia* earlier in 2008.

Ortega values how the High School Musical *franchise has helped revive the musical genre: "The biggest success for me is that it's turned on a whole new generation of kids to musicals, and for me that's the one I'm proudest of. It has this greater massive impact and this delicate, poignant simple one-on-one impact. And that's the miracle of this little project."*

Although his long and varied career has earned him fame and awards, Ortega values how the *High School Musical* franchise has helped revive the musical genre: "The biggest success for me is that it's turned on a whole new generation of kids to musicals, and for me that's the one I'm proudest of. It has this greater massive impact and this delicate, poignant simple one-on-one impact. And that's the miracle of this little project."

Ortega considers himself fortunate to have achieved a long and successful career in the sometimes wild entertainment business. He has said he wouldn't mind making more *High School Musical* films, and planned to work with HSM star Zac Efron on a musical remake of the 1984 film *Footloose.* "At this stage of my life, if I'm going to work on something, there has to be hope at the center of the project," the director said. Whatever he does, he will "never stop forgetting and appreciating the incredible luck and blessings that you manage to get. It's amazing—the arc, the adventure, the journey."

HOME AND FAMILY

Ortega is single and has no children. He lives in Southern California with his pet Yorkshire terrier, Manly, who plays Sharpay's dog in the *High School Musical* films.

HOBBIES AND OTHER INTERESTS

Ortega enjoys working with charity organizations that benefit kids. His favorite charity is the Make-A-Wish Foundation, which grants wishes to seriously ill children. The director maintains a "Yawn Jar" on his sets, and any cast or crew member who yawns during filming must contribute a dollar to the jar. At the end of the shoot, the money is donated to Make-A-Wish. In addition, Ortega has made time to host Make-A-Wish kids on the *High School Musical* set.

Ortega also has worked with a local children's hospital, a pediatric AIDS organization, and the Nyumbani orphanage in Nairobi, Kenya. He considers his visit to Nyumbani, during which the HIV-positive orphans sang "We're All in This Together" from *High School Musical,* one of the most moving experiences of his life. "I left Africa realizing the responsibility that we have and how far-reaching our ideas and our work can be," he said. He would like to change lives closer to home, as well. Some day he hopes to start an interactive program that works with kids through the performing arts; his goal is to give them "a creative learning space and a place where they could come together and arrive into themselves."

SELECTED CREDITS

Film Choreographer

Xanadu, 1980
St. Elmo's Fire, 1985
Ferris Bueller's Day Off, 1986
Pretty in Pink, 1986
Dirty Dancing, 1987
Salsa, 1988 (and associate producer)
To Wong Foo, Thanks for Everything, Julie Newmar, 1995
Hannah Montana: Miley Cyrus: Best of Both Worlds Concert Tour, 2008 (stage director and producer)

Film and Television Director/Choreographer

Newsies, 1992
Hocus Pocus, 1993 (director only)
"XIX Winter Olympics Opening Ceremony," 2002 (and producer)
The Cheetah Girls 2, 2006
High School Musical, 2006
High School Musical 2, 2007 (and producer)
High School Musical 3: Senior Year, 2008 (and producer)

Director of episodes of "Dirty Dancing," "Hull High," "Chicago Hope," "Grounded for Life," "Ally McBeal," and "Gilmore Girls."

HONORS AND AWARDS

Golden Eagle Award (Nosotros): 1988, Outstanding Achievement in Choreography, for *Dirty Dancing;* 2002, Lifetime Achievement in Choreography

American Choreography Award: 1997, Outstanding Achievement in Television (Variety or Special), for "1996 Olympic Games"; 1998, Outstanding Achievement in Television (Episodic), for "Chicago Hope"; 2002, Outstanding Achievement in Television (Variety or Special), for "XIX Winter Olympics Opening Ceremony"; and 2004, Career Achievement Award

Emmy Award (Academy of Television Arts and Sciences): 2002 (two awards), Outstanding Choreography and Outstanding Directing for a Variety, Music or Comedy Program, for "XIX Winter Olympics Opening Ceremony"; 2006, Outstanding Choreography, for *High School Musical*

ALMA Award (National Council of La Raza): Outstanding Director for Television, 2007, for *High School Musical*, and 2008, for *High School Musical 2*

DGA Award (Directors Guild of America): 2007, Outstanding Directorial Achievement in Children's Programs, for *High School Musical*

Diversity Award (Multicultural Motion Picture Association): 2007, best director, comedy/musical, for *High School Musical 2*

Raul Julia Award for Excellence (National Hispanic Foundation for the Arts): 2007, for lifetime achievement

FURTHER READING

Books

Eichenbaum, Rose. *Masters of Movement: Portraits of America's Great Choreographers*, 2004

Periodicals

Current Biography Yearbook, 2008
Entertainment Weekly, Aug. 10, 2007, p.40
Hispanic Business, Dec. 2006, p.56
Latino Leaders, Feb.-Mar. 2006, p.30
Los Angeles Times, May 11, 1988, p.1; Aug. 12, 2007, p.E1
Oakland Tribune, Aug. 24, 2006

Orlando Sentinel, Sep. 6, 2007, p.E5
USA Today, July 7, 2008, p.D1
Variety, Jan. 19, 2006, p.5; Aug. 13, 2007, p.39

Online Articles

http://insidelatinoentertainment.com
(Inside Latino Entertainment, "A Conversation with Kenny Ortega," Feb. 14, 2008)

ADDRESS

Kenny Ortega
Schwartzman and Associates
10801 National Blvd., Suite 410
Los Angeles, CA 90064-4139

WORLD WIDE WEB SITES

http://tv.disney.go.com/disneychannel/originalmovies/highschoolmusical/
http://tv.disney.go.com/disneychannel/originalmovies/highschoolmusical2/
http://disney.go.com/disneypictures/highschoolmusical3/
http://www.schwartzmanpr.com

Robert Pattinson 1986-

British Actor

Star of *Harry Potter and the Goblet of Fire* and *The Twilight Saga* Films

BIRTH

Robert Thomas Pattinson was born on May 13, 1986, in London, England. He was the third and youngest child of Richard Pattinson, a vintage car salesman, and Clare Pattinson, who worked for a modeling agency. He grew up with two older sisters, Victoria and Elizabeth (Lizzy).

YOUTH

Pattinson had a fairly traditional childhood growing up in the southwest London suburb of Barnes. He attended a private boys' school nearby, the Tower House School, where he occasionally performed in school plays. He wasn't a terrific student, and his report cards showed it. "They were always pretty bad—I never ever did my homework," he admitted. "I always turned up for lessons, as I liked my teachers, but my report said I didn't try very hard." At age 12, he moved to a mixed private school, the Harrodian School, which emphasized helping students reach their potential, both academically and socially. Pattinson enjoyed his new school, especially having girls as classmates. "I became cool and discovered hair gel," he recalled. At the same time he began modeling. He modeled for about three years, when he grew up and "stopped looking like a girl," as he put it.

Pattinson got involved with acting mostly because he hoped to meet girls. "My dad spotted a bunch of girls in a café and they were all really excited, so he asked them where they'd been," he recalled. "When they said that they'd been to drama classes, he reckoned I should get myself down there!"

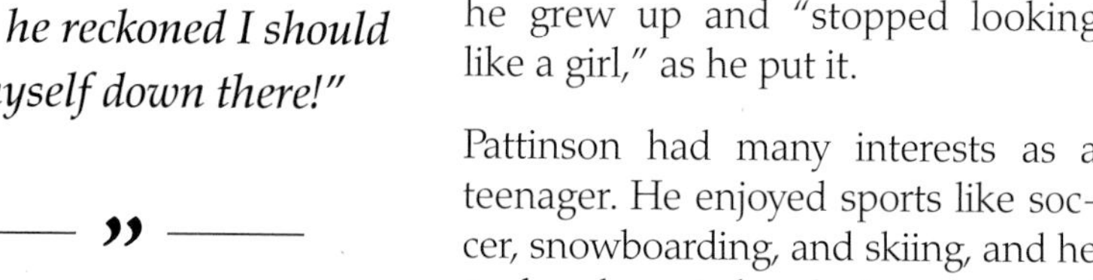

Pattinson had many interests as a teenager. He enjoyed sports like soccer, snowboarding, and skiing, and he explored music by playing piano and guitar. But he still wasn't a big success at school, either academically or socially. "I wasn't with the cool gang, or the uncool ones," he recalled. "I was transitional, in between." In fact, he got involved with acting mostly because he hoped to meet girls. "My dad spotted a bunch of girls in a café and they were all really excited, so he asked them where they'd been," Pattinson recalled. "When they said that they'd been to drama classes, he reckoned I should get myself down there!" He began by working backstage and eventually landed a leading role.

EDUCATION

In England, students complete secondary school at the age of 16. For those going to university, they take a couple of years of additional classes that prepare them for Advanced-Level exams, called A-Levels, in different subjects. After Pattinson completed secondary school at the Harrodian School, he wanted to continue his studies. Because he had been focusing more on acting than school, his father told him he would have to pay his own way; if he scored well on his exams, his father would reimburse him for the tuition. Pattinson used his fees from acting and modeling to continue A-Level studies at Harrodian, and he finished three A-Level exams. His scores weren't terrific, and he later revealed that he never really intended to go to college.

CAREER HIGHLIGHTS

Becoming an Actor

Pattinson got his start as an actor when he was still in high school. When he was 15 he joined the Barnes Theatre Company (BTC), a local theater group that produced a couple of stage productions each year. After working backstage for one production, he auditioned for a role in *Guys and Dolls,* an award-winning musical from 1950. He only got a small part, but he gave it his best, something his fellow actors noticed. "They respected me for doing it and gave me the lead in Thornton Wilder's *Our Town,*" he said. The role of George Gibbs in *Our Town* is challenging, portraying a teenager who falls in love, grows up and marries, and then faces the death of his wife. Pattinson's performance in the role earned him a professional agent.

Pattinson continued to appear in local stage productions, including the classic Cole Porter musical *Anything Goes,* the Shakespearean tragedy *Macbeth,* and the drama *Tess of the D'Urbervilles,* based on the 19th-century novel by Thomas Hardy. Pattinson played the villainous role of Alec, who ruins a young girl and forces her to become his mistress.

By the time he was 17, Pattinson had begun earning small parts in films and television shows. He earned a larger part in the 2004 European TV miniseries *Ring of the Nibelungs.* (The show was later broadcast in the United States on the SciFi Channel as *Dark Kingdom: The Dragon King.*) In this adaptation of a Germanic myth, Pattinson played a prince whose family is ensnared in the magical adventures of the dragon slayer Siegfried. The four-hour series was filmed entirely in South Africa, giving the young actor experience living on his own and working on a production with special effects. As he remembered, "I was there for three months in an apartment at just 17! So I came back really confident."

Winning a Role in the *Harry Potter* Films

Pattinson's confidence helped for his next audition, for the next installment of the blockbuster film franchise based on the *Harry Potter* books by J.K. Rowling. (For more information on Rowling, see *Biography Today,* Jan.

Pattinson as Cedric Diggory in scenes from Harry Potter and the Goblet of Fire: *conferring with his competitor, Harry; battling through the maze; and approaching the goblet of fire.*

2008.) Although the books had sold millions of copies around the world, Pattinson hadn't read any of them before he learned of the opportunity to audition for the fourth film, *Harry Potter and the Goblet of Fire.* He was up for the part of Cedric Diggory, an older student who competes against Harry in a magical tournament between wizarding schools. Pattinson quickly read the book to give himself an idea of the character, then had an initial audition for director Mike Newell before heading to South Africa to film *Ring of the Nibelungs.* The day after he returned, he was called back for a second audition. Soon after he got the news: he had won a key role in what would be the biggest movie of 2005.

In working on *Harry Potter and the Goblet of Fire,* Pattinson was joining a cast that had already worked on three films together. But after a few weeks of acting exercises with the other young actors, he felt like just another one of the gang. "I didn't notice the transition to being accepted, but they are all really nice people," he recalled. "It seems like it should have been daunting but it wasn't." More intimidating was the thought of working with such distinguished British actors as Sir Michael Gambon (Dumbledore), Dame Maggie Smith (Professor McGonagall), and Warwick Davis (Professor Flitwick), who starred in one of Pattinson's favorite films, the 1988 fantasy *Willow.* It inspired Pattinson to try his best. "I put quite a lot of work into it in the beginning," he recalled. "So I ignored all my nerves by sitting and looking at the script or reading the book 10 times." His preparations also included fitness and scuba training for some of the action scenes, as well as dance lessons for the ballroom scene.

The character of Cedric Diggory—school prefect, Quidditch captain, and Hogwarts' champion for the Triwizard Tournament—was appealing to Pattinson. "He's not really a complete cliché of the good kid in school. He's just quiet," he observed. "He is actually just a genuinely good person, but he doesn't make a big deal about it or anything. I can kind of relate to that."

The character of Cedric Diggory—school prefect, Quidditch captain, and Hogwarts' champion for the Triwizard Tournament—was appealing to Pattinson. "He's not really a complete cliché of the good kid in school. He's just quiet," he observed. "He is actually just a genuinely good person, but he doesn't make a big deal about it or anything. I can kind of relate to that." Although he might have looked the part, Pattinson didn't feel he

Pattinson and Kristen Stewart in a scene from Twilight.

was like his character at all. "I was never a leader, and the idea of my ever being made head boy would have been a complete joke," he acknowledged. "I wasn't involved in much at school, and I was never picked for any of the teams." Nevertheless, he enjoyed filming the various action scenes, which included many special effects and moving around huge sets. "It was amazing. It was a very different thing to anything I've ever experienced," he said at the time.

Harry Potter and the Goblet of Fire was a big hit at the box office, winning the approval of the series' many fans. Although it was the first *Harry Potter* film to be rated PG-13, it had the best opening weekend of any of the films to date, and it had the biggest worldwide receipts at the box office for 2005. In addition to his role in *Goblet of Fire,* Pattinson appeared in flashback in the fifth film, *Harry Potter and the Order of the Phoenix* (2007).

Trying New Roles

After completing his high-profile role in *Goblet of Fire,* Pattinson could have looked for similar good-guy roles. Instead he pursued a role on the London stage as a troubled youth, then won roles in a couple of British TV productions. In the 2006 mystery *The Haunted Airman,* based on the novel by Dennis Wheatley, he played a former Royal Air Force pilot who was wounded during World War II. Confined to a wheelchair, the pilot begins suffering hallucinations and nightmares, but it is unclear whether he is losing his mind or there is a sinister plot behind his decline. Pattinson had a smaller role in the 2007 family drama, *The Bad Mother's Handbook.* It follows the relationships between a grandmother, mother, and daughter; Pattinson played a nerdy friend of the daughter.

Pattinson was beginning to wonder whether he should keep acting when he decided to move to Los Angeles and try auditioning for some American roles. His first task was mastering the accent. That wasn't hard, he said, since "I grew up watching American movies and stuff, so I've learned how to'act' from American films." He soon got an audition for an adaptation of another popular book: the vampire romance *Twilight,* written by Stephenie Meyer. *Twilight* is the first in a series of books that now includes *New Moon, Eclipse,* and *Breaking Dawn.*

When *Twilight* film director Catherine Hardwicke saw Pattinson's audition, she was impressed by his chemistry with costar Kristen Stewart, as well as his otherworldly looks, and she cast him in the lead role of Edward. Thousands of fans protested, believing the part should be played by someone more famous and more handsome. After author Stephenie Meyer gave him her approval, calling him someone "who can look both dangerous and beautiful at the same time," the fans came around. "The funny thing is I've been trying to get pretty boy roles for the last four years and nobody cast me," Pattinson commented. "It's like the world has changed its mind this year." The concept of playing a "pretty boy" has been a struggle for Pattinson. "I literally have to be filmed from the right angle or I look deformed. I'm not just one of those guys you can shoot from any angle and they look perfect."

"

The concept of playing a "pretty boy" has been a struggle for Pattinson. "I literally have to be filmed from the right angle or I look deformed. I'm not just one of those guys you can shoot from any angle and they look perfect."

"

Appearing in *Twilight*

Pattinson worked hard to prepare for the role of Edward, reflecting on the character's personality, actions, and feelings. He headed to Oregon, where *Twilight* was filmed, ahead of the rest of the cast. There he spent a lot of time alone, reading the script and books and avoiding people. "Edward would be so bored with any kind of human interaction," he explained. "He would not feel like he was part of the human world." The actor thought about why a vampire over 100 years old would still be in high school. "You think he'd stay in college, or be a street kid," the actor mused. "It'd be way cooler. But I think the whole concept of it is: He's like an addict. I think he wants to make his life really, really, really boring." Although in the book Edward is described as almost perfect, both in looks and personality, "I just kind of ignored it," Pattinson said. "I just tried to concentrate on his flaws." His approach was to play Edward almost as a manic-depressive. "I tried to play it, as much as possible, like a 17-year-old boy who had this purgatory inflicted on him." His goal was to make Edward as real a character as possible. "I never saw it as a vampire," he remarked. "I saw it as a guy with something in him that makes him terrified of commitment."

"

Pattinson worked hard to prepare for the role of Edward. "I tried to play it, as much as possible, like a 17-year-old boy who had this purgatory inflicted on him." His goal was to make Edward as real a character as possible. "I never saw it as a vampire," he remarked. "I saw it as a guy with something in him that makes him terrified of commitment."

The story in *Twilight* focuses on the growing—and dangerous—love between Bella Swan, an ordinary human teenager, and Edward Cullen, a vampire. Bella moves to a new town to live with her father, the local sheriff. On her first day of school, she meets her new lab partner, Edward. He has sworn not to feed off humans, but he finds Bella's scent intoxicating. She falls in love with him, which becomes especially dangerous when other vampires show up in town. As Pattinson sees it, "Edward is essentially the hero of this story but violently denies that he is the hero.... He refuses to accept Bella's love for him but at the same time can't help but just kind of need it."

In addition to acting in the film, Pattinson contributed some songs as well. Someone gave director Hardwicke a recording of his songs, and she used two of them in the film without telling him about it. "It was like [the song] was supposed to be there.... It's this little song with acoustic guitar. I'm singing it, maybe that makes it different, but it's kind of overwhelming." His

Pattinson (right) with Taylor Lautner and Kristen Stewart at the 2009 MTV Awards, where the movie Twilight *and the cast took home several awards.*

song "Never Think," co-written with a friend, appeared on the film's official soundtrack, which hit No. 1 on Billboard's Top 200 Album Chart and was certified platinum with over one million copies sold. Although he loves music, Pattinson hasn't recorded anything seriously, preferring to play small gigs in bars with friends. "I really didn't want it to look like I was trying to cash in.... I'm not going to be doing any music videos or anything. Music is my backup plan if acting fails. I don't want to put all my eggs in one basket."

Twilight debuted in November 2008 and earned almost $70 million in its first weekend alone. While that may have surprised those unfamiliar with the books, it certainly didn't surprise devoted *Twilight* fans, who saw the film multiple times. This story of forbidden love eventually led to $191 million in sales at the box office in the U.S. alone, making *Twilight* the top vampire movie of all time. According to many critics, Pattinson was a big reason for the movie's success. "Pattinson walks away with every scene he's in," a London *Times* online reporter wrote, while *Entertainment Weekly* critic Owen Gleiberman noted that "Pattinson has a look so broodingly unearthly it's no wonder he doesn't sprout fangs. His creepy bedroom stare is a special effect all its own." In addition, the movie and its cast won a host of awards at the MTV movie awards, including best movie; best male breakthrough performance for Pattinson; best female performance for Kristen Stewart; best kiss for Pattinson and Stewart; and best fight for Pattinson and Cam Gigandet.

Following the success of *Twilight,* the movie studio was eager to film the sequels. *New Moon* is currently scheduled to be released in November 2009, followed by *Eclipse* in June 2010. Pattinson will reprise the role of Edward in both films.

Expanding His Acting Range

It seems likely that Pattinson has a long career as an actor ahead of him. His role in *Twilight* brought him lots of attention, with crowds of over 5,000 coming to some of his public appearances. The readers of the London *Times* Online voted him "British Star of Tomorrow." Low-budget, independent movies that he filmed before *Twilight* suddenly got more attention, and they demonstrated Pattinson could play a wide range of characters. He played one such character, Art, in the 2008 film *How to Be.* Art is a failed musician whose girlfriend kicks him out, forcing him to move back home with his parents. He then uses an inheritance to hire a self-help guru as his personal life-coach. The film appeared at several festivals in 2008 and earned Pattinson a Best Actor Award from the Strasbourg (France) International Film Festival.

Pattinson admits to being somewhat shy, especially when it comes to talking about himself, and he would prefer not to give interviews. "I just say the first thing that comes into my head out of nervousness."

Pattinson took a completely different role in *Little Ashes,* which also appeared at film festivals in 2008 and was released in theaters in 2009, after his success in *Twilight.* In this biography, he plays the Spanish painter Salvador Dalí, best known for surrealist landscapes that often featured melting clocks, eggs, ants, and spindly figures. The role was challenging and complex, playing the artist as a youth in the early 1920s, when he became involved with two other future artistic giants, poet Federico García Lorca and filmmaker Luis Buñuel. "I didn't want to get stuck in pretty, public school roles, or I knew I'd end up as some sort of caricature," Pattinson said. "Playing Dalí has been a complete turning point for me.... He was the most bizarre, complex man, but in the end I felt I could relate to him. He was basically incredibly shy."

Pattinson in a scene from How to Be.

Pattinson's success in *Twilight* has brought him fame and fortune—including a reported $10 million a picture for the sequels. But he dislikes all the media attention he has been getting. "It's boring! I'm thinking about my career in long terms, rather than just trying to milk one thing for whatever it's worth." He also admits to being somewhat shy, especially when it comes to talking about himself, and he would prefer not to give interviews. "I just say the first thing that comes into my head out of nervousness."

Pattinson has said that his future might involve writing and producing, both films and music. His goal is to create work that is creatively fulfilling, in whatever field. "I'm not massively concerned about doing lots of acting jobs," he remarked. "If it all just went, right now, I'd be like, 'All right. I don't really care.' That's probably a stupid thing to say. But I don't, really. I think it'd be much worse to do a load of stuff that's really bad. Because then you can't go into another career. If you've made an idiot out of yourself, you're never going to be taken seriously, as a lawyer or something, if you're, like, a joke actor. The only thing I want from anything is to not be embarrassed." As for his success, he keeps it all in perspective. "It's hard for [my parents] because they want to be proud of me, but I keep reminding them that it's all luck. Luck is what got me here, nothing else."

HOME AND FAMILY

Pattinson spends time in both London and Los Angeles. For a time he shared an apartment with a friend in London's Soho neighborhood, but since his success in *Twilight* he has begun renting his own place in Los Angeles. "Really, I'm a bit of a loner and not that good with dealing with loads of people," he has said. "Most of the time, I feel that going out is a complete waste of time. I'd rather stay in and create something than go out and talk."

HOBBIES AND OTHER INTERESTS

Besides playing and listening to music, Pattinson spends his free time playing cards and darts. He also enjoys writing in a journal. When at home in London, he loves to spend time with his dog, Patty, a white West Highland terrier.

MOVIE AND TELEVISION CREDITS

Ring of the Nibelungs, 2004 (European TV; aired in the U.S. as *Dark Kingdom: The Dragon King*, 2006)
Harry Potter and the Goblet of Fire, 2005
The Haunted Airman, 2006 (British TV)
The Bad Mother's Handbook, 2007 (British TV)
Harry Potter and the Order of the Phoenix, 2007
How to Be, 2008
The Summer House, 2008 (short film)
Twilight, 2008
Little Ashes, 2009

HONORS AND AWARDS

Festival Prize for Best Actor (Strasbourg International Film Festival): 2008, for *How to Be*
New Hollywood Award (Hollywood Film Festival): 2008
MTV Movie Awards: 2009 (three awards), for *Twilight*, for Best Male Breakthrough Performance, Best Kiss (with Kristen Stewart), and Best Fight (with Cam Gigandet)

FURTHER READING

Books

Adams, Isabelle. *Robert Pattinson: Eternally Yours*, 2008

Periodicals

Boston Globe, Nov. 16, 2008, p.N9
Chicago Tribune, Nov. 14, 2008
Daily Mail (London), Dec. 5, 2008, p.45

Daily Telegraph (London), Dec. 5, 2008, p.32
Entertainment Weekly, Nov. 14, 2008, p.24; Nov. 28, 2008, p.58
GQ, Apr. 2009, p.102
Los Angeles Times, Nov. 2, 2008, p.E5
Maclean's, Dec. 8, 2008, p.52
New York Times, Nov. 16, 2008, p.L4
USA Today, Nov. 20, 2008, p.D1; Nov. 21, 2008, p.E4

Online Articles

http://women.timesonline.co.uk
(London Times, "Fancy Man: Robert Pattinson," Dec. 14, 2008)
http://latimesblogs.latimes.com
(Los Angeles Times, "Robert Pattinson on his *Twilight* Songs," Oct. 9, 2008)
http://www.mtv.com/movies
(MTV, "What's in Store for Robert Pattinson's Post-*Twilight* Future?" Feb. 25, 2009)

ADDRESS

Robert Pattinson
Summit Entertainment
1630 Stewart Street
Suite 120
Santa Monica, CA 90404

WORLD WIDE WEB SITES

http://www.twilightthemovie.com
http://www.stepheniemeyer.com

Chris Paul 1985-

American Professional Basketball Player with the New Orleans Hornets
2005-06 NBA Rookie of the Year
Member of the 2008 Olympic Gold Medal-Winning USA Men's Basketball Team

BIRTH

Christopher Emmanuel Paul was born on May 6, 1985, in Winston-Salem, North Carolina. His father, Charles Paul, built surveillance equipment, while his mother, Robin Paul, oversaw the technical staff at a bank. Chris has one brother, C.J., who is two years older.

YOUTH

Chris Paul grew up in a modest, two-story brick house in the town of Lewisville, about 10 miles from Winston-Salem. His parents had strict rules and expected their boys to follow them. "We went to church, got whuppings when we were bad, and couldn't play our video games during the week," C.J. Paul remembered. "Some people would say it was a rough childhood, but it brought out the best in us. We were raised to give back and never take things for granted."

Throughout his youth, Paul spent a lot of time with his maternal grandfather, Nathaniel Jones, whom he called Papa Chilly. Papa Chilly owned a local gas station, Jones Chevron. When he opened the business in 1964, at the height of the African-American civil rights movement, it was the first black-owned service station in North Carolina. Chris and his brother C.J. worked there during the summer and on weekends. They cleaned windshields, pumped gas, and helped out with routine car maintenance like changing oil and rotating tires. They also learned from their grandfather's example. "My grandfather always worked hard. He took care of my family spiritually, emotionally, and financially," Chris explained. "My granddad was my best friend. I wouldn't be in the position I'm in now had it not been for him and the things he instilled in me—hard work and the importance of family."

"My grandfather always worked hard. He took care of my family spiritually, emotionally, and financially," Chris explained. "My granddad was my best friend. I wouldn't be in the position I'm in now had it not been for him and the things he instilled in me—hard work and the importance of family."

When he was not going to school or working at the gas station, Chris loved to play sports. Even as a boy, he was very competitive and hated to lose. He and his brother developed a fierce sibling rivalry that extended to all sorts of contests, from basketball and football to bowling and board games. "We didn't finish most of our games, that's how bad it would get," C.J. admitted. "Sometimes my mother would leave work early, just so she could control us." Even though Chris was younger and smaller, he never questioned whether he could compete with C.J. and his friends. "He's always said, 'If they can do it, I'm going to do it,'" Robin Paul noted. "He's always had that determined spirit."

When Paul was just in high school, he played on the 2003 Jordan Capital Classic Team. Paul is shown in the front row, third from right; Michael Jordan is in the center.

Chris Paul showed athletic talent from an early age. He played quarterback in Pop Warner youth football, for example, and led his team to the 10-and-under national championship game. From the start, though, his favorite game was basketball. "I always had a basketball in my hands as a kid," he recalled. "I was always dribbling and trying new things. Then I'd try to transfer the things I worked on to the court."

For many years, Paul found that the main obstacle to basketball success was his small size. He was only about five feet tall when he entered high school. Every night before bed, he would kneel down and ask God to make him taller. Finally, after an eight-inch growth spurt during his junior year, Paul reached his adult height of six feet. "I've always been vertically challenged. I never grew at all until my junior year of high school. If you call this growing," he laughed. "I knew God wasn't going to get carried away and make me seven feet, two inches. He just gave me enough to get by."

EDUCATION

Paul attended West Forsyth High School near his home in Lewisville. He was a popular student who was elected president of his sophomore, junior, and senior classes. He was an active member of several school clubs and committees, and he served as the school's homecoming king. Since his parents insisted that he maintain at least a 3.0 grade point average if he wanted to play sports, Paul also made the honor roll.

Partly due to his small stature, Paul did not make the varsity basketball team at West Forsyth until his junior year in 2001-02. Still, the young player's dedication to the game impressed the varsity coaching staff. "I played on the junior varsity during my freshman and sophomore years, so I would practice with my team, then when we got done, I would go practice with my older brother's team, the varsity," Paul recalled. "Then I'd go home, eat dinner, then go to the YMCA and play there. I didn't really look at it like I was training or working out with certain guys; I was just playing ball."

Paul's hard work paid off during his junior season, when he became the starting point guard for the West Forsyth Titans varsity basketball team. He averaged an impressive 25 points, 5.3 assists, and 4.4 steals per game to lead his team to a 26-4 won-loss record and the semifinals of the state tournament. The following season went even better for Paul. As a senior in 2002-03, he tallied 30.8 points and 8.0 assists per game and led the Titans to a 27-3 record. Unfortunately, the team was knocked out in the regional finals of the state tournament. Paul's amazing senior season earned him several honors and awards. He was named Mr. Basketball for North Carolina, for instance, as well as a High School All-American.

Honoring His Grandfather

Paul's performance on the basketball court attracted the attention of a number of the top college basketball programs in the country. A week before the start of his senior season, Paul formally accepted a full scholarship to play basketball at his hometown college, Wake Forest University in Winston-Salem. He signed a national letter of intent on November 14, 2002, during a ceremony at his high school that was attended by many family members and friends.

The very next day, Paul's family was rocked by tragedy. His beloved grandfather, Nathaniel Jones, was murdered. Jones had returned home from working at the gas station to find four teenagers robbing his house. The burglars stole his wallet and beat him to death. He was 61 years old.

Paul attended his grandfather's funeral on the day before the first game of his senior high school basketball season. After the service, the grief-stricken teen questioned whether he would be able to join his teammates on the court the next day. Since Jones had always been one of Paul's biggest supporters, though, several family members encouraged him to play in the game. An aunt suggested that Paul find some way to honor his grandfather during the contest.

Inspired, Paul decided that he would try to score 61 points—one for every year of his grandfather's life. He was not sure whether he was capable of the feat (his previous career high was 39 points), so he did not tell anyone about his plan. Once the game got underway, though, it did not take long for his teammates and fans to sense that something special was happening. After scoring 32 points in the first half, Paul continued to scorch the nets in the second half. He hit a layup with two minutes remaining in the game to bring his total to 61. He was fouled on the play, but he intentionally missed the resulting free throw. Even though the state high school record of 67 points was within his reach, Paul then took himself out of the game and collapsed in tears on the bench. His remarkable achievement received mention in several national magazines and newspapers.

"I played on the junior varsity during my freshman and sophomore years, so I would practice with my team, then when we got done, I would go practice with my older brother's team, the varsity," Paul recalled. "Then I'd go home, eat dinner, then go to the YMCA and play there. I didn't really look at it like I was training or working out with certain guys; I was just playing ball."

Playing for Wake Forest

Paul graduated from West Forsyth in the spring of 2003. That fall he entered Wake Forest, where he majored in communications and earned a spot on the dean's list. He also became the star point guard on the Demon Deacons basketball team. As a freshman, he averaged 14.8 points per game and led the team in a number of statistical categories, including assists (with 183), steals (84), three-point field goal percentage (.465), and free-throw percentage (.843). His strong performance helped him win the 2003-04 Atlantic Coast Conference (ACC) Rookie of the Year Award and the National Freshman of the Year Award. Wake Forest posted a 21-9 record that year and earned a coveted invitation to the season-ending National Collegiate Athletic Association (NCAA) tournament. Paul raised his scoring average to 21 points in the tournament, but the Demon Deacons lost to St. Joseph's in the third round.

Playing for the Wake Forest Demon Deacons,
Paul hustles to the basket in this game against Duke.

During his sophomore season in 2004-05, Paul emerged as one of the top point guards in the country. He averaged 15.3 points, 6.6 assists, and 2.4 steals per game to lead the Demon Deacons to a 27-6 record. Once again, however, the season ended in a disappointing fashion when Wake Forest lost to West Virginia in the second round of the NCAA tournament. Paul's many post-season honors included being named a consensus first-team All-American. He decided to leave Wake Forest without completing his degree in order to make himself eligible for the 2005 National Basketball Association (NBA) draft.

CAREER HIGHLIGHTS

NBA—The New Orleans Hornets

Paul was selected in the first round of the 2005 draft, with the fourth overall pick, by the New Orleans Hornets. The Hornets had entered the NBA in 1988 as an expansion team based in Charlotte, North Carolina. The franchise relocated to New Orleans, Louisiana, in 2002. The year before Paul joined the team, the Hornets had struggled to an 18-64 record in the NBA's tough Western Conference.

Despite the addition of a promising young point guard, few people expected the Hornets to do well in 2005-06. Prospects for the season looked even more bleak when Hurricane Katrina roared through the Gulf of Mexico and struck New Orleans in August 2005. The storm caused severe flooding that devastated the city. The Hornets' home stadium suffered serious damage, so the team was forced to play most of its home games that year in Oklahoma City, Oklahoma.

Paul and the Hornets overcame this disruption, however, and performed far better than expected. They finished the season with a respectable 38-44 record, more than doubling the previous year's win total. Paul averaged 16.1 points, 7.8 assists, and 2.24 steals per game in his professional debut. He led all rookies in those categories and easily won the NBA Rookie of the Year Award. In addition, his 175 total steals ranked first in the entire league.

In an effort to build a stronger supporting cast for Paul, New Orleans made a number of changes to its roster prior to the 2006-07 season. The Hornets signed free-agent guard Jannero Pargo, acquired small forward Peja Stojakovic from the Indiana Pacers, and traded with the Chicago Bulls for center Tyson Chandler. Unfortunately, it turned out to be a frustrating year for Paul and his teammates. Paul suffered a series of injuries to his foot, ankle, and thumb that kept him out of action for a total of 18 games. "It's been tough," he noted. "It seems like when you come back from one [injury],

Paul in action in 2008, as the team drove toward the playoffs.

another one comes up. But that's how this league is." The absence of their star player proved too much for the Hornets to overcome. Still playing most of their home games in Oklahoma City, they posted a 39-43 record and failed to make the playoffs.

Paul still averaged 17.3 points, 4.4 rebounds, 8.9 assists, and 1.84 steals per game during his second NBA season. In spite of his nagging injuries, he led the Hornets in assists, steals, and total points, and he ranked fourth in the league in assists per game. After the season ended, Paul underwent surgery to repair a stress reaction in his left foot.

Making the NBA Playoffs

With repairs to their stadium completed, the Hornets moved back to New Orleans prior to the start of the 2007-08 season. The team had attracted so many fans in Oklahoma City, however, that the NBA decided to award the city its own franchise. The former Seattle Supersonics announced plans to move there in 2008-09 and become the Oklahoma City Thunder.

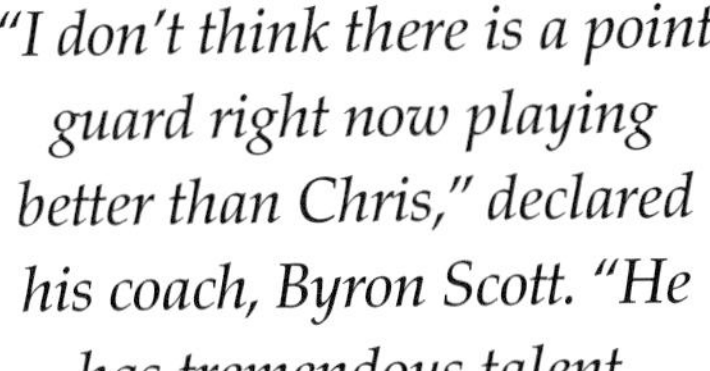

"I don't think there is a point guard right now playing better than Chris," declared his coach, Byron Scott. "He has tremendous talent, tremendous will. He loves to be out there, winning and doing whatever it takes to knock down an opponent."

The Hornets' return home helped propel the team to a great start in Paul's third NBA season. New Orleans led the Western Conference with a 29-12 record at the halfway point in the season. As a result, the team's head coach, Byron Scott, was named coach of the Western Conference All-Star Team. The roster included two of his own players, Paul and power forward David West. Paul contributed 16 points, 4 steals, and a game-high 14 assists, but his team lost to the Eastern Conference All-Stars by a score of 134-128. He still enjoyed playing in the All-Star Game, which he described as "totally different from anything I've ever experienced, because this is one of the biggest stages, if not the biggest, as an NBA player."

The Hornets stayed healthy and continued to play well for the remainder of the 2007-08 season. To the surprise of many observers, New Orleans posted the best record in franchise history at 56-26, won the Southwest Division title, and earned the second seed in the Western Conference for the playoffs. "CP [Chris Paul] and I always talked about closing the gap with the best teams in the West," said teammate David West. "We knew if we could stay healthy and stay together, we could do it, and it looks like we've done it. Just maybe a little quicker than we thought."

Paul led the Hornets in scoring, averaging a career-high 21.1 points per game. He also led the entire NBA in assists (with an average of 11.6 per game) and steals (2.7 per game). He thus became the first player to lead the league in both of those categories since Utah Jazz point guard John Stockton did it in 1991-92. Taking note of his individual performance as well as his impact on his team, many people argued that Paul deserved to be named the NBA's Most Valuable Player (MVP). "Chris has his team near the top in the toughest division. He's the best player on our team. He's the floor general, making everyone better," teammate Tyson Chandler explained. "Man, I don't know what an MVP is if it isn't that guy." In the end, however, Paul finished second in the regular-season MVP voting to Los Angeles Lakers star Kobe Bryant.

As the 2007-08 playoffs got underway, the Hornets smoked the Dallas Mavericks in the first round, winning the best-of-seven series four games to one. New Orleans then moved on to face the defending NBA champion San Antonio Spurs in the second round. Paul practically won the first two games in the series himself by scoring a total of 67 points and dishing out 27 assists. "I don't think there is a point guard right now playing better than Chris," declared Coach Scott. "He has tremendous talent, tremendous will. He loves to be out there, winning and doing whatever it takes to knock down an opponent."

Despite Paul's valiant effort, the young Hornets soon relinquished their 2-0 lead and ended up losing the series to the veteran Spurs 4-3. Paul averaged an impressive 24.1 points, 4.9 rebounds, 11.3 assists, and 2.3 steals per game during the playoffs. Afterward, he promised that his team would compete for the NBA title in 2008-09. "We have the tools. We have the talent. We have the personnel," he stated. "We have what it takes."

Winning an Olympic Gold Medal

During the summer of 2008, Paul traveled to Beijing, China, to compete in the Olympic Games as a member of the U.S. Men's National Basketball Team. He had represented the United States in international competition once before, winning a bronze medal at the 2006 World Championships in Japan. Paul was unable to play for the National Team during the summer of 2007, however, because he was recovering from surgery. He was thrilled to have an opportunity to play in the Olympics. "It is the ultimate honor to represent your country," he noted. "I am so proud to be playing for Team USA."

Paul joined a powerful American squad made up of such NBA stars as Kobe Bryant, Jason Kidd, Carmelo Anthony, LeBron James, Dwyane Wade, and Deron Williams. He and his teammates were determined to set their egos aside in order to return home with the gold medal. "We all are just trying to come together and do whatever we need to do to win this gold

In the gold medal game of the 2008 Olympics, Paul and his teammates faced Spain. Team USA took home the gold medal for the first time since 2000.

medal," he stated. "It's not about who plays the most minutes, who gets the most shots. It's about the USA winning at the end."

During the Olympic tournament, Paul led Team USA in assists with 4.1 per game. He also contributed 8.0 points and 3.6 rebounds per contest. After trouncing their opponents in the early rounds, the American squad faced Spain in the gold-medal match. It was a hard-fought contest, but Paul and his teammates prevailed by a score of 118-107. They thus claimed the first gold medal for the United States in men's basketball since the 2000 Games. "The gold medal is one of the highest achievements in my basketball career to date," Paul said afterward. "This was the first time in my life that I've really been a champion. I've always been on winning teams. But to actually be a champion? It has given me something to strive for in the NBA."

Joining the Ranks of Great Players

Prior to the start of the 2008-09 NBA season, Paul signed a three-year contract extension with the Hornets worth an estimated $68 million. The new contract reflected his impact on the team, as well as his popularity with fans in New Orleans. "We are honored to have [him] as the face and future of our franchise," said Hornets owner George Shinn. "The difference between a good player and a great player is character. I think without a doubt Chris Paul has character plus."

As he entered his fourth year in the league, Paul seemed ready to join the ranks of the greatest point guards in NBA history. "When you talk about great point guards in this league that have all had a very big impact on the game, you've got to talk about Magic [Johnson] and Zeke [Isiah Thomas] and [John] Stockton and guys like that," said Byron Scott. "When you start talking about those guys, he's in that sentence somewhere."

"

Paul enjoys being a role model for kids and takes the responsibility very seriously. "It means a lot," he said. "Every time I look at kids, I see myself at that age, knowing I would have loved someone like an NBA player talking to me and letting me know what he did to get there."

When the Hornets began the 2008-09 season, many viewed them as contenders. After the team's spirited playoff run in 2008, many believed the team could go all the way. Fans were disappointed, however, when the Hornets only made it to the first round of the playoffs. There they were trounced in five games by the Denver Nuggets, including one game at home that New Orleans lost by 58 points. Still, Paul's statistics for the season showed the level of his play. Overall, he averaged 22.8 points per game. He broke a league record when he played in 108 consecutive games with at least one steal. For the season, he ranked No. 1 in the league in assists and steals, No. 2 in triple-doubles, and No. 3 in double-doubles. Despite the team's poor end to the season, many are looking forward to Paul's future prospects, as is shown in the comment from sports analyst Don Yaeger: "[He] has become the NBA's point guard of the future. He's an unbelievable scorer, a great defender despite his six-foot size, a player who controls the game's tempo, creates opportunities for his teammates, and challenges them as well." With that kind of reputation, Paul still seems poised on the brink of greatness.

HOME AND FAMILY

Chris Paul, who is single, shares a home in New Orleans with his brother.

HOBBIES AND OTHER INTERESTS

Bowling is Paul's favorite hobby.

When he is not playing basketball, Paul enjoys watching football (especially the Dallas Cowboys), mountain biking, and listening to music. His favorite hobby, however, is bowling. "My dad used to bowl in leagues all the time," he recalled. "We used to go up there with him. It was a fun family event. Then, when I got to college, I really got into it. My parents bought me my own bowling ball that looks like the old ABA [American Basketball Association] three-color basketball."

Paul sometimes goes bowling twice a day with his brother. His bowling scores average between 180 and 190, and he once tallied a high game of 256. Paul serves as an official spokesman for the U.S. Bowling Congress (USBC). He also hosts an annual charity bowling tournament in Winston-Salem. The 2008 event featured NBA stars LeBron James, Dwyane Wade, and Dwight Howard, as well as professional bowling stars Jason Couch, Chris Barnes, Tommy Jones, and Doug Kent.

Paul also contributes his time and money to a variety of other charitable causes. Shortly after joining the NBA in 2005, for example, he established a foundation to sponsor projects in the Winston-Salem community. After the city of New Orleans was devastated by Hurricane Katrina in 2005, Paul fed 200 needy families on Thanksgiving, took 100 kids Christmas shopping, joined with other NBA stars to help Habitat for Humanity build homes in New Orleans, and joined Dwyane Wade in building a family learning center and furnishing it with computers. "People ask me if I feel obligated to give back, especially given what New Orleans went through," he said at the time. "I tell them you should never feel obligated to do it; you should want to do it." Paul also makes frequent appearances at schools and basketball camps to connect with his young fans. He enjoys being a role model for kids and takes the responsibility very seriously. "It means a lot," he said. "Every time I look at kids, I see myself at that age, knowing I would have loved someone like an NBA player talking to me and letting me know what he did to get there."

HONORS AND AWARDS

High School Basketball All-American (MacDonald's, *Parade*): 2003
Mr. Basketball for North Carolina (*Charlotte Observer*): 2003
NCAA Men's Basketball Freshman of the Year (*College Insider, Sporting News, Basketball Times*): 2003-04
NCAA Basketball All-American: 2004-05
NBA Rookie of the Year: 2005-06
NBA Community Assist Award: 2006
NBA Western Conference All-Star: 2007-08
Olympic Games, Men's Basketball: 2008, gold medal

FURTHER READING

Periodicals

Atlanta Journal and Constitution, Feb. 27, 2005, p.D1
Current Biography, Apr. 2009
Forbes, June 22, 2009, p.88
New York Times, Apr. 8, 2006, p.D1; Apr. 27, 2008, p.L5
Sports Illustrated, Feb. 28, 2005, p.54; Feb. 13, 2006, p.66; Dec. 17, 2007, p.50; Feb. 18, 2008, p.32
Sports Illustrated for Kids, Mar. 2005, p.46; May 2006, p.T4; Apr. 2008, p.20; Nov. 2008, p.28
St. Petersburg Times, Mar. 20, 2004, p.C1
Success, July 2009, p.78
USA Today, Mar. 22, 2007, p.C12; Apr. 11, 2007, p.C8; Feb. 14, 2008, p.E1
Washington Post, Jan. 29, 2004, p.D1

ADDRESS

Chris Paul
New Orleans Hornets
1250 Poydras Street, Floor 19
New Orleans, LA 70113

WORLD WIDE WEB SITES

http://www.chrispaul3.com
http://www.nba.com/hornets
http://www.nbcolympics.com/athletes

Michael Phelps 1985-

American Swimmer
Winner of 14 Gold Medals in the 2004 and 2008 Olympic Games

BIRTH

Michael Fred Phelps was born on June 30, 1985, in Baltimore, Maryland. His father, Fred Phelps, is a retired Maryland State Police officer. His mother, Debbie Phelps, is a former Maryland teacher of the year who later became a Baltimore County school administrator. Michael's parents divorced when he was nine years old. He and his two older sisters, Hilary and Whitney, were raised primarily by their mother.

YOUTH

Phelps has been involved in swimming almost from the time he was born. When he was a toddler, his older sisters started taking swimming lessons at the North Baltimore Aquatic Club (NBAC), one of the premier competitive swimming clubs in the country. His mother brought him along to all of their practices and meets. "I remember taking him out of his crib, putting him in the car, and driving to practice or a competition," Debbie Phelps recalled. "He grew up around the pool."

Phelps began taking swimming lessons himself at the age of seven. But his fear of putting his face in the water made the first few lessons difficult for both him and his instructors. "You would think that on the first day I hit the water I just sort of turned into a dolphin and never wanted to leave the pool," he wrote in his autobiography *Michael Phelps: Beneath the Surface.* "No way. I hated it. We're talking screaming, kicking, fit-throwing, goggle-tossing hate." As time passed, though, Phelps overcame his fears. "Once I figured out how to swim, I felt so free," he explained. "It was like I had this new toy that my sisters enjoyed all the time."

"

"You would think that on the first day I hit the water I just sort of turned into a dolphin and never wanted to leave the pool. No way. I hated it. We're talking screaming, kicking, fit-throwing, goggle-tossing hate." As time passed, though, Phelps overcame his fears. "Once I figured out how to swim, I felt so free. It was like I had this new toy that my sisters enjoyed all the time."

"

As Phelps was learning the basics of the various swimming strokes, his sister Whitney was emerging as one of the most talented young swimmers in the United States. She even appeared likely to claim a spot on the U.S. Olympic Team that would compete in the 1996 Games in Atlanta, Georgia. Unfortunately, Whitney suffered a back injury that prevented her from qualifying for the Olympics and eventually forced her to quit the sport.

Getting Serious about Swimming

Phelps possessed a strong competitive drive from the start of his swimming career, but his immaturity sometimes showed. "Michael was a goofy little kid, but when it came to a swim meet, he wanted to win," said his

Phelps has been training with his coach, Bob Bowman, since the age of 11.

first coach, Tom Himes. "He was just like any other little kid. When he got tired, little things became big issues. He would throw his goggles and have a fit in practice, which was always a challenge for him. When I'd get on him about doing something that he wasn't doing in the right way, his defense was tears."

When Phelps was 11 years old, he began training with a new coach, Bob Bowman. Unlike most competitive swimmers who tend to specialize in a particular stroke and distance, Phelps showed promise in 50-meter and 100-meter sprints as well as 400-meter endurance races. He was also highly competitive in all four strokes: freestyle, backstroke, breaststroke, and butterfly. As a result, Bowman decided to base Phelps's training around the individual medley (IM). In this event, a competitor swims each of the four strokes for one leg of the race. "All the events complement each other, so working on all of them makes sense," the coach explained. The two individual medley events are the 200-meter IM, in which swimmers use each stroke for 50 meters, and the 400-meter IM, in which swimmers use each stroke for 100 meters. There are also medley relay events involving teams of four swimmers, such as the 4x100 medley relay (four legs of 100 meters each). In the medley relay events, each of the four team members completes one leg of the race using a different stroke.

Bowman and his sometimes bratty star pupil clashed often in the early stages of their relationship. After a while, though, Bowman figured out the best ways to reach the youngster.

"The thing that got Michael the most, and still does, is to take swimming away from him," Bowman said. "He hated to be excused early. He considered that an embarrassment.... It was one thing that came naturally and felt good.... He always left practice in a better state than when he arrived."

"

Bowman expressed a lot of confidence in Phelps's potential and convinced him to focus all of his attention on swimming. "He told me, 'If you want to focus on something, you could be in the Olympics,'" Phelps recalled. "When I heard that, I perked my ears up. Everyone, I think, as a little kid, wants to do something big, like be in the Olympics. Everyone wants to be the best—an American icon."

"

Bowman sometimes felt frustrated by Phelps's immaturity. But the coach persevered because he sensed that the young swimmer had the physical gifts to become a star. A few months after he began working with Phelps, Bowman even pulled Debbie Phelps aside and informed her that her son had the potential to make it to the Olympics someday. "I'm thinking, this man is crazy," she remembered. "This is my 11-year-old baby!"

Bowman was dead serious, though, and his confidence in Phelps's potential convinced the youngster to quit playing other sports and focus all of his attention on swimming. "He told me, 'If you want to focus on something, you could be in the Olympics,'" Phelps recalled. "When I heard that, I perked my ears up. Everyone, I think, as a little kid, wants to do something big, like be in the Olympics. Everyone wants to be the best—an American icon." Over the next few years he reluctantly abandoned lacrosse, soccer, and other sports that he enjoyed so that he could spend more time at the pool. The sacrifices proved worthwhile, as Phelps became one of the top junior swimmers in the nation.

During his early teens, Phelps began practicing swimming twice a day—for a total of about five hours—six days per week. The demands of his training schedule limited his free time, but his mother scoffed at any suggestion that he "missed out" on anything during this period of his life. "Like what?" she asked the *New York Times*. "Like he missed some of the things that teenagers get into in this country? I don't feel bad about that. There was always a balance. He went to basketball games. He went to football games. He had friends. He was a normal kid. But he always came home early and got his sleep and went to practice the next day."

EDUCATION

During his first few years of attendance at Rodgers Forge Elementary School in Baltimore, Phelps had trouble sitting still and paying attention in class. "He was a very energetic boy who drove all his teachers crazy," his mother admitted. In addition, he often displayed the same sort of disruptive and disrespectful behavior at home. "I simply could never sit still," he recalled in *Beneath the Surface.* "I made faces at cameras, answered questions with questions and climbed on things that weren't meant for climbing." His behavior improved, though, after he was diagnosed with attention deficit hyperactivity disorder (ADHD). Phelps was given medication that helped him focus on his school tasks. In addition, his intensive swim practices gave him a healthy outlet for his high levels of energy.

> "
>
> *Phelps often displayed disruptive and disrespectful behavior at school and at home—until he was diagnosed with attention deficit hyperactivity disorder (ADHD). "I simply could never sit still," he recalled. "I made faces at cameras, answered questions with questions and climbed on things that weren't meant for climbing."*
>
> "

In 1999, Phelps entered Towson High School in Towson, Maryland. By that point, he was already a nationally ranked competitive swimmer. In fact, he missed the start of his sophomore year in order to compete at the 2000 Olympic Games in Sydney, Australia. Upon his return, he was greeted by 1,200 fellow students cheering on the front lawn of the school. Before the start of his junior year in 2001, Phelps had broken his first world record and signed an endorsement contract with Speedo that made him a professional athlete. After graduating from high school in 2003, he took a year off in order to train for the 2004 Olympic Games in Athens, Greece.

In January 2005 Phelps enrolled as a student at the University of Michigan in Ann Arbor, where Bowman had accepted a job as coach of the swim team. "School is important because it will give him a normal experience

At the 2000 Olympics, Phelps finished fifth in the 200-meter butterfly. He was only 15 years old.

that other people his age are getting," Bowman explained. "He really doesn't have a lot of normal experiences anymore."

Phelps attended classes at Michigan for the next three years. As a professional, he was not eligible to compete in college swimming events. But he served as an assistant for the university team and also trained with Club Wolverine, a world-class swimming club that included many Michigan swimmers as well as college graduates and professionals.

CAREER HIGHLIGHTS

Phelps began his swimming career at a young age. In fact, he showed so much promise as a young swimmer that he made the USA Swimming B Team at the age of 14, in 1999. Between the spring of 1999 and the summer of 2000, Phelps grew a remarkable eight inches and added 60 pounds to his lean frame. The growth spurt made him even faster in the water.

Setting Early Records

In 2000, before starting his sophomore year in high school, Phelps made the USA Swimming A Team and competed in the U.S. Olympic Trials. The top two swimmers in each event would qualify for the team that would represent the United States at the 2000 Games in Sydney, Australia. Phelps finished second in the 200-meter butterfly event and qualified for the U.S. Olympic Team. At age 15, he was the youngest male athlete in more than 60 years to qualify for the U.S. Olympic Team.

Phelps finished fifth in the 200 butterfly at the Sydney Games. The 15-year-old was roundly praised by his coaches for turning in such a solid performance. But Phelps was dissatisfied, and over the next several months he pushed himself even harder. These long hours of exhausting practice paid off at the 2001 U.S. Spring National Championships. Midway through that competition, Phelps became the youngest male athlete in history to set a world record by swimming the 200-meter butterfly in 1 minute and 54.92 seconds (written as 1:54.92). He was still only 15. "When I hit the wall, I turned around and saw the scoreboard flashing 'New World Record,'" he remembered. "I remember I jumped out of the water and went nuts. I don't think I've ever smiled so big before."

"

"When I hit the wall, I turned around and saw the scoreboard flashing 'New World Record,'" Phelps remembered. "I jumped out of the water and went nuts. I don't think I've ever smiled so big before."

A few minutes later, a still-dripping Phelps called his mother with the exciting news. "Before I could say anything, I just started giggling, like a kid in a candy store who is embarrassed by how good he feels," he recalled in *Beneath the Surface*. "'Mom, I broke a world record.' I could tell my mom was trying to stay calm on the other end, but we were both ready to start dancing on the walls. Make that two kids in a candy store."

Phelps continued his string of impressive performances at the 2001 World Championships in Japan. He broke his own world record in the 200 fly with a time of 1:54.58 to claim his first world title. "It felt awesome," he said afterward. "This is the first medal I've ever won in an international meet. For it to be gold is incredible. It feels great." USA Swimming recognized his achievements by naming him Swimmer of the Year for 2001.

Following his outstanding 2001 season, Phelps signed an endorsement contract with Speedo that made him one of the youngest male athletes ever to turn professional. The deal provided income to pay for his training and his travel expenses. But becoming a professional meant that he gave up his eligibility to compete in collegiate swimming.

Phelps in his natural habitat—poolside (at the qualifying events for the 2004 Olympics).

Emerging as a Dominant Force

Over the next two seasons, Phelps emerged as one of the most dominant male swimmers in the world. At the 2002 U.S. Summer National Championships he won four events—the 200-meter butterfly, the 100-meter butterfly, the 200-meter IM, and the 400-meter IM. His time of 4:11.09 in the 400 IM set a new world record. The following year he won national titles in three different strokes at the 2003 U.S. Spring National Championships, swimming to victory in the 200-meter freestyle, the 200-meter backstroke, and the 100-meter butterfly.

Phelps achieved another level of international stardom at the 2003 World Championships in Barcelona, Spain. He became the first swimmer ever to set five individual world records in a single meet. He lowered his own record in the 200 fly to 1:53.93, and he also set records in winning the 200 IM and 400 IM. For Phelps, though, the defining moment of the meet came when he set a personal best time of 51.10 seconds in the 100-meter butterfly—only to be defeated by a world-record performance from U.S. teammate Ian Crocker. The loss bothered Phelps so much that he put a picture of Crocker on his bedroom wall to inspire him to train harder.

At the 2003 U.S. Summer National Championships, Phelps became the first man ever to win five national titles at a single meet. His achievements included setting a new world record in the 200 IM with a time of 1:55.94, more than two seconds faster than anyone had ever swum the event. His extraordinary success in 2003 earned him a second Swimmer of the Year Award, as well as the prestigious James E. Sullivan Award as the nation's top amateur athlete. Meanwhile, Phelps displayed new levels of maturity and friendliness around his coaches and teammates. "He's a really good teammate," said one fellow swimmer. "He pays attention to other people. He knows when somebody needs encouragement. He jokes around. Most of the time, to tell you, he's just this big goof."

Phelps is a nearly perfect physical specimen for swimming. His natural advantages include a long torso and exceptionally long arms, but short legs. "With that arm length, he has a much greater range of motion with his stroke," Bowman explained. "His legs are not particularly long, and that helps him ride high in the water."

At the 2004 U.S. National Championships, Phelps repeated his feat of winning five national titles. His dominance gave him great confidence going into the U.S. Olympic Trials, where the nation's top swimmers would compete to represent the United States at the 2004 Olympic Games in Athens, Greece. Phelps turned in a phenomenal performance at the trials, becoming the first American swimmer ever to qualify to compete in six individual events at the Olympics. He even set a new world record in the 400 IM. His strong performance at the U.S. Olympic Trials earned him a spot on at least two American relay teams—the 4x200 freestyle relay and the 4x100 medley relay.

The 2004 Olympic Games

When Phelps qualified to compete in eight events at the 2004 Olympics—including six individual events and two relays—many observers felt that he was poised to break the all-time record of seven gold medals in a single Olympics. This incredible feat had been set by American swimmer Mark Spitz at the 1972 Games in Munich, Germany. Spitz collected his medals by winning four individual events and contributing to three relay victories. In those days, the American men were dominant in relay events, and their

Phelps swimming at the 2004 Olympics in the 200-meter IM, where he won a gold medal.

margins of victory in the three gold medal races ranged from three to six seconds. Counting preliminary heats, Spitz swam a total of 13 races in the Olympic Games.

Phelps, though, faced a much more difficult challenge. Preliminary heats had been added in several events since 1972, so he would have to compete at least 17 times over eight days in order to have a chance at winning seven gold medals. In a few cases, he would have to compete less than an hour after completing a previous race. In addition, international competition had become so fierce by 2004 that most swimmers specialized in a single stroke and distance. In the individual events, therefore, Phelps would face the world's best swimmers, most of whom had dedicated their training to that one event. Finally, the American relay teams were not as dominant as they had been back in Spitz's day. Given all these issues, some swimming experts flatly declared that Spitz's record was out of Phelps's reach.

Other observers, though, were not so quick to dismiss his chances. They noted that the fiercely competitive Phelps had grown into a nearly perfect physical specimen for swimming. His natural advantages include a long torso and exceptionally long arms, but short legs. "With that arm length, he has a much greater range of motion with his stroke," Bowman explained. "His legs are not particularly long, and that helps him ride high in the water." Phelps also possesses hyperflexible joints that give him more freedom of movement than most of his competitors, and size 14 feet that act like big flippers to propel him through the water. He also has a freakish ability to recover quickly after races because his body produces less lactate—the substance that makes muscles feel tired after exertion—than most athletes. Finally, Phelps has a natural "feel" for the water that is the envy of many other swimmers. "He's a dream in the water, mesmerizing to watch," said Olympic swimmer Debbie Meyer. "You think of a porpoise. You wonder how a human being can do that."

Phelps has a natural "feel" for the water that is the envy of many other swimmers. "He's a dream in the water, mesmerizing to watch," said Olympic swimmer Debbie Meyer. "You think of a porpoise. You wonder how a human being can do that."

As the Athens Games approached, many experts speculated that scheduling conflicts would force Phelps to drop one of the six individual events for which he had qualified. He remained secretive about his plans for several weeks. Although some of his rivals expressed annoyance at his refusal to reveal his plans, Phelps seemed to enjoy keeping them guessing. "Why do they have to know?" he asked. "Wouldn't it be better for them just to concentrate on their own events and not worry about what I'm doing?"

Finally, a few weeks before the Olympics began, Phelps announced that he was withdrawing from the 200-meter backstroke competition. His decision surprised many people, because he was virtually guaranteed to win at least a silver medal in that event. Instead, he decided to compete in one of his weaker events, the 200-meter freestyle, in order to face famed Australian swimmer Ian Thorpe. "If this was just about seven gold medals, he would have dropped this event," Bowman said of the 200 free. "But that's not the goal. The goal is to see what he can do."

Phelps also shed some light on his unexpected choice of events. "One thing I always wanted to do was race Thorpe in a freestyle event," he explained. "I think it is the best opportunity for me to be able to swim in probably the fastest 200 freestyle heat in history." He also indicated that he

Phelps shows his form at the 2004 Olympics in the 200-meter free, an exciting race in which he came in third after Ian Thorpe and Pieter van den Hoogenband.

was not concerned about chasing Spitz's record. "My goal is to win one Olympic medal," he declared. "One will not be a failure to me."

Winning Gold in Athens

Once the Olympic Games got underway, Phelps more than met the high expectations that had preceded his trip to Athens. He won gold medals in his three best individual events—the 200 butterfly (with a time of 1:54.04), the 200 IM (with a time of 1:57.14), and the 400 IM (with a world record time of 4:09.09). He earned a fourth individual gold in the 100 butterfly, overcoming a slow start to beat teammate Ian Crocker by .04 seconds. He thus tied Spitz's record of four individual swimming gold medals in a single Olympics.

Phelps's final individual event, the 200 freestyle, featured one of the strongest fields in the history of competitive swimming. In addition to Phelps and favorite Ian Thorpe, the "race of the century" included defending Olympic champion Pieter van den Hoogenband of the Netherlands, Grant Hackett of Australia, and Klete Keller of the United States. Van den Hoogenband took an early lead, but Thorpe charged past him in the final 50 meters to claim the gold with a time of 1:44.71. Phelps nearly caught the Dutchman as well, but he ended up settling for the bronze, despite setting a new American record of 1:45.32. "I was happy to be part of this field and to do my best time," he said afterward. "It was fun."

Halfway through the Olympic swimming competition, USA Swimming coaches announced that they were adding Phelps to the American 4x100 freestyle relay team. Some of his teammates were upset by the decision. Since Phelps had not qualified for the event at the Olympic Trials, they wondered if the coaches were adding him at the last minute in order to improve his chances of winning seven gold medals. Despite the presence of Phelps, though, the American men had to settle for bronze in the event behind South Africa and the Netherlands.

Phelps's favorite race of the Athens Games was the 4x200 freestyle relay, an event that the American men had not won in international competition in seven years. Competing just one hour after winning gold in the 200 fly, Phelps swam a blistering leadoff leg that gave the American team a body-length lead. He then climbed out of the water and watched intently as his teammates completed their legs of the race. When American anchor Klete Keller held off a charging Ian Thorpe and touched the wall first, Phelps raised his arms and whooped with joy. "That was the most exciting race I have ever been a part of," he said afterward. "I don't think I have ever celebrated like that in my life."

Phelps's final race of the 2004 Olympics was the 4x100 medley relay, in which he was scheduled to swim the butterfly leg. By this time, though, he was feeling the effects of the strenuous eight-day competition. He also knew that he would share any medal that the U.S. team earned in the final, since he had competed in the preliminary heat of the event. Phelps thus decided to give up his spot on the relay team to teammate Ian Crocker, who had yet to win a gold medal in Athens. Crocker found his teammate's generosity hard to believe. "I'm speechless," he said. "It makes me want to just go out there and tear up the pool tomorrow."

On the final day of the Olympic swimming competition, Phelps watched from the stands as Crocker and the rest of his teammates won the 4x100 medley relay with a world record time of 3:30.68. Phelps thus earned his sixth gold medal of the Athens Games, falling one short of matching Spitz's record. Counting his two bronze medals, though, his total of eight medals tied the all-time record for an individual competitor in a single games.

———— " ————

"He's the greatest swimmer in the world right now," said American backstroker Aaron Peirsol during the 2004 Olympics. "He's incredible, unbelievable. What he's done is really spectacular in this day and age. To come away with eight medals, that really is the Spitzian accomplishment of our age."

———— " ————

Phelps's coaches and teammates were quick to praise his accomplishments. "He's the greatest swimmer in the world right now," said American backstroker Aaron Peirsol. "He's incredible, unbelievable. What he's done is really spectacular in this day and age. To come away with eight medals, that really is the Spitzian accomplishment of our age."

Struggling to Regain His Form

After the Olympics, Phelps struggled with some problems. He was forced to withdraw from the 2004 Short-Course World Championships due to a nagging back injury. In November 2004, he attended a party with some friends. Since he did not have an early morning practice session the next day, he stayed late and drank alcohol. But then he made the decision to drive. On his way home, Phelps ran a stop sign, was pulled over by the police, and was arrested for driving under the influence of alcohol (DUI).

Phelps immediately admitted his mistake and apologized for it. He also spoke out publicly about the dangers of drinking and driving, and he answered questions about his own experience and the effect it had on him and his family. "I've made a mistake and it's something I'm going to have to live with now," he noted. "I want to reach out as much as I can to help as many kids as I can to get the message not to drink and drive. It's unacceptable and just flat-out wrong. It's a big learning experience, and I want to move forward from here. The hardest thing is knowing the people I have let down."

In December Phelps pleaded guilty to the DUI charge. The judge considered his long record of community service in handing down a sentence of 18 months probation. His record was wiped clean after Phelps completed the terms of his probation without any problems.

Phelps brings a lot of intensity to swimming—and to cheering on his teammates.

In 2005 Phelps moved to Ann Arbor, Michigan, and enrolled as a student at the University of Michigan. He also published his autobiography, *Michael Phelps: Beneath the Surface*. Once his back injury healed, he resumed training with Bowman at Club Wolverine in preparation for the 2005 World Championships. When Phelps returned to the water, he showed the same explosive talent that had been on display in Athens. He earned a total of five gold medals at the 2005 World Championships, claiming top spots in the 200-meter freestyle, 200-meter individual medley, 4x100 freestyle, 4x200 freestyle, and 4x100 medley. Most impressively, he also set or helped set (in team competitions) five new world record times.

Phelps's spectacular performance set off a new round of magazine and television stories about his torpedo-like physique. Observers agreed that his physical tools only partially explained his success. In the foreword to the 2007 revised edition of *Beneath the Surface,* for example, sports journalist Bob Costas compared Phelps to Michael Jordan and Tiger Woods. "Phelps has the most talent," stated Costas. "But like that esteemed pair, he wins so often because he understands that while talent is huge, hard work takes it to other levels. And also because, like Jordan and Woods, he loves nothing more than competing, and hates nothing more than losing."

Phelps confirmed that he enjoyed battling against other swimmers. "Once I get to the competition, it's like I'm in a cage, so just let me out, because I know exactly what to do," he said. "I know how to warm up. I know how to get my head in the game. Competition is my favorite part of the sport. That's what I do best."

The 2008 Olympic Games

With the approach of the 2008 Olympic Games in Beijing, China, Phelps loomed as a clear favorite to win multiple gold medals. Everyone knew that he was the best swimmer in the world and that he would have an opportunity to show his stuff in eight different events. The big question was whether he would be able to finally match—or even surpass—Spitz's 1972 record of seven gold medals. Ian Thorpe, for one, openly dismissed Phelps's chances just before the Games opened. "I have said before that I don't think he can [win] the eight [gold medals], and I still believe that."

"Once I get to the competition, it's like I'm in a cage, so just let me out, because I know exactly what to do," Phelps boasted. "I know how to warm up. I know how to get my head in the game. Competition is my favorite part of the sport. That's what I do best."

Phelps decided not to respond to Thorpe with words. Instead, he let his swimming do the talking for him. In his first event of the 2008 Games, the 400-meter individual medley, he crushed his own world record with a mark of 4:03.84. After claiming his first gold medal, though, Phelps immediately turned his attention to the next event. "I'm not downplaying this race by any means, but I have to put that race behind me," he explained. "I have to act like it never happened because I have so many tough races ahead of me."

Phelps claimed his second gold medal of the Beijing Games in the 4x100 freestyle relay—but not without a major assist from one of his teammates. Phelps swam the first leg of the relay for the Americans and gave Team USA a nice early lead. The French team pulled ahead midway through the race, though. By the time of the event's last or anchor leg, French swimmer Alain Bernard had a huge lead on American Jason Lezak. But Lezak pulled off one of the greatest comebacks in Olympic swimming history and touched the wall just ahead of Bernard. Lezak's performance, which Phelps later described as "unbelievable," enabled the USA men to claim gold with a world record time of 3:08.24.

Phelps moved on from there to the 200-meter freestyle. He easily clinched the gold medal in that event with a time of 1:42.96, breaking his own world record by nearly a second. "He's not just winning, he's absolutely destroying everything," said teammate Aaron Peirsol. "It's awesome to watch."

Phelps in action during the 2008 Olympics in the 400-meter IM, in which he won the gold medal and set a new world record.

Gold medal number four for Phelps came in the 200-meter butterfly. Once again he posted a new world record time (1:52.03) to clinch the top spot on the podium. According to Phelps, he would have posted an even better time if his goggles had not filled up with water during the race. "I couldn't see," he explained. "I know I can go faster than that." USA Swimming head coach Eddie Reese, though, was delighted with his star swimmer. "There is nobody in our sport that can win like he wins," Reese said. "He is not just winning, he is crunching world records."

Phelps's gold medal in the 200-meter butterfly made him the first Olympian in history to earn 10 career gold medals (Spitz, American sprinter Carl Lewis, Soviet gymnast Larysa Latynina, and Finnish runner Paavo

Nurmi all had won nine). When asked about this feat, Phelps admitted that "I'm almost at a loss for words. Growing up I always wanted to be an Olympian. Now to be the most decorated Olympian of all time, it just sounds weird saying. It started setting in a little after the butterfly. I was just trying to focus on my next race, but I just kept thinking, 'Wow, greatest Olympian of all time.' It's a pretty cool title."

Closing in on Olympic History

Phelps's next event in Beijing was the 4x200 freestyle relay. He swam the leadoff leg and put his team more than two seconds ahead of its nearest competitor. From there the Americans cruised to a gold medal with a time of 6:58.56. Holding his fifth gold medal of the 2008 Games, Phelps smiled and said that he still had "some left in the tank.... From now on, it's just a downward slope. The end is close. I love it."

"I'm almost at a loss for words. Growing up I always wanted to be an Olympian. Now to be the most decorated Olympian of all time, it just sounds weird saying. It started setting in a little after the butterfly. I was just trying to focus on my next race, but I just kept thinking, 'Wow, greatest Olympian of all time.' It's a pretty cool title."

Gold medal number six for Phelps came in the 200-meter individual medley, in which he posted a world-record time of 1:54.23 seconds. This triumph had the entire Olympics community—and an international audience of millions—wondering if he might actually be able to win gold in all eight of his events. They tuned in to watch his next race, the 100-meter butterfly, and were treated to his most spectacular victory yet. For most of the race, it looked as if he was going to finish second behind Serbia's Milorad Cavic. But Phelps launched a feverish final charge and managed to catch Cavic at literally the very last instant. The American swimmer won by a hundredth of a second—the smallest measurement of time in swimming competition. Phelps's time of 50.58 marked the first time in the 2008 Games that he did not win gold by setting a new world record, but the beaming swimmer did not care. After all, he had tied Mark Spitz's record of seven gold medals in a single Olympics competition. "I am sort of in a dream world," Phelps admitted. "Sometimes I have to pinch myself to make sure it is real."

Phelps celebrating his win in the 200-meter butterfly at the 2008 Olympics.

The last event for Phelps was the 4x100-meter medley relay. If he and his teammates could win gold in this event, Phelps would enter the annals of Olympics history as the first-ever athlete to win eight gold medals in a single Olympics Games. During the first half of the relay, the USA team fell behind both Australia and Japan. But when Phelps dove into the pool for the butterfly leg of the event, he quickly closed the distance. As ESPN.com reported, "With his long arms whirling across the water like propellers, Phelps caught the two guys ahead of him on the return lap and passed off to [Jason] Lezak a lead of less than a second for the freestyle." Lezak then held off a late charge from Australia to bring gold home to the U.S. team once again. Their time of 3:29.34 marked Phelps's seventh world record of the Games.

After watching Phelps receive his record eighth gold medal, journalists and athletes from all around the globe paid tribute to his accomplishment. Writing in *USA Today,* reporter Vicki Michaelis noted that "his success rep-

"

"I've never really had a real vacation," Phelps said about his plans after the Olympics. "I'm going to sit on the beach and do nothing. I'm sleeping in. I'm putting on weight. And I'm not going to care."

"

resents one of those rare moments in sports when the stars align to produce an awe-inspiring feat: an athlete with unique talent, focus, stamina, and versatility, fast in each of swimming's four strokes at a time when specialization and growth of the sport worldwide have made it tougher than ever to be dominant." And Spitz himself declared that "not only is this guy the greatest swimmer of all time and the greatest Olympian of all time, he's maybe the greatest athlete of all time. He's the greatest racer who ever walked the planet."

For his part, Phelps expressed happy satisfaction with his Olympic experience. "Everything was accomplished," he said. "I will have the medals forever." And those medals also give him a shot at yet another hallowed Olympic record when the next Summer Games take place in London, England, in 2012. After the Beijing Games, Phelps's career total of 16 Olympic medals—14 gold and two bronze—puts him within striking distance of the all-time leading medal winner, Soviet gymnast Larissa Latynina, who captured 18 medals (nine gold, five silver, four bronze) during her career.

But as the 2008 Summer Olympics drew to a close, Phelps was focused on more immediate plans. "I've never really had a real vacation," he said. "I'm going to sit on the beach and do nothing. I'm sleeping in. I'm putting on weight. And I'm not going to care."

HOME AND FAMILY

Phelps, who is single, lives in his hometown of Baltimore in a waterfront townhouse that looks over Chesapeake Bay.

HOBBIES AND OTHER INTERESTS

Phelps's status as the best swimmer in the world and an Olympic hero has made him both wealthy and famous. He earns millions of dollars each year in endorsements, and in 2008 he served as both a host for "Saturday Night Live" and a presenter at MTV's 2008 "Video Music Awards."

Despite all the accolades, though, Phelps has many of the same interests as many other young men. He enjoys listening to rap music, watching

Phelps (far left) with his teammates after winning the gold medal in the 4x100-meter medley relay. With this event, Phelps earned eight gold medals at the 2008 Olympics—more than any other athlete in history at a single Olympics.

comedy films and ESPN's "SportsCenter," and playing video games. He has also expressed an interest in learning how to golf and snowboard. "I'm just going to experiment," he said.

Phelps is also active in several charitable causes. He has served as the national spokesman for Boys and Girls Clubs of America and is an honorary board member of Pathfinders for Autism. In addition, he frequently participates in public events for young swimmers. "It wasn't long ago that I was that young boy or girl, wanting to be just like the swimmers I looked up to," he said. "I just try to be myself, and act normal. What they see is what they get with me."

WRITINGS

Michael Phelps: Beneath the Surface, 2005 (with Brian Cazeneuve)

SELECTED HONORS AND AWARDS

Swimmer of the Year (USA Swimming): 2001, 2003
James E. Sullivan Award (Amateur Athletic Union): 2003
Olympic Swimming, 100-meter butterfly: 2004, gold medal; 2008, gold medal
Olympic Swimming, 200-meter butterfly: 2004, gold medal; 2008, gold medal

Olympic Swimming, 200-meter individual medley: 2004, gold medal; 2008, gold medal
Olympic Swimming, 400-meter individual medley: 2004, gold medal; 2008, gold medal
Olympic Swimming, 4x100-meter medley relay: 2004, gold medal; 2008 gold medal
Olympic Swimming, 4x200-meter freestyle relay: 2004, gold medal; 2008 gold medal
Olympic Swimming, 200-meter freestyle: 2004, bronze medal; 2008, gold medal
Olympic Swimming, 4x100-meter freestyle relay: 2004, bronze medal; 2008, gold medal
Athlete of the Year (*Sports Illustrated for Kids*): 2004
World Swimmer of the Year (*Swimming World*): 2004

FURTHER READING

Books

McMullen, Paul. *Amazing Pace,* 2006
Phelps, Michael, with Brian Cazeneuve. *Michael Phelps: Beneath the Surface,* 2005
Sapet, Kerrily. *Xtreme Athletes: Michael Phelps,* 2008 (juvenile)

Periodicals

Baltimore Sun, Aug. 13, 2000, p.A1; Jan. 14, 2001, p.F9; July 25, 2001, p.A1; July 11, 2004, p.E1; Aug. 8, 2004, p.A1; Nov. 14, 2004, p.B1; Dec. 30, 2004, p.B1
Boston Globe, Aug. 13, 2008
Boys' Life, Aug. 2004, p.14
Chicago Tribune, July 4, 2004, Sports, p.1
Current Biography Yearbook, 2004
Detroit Free Press, Dec. 18, 2004, p.B1
ESPN Magazine, Apr. 11, 2005, p.106
New York Times, Aug. 8, 2004; Aug. 16, 2008, p.A1
New York Times Magazine, Aug. 8, 2004, p.22
Newsweek, Aug. 16, 2004, p.40; Aug. 30, 2004, p.16
People, Sep. 1, 2008, p.58
Sports Illustrated, Aug. 6, 2001, p.74; Aug. 23, 2004, p.46; Aug. 30, 2004, p.58; Aug. 25, 2008
Sports Illustrated for Kids, Aug. 2004, p.26; Jan. 2005, p.38
Swimming World, June 2001, p.27; Dec. 2004, p.16; Sep. 2003, p.30; Oct. 2003, p.22; Sep. 2004, p.18

Time, Apr. 30, 2007, p.6
USA Today, Aug. 14, 2000, p.C3; Aug. 13, 2002, p.C10; July 7, 2004, p.C1; July 14, 2004, p.C3; Aug. 13, 2004, p.F4; July 19, 2005, p.C3; Aug. 1, 2008, p.A1; Aug. 15, 2008, p.A1; Aug. 29, 2008, p.C7

Online Articles

http://sports.espn.go.com
(ESPN, "And After That, Mr. Phelps Will Leap a Tall Building In a Single Bound," July 28, 2008; "Phenomenal Phelps Wins 7th Gold by 0.01 Seconds to Tie Spitz," Aug. 15, 2008)
http://topics.nytimes.com/top/reference/timestopics/index.html
(New York Times, "Times Topics," multiple articles, various dates)
http://www.si.com
(Sports Illustrated, "My Sportsman Choice: Michael Phelps," Nov. 26, 2004)

ADDRESS

Michael Phelps
USA Swimming
1 Olympic Plaza
Colorado Springs, CO 80809

WORLD WIDE WEB SITES

http://www.michaelphelps.com
http://www.usaswimming.org
http://www.usolympicteam.com
http://www.fina.org

Rachael Ray 1968-

American Professional Cook
Host of Television Cooking Shows and Cookbook Author

BIRTH

Rachael Domenica Ray was born on August 25, 1968, in Glens Falls, New York. Her mother, Elsa Providenzia Scuderi, worked as a restaurant manager. Her father, James Claude Ray, worked in the food-service industry for some years, and later as a marketing director for a book publisher. She has a sister, Maria, who is nine years older, and a brother, Emmanuel, who is six years younger.

YOUTH

Ray came from a background with a rich heritage in food. Her father was brought up in the French region of Louisiana, where cooking is a key part of the culture. Her mother came from an Italian family where cooking was also very important, both in the home and as a business—the extended family owned several restaurants. Ray was still a baby when her family moved from upstate New York to Cape Cod, in Massachusetts. They lived there for some years. Her parents divorced when she was 12 years old, and after that her mother took the children and moved back up to the Adirondack region of New York, where Ray had been born.

"My grandfather lived with us and was my caretaker, so I liked everything that old Italian men liked," Ray remembered. "I liked sardines and squid and eating calamari with your fingers and anything with anchovies, anything with garlic and oil. I still eat much the same way today. I was not a very popular girl when I opened my lunch sack at the lunchroom."

Ray's mother did not like to leave her children in day care. Instead, from the time they were very young, she took them along to work with her at the family's restaurants. Everyone was expected to pitch in and help, whether they were paid for it or not. Ray grew up waiting tables, washing dishes, and preparing food. The family believed that the children would learn by doing. "Nobody says, 'Here's how you peel a potato'—they just say, 'Rachael, peel a potato,'" she recalled. "My first memory in life is grilling my thumb to the griddle in our restaurant on Cape Cod."

As a child, Ray enjoyed foods that many children wouldn't touch. "My grandfather lived with us and was my caretaker, so I liked everything that old Italian men liked," she remembered. "I liked sardines and squid and eating calamari with your fingers and anything with anchovies, anything with garlic and oil. I still eat much the same way today. I was not a very popular girl when I opened my lunch sack at the lunchroom."

EDUCATION

Ray graduated from Lake George High School in Lake George, New York. She attended Pace University in New York, but did not graduate.

FIRST JOBS

After graduating from high school and attending Pace University for a while, Ray decided to move to New York City. She spent two years working at Macy's Marketplace, staffing the candy counter and managing the fresh-food department. Within a few years, she had moved on to be the store manager and buyer at Agata & Valentina, a gourmet market in the heart of the city. She enjoyed her job, but she decided to leave the city. In 1997, she was violently attacked and robbed at her own apartment building twice, in a matter of just two weeks. She decided to head for a safer location and moved back to the Lake George area, where she managed pubs and restaurants for a while. Eventually, she took a position as a food buyer and chef at Cowan & Lobel, a gourmet market in Albany, New York, the state capital.

Good Meals in Half an Hour

While working at Cowan & Lobel, Ray noticed that prepared foods sold very well, but simple, whole ingredients did not. She asked customers some questions and learned that many people felt they didn't have enough time to cook, even if they enjoyed being in the kitchen and were interested in eating well. Ray set out to prove that they could indeed make themselves delicious, healthful dinners even if time was short. She began to give a series of cooking classes to show how to put together a great meal in 30 minutes. In addition, she bundled together packages of the ingredients she used, to make shopping that much easier for the customers.

The classes were a great success, and they attracted people from all walks of life. In fact, they became so popular that in 1998 Ray was asked by WRGB, an Albany-area television station, to start doing a weekly segment on their news broadcast featuring some of her 30-minute meals. Her television segment was nominated for two regional Emmy Awards that year. The success of her "30-Minute" concept continued to expand the following year, when she published a cookbook titled *30-Minute Meals*. In 2001, she published two more cookbooks, *Comfort Foods* and *Veggie Meals*.

CAREER HIGHLIGHTS

Star of the Food Network

Ray made her first national television appearance in 2001. She was asked to appear on the "Today" show, a big-budget morning program on the NBC network. In a segment with the show's weatherman, Al Roker, she made some hearty winter soups and shared tips about using Thanksgiving leftovers. Roker remembered being very impressed with her and later

Ray's first cookbook, 30-Minute Meals, *led to her TV show of the same name and launched her successful cooking career.*

said: "She is unabashedly who she is and makes no apologies, which is what people like about her. She's real.... You see her on camera, and she just pops."

The day after her appearance on "Today," Ray was approached by the Food Network, a cable television company. She was offered a $360,000 contract to work with the network on a variety of projects. Her program "30-Minute Meals" premiered soon after, and it was an immediate success. The show was based on the same concept that she had been pushing since working at the Cowan & Lobel store: that anyone can cook a healthful, delicious meal in about a half an hour. In her quest to make things simple, she didn't hesitate to use shortcuts, such as ready-made salads in a bag, sauce from a jar, or items from the frozen-food section.

"Ray has readily admitted her own faults: "I'm not a chef, I don't bake, I am loud, I am goofy, and after a while, my voice is annoying."

The concept was a good one, but a big part of the show's success was Ray's personality. Her delivery was friendly, upbeat, and casual. Unlike some television chefs, she didn't prepare fancy dishes or use complicated methods. Her consistent message was that you don't have to know much about cooking in order to create a good meal. She readily admitted her own faults and has said of herself: "I'm not a chef, I don't bake, I am loud, I am goofy, and after a while, my voice is annoying." She often dropped things on the set or got her lines wrong. She has set not only a loaf of bread on fire, but also her hair. All her quirks and goofs just seemed to boost her appeal, however.

In 2002, while still going strong with "30-Minute Meals," Ray was given a second program on the Food Network. On "$40 a Day," she traveled around the United States and Europe, sampling various restaurants where good meals can be purchased on a budget. In 2004, the Food Network decided to capitalize on her winning personality by moving her beyond the confines of a simple cooking or restaurant-review show. "Inside Dish with Rachael Ray" featured Ray hanging out with various celebrities. They might be in the stars' homes, at their favorite restaurants, or chatting casually while they cooked up some tasty food together. Like "30-Minute Meals" and "$40 a Day," "Inside Dish with Rachael Ray" was a success. In August, 2005, the Food Network launched yet another program, "Rachael Ray's Tasty Travels." This was something like her "$40 a Day" show, but aimed at travelers who were willing and able to spend more money. The

Ray's success has allowed her to branch out into other areas, including producing a magazine.

show's exotic locations led to some mishaps, according to Ray: "I've almost drowned on 'Tasty Travels' many times; falling off surfboards, getting caught in undercurrents, deep-sea diving."

Expanding Empire

By 2004, Ray's business ventures were moving far beyond cooking on television. She signed a multi-book contract with Random House, a major publisher. Five of her cookbooks were on the *New York Times* bestseller list during the holiday season that year. Titles from her expanding series of cookbooks sold millions of copies. In fact, *365: No Repeats: A Year of Deliciously Different Dinners* alone sold more than 1.3 million copies. "That was the stupidest idea I ever had," she later said humorously of *365: No Repeats.* "That many recipes nearly killed me."

In 2005, she designed and launched the Gusto-Grip knife collection. Manufactured by Furi, the knives feature a distinctive bright-orange handle. Ray eventually went on to expand her line of signature products to include more cookware, a brand of olive oil, high-quality dog food, and even a microwave oven. She even worked with Epic Records to put out two albums: "How Cool Is That," a selection of Christmas music, and "Too Cool for School," which was aimed at children. Ray didn't perform on either, but chose the selections on each.

Ray's fans could not get enough of her, and the first issue of a new magazine debuted in October 2005, with Ray acting as editor-in-chief. *Every Day with Rachael Ray* was a continuation of her message that good food, and good living, can happen without too much fuss, time, or money. It was illustrated with hundreds of pictures, making it a quick read with lots of visual inspiration. One regular feature was a recipe so simple to make that no written directions were given, only photographed illustrations. The magazine's first issue was eagerly awaited and quickly sold out at many stores on the first day it was available. An additional run of it was printed, and more than a million copies of that first issue were sold.

Multiple television shows, numerous books, product lines, product endorsements, and a monthly magazine led some critics to complain that Ray was overexposed. In response, she said: "I don't put my name on things I don't believe in. I love every page of our magazine. I'm extremely proud of it. I work very hard on each cookbook to make it different." She may have had some detractors, but in 2006 Ray was ranked number 81 on a list of the most powerful celebrities, compiled by the business magazine *Forbes.* She was the top chef on the list. She was also awarded a daytime Emmy Award for her "30-Minute Meals" program that year.

National Talk Show Host

Ray's appeal to TV audiences was noticed by Oprah Winfrey, another woman who had created a business empire based on her strong, winning personality. Winfrey rose to fame as a talk-show host but eventually became one of the most powerful women in the entertainment industry. Taking Ray under her wing, Winfrey encouraged the idea of a nationally syndicated, hour-long talk show featuring Ray. With the backing of Winfrey's production company, Harpo Productions, the "Rachael Ray" show debuted on September 18, 2006. By November of that year it was the top-rated syndicated talk show on the air, and it eventually settled into fourth place behind the popular programs "The Oprah Winfrey Show," "Dr. Phil," and "Live with Regis and Kelly."

Filmed in New York, "Rachael Ray" utilizes an elaborate set that gives the feel of a loft-style apartment. There is a kitchen, a game room with Foosball and air hockey, a living room, a patio, even a garage. The idea was for Ray to invite celebrities to relax with her in her "home." During filming, the audience is seated on a special platform in the middle of the set, which rotates to face whatever area of the set is being used. There would be "no crying, no big stuff," she explained. Instead, she would ask them things like "What your nickname was in fourth grade. What do you have in your fridge right this minute. Those fun, stupid party questions." She worked without a writing staff, using no script or teleprompters.

"In creating her new talk show, Ray had definite ideas for the show's tone and content. There would be "no crying, no big stuff," she explained. "I'm the queen of the little stuff. I want it to be really accessible. With a can-do, party feel rather than a talk-show feel. I want to hear real-life solutions to small problems."

During the course of the show Ray might touch on anything, from celebrity visits, to home remedies, to tips for traveling with children, to recipes for dog treats. "I'm the queen of the little stuff. I want it to be really accessible. With a can-do, party feel rather than a talk-show feel. I want to hear real-life solutions to small problems," she said.

Ray also left the set sometimes, as when she visited NASA headquarters to do a segment on 30-minute meals that could be prepared in space. The "Rachael Ray" show was also responsible for some extravagant gifts to people in need. For example, after the devastating hurricane Ike struck the Gulf Coast of the United States, Ray's show funded a special wedding event for 33 couples whose wedding plans were ruined due to the storm. In another instance, a deadly tornado struck Enterprise, Alabama, leaving eight students dead and destroying the high school. After that tragedy, Ray

In 2006, Ray progressed from TV cook to talk show host.

and her crew organized a prom dance for the school's students at a nearby Air Force base.

Sammies and EVOO

One trait that endears Ray to her fans—while annoying her critics—is her use of slang and made-up words. She frequently refers to dishes as "easy-peasey" to make, calls sandwiches "sammies," and has dubbed a thick soup with stew-like qualities a "stoup." She frequently exclaims "Yum-o!" in anticipation of good food, and "Delish!" when eating something she considers delicious. "EVOO," her term for extra-virgin grade olive oil, became so widely used that in 2007, it was added to the *Oxford English Dictionary*, which is considered the leading reference book on the English language.

Like her language, Ray's personality is cheerful and breezy. Yet she is also very hardworking. She usually only gets about five hours of sleep a night, but she thrives on her fast-paced life-style. "I like hard work," she admitted, "Generally speaking, unless it's pouring rain or I'm really, really sick, it freaks me out to be still." Although her schedule is extremely busy, she appreciates everything she has to do, especially when she compares it to some of the strenuous, physical work she has done in her past—such as unloading heavy crates of food into restaurant kitchens or trying to prepare meals for busloads of tourists at resorts. "I come from very hard-working people," she said. "But, more importantly, they really eat life. They're optimistic, fun, outgoing. Everybody in my family has an over-the-top personality. They just like to create and share."

"It's just a lot of fun to walk down the street and have people stop you and give you a recipe," she acknowledged. "They'll give me travel tips, coupons to go to different restaurants. And people are always looking out for me, too. People stop me in the street and say, 'Hey, can I help you with those bags there, Rach? How far do you have to go?' It's very down-to-earth and homey. It's nice."

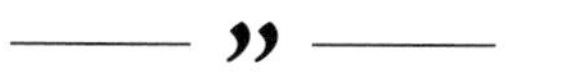

For Ray, fame is one more aspect of life to be enjoyed. "It's just a lot of fun to walk down the street and have people stop you and give you a recipe," she acknowledged. "They'll give me travel tips, coupons to go to different restaurants. And people are always looking out for me, too. People stop me in the street and say, 'Hey, can I help you with those bags there, Rach? How far do you have to go?' It's very down-to-earth and homey. It's nice." On the other hand, fame has also given rise to some negative attention, such as anti-Rachael Ray web sites that relentlessly pick apart her every move. Ray shrugs off that kind of criticism, knowing that it is impossible to please everyone.

Looking to the future, Ray has no specific plans, but said: "If you keep your mind open and your spirit open and you're very hardworking, I think life sort of unfolds and presents itself to you. And so far, it's been more fun than anything I could have planned. So, you know, whatever's the next logical thing that comes out of the growth of this thing that's now got a life of its own, I'll just follow the path."

HOME AND FAMILY

Ray is married to John Cusimano, an entertainment lawyer she met at a party in 2001. The two immediately hit it off and began dating. They were married on September 24, 2005, at a five-day wedding party they held at a castle in Montalcino, Italy. They now have homes in New York City and in the Adirondack region of New York state. Ray was glad to have found someone who understood her fast-paced lifestyle."Some days I am up at 4:00 a.m. and don't leave work until 9:00," she said. "Luckily I married a man who doesn't mind eating dinner at 10:30 every night." After coming home from work, Ray generally likes to just relax, have something to eat, and watch some television—but not her own programs, which she says she never views because she does not want to become self-conscious.

Cusimano plays in a band called The Cringe, and Ray occasionally enjoys going to hear their music at clubs around New York. She doubts she and her husband will have children, for as she put it: "I work too much to be an appropriate parent. I feel like a bad mom to my dog."

FAVORITE FOODS

Listing her favorite foods, Ray said they change with the seasons: "In the fall and winter, I make soups three nights a week, definitely one with beans and greens. I want more steak and pasta in the winter, but in the summer, I'll make salad suppers with all sorts of delicious things in them. I also like sammies (hollowed-out sandwiches) and, once in a while, a big fruit salad with scrambled eggs. Oh, and I am the queen of burgers."

As far as staying fit in a career that has revolved around food, Ray said, "I do some calisthenics at home when I can," but she noted she's not very consistent about exercising. She added: "I try to eat well—I grew up with a Mediterranean diet, so I don't eat a lot of butter and fat. I eat a lot of vegetables and good, fresh-looking food."

HOBBIES AND OTHER INTERESTS

Ray loves animals, and her pit bull-mix dog, Isaboo, is a very familiar figure to her fans. "I make a huge mess in the kitchen. That's why I have a big dog," she joked, referring to Isaboo's enthusiasm for eating food that falls on the floor. The dog has appeared on Ray's television program and in her magazine, both of which have featured articles on tasty foods meant for shared human and animal snacking.

Ray's concern for animals, especially dogs, led her to develop Nutrish, a special brand of dog food. Some of her pet-food products are named after her own beloved dog. Customers can buy Isaboo Booscotti crunchy treats and Isaboo Grill Bites chewy treats. All the proceeds from sales of her pet-food products go to support an animal-rescue program called Rachael's Rescue.

Another charitable cause Ray energetically supports is the Yum-O Organization, a nonprofit foundation created to help children and families improve their relationships with food. Yum-O's mission has three parts: to educate all people about cooking good food for a reasonable amount of

A dog lover, Ray launched a line of pet food, Nutrish.

money; to help feed hungry children in America; and to help young people who want to attend cooking schools by providing scholarships.

"Growing up, I had a very healthy relationship with food and cooking and, throughout my life, I've met people who were positively influenced by lessons learned in the kitchen," Ray explained. "We've created Yum-o! to introduce more kids to cooking, which can have such a meaningful impact on their lives and health. Food definitely brings a smile to my face and so many great memories can be made by spending time together as a family in the kitchen." With Yum-O!, Ray hopes to "get parents and kids cooking healthier breakfasts, lunches, lunchboxes, and dinners and we want to make food fun, fast, and affordable for American families.... The challenge I've heard from parents is that they don't have the time or money to cook healthier. They just don't believe they can make good food fast and that is just not true."

SELECTED CREDITS

Television

"30-Minute Meals," 2002-
"$40 a Day," 2002-
"Inside Dish with Rachael Ray," 2004-
"Rachael Ray's Tasty Travels," 2005-
"Rachael Ray," 2006-

Books

30-Minute Meals, 1999
Veggie Meals, 2001
30-Minute Meals 2, 2003
Cooking Rocks! Rachael Ray's 30-Minute Meals for Kids, 2004
$40 a Day: Best Eats in Town, 2004
Guy Food, 2005
Rachael Ray Express Lane Meals, 2006
Just in Time, 2007
Yum-O! The Family Cookbook, 2008

HONORS AND AWARDS

Daytime Emmy (National Academy of Television Arts and Sciences): 2006, for Outstanding Service Show, for "30-Minute Meals"
Daytime Emmy (National Academy of Television Arts and Sciences): 2008, for Outstanding Talk Show, for "Rachael Ray"

FURTHER READING

Periodicals

Current Biography Yearbook, 2005
Good Housekeeping, Aug. 2006, p.114
Newsweek, Sep.12, 2005, p.72
People, Dec. 5, 2005, p.109; May 14, 2007, p.118
Redbook, Oct. 2006, p.60

Television Week, Jan. 15, 2007, pp.41, 48
Time, Sep. 11, 2006, p.75
USA Today, Sep. 14, 2006, p.D1

ADDRESS

Rachael Ray
Food Network
75 Ninth Avenue
New York, NY 10011

WORLD WIDE WEB SITES

http://www.rachaelray.com
http://www.rachaelrayshow.com
http://www.foodnetwork.com

Emma Roberts 1991-

American Actress

Star of the Television Show "Unfabulous" and the Films *Nancy Drew* and *Hotel for Dogs*

BIRTH

Emma Rose Roberts was born on February 10, 1991, in Rhinebeck, New York (some sources say Los Angeles, California). Her father is Eric Roberts, an actor, and her mother is Kelly Cunningham, a producer. Roberts and Cunningham separated when their daughter was about two months old. Roberts's father married Eliza Garrett, an actress who had two children from a previous marriage—a son, Keaton Simons, and a daughter, Morgan Simons (Emma's step-brother and step-sister). Roberts's mother later married Kelly Nickles, a bassist who formerly played in the band L.A. Guns; they had one daughter, Grace (Emma's half-sister).

YOUTH

Roberts has grown up in a family that is deeply involved in show business. Her grandparents on her father's side, Walter Roberts and Betty Lou Motes, were both known as outstanding acting teachers in Atlanta, Georgia. Their three children, Eric, Julia, and Lisa, all took up acting careers. Emma Roberts's father, Eric, started in show-business when he was just seven years old. By the time his daughter was born, he had been nominated for an Academy Award for his work in the 1985 film *Runaway Train.* Eric's sisters Julia and Lisa also went into acting. Julia Roberts took her career to the top, becoming an Academy Award winner and the highest-paid actress in the world. Lisa Roberts Gillan has not become as famous as her brother and sister, but she has had small parts in many films.

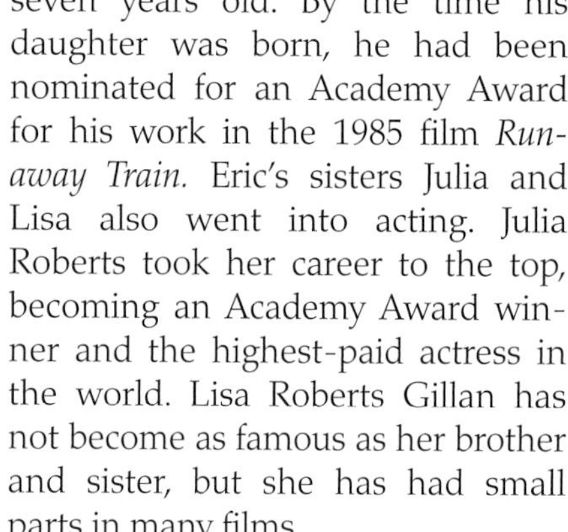

Roberts has grown up in a family that is deeply involved in show business, and she decided she was ready to start her own professional acting career when she was nine. "I think it's in my blood," she once said. "All the Robertses want to be in the movie business."

Emma Roberts had her first exposure to filmmaking when she was only two weeks old. Her father was working on the movie *Final Analysis* when she was born, and she was often taken to the set. Because of her family connections, she had chances to watch some of the top actors in the business at work, even when she was very young. When she was nine, she announced she was ready to start her own professional acting career. "I think it's in my blood. All the Robertses want to be in the movie business," she once said.

Roberts's mother was a little concerned, because she wanted her daughter to have as normal a childhood as possible. That is often difficult for child actors, and it would be even more of a challenge for someone who would attract extra media attention because of her celebrity relatives. Her mother agreed to let her audition for parts, but only under certain conditions. Roberts would have to keep up with her schoolwork, maintain a social life with her friends, continue doing her usual household chores, and attend college when she was old enough. As her mother said, "Life is a long road and she's got to be prepared for it."

EDUCATION

Until the end of seventh grade, Roberts attended the Archer School for Girls, located in the Brentwood area of Los Angeles, California. After seventh grade she left school, but continued her education by home-schooling and studying with tutors. Roberts has an outgoing personality, and it was hard to leave the social life at school. "I miss it a little bit," she said. "I miss seeing my friends every day. But I go to my friends' school for things like dances and football games. So it's not too bad."

FIRST JOBS

Roberts's career got off to a fast start. At her very first audition, she won a part in a major motion picture, *Blow* (2001), starring Johnny Depp and Penelope Cruz. Depp is one of the top stars in the movie industry, but, Roberts said, "I was so young. I didn't understand that I was working with one of the best actors ever until later." *Blow* is based on the true story of George Jung, a drug dealer. Depp and Cruz played Jung and his wife, and Roberts portrayed their daughter, Kristina. Because of the movie's subject matter, she has still never seen the whole movie, only the scenes in which she appeared. She next acted in a quirky, short movie called *BigLove* (2001), which was first shown at the Sundance Film Festival.

After *BigLove,* Roberts had leading roles in a couple of films with animal co-stars. *Grand Champion* (2001) is a story about a farm family and their beloved prize steer, Hokey Pokey. Financial troubles force the family to sell Hokey Pokey, but when the children learn his life is in danger, they set out on a mission to save him. "It was so much fun to do, especially as I got to go to Texas, where I'd never been before and I loved it there," she recalled. "I got to hang out with a lot of other kids, and we all learned so much about cattle and that whole way of life. I mean, I grew up in L.A., so it was a real education."

Roberts took on a very different role in her next project, *Spymate.* In this film, she played the part of a brilliant young inventor. She is kidnapped by people who want to use her knowledge to help them gain control over the world. In *Spymate,* she co-starred with a chimpanzee. Being an animal lover, she enjoyed the unique opportunity to get to know a chimp. "They're really sweet, and it's incredible to see that they're animals and they're working like that," she said.

Roberts's success in Spymate, *one of her early movies, helped her win the role in "Unfabulous."*

CAREER HIGHLIGHTS

"Unfabulous"

Following her success in *Spymate,* Roberts was asked to meet with executives from the Nickelodeon television network to discuss a new TV series.

Before long, 12-year-old Roberts was cast as Addie Singer, the lead in a new comedy called "Unfabulous." Her co-stars included Molly Hagan as Addie's mother, Sue; Markus Flanagan as her dad, Jeff; Tadhg Kelly as her brother, Ben; Jordan Calloway as her best male friend, Zach, and Malese Jow as her best girlfriend, Geena. Roberts enjoyed being on the set with lots of other people her own age, and her co-stars found her nice to be around. "Emma is always full of energy. She's got a charisma that makes everyone around her want to get up and do something fun," said Tadhg Kelly. "She can make even the longest scenes fly by with her upbeat personality and sense of humor."

"Unfabulous" centers on Addie, a middle-school student going through all the frustrations and insecurities common to kids her age: homework, having a crush on someone, worrying about being popular at school. "Like some girls, she wants to fit in. She wants to throw the best party, but at the same time she's happy with who she is," Roberts said. "She's glad that she's getting through middle school and getting through life." One way she copes with daily life is by writing and singing songs about the things she is experiencing, just as some people express themselves by writing in a diary. These songs are often silly or downright funny. They are all written by Jill Sobule, but Roberts really did sing and play the guitar on the program—luckily she had taken guitar lessons since she was nine years old. "Addie's actually really good at playing the guitar, but singing? She's not supposed to be the best," she acknowledged. In 2005, an album featuring music from the show was released, titled *Unfabulous and More: Emma Roberts.*

"Like some girls, she wants to fit in," Roberts said about her character, Addie, on "Unfabulous." "She wants to throw the best party, but at the same time she's happy with who she is. She's glad that she's getting through middle school and getting through life."

The first episode of "Unfabulous" aired on September 12, 2004, during the Sunday night programming block that included the shows "Romeo," "Drake and Josh," and "Ned's Declassified School Survival Guide." The show was an immediate hit with young viewers. Three seasons of "Unfabulous" were produced, with one finale episode shown in the fourth season. When filming ended in 2007, it was an emotional experience. "Nobody was going to cry, and then when they said, 'That's a wrap,' I started getting teary-eyed. Everyone was very sad," Roberts recalled.

Roberts as Addie in "Unfabulous."

Aquamarine

The success of "Unfabulous" kicked Roberts's career into high gear. In 2006, she played a lead role in the comic movie *Aquamarine,* co-starring with the singer Joanna "JoJo" Levesque and the actress Sara Paxton. Roberts played Claire, a shy girl whose parents have both died. Claire is "totally opposite of me," she said. "She's really shy and really afraid of everything and doesn't want to take any chances. But it's fun to play a character that's not like yourself." JoJo played Claire's best friend, Hailey. Together the girls make an amazing discovery: a mermaid has ended up in the pool at their beach club. The mermaid, Aquamarine (played by Paxton), is curious about how humans live. She especially wants to find out about the human emotion called "love." Aquamarine promises Claire and Hailey that she will grant them a wish if they will help her to find love.

Aquamarine was filmed in Australia. Traveling there and getting to hang out with her two costars was lots of fun for Roberts, especially because she had already been a fan of JoJo's music. When the girls weren't on the set working, they were able to spend time biking, swimming, and enjoying themselves at the beach. They had so much fun together that it was sometimes hard to get in the right mood to film some of the dramatic scenes about the characters' problems. "We all had a great time laughing so it was hard to get in the mode of sadness. I also just find it really embarrassing!" Roberts commented.

Nancy Drew

Roberts's next film was a movie adaptation of the *Nancy Drew* mystery books. The book series, popular with young readers since the 1930s, features a title character who is prepared for any situation—from riding a circus horse to translating ancient manuscripts. The daughter of a well-to-do lawyer, Nancy is also an amateur detective who never fails to solve the case. Although the series has been updated periodically to reflect modern innovations, the 2007 movie *Nancy Drew* took a unique twist. It opens in black-and-white, and by the look of the clothing and furniture, Nancy and her father could be living in the 1950s.

Before long, however, Nancy's father takes a job in Los Angeles, and Nancy is shown transferring to a very modern Hollywood High School, where all the students are hooked into 21st century technology and fashion. Nancy's sense of style and ethics are greatly at odds with what she finds at Hollywood High, but she stays true to herself. By the end of the movie, her styles have become trendsetting at the school. Meanwhile, Nancy solves an old mystery involving a movie star who once lived in the

As Nancy Drew, Roberts looks a little out of place in a modern classroom.

house she and her father have rented. The movie combined elements of comedy, mystery, adventure, and romance.

Roberts enjoyed playing the famous character. "She's very kind, very genuine, very sweet," she said. "I think she just really teaches you it's OK for girls to be smart and well-mannered. You don't have to play stupid, and it's cool to be independent and take charge." The actress hadn't read any of the *Nancy Drew* books before she got the part, but she was given lots of copies of them after she was associated with the role. She didn't want to read too many before making the movie, however, preferring to stick to the character as it was written in the script.

Recent Projects

With starring roles in major movies to her credit, and good reviews for her performances in them as well, Roberts could now pick and choose among many projects. In 2008, she took a role in an independent film, *Lymelife,* about the pressures of adolescence and life in the well-to-do suburbs of New York City. After that, she appeared in two films with wide appeal to young audiences: *Wild Child* and *Hotel for Dogs.*

In the 2008 movie *Wild Child,* Roberts played Poppy, a spoiled, bratty rich girl from Malibu, California, whose behavior worsens after the death of her mother. Aiden Quinn played Poppy's father, who has given his daughter very little discipline since his wife died. In his youth, he was responsible for some wild pranks, and Poppy follows in his footsteps. At last she gets in so much trouble that her father decides to send her to a very strict British boarding school, run by the headmistress Mrs. Kingsley, played by Natasha Richardson.

Roberts enjoyed playing Nancy Drew. "She's very kind, very genuine, very sweet," she said. "I think she just really teaches you it's OK for girls to be smart and well-mannered. You don't have to play stupid, and it's cool to be independent and take charge."

Arriving in England, Poppy is horrified to find that the school doesn't allow fashionable clothes, iPods, cell phones, and all the other luxuries she depends on. Even worse, she finds herself at the bottom of the social order, whereas at home, she was always popular. The ruling clique of girls, led by a girl named Harriet, particularly scorn her because she is American. Eventually, Poppy is humbled enough to make friends with her roommates Josie, Kate, Kiki, and Drippy—four girls who are nearly as unpopular as she is. They agree to help her get in so much trouble that she will be expelled. Harriet temporarily spoils Poppy's plans and her newfound friendships, however. In the end, Poppy must make peace with her classmates and learn how to thrive at her new school—with the help of the headmistress's handsome son, played by Alex Pettyfer.

In 2009, Roberts played a lead role in *Hotel for Dogs,* an adaptation of the popular book of the same name by the author Lois Duncan. The movie concerns two siblings who hide stray dogs in an abandoned hotel. Roberts played Andi and Jake T. Austin played Bruce, her younger brother. Andi and Bruce are orphans who were placed in foster care after the death of their parents. They live in a series of foster homes before landing with the Scudders (played by Lisa Kudrow and Kevin Dillon), a couple of middle-aged aspiring rock-n-rollers who don't have much talent. The kids and their dog Friday, who they hide from the Scudders, find an old, abandoned building, the Francis Duke Hotel, where a few stray dogs live. With the help of some kids who work at a nearby pet shop, Andi and Bruce start taking in other stray animals. Bruce is a gifted inventor, and he creates some clever inventions to help care for the animals when he and Andi are not available.

Scenes from Hotel for Dogs.

Hotel for Dogs was called a fun film for kids and their parents, with a strong message about the importance of family. "I thought this film was special," Roberts declared. "While it is about dogs, it is also a movie about family. It has a great message about how family just doesn't have to be those you are related to. It can be those you feel comfortable with."

HOME AND FAMILY

Roberts lives with her mother, her stepfather, and her half-sister Grace. Even though she is a celebrity, her life is, in some ways, just like a typical teenager's. She has to do chores around the house and she must keep up with her schoolwork. She has two cats, Pirate and Coco Chanel. Coco was named after a famous French fashion designer.

MAJOR INFLUENCES

One of the major influences on Roberts's life has been growing up in a family of actors. Yet being asked about her famous relatives is one of her least favorite things about being a celebrity. Referring to her aunt, Julia Roberts, she revealed that while they are very close, they spend time together doing normal activities. "People always ask me if she gives me lots of advice, but we really don't talk about movies or the business. We'll cook or talk about fashion, that kind of thing." Overall, she feels that "a well-known relative can get you in the door, but talent and hard work are what counts." As proof of that, she said, "I've gone on maybe a hundred auditions where I've never even been called back."

Roberts is close to her aunt, actress Julia Roberts. "People always ask me if she gives me lots of advice, but we really don't talk about movies or the business. We'll cook or talk about fashion, that kind of thing." Overall, she feels that "a well-known relative can get you in the door, but talent and hard work are what counts."

FAVORITE BOOKS AND MUSIC

Roberts enjoys lots of different kinds of music, but some of her favorite recording artists are Usher, Jesse McCartney, Ashlee Simpson, Jessica Simpson, Michelle Branch, JoJo, Eminem, and John Mayer. Her favorite actresses include Reese Witherspoon, Drew Barrymore, Wynona Ryder, and Rachel McAdams. Some of her favorite books are *To Kill a Mockingbird, The Perks of*

Being a Wallflower, My Sister's Keeper, and the "Gossip Girl" series. She reads about one book each week. She is a spokeswoman for Drop Everything and Read (DEAR), a program that sets aside free reading time during the school day. "Kids today have so much technology (computers, Sidekicks, BlackBerrys, etc. which I love by the way!) that I think it is important to encourage them to read and spend quality time with their families."

HOBBIES AND OTHER INTERESTS

One of Roberts's greatest interests is fashion. She has thought about being a fashion designer instead of an actress someday. "I like cute dresses and colorful, comfortable stuff like jeans or a jean skirt and a casual top," she said. Roberts likes to knit, but admits that she doesn't try anything too complicated and has made mostly scarves. She also enjoys being active in sports such as volleyball and tennis, and she loves to cook. Photography is a special interest of hers, one she is considering studying in college.

SELECTED CREDITS

Movies

BigLove, 2001 (short)
Blow, 2001
Grand Champion, 2002
Aquamarine, 2006
Spymate, 2006
Nancy Drew, 2007
Lymelife, 2008
Wild Child, 2008
Hotel for Dogs, 2009

Television

"Unfabulous," 2004-07

Recordings

Unfabulous and More: Emma Roberts, 2005

HONORS AND AWARDS

ShoWest Awards: 2007, Female Star of Tomorrow

FURTHER READING

Books

Brown, Lauren. *Emma Roberts: Simply Fabulous!,* 2007

Periodicals

Girls' Life, Oct.-Nov. 2005, p.44; June-July 2007, p. 44
Kidsworld Magazine, Winter 2007, p.14
Teen Vogue, May 2007, p.138
Times (London), Oct. 6, 2007, p.6
USA Today, Mar. 3, 2006, p.E6; Jan. 7, 2005, p.E4; June 14, 2007, p.D3
Variety, Mar. 6, 2006, p.20

ADDRESS

Emma Roberts
Sweeney Management
8755 Lookout Mountain Avenue
Los Angeles, CA 90046

WORLD WIDE WEB SITES

http://www.emmaroberts.net
http://www.nick.com/shows/unfabulous/index.jhtml
http://nancydrewmovie.warnerbros.com
http://www.wildchildmovie.com
http://www.hotelfordogsmovie.com

Robin Roberts 1960-

American Television Journalist
Co-Host of "Good Morning America"

BIRTH

Robin Roberts was born on November 23, 1960, in Pass Christian, Mississippi. Her parents were Lawrence Roberts and Lucimarian (Tolliver) Roberts. Robin was the youngest of their four children. She has one older brother, Lawrence Jr., and two older sisters, Sally-Ann and Dorothy.

Roberts's parents were both accomplished professionals at a time when white society made life very difficult for African

Americans. Her father, Lawrence Roberts, was one of the nation's famed Tuskegee Airmen of World War II. These pilots, who received their training in Tuskegee, Alabama, were the first African-American pilots to defend the United States in wartime. Their valiant performance helped pave the way for broader acceptance of African Americans in the U.S. armed services. Lawrence Roberts remained in the Air Force after the war and rose to the rank of colonel. Her mother, Lucimarian (Tolliver) Roberts, was another pioneer. She was the first woman in her family to go to college, and she became the first African American in Mississippi history to serve on the state board of education.

YOUTH

Looking back on her childhood, Roberts believes that her experiences as a youngster laid the foundation for much of her future success. "I was allowed to be a child," she explained. "I also had the privilege, with my father being in the military, of being able to travel. I saw the world. I lived in Turkey and traveled around Europe. I was exposed to different cultures."

But Roberts believes that the example and guidance of her parents were the biggest factors in her development. The life histories of her parents, for instance, gave her enormous confidence that she was also capable of realizing her dreams. "Lawrence Roberts was a remarkable man," she explained. "When he was a kid he'd 'ride' a broomstick handle around the house and pretend to fly. He was determined to fly airplanes. Now keep in mind, this was way outside the traditional career options for blacks at the time. And he was often told how crazy it was for a black man to even think it. But he joined the military and became a Tuskegee airman."

Similarly, Lucimarian Roberts's life was an inspiration to her youngest daughter. Robin knew that her mother had overcome poverty and racism to rise to her influential position with the state board of education. "I had two people raising me that had overcome some really long odds," she summarized. "I felt that I could do anything."

High Expectations

Robin and her siblings also were raised in a household that strongly emphasized good manners and responsible behavior. Her mother, for example, always kept after her to speak correctly and clearly. Roberts sometimes grew tired of these reminders, but she now credits them as an important factor in her later success in broadcasting. Both of her parents also actively monitored her activities and friendships. "When I was growing up, my parents were harder on me about my friends than almost anything else in my life," she said. "They understood the concept of peer pressure before it became a catchphrase. They would grill me: 'Who are they? What do their parents do? Are they good students? Do they go to church? Do they smoke?' I was impatient with the questions then. Now I understand."

Looking back on her childhood, Roberts believes that the structured home environment maintained by her parents helped prepare her for adulthood. "It wasn't just rules for the sake of rules," she wrote in her 2007 book *From the Heart.* "We learned that rules have a purpose. They teach us invaluable lessons. Lessons that we may not even be aware of at the time, like discipline. It's not always easy to do what is expected of us, especially when others aren't holding up their end of the bargain. But my parents never let us get away with measuring ourselves against other people's performance or blaming someone else's failure for our own. Our house was a no-whine zone. We were taught to take responsibility for our own actions."

"When I was growing up, my parents were harder on me about my friends than almost anything else in my life," Roberts said. "They understood the concept of peer pressure before it became a catchphrase. They would grill me: 'Who are they? What do their parents do? Are they good students?' ... I was impatient with the questions then. Now I understand."

These lessons served Roberts well in her athletic endeavors. Her maturity and self-discipline helped her make a mark in a variety of sports during her youth. She was one of the state's top junior bowlers as a pre-teen, and she also showed promise on the tennis court. "Oh, I loved everything about being an athlete," she told National Public Radio. "I loved running. I loved jumping. I loved sweating. I loved it all. Loved competing against myself, against other people.... My first dream was to be Venus and Serena [Williams]. I wanted to be a pro tennis player. But there's something called ability you have to have along with that desire and the heart."

Roberts ultimately settled on basketball instead, in large part because she was taller than most of her classmates. "My heart belonged to tennis," she recalled, "[but] my body was more suited for basketball. When you're 5'10" in the eighth grade, people expect you to play hoops, so that's what I did. I put my heart into the game and loved it."

Roberts playing for Southeastern Louisiana University, where she was the school's third all-time leading scorer and the third all-time leading rebounder.

EDUCATION

Roberts attended high school in Pass Christian. After graduating, she attended Southeastern Louisiana University (SLU) in Hammond on a tennis scholarship. After arriving on campus, though, she left tennis behind to concentrate on basketball. She knew that with the demands of studying, it would be impossible for her to participate in both sports.

Roberts excelled on the basketball court, and as of 2008 she continued to hold two long-standing SLU records: the third-leading scorer (1,446 points) and the third-leading rebounder (1,034 rebounds) in the history of the school's women's team. She averaged a career-high 15.2 points per game as a senior. But she also performed at a high level in the classroom at Southeastern Louisiana. Roberts graduated cum laude (with academic honors) in 1983, with a major in communications.

"Oh, I loved everything about being an athlete," Roberts acknowledged. "I loved running. I loved jumping. I loved sweating. I loved it all. Loved competing against myself, against other people."

CHOOSING A CAREER

By the time Roberts graduated from Southeastern Louisiana, she had already decided to pursue a career in sports broadcast journalism. A career as a professional athlete was beyond her grasp—the Women's National Basketball Association (WNBA) did not even exist yet—but she knew that she wanted to pursue a sports-oriented career. She also looked to the example of her older sister Sally-Ann, who enjoyed her own career as a television broadcaster in New Orleans. "She kind of planted that bug about, well, maybe broadcasting—maybe journalism—and then also combining that with sports and you could have that lifestyle," explained Roberts.

Roberts did not even wait until her graduation to explore this career path. "I practically stalked the owner of a small radio station near the SLU campus because I wanted to host a sports show," she remembered. "I knew I needed practical experience, and a small station seemed perfect. He finally gave me a shot as an early-morning DJ. But this was a country-and-western station—it's not like I was spinning Earth Wind & Fire records. Still, every day I got to that station at 6:00 A.M. Then after that shift I'd head to class at 8:00 A.M. I came back to the station at noon to write copy. I scratched a lot of good Merle Haggard records before the station let me host a sports show."

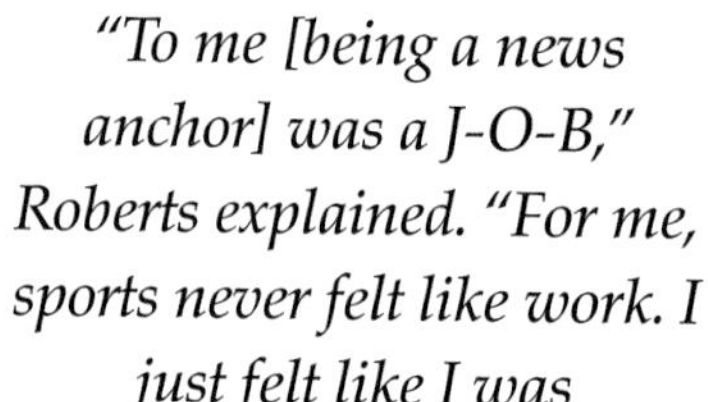

"To me [being a news anchor] was a J-O-B," Roberts explained. "For me, sports never felt like work. I just felt like I was stealing money."

CAREER HIGHLIGHTS

Once she earned her college degree, Roberts received a flurry of full-time job offers from local television stations scattered across the South. But these job openings were in the stations' news departments, and Roberts wanted to stay in the world of sports. With this in mind, she instead accepted a part-time job as the weekend sports anchor for WDAM, a local station in Hattiesburg, Mississippi. The job paid only $5.50 an hour, but she never regretted the decision.

The experience Roberts gained while working in Hattiesburg from 1983 to 1984 enabled her to move on to similar but higher-paying jobs at WLOX in Biloxi, Mississippi (1984 to 1986) and WSMV in Nashville, Tennessee (1986 to 1987). At both these stops, she turned down offers to anchor the news because she wanted to stay with sports. "To me [being a news anchor] was a J-O-B," she said. "For me, sports never felt like work. I just felt like I was stealing money." She occasionally encountered hostility from male athletes and sports reporters who did not believe that a woman had any business covering "men's" sports like football. But Roberts never let their disapproval stop her from pursuing her career goals.

In 1987 Roberts received two exciting job offers at nearly the same time. One was from ESPN, a national cable sports network whose on-air anchors and reporters are among the world's most recognized sports journalists. While excited by the prospect of working for ESPN, she didn't feel she was ready. So she instead accepted the second job offer—to be a sports reporter for WAGA, a local television station in Atlanta, Georgia. "I always wanted to live in Atlanta, ever since I was a kid," she explained. "It seemed really cool. I had never worked in a major market covering professional teams. I knew I wanted to get to the networks, but I wanted to stay there when I got there."

Roberts spent the next three years reporting on sporting events in Atlanta. Looking back on this period of her career, she praises the Atlanta sports stars that she covered. According to Roberts, stars like Dominique Wilkins and Doc Rivers of the NBA's Atlanta Hawks were "accepting of me and

While working at ESPN, Roberts had the opportunity to interview many sports legends. Here she's shown with former pro basketball player Bill Bradley after he announced that he was running for president. From left: Roberts, Bradley, Dave DeBusschere, Jerry Lucas, Willis Reed, Walt Frazier, Earl Monroe, and Dick Barnett.

treated me with respect." Wilkins even agreed to participate in a free throw contest against Roberts—and he responded with good humor when she beat him.

Working at ESPN

In late 1989 ESPN approached Roberts once again with a job offer, and this time she accepted. She believed that she had finally acquired the experience and seasoning that she needed to take full advantage of this step into the national spotlight. Roberts made her first appearance on ESPN on January 29, 1990, as an anchor for the network's famed "Sports Center" highlights show. She thus became the first black woman ever to fill that role on the program.

Roberts's role at ESPN expanded steadily over the next few years. Initially hired solely as an anchor for late-night editions of "Sports Center," she was named a host of both "Sunday SportsDay" and "NFL Prime Time" within a year of her arrival. She also roamed across the country—and the world—to cover such sporting events as the U.S. Open and Wimbledon tennis tournaments, the NBA Finals, the Super Bowl, and the Olympics.

By the mid-1990s, Roberts was one of the most recognizable journalists on ESPN. And her friendly personality, sports knowledge, and quiet professionalism led to new opportunities as well. She served as host of ESPN programs like "In the Sportslight" and "Vintage NBA." In 1997 she began a four-year stint as lead play-by-play announcer for WNBA games. She also hosted the legendary "Wide World of Sports" program on the ABC network from 1995 to 2001. (ESPN and ABC are both owned by the Walt Disney Company, so broadcast employees often appear on both networks.)

Roberts's years of success with ESPN were inspirational to younger female sports journalists. In fact, people throughout the world of sports say that the trailblazing Roberts proved that female journalists were just as capable of covering football, basketball, and hockey as their male counterparts. "She had a spirit and a style to her, and developed credibility with the sports fan that I think helped pave the way for future female anchors in sports," said John Walsh, a top executive at ESPN.

"

Sports analysts argue that Roberts proved that female journalists were just as capable of covering football, basketball, and hockey as their male counterparts. "She had a spirit and a style to her, and developed credibility with the sports fan that I think helped pave the way for future female anchors in sports," said John Walsh, a top executive at ESPN.

"

Moving to "Good Morning America"

In addition to all her responsibilities with ESPN and ABC, Roberts occasionally filed sports-related stories for "Good Morning America" (GMA), ABC's popular morning news and entertainment program. The GMA producers liked Roberts, who consistently displayed a friendly and poised on-air personality. As time passed, they gradually expanded her profile on the show. In 1999 they made her a co-host of the weekend edition of GMA, and three years later she became the lead host of the show's regular news update segments.

In 2005 Roberts's steady rise at "Good Morning America" took the most dramatic turn yet. That year she joined veteran GMA anchors Diane Sawyer and Charles Gibson to become the show's first-ever African-American co-anchor. "I remember my first morning as co-anchor," she re-

Roberts with her "Good Morning America" co-host and friend, newscaster Diane Sawyer.

called. "The announcer said: 'This is 'Good Morning America' with Charles Gibson, Diane Sawyer, and Robin Roberts.' All of a sudden I was on camera sitting next to Charlie and Diane. I wanted to shout to the TV audience, 'I don't know how I got here either!'"

Roberts's co-hosting duties at GMA made it impossible for her to continue working for ESPN as well, so she reluctantly bid farewell to the sports network. But she did not regret the move. As she grew older, she had become more interested in issues outside of the world of sports. And her GMA hosting responsibilities gave her the opportunity to travel around the globe and cover a wide range of events, both lighthearted and grim. Roberts admitted that some of her assignments—like covering wars in Iraq and Africa—troubled her. But she hastened to add that the human spirit endures in even the darkest parts of the world. "Being a journalist has exposed me to tragedy and suffering all over the world," she said. "I have seen despair, but I have also seen that no matter how great the problem, there are always people dedicated to the solution."

Reporting on the Hurricane Katrina Tragedy

Roberts received a heavy dose of both despair and inspiration in August 2005, when she was sent to the Gulf Coast to provide on-the-scene coverage of the Hurricane Katrina tragedy. Katrina was a Category IV hurricane that hit the United States on August 29, 2005, devastating New Orleans and large swaths of coastal Louisiana and Mississippi. The hurricane's impact was made even worse by a slow and ineffective response by the federal government. Many especially blamed the Federal Emergency Management Agency (FEMA), the government agency responsible for coordinating efforts after natural disasters and other types of emergencies. All told, Katrina killed 1,800 people and caused an estimated $80 billion in damage.

"

"Hurricane Katrina taught me a lesson in a big way," Roberts revealed. "At first all I could see was the storm's devastation and the incredible loss. But at the same time, there were thousands of volunteers cleaning up and helping to feed folks—people who had come from all over; they just refused to give up. It showed me the amazing power of the human spirit."

"

Roberts arrived in Louisiana on August 30, the day after the storm. But her first priority was to find her 81-year-old mother and other family members who had lived in the region (her father had passed away one year earlier). She drove hundreds of miles to Biloxi, Mississippi, where her mother had fled. Roberts's drive was tense and dangerous, as she detoured around downed power lines, overturned cars, and fallen trees every step of the way. Once she reached Biloxi, though, she found her mother, sister, and nieces safe and sound. After enjoying a brief reunion, Roberts sped back to a GMA satellite truck to prepare a report. She opened the live report in her usual professional way, but when Gibson asked her on the air if her family was safe, the emotional strain of the previous 24 hours finally shone through and she broke down in tears.

Roberts worried that her on-air struggles might elicit a negative response from colleagues and GMA viewers. But instead, co-workers and viewers alike rallied around her. They agreed that her response was totally natural, given the threat that Katrina had posed to her family. A few weeks later, the producers of GMA even launched a campaign to rebuild parts of Roberts's hometown of Pass Christian.

Roberts was gratified by this response—as well as by the reaction of her mother and many other Americans to the Katrina disaster. "Hurricane Katrina taught me a lesson in a big way," she said. "When the storm hit, our

After Hurricane Katrina, Roberts pitched in when GMA helped rebuild part of her hometown, Pass Christian, Mississippi. Here she and other volunteers are shown unloading a supply trailer.

family home was in ruins. And I remember standing with my mom, our mementos and belongings strewn all over the place. Just the year before, my dad had died in his sleep, and I was still reeling from that. Now this. It was absolutely the hardest time of my life. Mom just looked everything over and said very calmly, 'We'll rebuild.' At first all I could see was the storm's devastation and the incredible loss. But at the same time, there were thousands of volunteers cleaning up and helping to feed folks—people who had come from all over; they just refused to give up. It showed me the amazing power of the human spirit."

From the Heart

In 2006, the "Good Morning America" anchor team was broken up when Gibson left to host ABC's evening news program. With his departure, Roberts and Sawyer became the only all-female team to anchor a morning network show. Fortunately, Roberts and Sawyer had forged a close friendship by this time, and this warmth was evident to GMA's five million viewers. As one television executive told the *New York Times* in 2006, Roberts and Sawyer were "just so relaxed and likeable together." This chemistry enabled the show to maintain its high popularity even after the loss of Gibson.

In March 2007 Roberts branched out into a new media form, publishing *From the Heart: Seven Rules to Live By.* In this small but inspirational book, Roberts shared personal stories and reflections that she believes have been essential factors in her happiness and success. She distilled these thoughts into the following seven rules:

- Position yourself to take the shot
- Dream big, but focus small
- If at first you don't succeed, dive back in
- Never play the race, gender, or any other card
- Venture outside your comfort zone
- Focus on the solution, not the problem
- Keep faith, family, and friends close to your heart.

Devoting a chapter to each of these rules, Roberts explained how these guidelines helped her build a happy and fulfilling life. But she also acknowledged that "when it comes right down to it, there is no playbook for your own unique, wonderful life." The main thing, she claimed, is to remember that "no matter what your circumstances, how high your barriers, or how daunting your challenges, you can change the way you think. And once that happens, you can do anything."

Fighting Back Against Cancer

Four months after the publication of *From the Heart,* Roberts received terrible news out of the blue. In the midst of a GMA assignment on July 17, 2007, she received a call from her doctor informing her that she had been diagnosed with cancer. Roberts managed to file her usual professional report, but she admitted that when she got home one day later, "I just collapsed on the floor and cried. Just cried and cried."

In From the Heart, *Roberts included personal stories and her advice about happiness and success.*

Doctors removed a marble-sized tumor from Roberts's right breast. But this operation turned out to be only the first step in a long ordeal. Tests on the removed tumor revealed that it was a more dangerous type of cancer than doctors had originally believed. They urged her to undergo chemotherapy treatments to extinguish any cancer cells that might still be lurking in her body. One of her doctors compared the invasive type of cancer in Roberts to a nearly—but not quite—dead fire in a fireplace: "You know there are a couple of embers in there, that if you poke them you could start up a fire and burn down the whole house. But if you throw water into the fireplace, you put out all those embers. That's what chemotherapy does."

Roberts agreed to undergo chemotherapy, even though she knew that she would endure some miserable days and nights as a result. The chemicals used in chemotherapy treatments are essentially poisons, so they damage healthy cells at the same time that they attack cancer cells. As a result, side effects of "chemo" treatments often include severe nausea, fatigue, hair loss, and increased susceptibility to certain diseases.

Despite the threat of these side effects, Roberts decided to continue with her co-anchor duties at GMA. "You want to say, 'Everything's the same; I'm living with cancer and it's not going to stop me,'" she explained. Roberts returned to the GMA set and revealed her diagnosis to millions of stunned television viewers. Even more impressively, she decided to use her illness to educate the public about cancer treatments—and to give strength to other families struggling with cancer.

Roberts with fashion designer Isaac Mizrahi after his fashion show, part of the GMA "I Dare You" series. It was the first time Roberts appeared on TV without a wig.

A Public Struggle

Over the next several months, GMA cameras accompanied Roberts as she met with doctors and underwent chemotherapy and radiation treatments. GMA even showed her getting her head shaved—a step that she took only after her hair began to fall out. "You know everyone tells you to shave your head" before beginning chemo, she said. "And I thought, no, not me, that's not going to be me, because some chemotherapy patients don't lose their hair. But let me tell you, I've joined that choir. That's a bit of advice I now preach, because when it starts to fall out, phew, that's rough."

Throughout her eight months of chemo treatment, Roberts tried to provide an honest picture of her experiences. "I did feel a sense of responsibility to be truthful about how I was doing," she said. "There are so many people living with cancer. I wanted to be able to change the face of what it really looks like." Many viewers believe that Roberts succeeded in this goal. As Diane Salvatore wrote in *Ladies' Home Journal,* "Her struggle moved, empowered, and awed all of us [women], whether you've had breast cancer, know someone who does, or ever had a jolt of fear that you might one day, too."

Roberts completed her course of treatments in the spring of 2008. She reported that she suffered some lingering side effects of chemotherapy, such as cloudy vision and loss of feeling in some of her toes. But she also indicated that doctors are optimistic that she has defeated the cancer.

Roberts believes that good physical fitness helped her during the grueling chemotherapy treatments. "Being athletic did not prevent me from getting cancer, but it has helped me in battling it," she said. Roberts also says that she relied heavily on her religious faith and on support from family and friends during those difficult months of treatment. Sawyer was a particular source of strength to her on the GMA set, she has said. "[People] say women in positions of authority, they're the worst enemies. And that happens from time to time, but Diane and I feel we complement each other," she said. "We don't threaten one another. We help one another."

Looking to the future, Roberts believes that her best days are still ahead of her. "It's like a rebirth," she explained. "I had a fairly good appreciation for life before this. I didn't really need cancer to get my attention.... And I'm excited to feel better again."

HOME AND FAMILY

Roberts lives on Manhattan Island in New York City. She has never been married and has no children.

HOBBIES AND OTHER INTERESTS

Roberts enjoys Pilates, biking, and light weightlifting to keep in shape. She has also expressed interest in taking flying lessons and earning a private pilot's license someday.

SELECTED WRITINGS

Careers for Women Who Love Sports, 2000 (juvenile)
Sports for Life: How Athletes Have More Fun, 2000 (juvenile)
Which Sport Is Right for You, 2000 (juvenile)
From the Heart: Seven Rules to Live By, 2007

SELECTED HONORS AND AWARDS

T.V. Award of Merit (Daughters of the American Revolution): 1990
Women at Work Broadcast Journalism Award: 1992
Excellence in Journalism Award, Broadcast Media (Center for the Study of Sport in Society): 1993

Women's Institute on Sport and Education Foundation Hall of Fame: 1994
Women's World Cup Advisory Board (FIFA): 1999
President's Award (Women's Sports Foundation): 2001
Journalist of the Year (*Ebony*): 2002
Inspiration Award (WNBA): 2008

FURTHER READING

Books

Roberts, Robin. *From the Heart: Seven Rules to Live By,* 2007

Periodicals

Atlanta Journal-Constitution, Apr. 17, p.C5
Black Enterprise, Apr. 1997, p.56; Sep. 2007, p.146
Current Biography Yearbook, 2008
Ebony, Mar. 2006, p.118
Essence, May 2007, p.192
Good Housekeeping, Aug. 2004, p.184
Jet, May 30, 2006, p.30
Ladies' Home Journal, Aug. 2008, p.78
Los Angeles Times, Oct. 15, 2005, p.E1
New York Times, May 9, 2005, p.C5; Nov. 16, 2006, p.E3; July 28, 2008, SPORTS, p.7
People, Aug. 13, 2007, p.95; Nov. 26, 2007, p.64
Redbook, April 2007, p.30; May 2008, p.94
Sports Illustrated, June 17, 1991, p.78
USA Today, May 16, 2005, p.D4; Aug. 1, 2007, p.D8

ADDRESS

Robin Roberts
"Good Morning America"
ABC News
147 Columbus Ave.
New York, NY 10023

WORLD WIDE WEB SITE

http://www.abcnews.go.com/gma

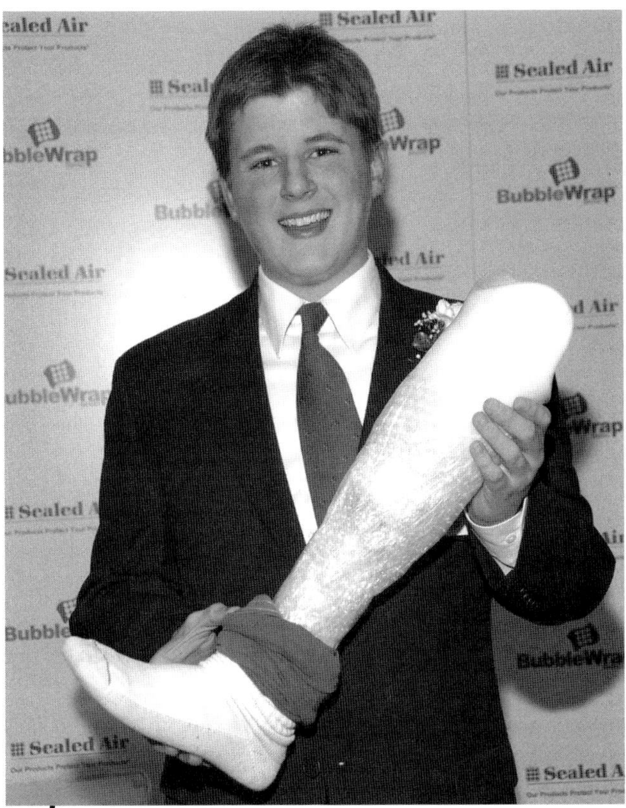

BRIEF ENTRY

Grayson Rosenberger 1992-

American Inventor

Created a Low-Cost, Lifelike Cosmetic Covering for Artificial Limbs

EARLY YEARS

Grayson Rosenberger was born on January 29, 1992, in Nashville, Tennessee. He is a tenth-generation Tennessean—his ancestors have served in the Continental Congress, as governors of Tennessee, and in the U.S. Congress. Grayson's parents, Peter and Gracie Rosenberger, lead an international organization called Standing With Hope, which provides artificial limbs to amputees in developing countries. Grayson has one older brother, Parker.

The Rosenbergers created the organization Standing With Hope as a result of the experiences of Gracie Rosenberger as a double amputee. She was involved in a serious car accident when she was a teenager, and her injuries eventually resulted in the amputation of both of her legs. She then began to use artificial legs called prostheses (pronounced *pros-THEE-sees*) to help her walk.

As a child, Grayson Rosenberger was constantly surrounded by the projects of Standing With Hope, and he saw the many challenges faced by amputees like his mother. Whenever his parents returned from a trip overseas, they would tell the stories of the people whose lives had been improved once they received artificial legs. Rosenberger was inspired by his parents' work, and he wanted to find a way to contribute on his own.

Rosenberger was particularly affected by the story of Daniel, a 16-year-old amputee living in Ghana, a country in West Africa. Daniel had broken his leg playing soccer, and because the proper medical treatments to repair his injury were not available, he had to have his leg amputated. Rosenberger's parents had given Daniel a basic artificial leg made of metal rods, but they had been unable to provide the costly prosthetic covering that would make the leg appear more lifelike. After hearing about Daniel, Rosenberger was determined to find a way to help.

"

Rosenberger thought that the bare metal rods of basic artificial legs looked "kind of robotic," and he wanted to help people feel less self-conscious about using a prosthesis. "By giving them what looks like a real leg, you give them back their dignity," he explained.

"

MAJOR ACCOMPLISHMENTS

In 2007, when he was 15 years old, Rosenberger decided to enter a contest sponsored by the makers of Bubble Wrap, a flexible plastic air-cushioned packing material. The contest challenged young inventors to create a unique new product using Bubble Wrap. After brainstorming ideas with his father, Rosenberger decided to try using Bubble Wrap to create an inexpensive, lifelike covering for prosthetic limbs. He thought that the bare metal rods of basic artificial legs looked "kind of robotic," and he wanted to help people feel less self-conscious about using a prosthesis. "By giving them what looks like a real leg, you give them back their dignity," Rosenberger explained.

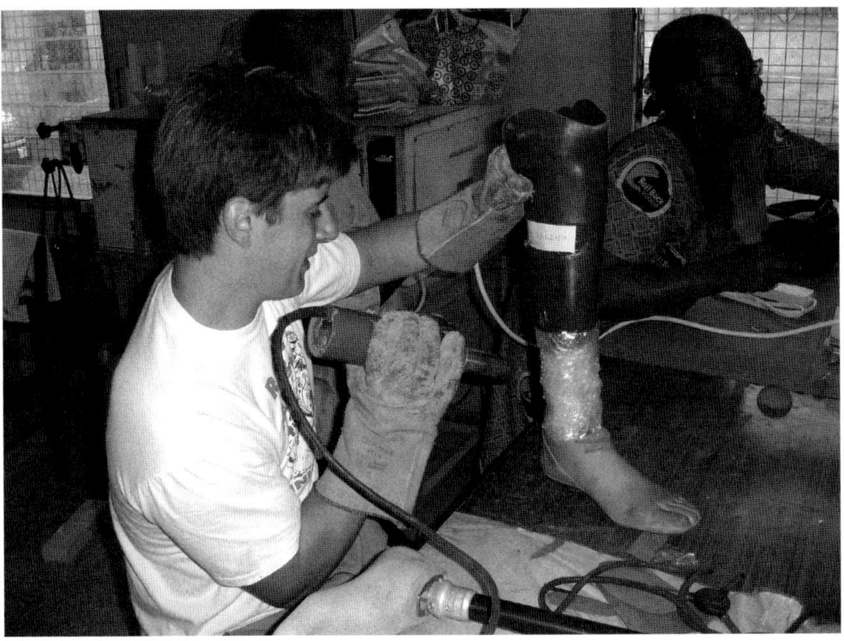

Rosenberger assembling a cover for a prosthetic leg.

Bringing an Idea to Life

To get started on his invention, Rosenberger first turned to his mother. Gracie Rosenberger has several pairs of legs, including a covered set. Her favorite legs to wear are high performance limbs that allow her to participate in such activities as snow skiing. Using one of his mother's legs, Rosenberger worked out the beginnings of his Bubble Wrap covering. He then took his concept to his mother's prosthetist, Jim McElhiney, who served as the official mentor needed for the contest. McElhiney gave Rosenberger a discarded prosthetic leg that had one of the expensive traditional cosmetic covers.

Rosenberger studied this prosthesis closely, using it as a model for his own design. He wanted to make a cosmetic covering that would be affordable so that more people could use it. But he also wanted to make it look as lifelike as possible, to disguise the metal parts of the prosthesis with something that looked and felt more like a human leg. He did not want to simply wrap a cylinder around the artificial leg. He needed to find a way to shape the covering to resemble muscle structure, while keeping a softer and somewhat flexible texture. Bubble Wrap, with its small, individual air cushions encased in meltable plastic, seemed perfect for the project.

To create a realistic looking cover for the artificial leg. Rosenberger first taped layers of Bubble Wrap over the metal rod that acted as the leg's bone. He then used a heat gun (a tool that resembles an extremely high-powered blow dryer) to melt and shape the plastic wrapping to imitate the muscles of a human leg. With the addition of a flesh-colored stocking pulled over the plastic form, the prosthesis appeared even more lifelike. In about two hours, Rosenberger had created his first attempt at a new kind of prosthetic cover.

"Conventional coverings are very expensive, and if you have to make an adjustment to the leg, then you have to cut and ruin the covering," Rosenberger explained. "With the Bubble Wrap covering, it's cheap to replace, … and if you're careful, you can put it right back on."

Making a Difference

Rosenberger entered his invention in the 2007 Bubble Wrap Competition for Young Inventors, where it won the Grand Prize. But that was only the beginning. His new cosmetic prosthesis covering had much greater impact than he originally imagined. Within hours of winning the contest, he was interviewed by the Associated Press, the BBC, the "Today Show," *USA Today*, and many other news organizations.

Prosthetic specialists, clinic workers, and amputees were all impressed with the advantages and the potential of Rosenberger's alternative prosthesis covering. He was even invited to speak at the American Orthtotics and Prosthetic Association's convention in Las Vegas, where he met with many prosthetists from around the country. Some of them have actually tried his invention in their own laboratories.

Rosenberger's new design was simple, highly customizable for each person who would use it, and easy to make with basic materials found in hardware or office supply stores. Most importantly, his invention cost very little to make. Traditional prosthesis coverings normally cost at least several hundred dollars each, and they can cost as much as several thousand dollars. But Rosenberger's original design cost only $15 to make. "Conventional coverings are very expensive, and if you have to make an adjustment to the leg, then you have to cut and ruin the covering," he explained. "With the Bubble Wrap covering, it's cheap to replace, … and if you're careful,

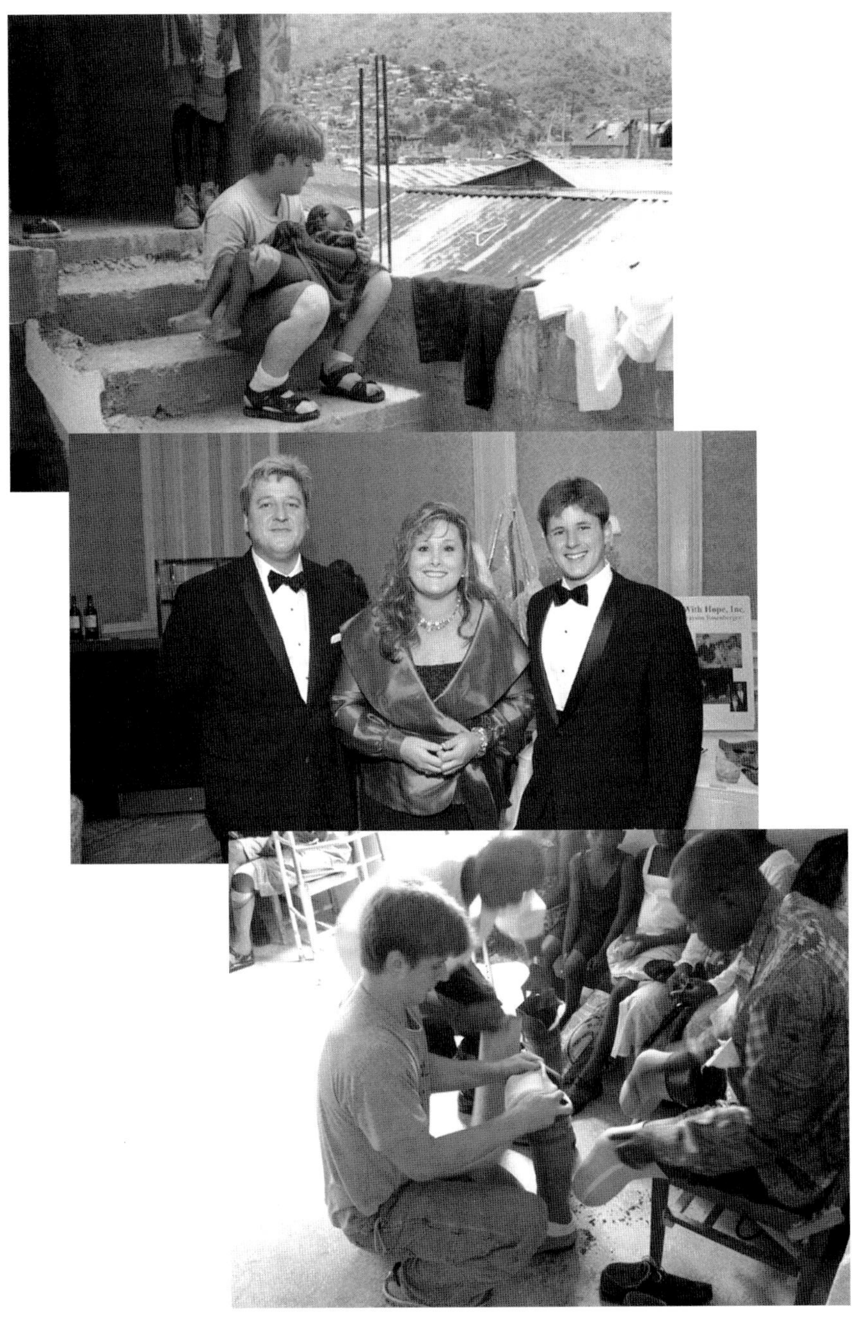

Rosenberger with his parents and with some of the people helped by Standing With Hope.

you can put it right back on." Paddy Rossbach, president of the Amputee Coalition of America, praised Rosenberger's invention, telling *People* magazine, "I think it's a fabulous idea."

Following through with his desire to help amputees regain a sense of normalcy in their lives, Rosenberger decided not to apply for a patent on his invention. A patent is a legal document from the U.S. government that gives an inventor the sole right to make, use, and sell an invention for a certain period of time. The government registers the idea as the property of the inventor, and no other person or company is allowed to use it without the inventor's permission until the patent expires. If Rosenberger had filed for a patent, then anyone who used his idea would have been required to pay him a fee. Instead, he began offering his invention to others for free.

"I want my message to be, anyone can make a difference, even a woman who's missing both legs or a teenager with Bubble Wrap.... If you have an idea, don't just sit there and think, 'it will never happen.' Don't wait for something to happen. Make that dream come true."

Soon after winning the contest, Rosenberger traveled with his parents to Ghana to make coverings for amputees. During the 10-day trip, he created cosmetic coverings for 25 people. He molded and shaped each covering to match the person's body size and build, giving everyone a custom fit that looked as natural as possible. Rosenberger also trained clinic workers in Ghana to make the coverings on their own. Since then, he has trained workers in other clinics, so that more people can benefit from his invention. "When I first came up with this, it seemed like a really good idea, but ... I was scared that people wouldn't like them," Rosenberger recalled. "But I didn't need to be afraid. Everyone wanted a covering. They loved it!"

Inspiring Others

The impact of his prosthetic covering has helped convince Rosenberger that no idea is too strange to be developed, although so far none of his other inventions have been as successful. (For example, he has also invented a motorized skateboard vehicle known to his family as the "death mobile.") His father told *People* magazine, "He comes up with some bizarre things, but he hit one out of the ballpark with the leg." Rosenberger hopes that his unexpected success creating an innovative medical device from unlikely materials will encourage other young inventors to pursue their own projects. "I want my message to be, anyone can make a difference, even a woman who's missing both legs or a teenager with Bubble Wrap.... If you have an idea, don't just sit there and think, 'it will never happen.' Don't wait for something to happen. Make that dream come true."

Rosenberger returned to West Africa in 2008 and plans on traveling with Standing With Hope in 2009 to launch a new program in China. For high school, he attends Franklin Road Academy in Nashville, Tennessee. His future plans include attending the U.S. Military Academy at West Point. He plans to become a helicopter pilot so that he can serve with a medical evacuation unit.

HONORS AND AWARDS

Bubble Wrap Competition for Young Inventors (Sealed Air Corp.): 2007
da Vinci Apprentice Award (National Multiple Sclerosis Society, Michigan chapter): 2007
Sonny Sneed Young Entrepreneur Award (National Museum of Education): 2008

FURTHER READING

Periodicals

Boy's Life, Oct. 2007, p.18
Campus Life's Ignite Your Faith, Jan.-Feb. 2008, p.11
Current Health, Oct. 2007, p.24; Mar. 2008, p.5
Exceptional Parent, Nov. 2007. p.50
Junior Scholastic, Mar. 26, 2007, p.10
Odyssey, Feb. 2008, p.14
People, Mar. 26, 2007, p.110

ADDRESS

Grayson Rosenberger
Standing With Hope
PO Box 159115
Nashville, TN 37215

WORLD WIDE WEB SITE

http://www.standingwithhope.com/Grayson.cfm

Dinara Safina 1986-

Russian Professional Tennis Player
Silver Medal Winner at the 2008 Olympic Games

BIRTH

Dinara Mikhailovna Safina (pronounced *di-NAH-ruh SAF-i-nah*) was born on April 27, 1986, in Moscow, Russia. Her father, Mikhail Alekseyvich Safin, runs the Spartak Tennis Club in Moscow. Her mother, Rauza Islanova, is a tennis coach who has worked with a number of young Russian stars, including Elena Dementieva. Dinara has a brother, fellow professional tennis player Marat Safin, who is six years older.

Safina uses a different form of her last name than the rest of her family, who spell their name "Safin." She spells her last name differently because, in accordance with Russian tradition, she added the feminine ending "a" to the end.

YOUTH AND EDUCATION

Thanks to their parents' professions, Dinara and her brother Marat practically grew up on a tennis court. "I had no choice but to become a tennis player," she conceded, "but I don't mind being a tennis player." With their mother serving as their coach, both children showed talent from an early age.

Thanks to their parents' professions, Dinara and her brother Marat practically grew up on a tennis court. "I had no choice but to become a tennis player," she conceded, "but I don't mind being a tennis player."

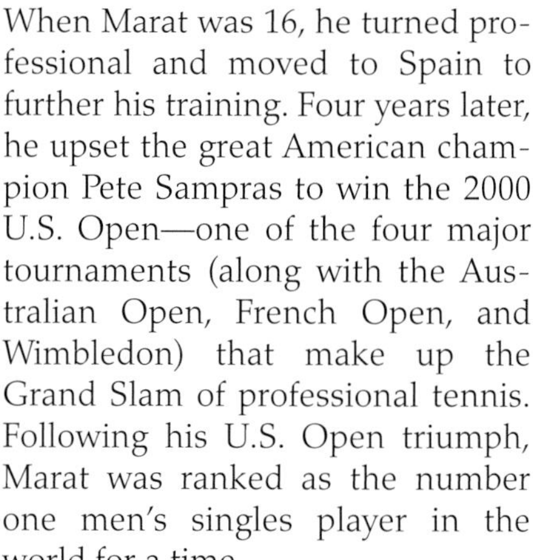

When Marat was 16, he turned professional and moved to Spain to further his training. Four years later, he upset the great American champion Pete Sampras to win the 2000 U.S. Open—one of the four major tournaments (along with the Australian Open, French Open, and Wimbledon) that make up the Grand Slam of professional tennis. Following his U.S. Open triumph, Marat was ranked as the number one men's singles player in the world for a time.

Meanwhile, Dinara learned to hit tennis balls at the age of three and began entering junior tournaments at the age of eight. She was 14 when Marat won his first Grand Slam tournament. As a promising young player in her own right, she often found it difficult to be the little sister of a famous champion. "Every time, it's the same thing," she complained. "People want to know what [Marat] is doing and how he is faring. All the time the questions are about him."

Like her brother, Dinara gained a reputation for having a strong serve, hitting powerful ground strokes, and showing emotion on the court. They both had a tendency to argue line calls, for instance, and throw their rackets in frustration. "I think he's an entertainer to watch," she said of Marat. "That's why people love to watch him play, because he always gives some show. I mean, he's real on the court. If he has his emotions, he will not hide them. He will explode."

Safina won her first victory in a WTA tennis tournament in Poland in 2002, when she was just 16.

Dinara claimed that she and her brother inherited their hot tempers from their father, who always hated to lose. "My dad, he's also like a character," she explained. "Even if he plays football [soccer] for fun, when he loses with friends he comes home and he's so angry. And I'm like, 'Pop, it's only a friends match.' But he ... always wants to win."

CAREER HIGHLIGHTS

Turning Pro

Safina turned professional in 2000, just as her brother was reaching the height of his fame. She started out by playing on the International Tennis Federation (ITF) Women's Circuit, which is considered a training ground for the Sony Ericsson Women's Tennis Association (WTA) Tour. She began playing in professional tennis tournaments, which are organized in rounds of competition. Winning players advance to the next round, while losing players are eliminated. Most tournaments consist of three or four preliminary rounds, followed by quarterfinals (featuring 8 players), semifinals (4 players), and finals (2 players). The player who wins the final match is the tournament champion and claims the title. Throughout the season, a player plays in many tournaments, and points are totaled for the season.

Scoring in tennis can be confusing. In women's tennis, a player wins a match by defeating her opponent in 2 out of 3 sets. The first player to win 6 games usually wins the set, but if their margin of victory is less than 2 games, the set is decided by a tiebreaker. Shorthand notation is often used to show the score of a tennis match. For example, 6-4, 2-6, 7-6 means that the player in question won the first set by a score of 6 games to 4, lost the next set 2 games to 6, and came back to win the match in a third-set tiebreaker.

When Safina starting playing tennis professionally, she was just 14, so her mother traveled with her and served as her coach. "I do have my mum with me, and that helps a lot as I know I can look to her and have her tell me where I am going right or wrong," Safina acknowledged. "But sometimes one can get tired of being with a person for a full 24 hours at a stretch."

In 2001, Safina showed some promise as a pro. Although she failed to qualify for the WTA Tour, she won one singles and one doubles title on the ITF Circuit that year. She also reached the girls' singles final at Wimbledon as a junior player. By the end of the season, she was ranked 394th among female tennis players around the world.

In 2002, Safina began playing consistently on the WTA Tour. In only her fourth event on the Tour, she claimed her first singles title at Sopot, Poland, beating Henrieta Nagyova of Slovakia 6-3, 4-0 (retired). Safina also continued to compete on the ITF Circuit, winning three singles and two doubles titles. Her strong performance also helped her break into the top 100 in the world rankings. By the time the season drew to a close, she had climbed to number 68.

The 2003 season saw Safina win the second WTA Tour singles title of her career at Palermo, Italy, beating Katarina Srebotnik of Slovenia 6-3, 6-4. She also turned in her best performance at a Grand Slam tournament, advancing to the fourth round at the U.S. Open. Safina ended the season ranked number 54 in the world.

The 2004 season started out well for Safina. During the early part of the year, she beat three players ranked in the top 20 in the world. She also claimed her first WTA Tour doubles title in Beijing, China. Unfortunately, she injured her lower back at Wimbledon and was forced to withdraw from several later tournaments with what turned out to be a lumbar spine stress fracture. Still, Safina managed to rise to number 44 in the world rankings by the end of the year.

Growing Up

By the start of the 2005 season—her sixth as a professional tennis player—some analysts began to wonder whether Safina had already reached the greatest heights of her professional career. After all, she had hovered in the middle of the Top 100 in the world rankings for three straight seasons without showing many signs that she could regularly challenge the sport's reigning stars. But her brother thought that a coaching change might help her. He suggested that it might be time for Safina to end her coaching relationship with her mother, and she decided to follow Marat's advice. "Sometimes he's a little hard, but he wants the best for me," she stated. "He told me I was traveling too much with my mom and when I was play-

Safina reacting after the victory point over Amelia Mauresmo during the 2005 Paris Indoors tournament. She beat Mauresmo 6-4, 2-6, 6-3.

ing I was looking too much at her and waiting for help. Now I'm playing alone, I'm more mature and concentrate more. That's what my mom wanted for me, too."

Safina acknowledged that her relationship with her mother improved once she found a new tennis coach. "It was tough. We saw a lot of each other. We lived together and worked together," she revealed. "She'd get uptight and we'd begin to fight about stupid things, like where I put my phone. It's just like any family when you spend too much time together. It's better now."

Under the guidance of Dutch coach Glen Schaap, Safina resumed her rise through the ranks of women's tennis. She won her third WTA Tour singles title at the Paris Indoors, defeating French star Amelie Mauresmo in the finals by a score of 6-4, 2-6, 6-3. Safina described it as "the best day of my career so far and my biggest victory ever." She took another Tour singles title in Prague, Czech Republic, beating Czech player Zuzana Ondraskova 7-6, 6-3. Safina also reached the semifinals in four other events that year. Her strong performance helped her jump to number 20 in the world rankings.

As it turned out, though, 2005 was an even bigger year for Marat Safin. After struggling with injuries for several seasons, he came back to win a second career Grand Slam title at the Australian Open. In the midst of all the media attention he received, Safin made several critical comments about his younger sister. He told reporters that Safina needed to get in better shape and learn to control her emotions if she wanted to reach the top of women's tennis. "She needs to have a character, and she needs to be a little bit of a grown-up woman," he declared. "With all respect, [when I was her age] I had been number one in the world."

"Safina acknowledged that her relationship with her mother improved once she found a new tennis coach. "It was tough. We saw a lot of each other. We lived together and worked together," she revealed. "She'd get uptight and we'd begin to fight about stupid things, like where I put my phone. It's just like any family when you spend too much time together. It's better now."

Although Safina was stung by her brother's criticism, she admitted that he had a point.

"I would behave like a baby and be crying and all this. He hated it. He was always, 'Come on! You have to grow up in your mind,'" she related. "I also knew that I had to be in much better shape to play against top players. I had to be much fitter."

Working Hard

Safina took her brother's words to heart and worked hard to improve her conditioning prior to the start of the 2006 season. Her dedication paid off in several impressive performances. Although she failed to win any titles, Safina defeated four players ranked among the top 10 in the world, reached the semifinals in two events, and made career-best quarterfinal appearances in two Grand Slam tournaments (the French Open and U.S. Open).

Safina's new and improved game was on full display when she stunned Russian star Maria Sharapova in the fourth round of that year's French Open. After trailing her opponent 5 games to 1 in the third set, Safina scored 18 of the last 21 points for an exciting comeback victory, 7-5, 2-6, 7-5. "I think it's unbelievable what I did, just to come back," Safina said afterward. "I took everything in my hands. Before, she was dictating and I had always to run from corner to corner. I said, 'OK, now I'll try to make

Safina beat Martina Hingis to win the 2007 Gold Coast tournament in Australia, 6-3, 3-6, 7-5.

her run.' I started to be more aggressive." Safina ended the 2006 season ranked number 11 in the world in women's singles. She also moved up to number 15 in doubles after winning two titles and reaching the final of the U.S. Open with partner Katarina Srebotnik.

Before the start of the 2007 season, Safina decided to change coaches again. She had trouble getting along with Schaap, and she felt that their conflicts off the court affected her performance on the court. "He would not accept what I would say. He didn't want to hear my opinions," she stated. "I have enough stress on the court playing a match and if I go practice and I'm still fighting with my coach, I don't need this."

Safina credited her new coach, Zeljko Krajan of Croatia, with helping her learn to control her emotions. "I had many coaches, but they could not deal with this," she explained. "He just changed me. I trust him fully." Safina also began working with a new trainer, Dejan Vojnovic of Croatia, who helped her improve her strength, speed, agility, and endurance.

These changes helped Safina claim her fifth career Tour singles title at the 2007 Gold Coast tournament in Australia. Following her victory over

Martina Hingis in the final, 6-3, 3-6, 7-5, Hingis predicted that "Everyone's going to have to watch her." Safina followed that up with another big win—the first Grand Slam victory of her career. She and partner Nathalie Dechy won the 2007 U.S. Open doubles title, beating a team from Chinese Taipei, Yung-Jan Chan and Chia-Jung Chuang, with a score of 6-4, 6-2. By the end of the year Safina was ranked number 15 in the world in women's singles.

On a Roll

The 2008 season began disappointingly for Safina when she lost in the first round of the Australian Open in January. Her struggles continued until May, when she suddenly emerged as one of the hottest players on the Sony Ericsson WTA Tour. The breakthrough began at the German Open in Berlin, when Safina defeated three top 10 players (Justine Henin, Serena Williams, and Elena Dementieva) on her way to winning the sixth Tour singles title of her career, ultimately defeating Dementieva in the finals 3-6, 6-2, 6-2.

Safina's success continued at the French Open in May, where she once again beat three top 10 players (Sharapova, Dementieva, and Svetlana Kuznetsova) to reach her first Grand Slam final as a singles player. Safina demonstrated her newfound physical fitness and mental toughness in each of these triumphs. In the fourth round, for example, she was down 5-3 in the second set against top-seeded Sharapova, facing her opponent's serve at match point. Safina escaped elimination with a backhand winner up the line, then got aggressive and won the match 6-7, 7-6, 6-2. In the quarterfinals against Dementieva, meanwhile, Safina rallied from a 5-2 deficit in the second set to win 4-6, 7-6, 6-0.

After defeating Kuznetsova in the semifinals, Safina had a chance to become part of the only brother-sister combination to both win Grand Slam titles during the Open era of professional tennis (since 1968). She tried to remain focused as she prepared for her first appearance in a major singles final. "I have to do the things that I know to do and try to avoid thinking as much as I can about 'this is the final,'" she noted. "It's still the same court and still the same ball. It's just how I take it in my mind." Unfortunately for Safina, she lost in the final to Ana Ivanovic, snapping her winning streak at 12 matches.

Winning an Olympic Medal

In May, while Safina was in the middle of her winning streak, Russia announced the members of its national tennis team that would compete in the 2008 Olympic Games in Beijing, China. Since several Russian players were ahead of her in the world rankings at that time, Safina did not make the team. After the French Open, however, Russian team member Anna Chakvetadze decided not to compete in the Games. Based on her strong performance in recent tournaments, Safina was selected to replace her.

As the Olympics approached, Safina continued playing on the WTA Tour, and her hot streak continued also. Although she was knocked out in the third round of Wimbledon in June, she won two tournaments in a row in July. Her seventh career title on the WTA Tour came at the East West Bank Classic in Los Angeles, where she beat Flavia Pennetta of Italy 6-4, 6-2. She quickly followed that up with her eighth WTA title at the Rogers Cup in Montreal, Canada, beating Dominika Cibulkova of Slovakia 6-2, 6-1. Going into the Olympic Games, Safina had reached the finals in five out of six tournaments in a row and attained a career-high number 6 in the world rankings.

"For some people I will always just be [Marat's] younger sister. But we have completely different lives. Whatever I have achieved and will achieve, I have done by myself," she noted. "I always wanted to be myself, and now finally the results are coming, and people can know me as Dinara Safina."

Safina flew directly from Montreal to Beijing and did not even have a day off before she began playing in the Olympic tournament. Despite struggling with fatigue, she defeated hometown favorite Li Na of China in the quarterfinals and top-ranked Jelena Jankovic in the semifinals to face Dementieva in the gold medal match. Safina did her best, but she had to settle for the silver medal. "I'm not a machine, I'm a human being," she said afterward of the grueling schedule. "Of course it's sad that it's not the gold medal, but it doesn't matter given what I've done, not many girls can do it."

Reaching for the Top

Immediately after the Olympic Games ended, Safina traveled to America to compete in the 2008 U.S. Open. If she managed to capture her first Grand Slam singles title, she stood to win a $1 million bonus and claim the world number one ranking. Safina fought hard in the tournament and made it all the way to the semifinals before losing to Serena Williams.

After winning the silver medal at the 2008 Olympics, Safina (left) is shown here with fellow medalists Elena Dementieva (gold, center) and Vera Zvonareva (bronze, right).

Safina came back strong to win the next tournament she entered, the Pan Pacific Open in Tokyo, Japan, beating fellow Russian Svetlana Kuznetsova 6-1, 6-3. She thus claimed the ninth WTA Tour title of her career and moved up to the number 2 position in the world rankings. After the match, Kuznetsova was full of praise for Safina's game. "She works very hard and she has lots of energy, and I think she has much more confidence now," Kuznetsova said. "She has been one of the strongest players on the tour in the second half of the season." From the time her hot streak started at Berlin in May 2008, Safina posted an amazing match record of 37 wins and 5 losses.

By the midpoint of the 2009 season, Safina had faced both highs and lows. As of August, she hadn't yet won a Grand Slam event, although she'd made it to the finals twice—at the Australian Open, where she lost to Serena Williams, and at the French Open, where she lost to Svetlana Kuznetsova. But Safina did win several singles titles, winning her 10th and 11th WTA Tour titles in May at tournaments in Rome and Madrid, and then winning her 12th WTA Tour title in July in Portoroz. But more impressively, she became the No. 1 women's singles player in the world in April. By September 2009, she had raised her career win-loss record to 333-145 and boosted her career earnings to $8.9 million in prize money.

Although Safina had not yet won a Grand Slam singles title, she felt confident that she will one day match her brother's achievement. "I think it's going to be the dream of our family," she stated. "Once we do this we can put really the racket on the wall and say we did everything we could. But to get to his level, I still have to work a little bit harder."

For Safina, her rise to the top of women's tennis marked her emergence from her famous brother's shadow. "For some people I will always just be [Marat's] younger sister. But we have completely different lives. Whatever I have achieved and will achieve, I have done by myself," she noted. "I always wanted to be myself, and now finally the results are coming, and people can know me as Dinara Safina."

HOME AND FAMILY

When she is not traveling on the WTA Tour, Safina makes her home in Monte Carlo, Monaco.

HOBBIES AND OTHER INTERESTS

In her spare time, Safina enjoys going to the movies, reading, and listening to music. She is also a big fan of the European professional soccer team Real Madrid.

HONORS AND AWARDS

U.S. Open, Women's Doubles: 2007
Olympic Tennis, Women's Singles: 2008, silver medal

FURTHER READING

Periodicals

Los Angeles Times, June 3, 2008, p.D3; July 28, 2008, p.D4
New York Times, Sep. 7, 2006, p.D3; Aug. 25, 2008, p.5; Aug. 27, 2008, p.D5
Palm Beach Post, June 5, 2006, p.C10
South Florida Sun-Sentinel, June 6, 2008
Sports Illustrated, June 12, 2006, p.73
USA Today, June 3, 2008, p.C8; June 6, 2008, p.C10

Online Article

http://www.sonyericssonwtatour.com
(Sony Ericsson WTA Tour, "Dinara Safina to Become Sony Ericsson WTA Tour No. 1," Apr. 8, 2009)

ADDRESS

Dinara Safina
Sony Ericsson WTA Tour
One Progress Plaza
Suite 1500
St. Petersburg, FL 33701

WORLD WIDE WEB SITES

http://www.dsafina.com
http://www.sonyericssonwtatour.com

BRIEF ENTRY

Gloria Gilbert Stoga 1955?-

American Dog Training Program Organizer
Founder and President of Puppies Behind Bars

MAJOR ACCOMPLISHMENTS

Gloria Gilbert Stoga is the founder and president of Puppies Behind Bars. This nonprofit organization uses prison inmate volunteers to raise and train guide dogs for the blind, service dogs for the disabled, and explosive-detection dogs for law enforcement. As of 2009, it had produced over 335 working dogs.

The first seed of this innovative program took root in 1990, when Stoga and her husband adopted a Labrador retriever named Arrow. Arrow had participated in a program to train guide dogs for the blind, but he was released for medical reasons. When she adopted Arrow, Stoga learned about all the time, money, and effort that went into training dogs like him. She discovered that guide dogs and service dogs spend their early lives with specially trained puppy raisers. These individuals care for the dogs for 16 months. During this time, the puppy raisers teach the dogs basic obedience skills, help them become comfortable in different situations, and help them to gain confidence. Dogs that excel in this phase go on to receive further training at guide dog schools.

———— “ ————

Stoga believed Puppies behind Bars could benefit the disabled and the inmates alike. "It made so much sense," she thought, "to have people who can give love, who have a lot of time, who need to be rehabilitated, and put them together with dogs—and not just dogs as pets, but dogs that will make a difference in somebody's life."

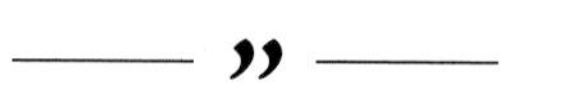

A few years later, Stoga heard about some newly developed programs that used prison inmates as puppy raisers. A veterinarian, Dr. Thomas Lane, started one of the first programs of this kind in Florida. Stoga also read a newspaper article about a similar program in Ohio. She was struck by the ways in which these programs could benefit the disabled and the inmates alike. "It made so much sense," she thought, "to have people who can give love, who have a lot of time, who need to be rehabilitated, and put them together with dogs—and not just dogs as pets, but dogs that will make a difference in somebody's life."

Stoga had some previous experience working for charitable causes. During the 1990s, for example, she served on New York City's Youth Empowerment Services Commission, which helped find jobs for low-income, inner-city teens. She eventually decided to draw on this experience to start her own dog-training program.

Founding Puppies Behind Bars

In July 1997 Stoga founded Puppies Behind Bars, a nonprofit organization dedicated to training prison inmates to serve as puppy raisers. A short time later, she received permission from Glenn Goord, the commissioner of the

New York Department of Corrections, to bring puppies into the state prison system for training.

But when Stoga approached Guiding Eyes for the Blind, a respected guide dog school and breeding facility in New York, she found that the organization was unwilling to provide her with dogs. "The initial reaction from all of the guide dog schools was: no way," she recalled. "I found myself in the position of having no guide dogs to bring to the prison." Some people felt that a prison was not an appropriate atmosphere for a puppy. Critics worried that the inmates would mistreat the dogs or train them to attack prison guards. Stoga understood these objections. In fact, she admitted that she held a negative view of prison inmates herself until she got to know them as people.

Stoga finally reached a compromise with Guiding Eyes for the Blind. To prove that her program could work, she arranged to buy five puppies that had failed to qualify for guide dog training and had been released from the school. In November 1997 she took these dogs to the Bedford Hills Correctional Facility—a maximum-security prison for women in upstate New York. If the inmates were able to train the puppies successfully, the school agreed to let Puppies Behind Bars raise qualified dogs. "Basically we had people that were written off by society raising dogs that were written off as potential guide dogs," Stoga noted.

As it turned out, the Puppies Behind Bars program was a huge success. Two of the first group of puppies qualified to become guide dogs for the blind, and the others went on to become working dogs in other capacities. "I have to say we were skeptical," said Jane Russenberger, director of breeding and placement for Guiding Eyes for the Blind. "The inmates at the Bedford prison have impressed me considerably. The work that they're doing and their commitment, the quality of the dogs that they're producing, the impeccable manners these dogs have—it's one of the finest puppy-raising jobs I've seen."

Stoga's early success paved the way for her to expand the program. Funded entirely by donations and staffed by volunteers, Puppies Behind Bars grew to include seven correctional facilities in three states over the next decade.

How the Program Works

When the puppies arrive at a prison, they are only eight weeks old. They are not yet housebroken and have not learned their names or any commands. Over the next 16 months, each puppy lives in a prison cell with its primary handler, who is responsible for providing it with basic care and af-

Inmates with their Labrador retriever puppies at the Fishkill Correctional Facility in New York. The inmates are listening to Stoga (off to the right, not shown), who is leading a class to train the dogs for guide work.

fection. Like other puppy raisers, the inmates also teach the puppies obedience and expose them to a variety of social situations. "The prison is a community unto itself," Stoga related. "These dogs go to the library, the dentist, chapel, the nursery, and offices within the prison where the inmates work each day."

Stoga also came up with ways for prison-raised puppies to experience the outside world. She organized a team of volunteer puppy sitters to take the dogs home with them on weekends and expose them to things they might encounter as working dogs, like crowds, traffic, sirens, shops, and restaurants. "Just going home to a person's apartment is different," Stoga explained. "Having rugs. Having sofas and chairs. Dishwashers, doorbells, coffee grinders. Everyday noises that aren't heard in prison." Stoga also started a program called Paws and Reflect, in which volunteers take puppies to visit elderly people who are confined to their homes. This experience helps the future service dogs get used to seeing wheelchairs, walkers, oxygen tanks, and hospital equipment.

Stoga chooses inmates to participate in the program carefully. She only considers those with spotless disciplinary records and at least two years remaining on their sentences. Interested inmates have to fill out an application and go through a screening process. Those selected as puppy raisers must attend classes on puppy training, complete homework assignments, and take tests. Stoga places a strong emphasis on the responsibility and commitment required to raise a puppy. "I ask them to fully understand what it is that they're doing, and if they can't handle the responsibility I ask them to leave," she explained. "I'm tough with them. I don't give them a lot of second and third chances. But I respect them, and I enjoy working with them."

Puppies changed the atmosphere at the medium-security men's prison, Fishkill Correctional Facility. According to deputy superintendent Jim Hayden, "The dogs have a calming, humanizing effect on the entire staff," he said. "They've broken these inmates down, taken their hard shells and cracked them open. Their level of love for and commitment to these dogs is something I never expected to see."

"

Bonding with Prison Inmates

In addition to producing well-trained dogs for the disabled, Puppies Behind Bars also has a positive impact on the lives of the inmates. Participating in the program helps the inmates learn to express love, have patience, and accept responsibility. It also gives them increased self-esteem, a sense of purpose, and an opportunity to give something back to society. "Gloria saved my life," said Susan Hallett, an inmate serving a sentence of 25-years-to-life at Bedford Hills. "In prison it is so easy to slide into mental illness or to just give up. There are people who come along and don't realize they are life savers, but they are, and Gloria is one of them."

Jim Hayden, a deputy superintendent at Fishkill Correctional Facility in New York, noticed that Puppies Behind Bars changed the atmosphere at his medium-security men's prison. "The dogs have a calming, humanizing effect on the entire staff," he said. "They've broken these inmates down, taken their hard shells and cracked them open. Their level of love for and commitment to these dogs is something I never expected to see." Ronald Jones, a puppy raiser serving a 15-years-to-life sentence for murder at Fishkill, also witnessed a major change. "I've seen 6-foot-2, 250-pound guys rolling around on the floor kissing and talking in a high voice to their dogs," he noted. "We *all* do it, even in the yard with 200 other inmates and guards walking by. We don't care what anybody thinks. It's all about what's good for the dogs. We owe them. They did what nothing or nobody could—they took away our selfishness."

"I've seen 6-foot-2, 250-pound guys rolling around on the floor kissing and talking in a high voice to their dogs," said Ronald Jones, a puppy raiser serving a 15-years-to-life sentence for murder. "We all *do it, even in the yard with 200 other inmates and guards walking by. We don't care what anybody thinks. It's all about what's good for the dogs. We owe them. They did what nothing or nobody could—they took away our selfishness."*

For the inmates who raise dogs for Puppies Behind Bars, the toughest part of the job is letting the dogs go after the 16 months of training are up. Some handlers take comfort in the fact that their dog will give a disabled person dignity, independence, and mobility. And some program participants find the bittersweet parting to be a valuable learning experience. "I felt what my mother must have felt on the day I was sentenced, when she stood next to the 24-year-old son she loved, who was going away for a long time," said inmate Thomas Lonetto of the moment when he said goodbye to the first dog he trained. "It's called empathy. I didn't know it existed in me until that moment."

For some inmates, the opportunity to train dogs for Puppies Behind Bars marks the first time anyone has trusted them or given them responsibility. Many participants in the program are inspired to study to become veterinary assistants or to earn bachelor's degrees. The program thus gives some participating inmates marketable skills to use upon their release from prison.

Inmates form a deep bond with the puppies they train, as shown by this pair at the Edna Mahan Correctional Facility in New Jersey.

"Most people can change," said former Bedford Hills superintendent Elaine Lord. "We need to give inmates meaningful work that will bring about that change—because most of them will get out, and our job is to make sure they aren't dangerous to society, but contributing members of society."

Changing People's Lives

In the years since she founded Puppies Behind Bars, Stoga has expanded its mission beyond training guide dogs for the blind. Following the terrorist attacks of September 11, 2001, the organization launched its Explosive Detection Canine Program. The inmates who participate in this program train dogs to assist law enforcement agencies by sniffing out bombs at airports, train stations, sporting events, and meeting places.

Paul Perricone, an officer with the New York Police Department's Bomb Squad, received an explosive detection dog named Sheeba from the Puppies Behind Bars program. Perricone visited the Edna Mahan Correctional Facility for Women in New Jersey to thank the inmates there for doing such a great job raising Sheeba. He explained how he depends on the dog to make the right decisions and keep him and other people safe. Sheeba has sniffed for bombs at a number of New York landmarks, including Yankee Stadium, the United Nations, and the U.S. Open tennis tournament. Two other explosive detection dogs raised by Puppies Behind Bars provide security for Egyptian president Hosni Mubarak.

———— " ————

"I felt what my mother must have felt on the day I was sentenced, when she stood next to the 24-year-old son she loved, who was going away for a long time," said inmate Thomas Lonetto of the moment when he said goodbye to the first dog he trained. "It's called empathy. I didn't know it existed in me until that moment."

———— " ————

In 2006 Stoga expanded Puppies Behind Bars to raise service dogs for adults and children with special needs, including autism and multiple sclerosis. The inmates teach the dogs 80 commands so that they can help disabled people perform such daily tasks as changing clothes, answering a telephone, opening a refrigerator, loading a washing machine, holding open a door, turning on a light switch, pushing an elevator button, or retrieving an item from a store shelf. As service dogs, they offer their disabled owners companionship, confidence, and independence.

Stoga also launched a program called Dog Tags: Service Dogs for Those Who've Served Us. This element of Puppies Behind Bars provides service dogs to U.S. military veterans of the wars in Afghanistan and Iraq. The dogs can assist veterans who have suffered physical injuries, traumatic brain injuries, or Post-Traumatic Stress Disorder (PTSD, a condition characterized by extreme fear and anxiety that develops following exposure to a severe emotional or physical trauma).

In 2008, the first dog to come out of the Dog Tags program, Pax, was paired with Sergeant William Campbell, an Iraq War veteran with PTSD. Once too frightened by flashbacks and nightmares to leave his home in Washington State, Campbell felt secure enough to bring Pax across the country to thank the women who raised him at Bedford Hills. "As inmates, we can understand the loss of freedom," said Jaymie Powers, a puppy raiser who is serving a sentence for murder. "Through these dogs we can give someone a chance at freedom."

HOME AND FAMILY

Stoga lives in New York City. She is married and has two adult children.

FURTHER READING

Periodicals

Christian Science Monitor, Aug. 16, 2000, p.15
Good Housekeeping, Apr. 2001, p.88
New York Times, Aug. 22, 1999, p.1; June 9, 2004, Metro, p.1; June 1, 2008, p.WE1; Nov. 30, 2008, p.WE1
Saturday Evening Post, Sep. 1, 2005, p.64
Smithsonian, Aug. 2004, p.62

Online Articles

http://www.bloomberg.com
(Bloomberg.com, "Maimed U.S. War Veterans Find Freedom with Prison-Raised Dogs," Nov. 18, 2008)
http://www.npr.org
(National Public Radio, "Putting Puppies Behind Bars (For A Good Cause)," Sep. 2, 2009)
http://www.oprah.com
(Oprah Winfrey Show, "Puppies Behind Bars," no date)
http://www.time.com/time/photogallery
(Time Magazine, "Puppies Behind Bars: Inmates Sign Up to Train Service Dogs—And Find a Sense of Responsibility in Return," no date)

ADDRESS

Gloria Gilbert Stoga
Puppies Behind Bars
10 East 40th Street
19th Floor
New York, NY 10016

WORLD WIDE WEB SITE

http://www.puppiesbehindbars.com

Taylor Swift 1989-

American Country Singer
Creator of the Songs "Teardrops on My Guitar" and "Our Song"

BIRTH

Taylor Alison Swift was born on December 13, 1989, in Wyomissing, Pennsylvania. She is the daughter of Andrea Swift and Scott Swift, a stockbroker. Taylor has one younger brother, Austin, of whom she wrote: "We're complete opposites—he's good at sports and all the things I'm awful at. And he has no interest in music."

YOUTH

Taylor Swift spent her early years on a Christmas tree farm in Berks County in eastern Pennsylvania. She began singing when she was nine years old, inspired in part by her maternal grandmother, who was a professional opera singer. At first Swift performed at local sporting events, fairs, karaoke nights, and talent contests. However, by age 11 she was determined to pursue a recording career. On a visit to Nashville, Tennessee, the center of the country music industry, she delivered demos to record companies in hopes of gaining their attention. (A demo is a recording made by a singer, songwriter, or band so that record companies can hear what their work sounds like.) She recalled the trip saying, "My mom waited in the car while I knocked on doors up and down Music Row. I would say, 'Hi, I'm Taylor. I'm 11. I want a record deal. Call me.'"

"

Determined to pursue a recording career, Swift visited Nashville, Tennessee, the center of the country music industry, to deliver demos to record companies in hopes of gaining their attention. "My mom waited in the car while I knocked on doors up and down Music Row. I would say, 'Hi, I'm Taylor. I'm 11. I want a record deal. Call me.'"

"

While no companies offered Swift a contract at that time, the experience showed her fearlessness and strong desire for success in the music industry. These qualities came from within, according to her mother. Her parents were supportive of their daughter's musical aspirations, but they did not push their child into a show business career. As Andrea Swift told *Entertainment Weekly*, "Music was never my dream [for Taylor].... We were on a farm, and I had her sitting on a pony when she was nine months old. If my dream had gone well, she'd be in a horse show right now." But her daughter had other ideas.

Back home in Pennsylvania, Swift began playing guitar and writing her own songs at age 12. Her determination paid off in 2003 when she signed a deal with RCA Records. She was disappointed, however, when she learned that RCA wanted her to sing songs written by others rather than her own music. The following year, at 14 years old, Swift became the youngest person ever signed to a songwriting contract with Sony ATV Publishing. As she began to work on songs for an album, her parents moved the family to Nashville.

EDUCATION

Swift attended Hendersonville High School in Hendersonville, Tennessee. By her junior year, she was often away from home performing. After that point, she was home-schooled. Her lessons were conducted through a program connected with Aaron Academy, a private Christian school in Hendersonville. Swift worked on school assignments on her tour bus between appearances and graduated from high school at the same time as her high school class, in spring 2008.

CAREER HIGHLIGHTS

Swift's childhood dream of a recording contract finally came true in 2005 when she signed a deal with Big Machine Records. This new company was being launched by Scott Borchetta, a music industry executive who had previously worked with such artists as Toby Keith and Randy Travis. He signed Swift after seeing her perform at the Bluebird Café, a famous music venue in Nashville. According to Borchetta, "I met Taylor Swift and thought, 'what a great lovin' artist!' ... It was completely a have-to-have.... She's totally unique and engaging. I could write a dissertation on all the reasons why."

"I met Taylor Swift and thought, 'what a great lovin' artist!' said Scott Borchetta, a music industry executive. "It was completely a have-to-have.... She's totally unique and engaging. I could write a dissertation on all the reasons why."

”

"Tim McGraw"

Big Machine quickly put the young singer to work, and her first single debuted in summer 2006. Called "Tim McGraw," the song was inspired by her feelings for an older boy who was leaving for college, as she realized that they would soon be separated. In the song, she sings about all the memories they shared and voices her hope that he would remember her whenever he heard music by her favorite country artist, Tim McGraw.

Swift came up with the melody and lyrics for "Tim McGraw" in math class in 15 minutes during her freshman year of high school. She developed the final version of the song at an after-school writing session, where she worked with cowriter Liz Rose, whom she calls her "songwriting soulmate." Rose called Swift "a genius.... I never second guessed her. I respect her a lot."

Swift has enjoyed touring and performing live for fans.

McGraw was flattered by the song and invited Swift to join his tour as an opening act in 2007. According to Swift, the boy she sings about in "Tim McGraw" later "bought the album and said he really loved it, which is sweet."

Taylor Swift

Swift's album, *Taylor Swift,* was released in fall 2006. Initially, few reviewers recognized its potential for success. Because it was an album by a teenager and treated such teen themes as fitting in at school and having a crush on someone who doesn't notice you, many critics were ready to dismiss it as unimportant. Reviewing the CD in *People*, Ralph Novak gave the album only two stars out of five and judged it "lively and engaging if inevitably lacking in polish and depth." When music promoter Jerry Bentley was asked what advice he had for Swift at the time of her album release, he snapped, "Tell her to get back in school and come back and see me when she's 18, and bring her parents."

"Fans are my favorite thing in the world," Swift said. "I've never been the type of artist who has that line drawn between their friends and their fans. I'll hang out with them.... If I see them in a mall, I'll stand there and talk to them for 10 minutes. I don't care. I'm just a senior in high school who has a different job."

Others, however, were willing to give Swift a chance, observing that she wrote or cowrote all 11 songs on the disc. That is a notable achievement for any artist, especially for someone still in high school. *Entertainment Weekly* reviewer Chris Willman, for example, called *Taylor Swift* "a lively, acoustic-based disc that unabashedly captures the sweetness, petulance, and passion of being a teen."

Following on the success of "Tim McGraw," Swift released a second single from the album, "Teardrops on My Guitar," which hit the airwaves in February 2007. The song tells about the singer's crush on a boy named Drew who doesn't know how she feels about him and just likes her as a friend. The song reached No. 2 on the Billboard Hot Country chart and was remixed as a pop song, reaching No. 13 on the Hot 100 chart.

"Our Song"

While her first two singles established Swift as a country artist with enormous potential, her third single rocketed her to international stardom. That was the sensation "Our Song," which Swift originally wrote for a high school talent show. A celebration of teen romance, the song tells how a young couple without a special song creates their own music out of the simple memories they share.

Billboard called "Our Song" "a delightfully crisp and breezy offering with a conversational lyric that will take the masses back to tender memories of

Swift's first CD was certified triple platinum in 2008—not a bad start for an 18-year-old singer-songwriter.

uncomplicated young love." It debuted in August 2007 and by December of that year was the No. 1 country song. As reviewer Randy Lewis observed in the *Los Angeles Times,* "It may be the first No. 1 country hit that got its premiere at a ninth-grade talent show." At 18 years old, Swift was the youngest person ever to write and perform a chart-topping country single. "Our Song" stayed in the No. 1 position for six weeks, tying for second place among the longest-reigning chart-toppers. By 2008 it had more than 6.1 million plays on Swift's MySpace page.

"Our Song" was still high on the charts when Swift's next single was released in January 2008. "Picture to Burn" recalls a bad break-up with a boyfriend who cheated on her. The video portrays a humorous revenge fantasy in which the jilted singer imagines having her band vandalize her ex's home. In *Billboard,* reviewer Deborah Evans Price called the song "a feisty uptempo number marked by Swift's youthful exuberance and personality-packed vocals." The song's sassy attitude showed that there was more to Swift's songwriting than romantic ballads, but she offered no apologies for writing about teenage life. "I'll have plenty of time to act 25 when I am 25," she acknowledged. "I want to sing about things I've actually gone through."

The album *Taylor Swift* was certified triple platinum in 2008. That means that it had sold more than three million copies. In addition, as of June 2008 the album had spent 20 weeks at the top of the *Billboard* country album chart, an amazing accomplishment for an album that had been in release for a year and a half.

"In some cases, writing songs about people is a great way to help you get over them," Swift said about writing about her life. "If you get out of a bad relationship that was a complete waste of your time and emotions, you can write a song about it and it can become a benefit to your career. How sweet is that?"

Writing about Real Life

By 2008 Swift had written more than 200 songs, which she based on her life and experiences and those of her friends. Unlike many artists who change the names of people they write about, she uses real names. "Every name in every song of mine is the actual name of the person I wrote the song about," she revealed. "In some cases, writing songs about people is a great way to help you get over them." Expressing a matter-of-fact attitude about using relationship experiences as material for her music, she explained, "If you get out of a bad relationship that was a complete waste of your time and emotions, you can write a song about it and it can become a benefit to your career. How sweet is that?"

Swift confided to fans on her MySpace page, "I've never been the kind of girl who needs a boyfriend. I believe that love will find you when you're not looking for it. So I've been actively not looking for it for about three years now. I'll let you know how that works out for me. It probably doesn't help that I write songs about every guy I talk to." She later added, "But I'm also the girl who still believes Prince Charming exists somewhere out there—fully equipped with great hair and an immature sense of humor."

Swift performing at the 2008 CMT Music Awards.

Though she is best known for songs about relationships, Swift has also written about other experiences that most teens recognize. "The Outside," which she wrote when she was 12 years old, is about the social trauma of being excluded from the popular clique in school. "Tied Together with a Smile" is about a beauty queen Swift knew who always looked perfect on the outside but hid a dark secret—an eating disorder. When she found out her friend was bulimic, Swift later revealed, "It was really hard for me to take.... So I played that song for her, and I said, 'Who do you think that's about?" And honestly, I don't think she ever did it after that." Such honesty in Swift's lyrics has resonated with fans of all ages, but she has formed a special connection with those in her peer group and younger fans. As Miami radio station programmer Ken Boesen remarked, "It's been a long time since young people have had somebody they could relate to who was their age writing songs and singing about things in their lives."

Becoming a Teen Role Model

Swift has been able to develop a unique bond with her fans, in part because many teens connect to the themes of her songs and in part because they are close to her age. At the end of concerts she takes friendship bracelets from her arm to give to fans in the audience. And she regularly communicates with her fans of all ages through her MySpace page. "Fans are my favorite thing in the world," she said. "I've never been the type of artist who has that line drawn between their friends and their fans. I'll hang out with them.... If I see them in a mall, I'll stand there and talk to them for 10 minutes. I don't care. I'm just a senior in high school who has a different job."

Swift personally designed her MySpace page and updates it herself. "I upload all the pictures, I check the comments, I am in charge of everything on that page.... My bio on there isn't some fabricated promo bio like 'Taylor Swift is blah, blah, blah, blah, blah.' It's written in first person just like a normal person because I am a normal person and I should have a normal MySpace that tells people who I am as a person."

Swift is keenly aware of her importance as a role model to her fans and embraces the position. She has said that recognizing her responsibility to her fans helps to keep her from making the kinds of destructive choices many teen stars make when they are thrust into the limelight. According to Swift, she thinks about a young six-year-old fan—and her mother—when she makes choices. "Would [that mother] let her listen to my music if she saw me do this? ... That is the easiest way to make decisions for me because it completely clears up any clouds that my judgment might have. I am not going to let those people down." She continued, "I have asked for this; I wanted it. Yes, there is pressure sometimes, but I have wanted this. I am going to respect people who have trusted me with their kids."

Fearless

Swift's early success appears to be just the beginning. In fall 2008 she released the single "Love Story," the first song from her new album, *Fearless*. The single was a big hit, and in fact, each of her first five new singles from the album reached the top 20 on the Billboard Hot 100 list. With those five hits, Swift tied the Jonas Brothers for third place on the Billboard Hot 100 chart record; only Janet Jackson and Madonna (with seven) and Mariah Carey and the Beatles (with six) have had more 20 top debuts in a single year. As of late 2009, *Fearless* had spent 21 weeks at No. 1 on Billboard's Top Country Albums chart. To date, Swift has sold more albums than any artist in the world this year.

"

"I hope that I stand for the girl who is 15 and is in school and doesn't fit in. Maybe she can find some sort of comfort by going home and putting on my CD."

But the album was not only a sales success—it was a success with critics as well. As Leah Greenblatt wrote in *Entertainment Weekly*, "[Swift] does something rarely seen from stars in either market [country and pop]: write or co-write all her material. On *Fearless*, Swift is once again a storyteller; her songs are narratives set to music, albeit mostly ones that concern love." Reviewer Ken Tucker wrote in *Billboard*, "Those who thought Taylor Swift was a big deal after the release of her first record should be prepared: she's about to get bigger. Though they're written by a teenager, Swift's songs have broad appeal, and therein lies the genius and accessibility of her second effort." The album was also a success at the awards shows. *Fearless* and Swift won several awards, including the Album of the Year award from the Academy of Country Music; the Video of the Year and Female Video of the Year awards from Country Music Television; the Choice Female Music Artist and Choice Music Album Female Artist awards from the Teen Choice Awards; and the Best Female Video from the MTV Video Music Awards.

In this new release, many commentators see the seeds of Swift's future success. "For now, her primary fan base will probably remain the young

Swift hoped to repeat the success of her first CD in her new release, Fearless.

girls she speaks to so well—but it will be exciting to watch her precocious talent grow," Greenblatt wrote. Those comments were echoed by other reviewers, including Chuck Taylor in *Billboard*. "Anyone who has met this teen prodigy recognizes that she is not only an old-soul master of writing and singing, but also possesses gobs of the 'it' magnetism that defines stardom." Swift calls her career a gift and hopes that her music is a positive force in people's lives. "I hope that I stand for the girl who is 15 and is in school and doesn't fit in. Maybe she can find some sort of comfort by going home and putting on my CD. Or for the mother and daughter who don't get along—but maybe when they listen to my music, they do. Or you know, a cute couple who didn't have a song, but they listen to one of my songs and that becomes their song.

That's what music was for me. That's what it stood for in my life and how it helped me."

HOME AND FAMILY

Swift lives in Hendersonville, Tennessee, with her parents and brother. Though she is only home a few days per month, she loves returning to her own bedroom, which her mother keeps "frozen in time" while Swift is away. The room is decorated with photos and memorabilia of her high school friends as well as music industry awards. "That's one of my favorite things about my room," she said. "There are so many mementos from my life before all this happened, and then there are things that remind me of where I am now.... I kind of took it for granted before, but now when I wake up here, it's like,'Oh my gosh, this is not a bus. This is awesome!'"

SELECTED RECORDINGS

Taylor Swift, 2006
Fearless, 2008

HONORS AND AWARDS

Country Music Association Awards: 2007, Horizon Award
Country Music Television Awards: 2007, Breakthrough Video of the Year, for "Tim McGraw"; 2008 (two awards), Female Video of the Year and Video of the Year, both for "Our Song"; 2009 (two awards), Video of the Year and Female Video of the Year, both for "Love Story"
Nashville Songwriters Association International Awards: 2007, Songwriter/Artist of the Year
Teen Choice Awards: 2008, Breakout Artist; 2009 (two awards), Choice Female Music Artist and Choice Music Album Female Artist
Academy of Country Music Awards: 2008, Top New Female Vocalist; 2009, Top Album of the Year, for *Fearless*
MTV Video Music Awards: 2009, Best Female Video

FURTHER READING

Periodicals

Billboard, May 21, 2005, p.14; Sep. 29, 2007; Jan. 12, 2008, p.40; Feb. 23, 2008; Mar. 22, 2008, p.22
Entertainment Weekly, July 27, 2007, p.26; Feb. 8, 2008, p.40
Houston Chronicle, Nov. 3, 2007, p.3; Feb. 10, 2008, p.3
Los Angeles Times, May 14, 2007, p.E6; Feb. 6, 2008, p.S26

Miami Herald, Jan. 25, 2008
Nashville Music Guide, Aug.-Sep. 2007
New York Times, Sep. 7, 2008, p.61
People, Nov. 20, 2006, p.45; Fall 2007, p.52; Mar. 12, 2008 p.18
Seventeen, June 2008, p.96
USA Today, Nov. 21, 2006 p.D5; Oct. 5, 2007, p.E1; Aug. 8, 2008, p.D11
Washington Post, Feb. 28, 2008, p.C1

ADDRESS

Taylor Swift
Big Machine Records
1219 16th Avenue South
Nashville, TN 37212

WORLD WIDE WEB SITES

http://taylorswift.com
http://www.bigmachinerecords.com
http://www.cmt.com/artists
http://www.myspace.com

Shailene Woodley 1991-

American Actress
Star of "The Secret Life of the American Teenager"

BIRTH

Shailene Diann Woodley was born on November 15, 1991, in Simi Valley, California. Her mother, Lori, works as a middle school counselor. Her father, Loni, is a school principal. She has one younger brother, Tanner.

YOUTH AND EDUCATION

Woodley was born and raised in Simi Valley, a prosperous middle-class community in the metropolitan Los Angeles area. Her childhood featured the usual bumps and scrapes, but her parents provided a loving and nurturing home for both of their children. As Woodley herself said, "I feel fortunate to have grown up in a safe and family-oriented environment."

Woodley's acting career began when she was only five years old. "It was kind of an accident, actually," she recalled. "I'm not even entirely sure how it happened. My cousin used to be a model and one day brought a talent-call audition thing with her and my mom was like, 'Hey, you want to act today?' and I was like, 'Sure!' And it just kind of happened. I was never forced to do it, and I never forced them to take me to auditions. It was just kind of one of those things that worked for everybody."

Woodley was thrilled when she began appearing on television in small roles. But she still had plenty of time to be a regular kid. She attended neighborhood public schools all the way through high school, and she never really felt different from her friends. "[Acting has] just been my hobby," she explained. "My friends went to soccer practice; I went to auditions." Her parents also made sure that she kept a level head about her acting career. "I had rules," she said. "I had to stay the person I knew I was. I had to stay really respectful [of my parents] … and I had to still do good in school."

"[Acting has] just been my hobby," she explained. "My friends went to soccer practice; I went to auditions." Her parents also made sure that she kept a level head about her acting career. "I had rules," she said. "I had to stay the person I knew I was. I had to stay really respectful [of my parents] … and I had to still do good in school."

Dealing with Scoliosis

By the time Woodley reached high school, her acting roles were getting more demanding and exciting. But her mid-teens were filled with pain and disappointment in other ways. When she was a freshman her parents got divorced, and when she was 15 she was diagnosed with scoliosis, a potentially dangerous curvature of the spine.

Woodley remembered when she got her first clue that she suffered from scoliosis. "We were getting ready to go swimming and I was in a bikini," she recalled, when suddenly her best friend said, "Shai, your spine is

One of Woodley's first big roles was in the TV movie Felicity *from the* American Girl *series.*

weird." What her friend had noticed was that Woodley's spine had an abnormal curve to it. She was quickly rushed off to see doctors, who reassured Woodley and her parents that she would be fine with treatment.

Woodley's doctors explained that scoliosis affects roughly two percent of the population and that most cases do not even require medical treatment. The doctors acknowledged that Woodley's condition would require intervention. But they assured her that she would not have to undergo surgery, which is required in cases where scoliosis threatens to cause severe deformities or damage heart and lung functions. Instead, she would be outfitted in a chest-to-hips plastic brace to straighten her spine.

Woodley spent most of the next two years in the brace. She did not have to wear it when she swam, went out with her friends, or was filming. But she was required to keep the brace on at virtually all other times—an average of 18 hours a day. The situation quickly became frustrating for the energetic youth. By the fourth week of wearing the brace, she found herself repeatedly thinking, "Whoa, this is a bummer." But she accepted the treatment as necessary, and she was able to take the brace off for good in December 2008, a few months before her graduation from high school.

CAREER HIGHLIGHTS

Woodley's first few parts on television were very small. In 2002, though, she won guest starring roles in the crime dramas "Without a Trace" and "The District." Her strong performances in these parts led to appearances over the next few years on several other popular TV series, including "Everybody Loves Raymond," "My Name Is Earl," "CSI: New York," and "Cold Case." Woodley also earned a recurring role in two series during this period. She played the character of Kaitlin Cooper in the 2003 season of "The O.C.," and from 2001 to 2004 she made four different appearances in the drama "Crossing Jordan" as the childhood version of the title character.

Woodley's biggest roles during her early teen years, though, came in two made-for-television films. In 2004 she had a significant part in a Hallmark Channel movie called *A Place Called Home,* starring Ann-Margret. One year later, she made an even bigger splash as the title character in the TV movie *Felicity: An American Girl Adventure.* In this film, which was inspired by the popular line of children's dolls, Woodley played a brave young girl in colonial America. The plot centers around her decision to rescue a beautiful wild horse that is being cruelly mistreated by its owner.

Felicity received praise for delivering positive messages to young girls about the importance of kindness and standing up for your beliefs. "*Felicity* is high adventure for its young target audience," said a reviewer for the *Hollywood Reporter.* "[It] makes history come alive in a compelling way for young viewers."

"The Secret Life of the American Teenager"

Woodley's strong performance in *Felicity* and on various TV shows caught the attention of executives at the ABC Family network. They asked her to audition for the starring role in a new series they were preparing called "The Secret Life of the American Teenager." Woodley's impressive audition convinced producers that she was ideal for the part, and in February 2008 they announced that she had won the role.

In "Secret Life," Woodley plays the part of Amy Juergens, a generally smart, cheerful, and responsible 15-year-old girl. Amy's life changes radically when she impulsively has sex for the first time at band camp with a "cool" older boy from her high school, then finds out that she is pregnant. She decides to keep the baby, but fights through feelings of confusion and fear as the pregnancy progresses. "She's a go-getter, she's excited for life, she wants to go to Juilliard, she has all these amazing goals," explained Woodley. "And then she finds out she's pregnant, and her world kind of comes crashing down and her sense of optimism turns to pessimism. And she freaks out, because all she's ever known has been completely turned upside down."

"She's a go-getter, she's excited for life, she wants to go to Juilliard, she has all these amazing goals," Woodley said about her character, Amy Juergens. "And then she finds out she's pregnant, and her world kind of comes crashing down and her sense of optimism turns to pessimism. And she freaks out, because all she's ever known has been completely turned upside down."

Woodley's character serves as the focal point of a wider story about the trials and tribulations of a group of middle-class high school students and their families. As the first season unfolded, viewers also got to know other characters such as Amy's mother, played by former teen movie star Molly Ringwald. But the action always returns to Amy and her relationships with the father of her child, played by Daren Kagasoff, and her current boyfriend, played by Ken Baumann.

When "Secret Life" first arrived on TV screens in 2008, critics were divid-

Scenes from "The Secret Life of the American Teenager."

ed about the show. The *New York Times* dismissed "Secret Life" as predictable and silly and said that the show "doesn't take the fun out of teenage pregnancy; it takes the fun out of television." The *San Francisco Chronicle,* on the other hand, said that the show "makes an effort to discuss some of the real challenges that would face any family of a pregnant teenager." The reviewer added that "Shailene Woodley and Ken Baumann are sweet and believably scared about the future as Amy and Ben."

As the reviews poured in, about the only thing that critics agreed about was that Woodley delivered a terrific and sympathetic portrayal of Amy. "Woodley is cute in an everyday way, and her shyness and visible thought processes are very endearing," declared one North Carolina newspaper. "Instantly, she's someone to root for, as she considers the consequences of her options." *Entertainment Weekly,* meanwhile, stated that "like a great silent-film actress, [Woodley] has a face that conveys shades of anguish and joy. Her performance lifts a well-meaning, rather brave, but ramshackle show a notch."

"[I've] heard a lot of teenage girls say they like how the script talks about high school drama because it is happening in real life," Woodley said. "There are so many different aspects of life that it definitely dives into and I thought that was really interesting to be able to portray that to … America's teenagers and teenagers all over the world and [say that] you're not alone."

Enjoying a Hit Series

By the end of the first season, it was clear that TV viewers did not care about the show's mixed critical reception. "Secret Life" was a big hit, especially with teenagers and their families. According to Woodley, the show's popularity is easy to understand. "[I've] heard a lot of teenage girls say they like how the script talks about high school drama because it is happening in real life," she said. "There are so many different aspects of life that it definitely dives into and I thought that was really interesting to be able to portray that to … America's teenagers and teenagers all over the world and [say that] you're not alone.… Everyone goes through trials and tribulations as a teenager and this is how we're dealing with it."

Woodley also rejects criticism from a few reviewers about the way that "Secret Life" depicts teen pregnancy. "I don't feel like this show glorifies

"I don't feel like this show glorifies pregnancy, because if you see my character she's obviously not jumping up and down, she's in the bathroom crying 24/7," Woodley explained. "If anything, I think it makes it seem like a very hard and difficult situation to go through, especially as a teenager."

pregnancy, because if you see my character she's obviously not jumping up and down, she's in the bathroom crying 24/7," she said. "If anything, I think it makes it seem like a very hard and difficult situation to go through, especially as a teenager."

Woodley is proud of the show, and she knows that Ringwald and the rest of the actors, writers, and crew on "Secret Life" feel the same way. She also loves the atmosphere on the set of the show. "Everyone is so great and everyone gets along so well," she said. "We're all so close and we have kinds of things like parties and dinners for each other for our birthdays and we all kind of play guitar, so we're always jamming in the trailers. It's a fun environment."

Playing the Role of Amy

Ever since "Secret Life" debuted, interviewers and fans have expressed curiosity about Woodley's view of the character she plays. She admits that "it's tricky sometimes because there are things that Amy does that I'm like, 'Why would she do this?' I just have to accept it and go along with it and find ways to make it work and find ways to believe it for myself, even though I would never even tell a boy I loved him at 15."

Woodley enjoys the challenge of playing someone so different from herself, though. "This is my first role where she's basically sad and lost in tragedy but still a teenager, still excited about school dances, and she has a new boyfriend, and she's finding love for the first time," she explained. "So it's a bunch of different colors that I kind of have to put into one rainbow, so it's been fun to figure out."

Woodley also believes that the role has allowed her to grow as an actress, because Amy has changed over the course of the show's existence. "I feel like she's become much stronger, personality-wise," she said. "She's learned to accept the fact that life isn't going to be perfect and that there are going to be many, many obstacles that she has to go through throughout her life.... I don't mean to discount the fact that she's still hurting and

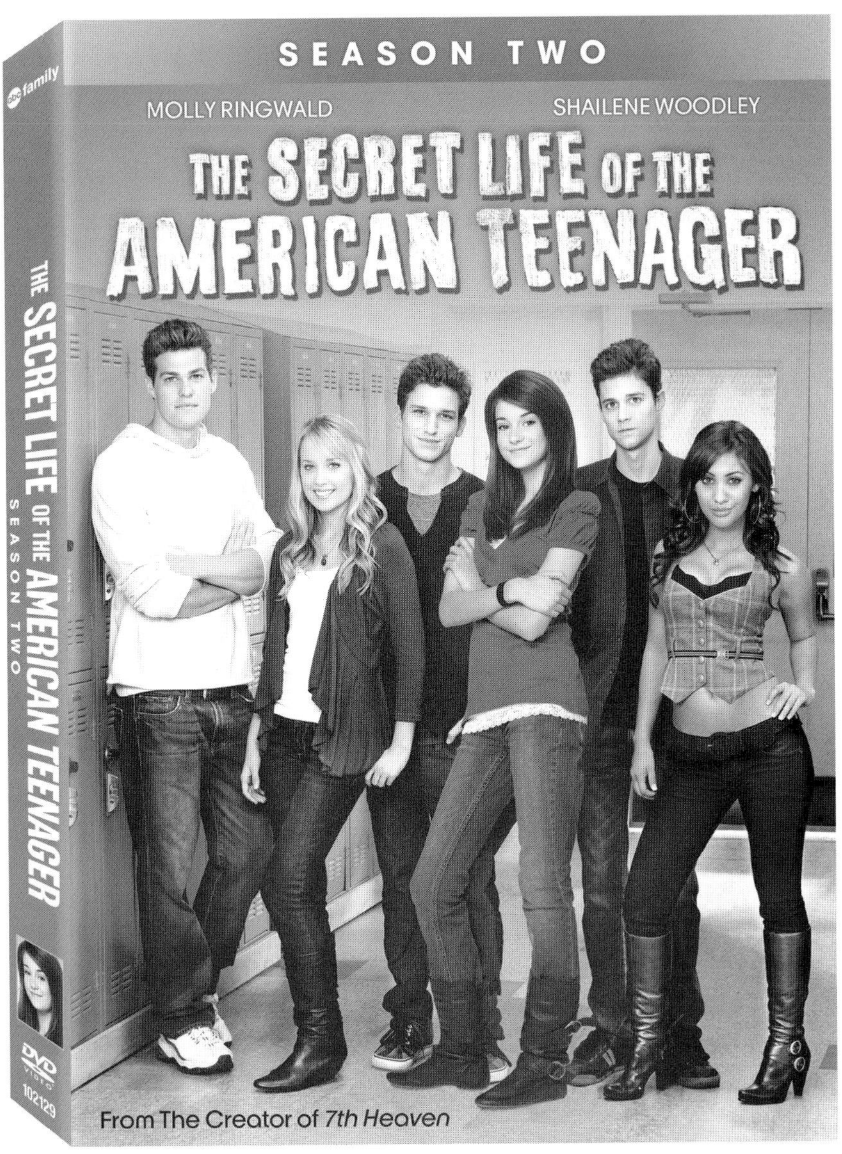

Fans of "Secret Life" have been glad to see the characters grow and develop over multiple seasons.

crying and emotionally stricken by the whole situation, but she's just accepted that it's going to have to happen. I think there's a state of acceptance and she's become stronger."

Adjusting to Stardom

"The Secret Life of the American Teenager" has changed Woodley's life in other ways as well. She enjoys interacting with fans, for example, but admits that it still feels strange to be the subject of fan web sites and to be identified by *Entertainment Weekly* as a "breakout star." "It's definitely different," she said. "When you go to a grocery store and you go anywhere there are people staring or pointing or whispering, and every now and then you have a brave girl come up and be like, 'Are you the girl from 'Secret Life'?'"

Woodley insists, though, that her growing stardom has not changed her personality or values. "As far as just my friends and where I can go, I still go all the places that I normally went. I might have to wear a hat or something [to disguise myself], but other than that it's no different because my friends, they treat me the same. They know I'm goofy, spontaneous, weird Shai and they accept me for that."

"There are so many emotions that you go through, whether it's when you're going through puberty and you have all these hormones … or whether it's a breakup with the boyfriend or divorcing parents," Woodley advised. "Just stay strong and remain who you are because the only thing that will keep you in check and keep you the person that everybody knows and loves is if you stay true to yourself … and know that you're super special."

Woodley also believes that she can use her high profile to help teenage fans going through their own turmoil. She urges teen girls to be brave and trust in themselves when life throws obstacles in their way. "There are so many emotions that you go through, whether it's when you're going through puberty and you have all these hormones going through your mind and you don't even know what to think, or whether it's a breakup with the boyfriend or divorcing parents," Woodley advised. "Just stay strong and remain who you are because the only thing that will keep you in check and keep you the person that everybody knows and loves is if you stay true to yourself … and know that you're super special."

Woodley describes acting as a "passion" and wants to continue with that career. But she also has many other plans for her future. For example, she would like to go to college in

New York City or someplace else on the East Coast "where it's cold and where you actually get seasons." She is particularly interested in studying psychology and interior design. "They're completely opposite [subjects]," she admits, "but I'm creative and I love the arts, so that's why I like interior design; and I think psychology is just so fascinating to be able to study the human mind and the human characteristics and the way they work. So I think that's definitely up my alley. I want to have options."

HOME AND FAMILY

Woodley lives in California, where "Secret Life" is filmed. She remains close to both her mother and father.

HOBBIES AND OTHER INTERESTS

Woodley has a wide range of interests that she likes to pursue when she is not on the set. She likes camping, hiking, Pilates, and painting, and she loves to sew. "I love to make bags or shirts or dresses or whatever," she said. After a tiring day of filming, though, she admits that she also enjoys just watching television with friends or family. "If I'm super exhausted, nothing soothes me better than 'Top Chef' or 'Project Runway,'" she stated.

SELECTED CREDITS

A Place Called Home, 2004
Felicity: An American Girl Adventure, 2005
"The Secret Life of the American Teenager," 2008- (ongoing)

FURTHER READING

Periodicals

Boston Herald, Jan. 5, 2009, p.27
Entertainment Weekly, Aug. 8, 2008, p.53; Nov. 21, 2008, p.86; Jan. 9, 2009, p.32
Girls Life, Aug.-Sep. 2008, p.48
Hollywood Reporter, Nov. 29, 2005, p.32
New York Times, July 1, 2008, p.E1
People, Jan. 26, 2009, p.42
Raleigh (NC) News & Observer, Aug. 10, 2008
San Francisco Chronicle, Jan. 3, 2009, p.E1
USA Today, June 30, 2008, p.D6

Online Articles

http://www.sidereel.com
(SideReel, "New Media Strategies: The Secret Life of the American Teenager—Shailene Woodley Q&A," Dec. 29, 2008)
http://www.tvaholic.com
(TVaholic, "Interview with Shailene Woodley," July 7, 2008)
http://www.webmd.com
(WebMD, "Actress Shailene Woodley Takes Scoliosis in Stride," no date)

ADDRESS

Shailene Woodley
"The Secret Life of the American Teenager" ABC Family
500 South Buena Vista Street
Burbank, CA 91521

WORLD WIDE WEB SITES

http://www.abcfamily.com
http://www.myspace.com/ishailenewoodley
http://www.shailene-woodley.com

Photo and Illustration Credits

Front Cover: Joe Biden: Department of Defense Photo by U.S. Air Force Senior Airman Kathrine McDowell; James Harrison: Gregory Shamus/Getty Images; Demi Lovato: Disney Channel/Heidi Gutman; Michelle Obama: Official portrait of First Lady Michelle Obama/WhiteHouse.gov.

Elizabeth Alexander: Photo by C. J. Gunther. Courtesy, Elizabeth Alexander (www.elizabethalexander.net) (p. 11); Book Cover: MISS CRANDALL'S SCHOOL FOR YOUNG LADIES & LITTLE MISSES OF COLOR (Wordsong/Boyd Mills Press, Inc.) Text copyright © 2007 by Elizabeth Alexander and Marilyn Nelson. Illustration copyright © 2007 by Floyd Cooper. All Rights Reserved. (p. 13); Ron Edmonds/AP Photo (p. 16).

Will Allen: Courtesy of Growing Power, Inc. (pp. 21, 24, 27, 29).

Judy Baca: Portrait of artist Judith F. Baca at the "Great Wall of Los Angeles," 2005 © SPARC www.sparcmurals.org (p. 33); Artist Judith F. Baca with mural crew at the "Great Wall of Los Angeles," 1983 © SPARC www.sparcmurals.org (p. 36); "MI ABUELITA" 1970, 20 ft. x 35 ft. Acrylic on cement. © SPARC www.sparcmurals.org (p. 39); "GREAT WALL OF LOS ANGELES" begun 1976. DETAIL: A view of the 13′ x 2,400′ "Great Wall" mural located in the Tujunga Wash, a flood control channel. The World's longest mural depicts a multi-cultural history of California from prehistory through to the 1950's. This mural is still growing. The Great Wall is located in California's San Fernando Valley Tujunga Wash, a flood control channel built in the 1930's. Acrylic on cast concrete, summer 1983. © SPARC www. sparcmurals.org (p. 41); "WORLD WALL: A Vision of the Future Without Fear" begun 1990. DETAIL: "WORLD WALL" installation in Mexico City 2006, eight panels totaling 10′ x 240′ acrylic on canvas. Begun in 1990, the World Wall is an international traveling mural installation consisting of numerous transportable panels with the theme "a vision of the future without fear." The completed work consists of *eight* 10′ x 30′ portable murals that bring forth a spiritual and material transformation of an individual, a community, and a nation towards peace. The World Wall had its premiere in Joensuu, Finland and traveled to Gorky Park, Moscow, USSR, in the summer of 1990 and continues to travel to new countries every year. © SPARC www.sparcmurals.org (p. 44); THE CESAR E. CHAVEZ MONUMENT "ARCH OF DIGNITY, EQUALITY AND JUSTICE" DETAIL: "Arch of Dignity, Equality and Justice," 2008. The Cesar E. Chavez monument at San Jose State University consists of farm workers featured in two murals painted and printed digitally, a portrait of Cesar Chavez painted and then produced in full color Venetian tile, along with portraits of Ghandi and Dolores Huerta. The monument at San Jose State University in San Jose California, was designed by Judith F. Baca and the UCLA/SPARC Cesar Chavez Digital Mural Lab. The monument commemorates Chavez through his ideals and beliefs, carried out in his actions to improve the conditions of the campesino, which inspired so many to join his efforts to achieve social justice. A key element to the monument is to teach the next generation how to choose to live a life in the center of your values and beliefs as Cesar Chavez did. © SPARC www.sparcmurals.org (p. 47).

Joe Biden: U.S. Army photo by K. Kassens (p. 51); Book cover: PROMISES TO KEEP (Random House) Copyright © 2007 by Joseph Biden. All Rights Reserved. Cover photo by Luigi Ciuffetelli. Cover design by David Stevenson. (p. 53); AP Photo (p. 56); Antonio Dickey, photographer. Chicago Public Library, Special Collections and Preservation Division, HWAC 1987-5-11 (p. 59); AP Photo/Barry Thumma (p. 61); Paul J. Richards/AFP/Getty Images (p. 62); Department of Defense photo by Master Sgt. Cecilio Ricardo/U.S. Air Force (p. 64).

Cynthia Breazeal: Photos courtesy of Personal Robots Group, MIT Media Lab (pp. 69, 80, 82); Photo still from THE EMPIRE STRIKES BACK © 1980 Lucas Film., LTD. (p. 71); Donna Coveney/MIT (pp. 73, 74); DESIGNING SOCIABLE ROBOTS by Cynthia Breazeal (MIT Press) © 2002 Massachusetts Institute of Technology. Images © 2000 Peter Menzel. Images © Sam Ogden. (p. 77).

Michael Cera: NICK AND NORA'S INFINITE PLAYLIST Photo: Barbara Nitke. © 2008 Playlist LLC. All Rights Reserved. Sony Pictures Entertainment Inc. (p. 85); ROLIE POLIE OLIE: THE GREAT DEFENDER OF FUN. ©Nelvana in Trust ©Disney Enterprises, Inc. All Rights Reserved. (p. 88, top); DVD set: ARRESTED DEVELOPMENT - SEASON ONE. © 2003, 2004 Twentieth Century Fox Film Corporation and Imagine Entertainment. All rights reserved. © 2004 Twentieth Century Fox Home Entertainment, Inc. All Rights Reserved. (p. 88, center); CLARK AND MICHAEL Photo: Monty Brinton/CBS ©2007 CBS Broadcasting Inc. All Rights Reserved. (p. 88, bottom); SUPERBAD © 2007 Columbia Pictures Industries, Inc. All Rights Reserved. Sony Pictures Home Entertainment (p. 91); JUNO © Twentieth Century Fox Film Corporation (p. 92); NICK AND NORA'S INFINITE PLAYLIST Photo: K.C. Bailey © 2008 Playlist LLC. All Rights Reserved. Sony Pictures Entertainment Inc. (p. 94).

Miranda Cosgrove: PRNewsFoto/Nickelodeon; Columbia Records/Newscom (p. 97); SCHOOL OF ROCK, TM & © 2003 by Paramount Pictures (p. 99); DVD: DRAKE & JOSH: VOLUME 1: SUDDENLY BROTHERS © 2005 Viacom International Inc. All rights reserved. © & TM 2005 Paramount Home Entertainment/Paramount Pictures. All rights reserved. (p. 102); CD: iCARLY-MUSIC FROM AND INSPIRED BY THE HIT TV SHOW Nickelodeon JV/Columbia Records Group © 2008 Sony BMG (p. 104, top); PRNewsFoto/Nickelodeon/Jon Mckee/Newscom (p. 104, center); PRNewsFoto/Nickelodeon, Lisa Rose/Nickelodeon/Newscom (p. 104, bottom).

Lupe Fiasco: NBC photo/Dave Bjerke (p. 109); Saverio Truglia/WireImage (p. 111); CD Cover: LUPE FIASCO'S FOOD & LIQUOR Copyright © Warner Elektra Atlantic Corporation (p. 115); Copyright © Warner Elektra Atlantic Corporation. Photo by Ray Tamarrra (p. 118); Tim Mosenfelder/Getty Images (p. 120).

James Harrison: AP Photo/John Bazemore (p. 123); Courtesy of Kent State Athletic Communications (p. 125); AP Photo/Jack Smith (p. 128); Andy Lyons/Getty Images (p. 130); Mark Cornelison/MCT/Landov (p. 133).

Jimmie Johnson: AP Photo/Glenn Smith (p. 137); AP Photo/Mark J. Terrill (p. 140); AP Photo/Wilfredo Lee (p. 143); AP Photo/J. Pat Carter (p. 145); Doug Benc/Getty Images (p. 148); AP Photo/Paul Connors (p. 151).

Heidi Klum: PROJECT RUNWAY Bravo Photo: Virginia Sherwood (pp. 155, 161 top); Mike Segar/Reuters/Landov (pp. 157, 164); Rose Hartman/WireImage.com (p. 159); PROJECT RUNWAY Bravo Photo: Barbara Nitke (p. 161, center and bottom).

Lang Lang: Deutsche Grammophon (Universal Music Group) (p. 169); Book Cover: LANG LANG: PLAYING WITH FLYING KEYS (Delacorte Press/Random House Children's Books) by Lang Lang with Michael French. Text copyright © 2008 by Lang Lang. Photograph © 2008 by Jesse Frohman (p. 172); © Photo: J. Henry Fair/Deutsche Grammophon (Universal Music Group) (p. 175); CD Cover: HAYDN, RACHMANINOFF, BRAHMS, TCHAIKOVSKY, BALAKIREV/Lang Lang℗© 2001 TELARC All Rights Reserved. Photo: Christopher Jacobs. Cover design: Anilda Carrasquillo (p. 177); Photo by Tim Hipps, Family and MWR Command. Courtesy U. S. Army (p. 180).

Leona Lewis: ABC/Adam Larkey (p. 183); Dave Hogan/Getty Images (p. 185); CD cover: SPIRIT © 2008 J Records, a unit of Sony BMG Music Entertainment (p. 188); NBC Photo: Margaret Norton (p. 190).

Nastia Liukin: Tony Marshall/PA/Landov (p. 193); Jonathan Ferrey/Getty Images (p. 197); zumalive/Newscom (p. 199); Pat Benic/UPI/Landov (p. 201).

Demi Lovato: Disney Channel/Nick Ray (p. 205); Barney & Friends ™, Courtesy of PBS KIDS Sprout/via Comcast (p. 206); DVD: CAMP ROCK: EXTENDED ROCK STAR EDITION, 2008. Copyright © Disney. All Rights Reserved. (p. 210, top and center); Disney Channel/Heidi Gutman (p. 210, bottom); TV: SONNY WITH A CHANCE. Disney Channel/Randy Holmes (p. 213); TV: PRINCESS PROTECTION PROGRAM, Disney Channel/Francisco Roman (p. 214).

Jef Mallett: Kim Kauffman Photography, courtesy Jef Mallett (p. 217); Courtesy Jef Mallett (pp. 218 and 226, left); FRAZZ © Jef Mallett/Dist. by United Feature Syndicate, Inc. Courtesy Mary Anne Grimes, United Media (pp. 220 and 226, right); FRAZZ © Jef Mallett/Dist. by United Feature Syndicate, Inc. (pp. 222, 223); Book cover: FRAZZ: LIVE AT BRYSON ELEMENTARY (Andrews McMeel Publishing) © 2005 by Jef Mallett. All Rights Reserved. (p. 224).

Warith Deen Mohammed: Stephen J. Carrera, File/AP Photo (p. 229); Hulton Archive/Getty Images (p. 230); Walter P. Reuther Library, Wayne State University (pp. 233, 235); AP Photo (p. 237); © John Van Hasselt/Corbis Sygma (p. 240); Tim Boyle/Getty Images (p. 243); Danny Johnston/AP Photo (p. 245).

Walter Dean Myers: Photo courtesy of HarperCollins Publishers (p. 247); Photo by Nichols, Photographs and Prints Division, Schomburg Center for Research in Black Culture, The New York Public Library, Astor, Lenox and Tilden Foundations (p. 248); BAD BOY: A MEMOIR (Amistad/HarperCollins) Copyright © 2001 by Walter Dean Myers. All rights reserved. Jacket art © 2001 by Robert Andrew Parker. Jacket design by Alison Donalty. Jacket © 2001 by HarperCollins. (p. 251); BROWN ANGELS: AN ALBUM OF PICTURES AND VERSE (HarperCollins) Copyright © 1993 by Walter Dean Myers. All rights reserved. Cover © 1996 HarperCollins. (p. 255);

WHERE DOES THE DAY GO? (Parents' Magazine Press) Text copyright © 1969 by Walter M. Meyers. Illustrations copyright © 1969 by Leo Carty. All rights reserved. (p. 257); FALLEN ANGELS (Scholastic, Inc.) Copyright © 1988 by Walter Dean Myers. All rights reserved. Cover art by Tomer Hanuka. Cover design by Steve Scott. (p. 260); MONSTER (Amistad/HarperCollins) text copyright © 1999 by Walter Dean Myers, illustrations copyright © 1999 by Christopher Myers. All rights reserved. Cover art by Christopher Myers. Cover design by Alison Donalty. (p. 262); SUNRISE OVER FALLUJAH (Scholastic, Inc.) Copyright © 2008 by Walter Dean Myers. All rights reserved. Front cover illustration © 2008 by Tim O'Brien. Jacket design by Elizabeth B. Parisi. (p. 265); Hugh Grannum/Detroit Free Press/Newscom (p. 267); HARLEM: A POEM (Scholastic, Inc.) text copyright © 1997 by Walter Dean Myers, illustrations copyright © 1997 by Christopher Myers. All rights reserved. (p. 270).

Michelle Obama: Official portrait of First Lady Michelle Obama/WhiteHouse.gov (p. 273); AP Photo/Obama for America (p. 276); Courtesy/University of Chicago (p. 278); AP Photo/Charlie Neibergall (p. 282); Department of Defense photo by Master Sgt. Gerold Gamble/U.S. Air Force (p. 285); The White House/Joyce N. Boghosian (p. 288, top); Courtesy of Corporation for National and Community Service. Photo by M.T. Harmon, Office of Public Affairs. (p. 288, center). Official White House Photo by Samantha Appleton (p. 288, bottom).

Omarion: PRNewsFoto/Newscom (p. 293); CD: B2K, Columbia Legacy copyright © 2002 Sony BMG. (p. 296); DVD: YOU GOT SERVED © 2004 Screen Gems, Inc. All rights reserved. Layout and design © 2004 Columbia TriStar Home Entertainment. All rights reserved. (p. 298); CD: O, Columbia Legacy Records Copyright © 2005 Sony BMG. (p. 301, top); Columbia/Urban Records, © 2007 Sony BMG. (p. 301, center); CD: FACE OFF, Columbia/Urban Records Copyright © 2007 Sony BMG. (p. 301, bottom); DVD: FEEL THE NOISE © 2007 Reggaeton, LLC. All rights reserved. © 2008 Layout and design Sony Pictures Home Entertainment Inc. All rights reserved. (p. 303).

Suze Orman: © Marc Royce. All Rights Reserved. Courtesy PBS (p. 307); Chris Kleponis/Bloomberg News/Landov (p. 310); Book Cover: YOU'VE EARNED IT, DON'T LOSE IT: MISTAKES YOU CAN'T AFFORD TO MAKE WHEN YOU RETIRE by Suze Orman, with Linda Mead © 1994, 1997, 1998 by Suze Orman. All Rights Reserved. Cover design by Jerry Pfiefer. Author photograph by Kelly Campbell (p. 312); DVD Cover: THE 9 STEPS TO FINANCIAL FREEDOM by Suze Orman. © 1998 Twin Cities Public Television and Q-Direct Ventures Inc. © 2004 Artwork PBS. All Rights Reserved. Photo: Kelly Campbell (p. 314); SATURDAY NIGHT LIVE, NBC Photo: Dana Edelson (p. 317).

Kenny Ortega: Reuters/Fred Prouser/Landov (p. 323); Central Press/Getty Images (p. 325); Michael Ansell/Warner Bros/Getty Images (p. 327); Photo still from DIRTY DANCING title copyright © 1997 Artisan Pictures Inc. Lionsgate Home Entertainment's *Dirty Dancing 20th Anniversary Edition* on Blu-Ray DVD, 2007 (p. 330); DVD: HIGH SCHOOL MUSICAL 2: DELUXE DANCE EDITION © WDSHE. All rights reserved. (p. 333, top); DVD: HIGH SCHOOL MUSICAL 2: Extended Edition © Disney. All rights reserved. (p. 333, center); HIGH SCHOOL MUSICAL 3: SENIOR YEAR © Disney Enterprises, Inc. All rights reserved. (p. 333, bottom).

Robert Pattinson: Elisabetta A. Villa/WireImage.com (p. 339); Movie stills: HARRY POTTER AND THE GOBLET OF FIRE. Copyright © 2006 Warner Bros Entertainment. Publishing rights © J. K. Rowling. Harry Potter characters, names, and related indicia are trademarks of and © Warner Bros Entertainment. All Rights Reserved. (p. 342, all photos); Movie still: TWILIGHT © Summit Entertainment/Peter Sorel (p. 344); Picture Group/MTV (p. 347); Movie still: HOW TO BE Copyright © 2009 How To Films Ltd. (p. 349).

Chris Paul: Bill Haber/AP Photo (p. 353); Linda Spillers/WireImage.com (p. 355); Photo by Brian Westerholt. Courtesy Wake Forest University (p. 358); Phil Ellsworth/ESPN (p. 360); Lucy Nicholson/Reuters/Landov (p. 363); Courtesy USBC (p. 365).

Michael Phelps: Al Bello/Getty Images (pp. 367, 376); Doug Pensinger/Getty Images (p. 369); Ross Kinnaird/Allsport/Getty Images (p. 372); Mike Blake/Reuters/Landov (p. 374); Donald Miralle/Getty Images (p. 378); QI Heng/Xinhua/Landov (p. 381); Kyodo/Landov (p. 383); Ding Xu/Xinhua/Landov (p. 385); Roger L. Wollenberg/UPI/Landov (p. 387).

Rachael Ray: PRNewsFoto via Newscom (pp. 391, 396); Book cover: RACHAEL RAY 30-MINUTE MEALS (Lake Isle Press) © 1998 by Rachael Ray. Photo: Colleen Brescia, courtesy of Food Network. Book design by Ellen Swandiak (p. 394); Peter Kramer/Getty Images (p. 399); PRNewsFoto/Ainsworth Pet Nutrition via Newscom (p. 402).

Emma Roberts: HOTEL FOR DOGS Photo: Jaimie Trueblood © 2008 DreamWorks LLC and Cold Spring Pictures. All Rights Reserved. (pp. 405 and 414, all photos); DVD: SPYMATE © Buena Vista Entertainment, Inc. All Rights Reserved. (p. 408); UNFABULOUS Courtesy of Nickelodeon (p. 410); NANCY DREW © 2007 Warner Bros. Entertainment, Inc. All Rights Reserved. Courtesy Warner Home Video (p. 412).

Robin Roberts: Copyright © 2008 ABC Studios/Heidi Gutman (p. 419); Photo courtesy of Southeastern Louisiana University Public Information Office (p. 422); AP Photo/Suzanne Plunkett (p. 425); Copyright © 2008 ABC Studios/Ida Mae Astute (p. 427); David Purdy/Biloxi Sun Herald/krtphotoslive/Newscom (p. 429); FROM THE HEART: SEVEN RULES TO LIVE BY Copyright © 2007 Robin Rene Roberts. All rights reserved. Published by Hyperion Books. (p. 431); Scott Gries/Getty Images (p. 432).

Grayson Rosenberger: Feature Photo Service/Newscom (p. 435); Photos courtesy of Standing With Hope (pp. 437 and 439, all photos).

Dinara Safina: Courtesy adidas (p. 443); Alik Keplicz/AP Photo (p. 445); Francois Mori/AP Photo (p. 447); Charlie Knight/AP Photo (p. 449); Clive Brunskill/Getty Images (p. 452).

Gloria Gilbert Stoga: Courtesy/Puppies Behind Bars. Photo by Keith Barraclough (p. 455); AP Photo/Jim McKnight (p. 458); AP Photo/Daniel Hulshizer (p. 461).

Taylor Swift: PRNewsFoto/Procter & Gamble/Newscom (p. 465); NBC Photo/Margaret Norton (p. 468); CD: TAYLOR SWIFT © 2008 Big Machine Records. Photo by Andrew Orth. (p. 470); Photo by Frank Micelotta/courtesy CMT (p. 472); CD: FEARLESS © 2008 Big Machine Records. Photo by Anthony Baker. (p. 475).

Shailene Woodley: ABC Family/Bob D'Amico (p. 479); DVD cover: FELICITY: AN AMERICAN GIRL ADVENTURE. *American Girl, Felicity, Felicity Merriman* and the associated characters and trademarks of The American Girl Collection are owned by American Girl, LLC. Package design, supplementary material compilation and distribution © 2005 Warner Bros Entertainment Inc. All Rights Reserved. (p. 481); ABC Family/Bob D'Amico (p. 484, top); ABC Family/Craig Sjodin (p. 484, center); ABC Family/Randy Holmes (p. 484, bottom); DVD: THE SECRET LIFE OF THE AMERICAN TEENAGER: SEASON 2 Copyright © WDSHE. All Rights Reserved. (p. 487).

Cumulative General Index

This cumulative index includes names, occupations, nationalities, and ethnic and minority origins that pertain to all individuals profiled in *Biography Today* since the debut of the series in 1992.

Places of Birth Index

The following index lists the places of birth for the individuals profiled in *Biography Today.* Places of birth are entered under state, province, and/or country.

Canada

Birthday Index

March (continued) **Year**

April **Year**

July (continued) **Year**

Krone, Julie 1963
Lopez, Jennifer 1970
Moss, Cynthia 1940
Wilson, Mara 1987
25 Payton, Walter 1954
26 Berenstain, Jan 1923
Clark, Kelly 1983
27 Dunlap, Alison 1969
Kimball, Cheyenne 1990
Rodriguez, Alex 1975
28 Babbitt, Natalie 1932
Davis, Jim 1945
Potter, Beatrix 1866
29 Burns, Ken 1953
Creech, Sharon 1945
Dole, Elizabeth Hanford 1936
Hayes, Tyrone 1967
Jennings, Peter 1938
Morris, Wanya 1973
30 Allen, Tori 1988
Hill, Anita 1956
Moore, Henry 1898
Norman, Christina 1963
Schroeder, Pat 1940
31 Cronin, John 1950
Kwolek, Stephanie 1923
Radcliffe, Daniel 1989
Reid Banks, Lynne 1929
Rowling, J.K. 1965
Weinke, Chris 1972

August **Year**

1 Brown, Ron 1941
Coolio .1963
Garcia, Jerry 1942
2 Asbaty, Diandra 1980
Baldwin, James 1924
Healy, Bernadine 1944
Howe, James 1946
3 Brady, Tom 1977
Roper, Dee Dee . . . .?
Savimbi, Jonas 1934
Stewart, Martha 1941
4 Gordon, Jeff 1971
Obama, Barack 1961
Whitman, Meg 1956
5 Córdova, France 1947
Ewing, Patrick 1962
Jackson, Shirley Ann 1946
6 Carter, Regina . . . .?1963
Cooney, Barbara 1917
Robinson, David 1965
Warhol, Andy . . . .?1928
7 Byars, Betsy 1928
Crosby, Sidney 1987
Duchovny, David 1960
Leakey, Louis 1903
Villa-Komaroff, Lydia 1947
8 Boyd, Candy Dawson 1946
Chasez, JC 1976
Federer, Roger 1981
9 Anderson, Gillian 1968
Holdsclaw, Chamique 1977
Houston, Whitney 1963
McKissack, Patricia C.. 1944
Sanders, Deion 1967
Travers, P.L. . . . .?1899
10 Hayden, Carla 1952
Tienda, Marta 1950
11 Haley, Alex 1921
Hogan, Hulk 1953
Rowan, Carl T. 1925
Wozniak, Steve 1950
12 Barton, Hazel 1971
Martin, Ann M. 1955
McKissack, Fredrick L. 1939
Myers, Walter Dean 1937
Sampras, Pete 1971
13 Aldrich, George 1955
Battle, Kathleen 1948
Castro, Fidel 1927
14 Berry, Halle . . . .?1967
Johnson, Magic 1959
Larson, Gary 1950
Mitchell-Raptakis, Karen 1956
15 Affleck, Benjamin 1972
Ellerbee, Linda 1944
Jonas, Joseph 1989
Thomas, Rob 1965
Walsh, Kerri 1978
16 Bennett, Olivia 1989
Farrell, Suzanne 1945
Fu Mingxia 1978
Gayle, Helene 1955
Jones, Diana Wynne 1934
Robison, Emily 1972
Thampy, George 1987
18 Danziger, Paula 1944
Murie, Margaret 1902

October (continued)		Year
	Sorenstam, Annika	1970
	Williams, Tyler James	1992
10	Earnhardt, Dale Jr.	1974
	Favre, Brett	1969
	Saro-Wiwa, Ken	1941
11	Freedman, Russell	1929
	Murray, Ty	1969
	Perry, Luke	?1964
	Wie, Michelle	1989
	Young, Steve	1961
12	Bloor, Edward	1950
	Childress, Alice	?1920
	Jones, Marion	1975
	Maguire, Martie	1969
	Ward, Charlie	1970
13	Ashanti	1980
	Carter, Chris	1956
	Kerrigan, Nancy	1969
	Rice, Jerry	1962
14	Daniel, Beth	1956
	Maines, Natalie	1974
	Mobutu Sese Seko	1930
	Usher	1978
15	Donovan, Marion	1917
	Iacocca, Lee A.	1924
16	Bruchac, Joseph	1942
	Mayer, John	1977
	Stewart, Kordell	1972
17	Eminem	1972
	Jemison, Mae	1956
	Kirkpatrick, Chris	1971
18	Bird, Sue	1980
	Efron, Zac	1987
	Foreman, Dave	1946
	Marsalis, Wynton	1961
	Navratilova, Martina	1956
	Suzuki, Shinichi	1898
19	Blum, Deborah	1954
	Pullman, Philip	1946
20	Grimes, Nikki	1950
	Kenyatta, Jomo	?1891
	Mantle, Mickey	1931
	Pinsky, Robert	1940
21	Cruz, Celia	?1924
	Gillespie, Dizzy	1956
	Le Guin, Ursula K.	1929
22	Hanson, Zac	1985
	Suzuki, Ichiro	1973
23	Anderson, Laurie Halse	1961
	Crichton, Michael	1942
	Milbrett, Tiffeny	1972
	Pelé	1940
24	Tandy, Karen P.	1953
25	Martinez, Pedro	1971
	Tolan, Stephanie S.	1942
26	Clinton, Hillary Rodham	1947
	Cohen, Sasha	1984
	Farmer, Paul Jr.	1959
	Newsom, Lee Ann	1956
27	Anderson, Terry	1947
	Carter, Majora	1966
	Morrison, Lillian	1917
28	Gates, Bill	1955
	Roberts, Julia	1967
	Romero, John	1967
	Salk, Jonas	1914
29	Flowers, Vonetta	1973
	Ryder, Winona	1971
30	Liukin, Nastia	1989
	Mohammed, Warith Deen	1933
31	Candy, John	1950
	Jackson, Peter	1961
	Paterson, Katherine	1932
	Patterson, Ryan	1983
	Pauley, Jane	1950
	Tucker, Chris	1973

November		Year
2	lang, k.d.	1961
	Nelly	1974
3	Arnold, Roseanne	1952
	Ho, David	1952
	Kiraly, Karch	1960
4	Bush, Laura	1946
	Combs, Sean (Puff Daddy)	1969
	Handler, Ruth	1916
5	Jonas, Kevin	1987
7	Bahrke, Shannon	1980
	Canady, Alexa	1950
8	Joy, Bill	1954
	Mittermeier, Russell A.	1949
9	Denton, Sandi	?
	Sagan, Carl	1934
10	Bates, Daisy	?1914
	Eve	1979
11	Blige, Mary J.	1971
	DiCaprio, Leonardo	1974
	Vonnegut, Kurt	1922
12	Andrews, Ned	1980
	Blackmun, Harry	1908

November (continued)		Year
	Harding, Tonya	1970
	Hathaway, Anne	1982
	Omarion	1984
	Sosa, Sammy	1968
13	Goldberg, Whoopi	1949
14	Boutros-Ghali, Boutros	1922
	Hussein, King	1935
	Lindgren, Astrid	1907
	Rice, Condoleezza	1954
	Schilling, Curt	1966
15	Breazeal, Cynthia	1967
	Long, Irene D.	1951
	Miyamoto, Shigeru	1952
	Ochoa, Lorena	1981
	O'Keeffe, Georgia	1887
	Pinkwater, Daniel	1941
	Woodley, Shailene	1991
16	Baiul, Oksana	1977
17	Fuentes, Daisy	1966
	Hanson, Ike	1980
18	Driscoll, Jean	1966
	Felix, Allyson	1985
	Klug, Chris	1972
	Mankiller, Wilma	1945
	Vidal, Christina	1981
19	Collins, Eileen	1956
	Devers, Gail	1966
	Glover, Savion	1973
	Strug, Kerri	1977
20	Biden, Joe	1942
	Wardlaw, Lee	1955
21	Aikman, Troy	1966
	Griffey, Ken Jr.	1969
	Schwikert, Tasha	1984
	Speare, Elizabeth George	1908
	Strahan, Michael	1971
22	Boyle, Ryan	1981
	Carmona, Richard	1949
	Cyrus, Miley	1992
23	Roberts, Robin	1960
24	Ndeti, Cosmas	1971
25	Grant, Amy	1960
	Mathis, Clint	1976
	McNabb, Donovan	1976
	Thomas, Lewis	1913
26	Patrick, Ruth	1907
	Pine, Elizabeth Michele	1975
	Schulz, Charles	1922
27	Nye, Bill	1955
	Watley, Natasha	1981
	White, Jaleel	1977
28	apl.de.ap	1974
	Stewart, Jon	1962
29	L'Engle, Madeleine	1918
	Lewis, C.S.	1898
	Tubman, William V.S.	1895
30	Jackson, Bo	1962
	Parks, Gordon	1912
	Rodriguez, Ivan "Pudge"	1971

December		Year
1	Delson, Brad	1977
2	Hendrickson, Sue	1949
	Macaulay, David	1946
	Seles, Monica	1973
	Spears, Britney	1981
	Watson, Paul	1950
3	Kim Dae-jung	?1925
	Filipovic, Zlata	1980
4	Banks, Tyra	1973
	Lennox, Betty	1976
5	Muniz, Frankie	1985
6	Park, Nick	1958
	Risca, Viviana	1982
7	Bird, Larry	1956
	Carter, Aaron	1987
8	Newman, Ryan	1977
	Rivera, Diego	1886
	Weatherspoon, Teresa	1965
	Williams, Lori Aurelia	?
9	Hopper, Grace Murray	1906
	Tré Cool	1972
10	Raven	1985
12	Bialik, Mayim	1975
	Frankenthaler, Helen	1928
	Sinatra, Frank	1915
13	Fedorov, Sergei	1969
	Pierce, Tamora	1954
	Swift, Taylor	1989
14	Hudgens, Vanessa	1988
	Jackson, Shirley	1916
15	Aidid, Mohammed Farah	1934
	Mendes, Chico	1944
	Smith, Betty	?1896
	Taymor, Julie	1952
16	Bailey, Donovan	1967
	McCary, Michael	1971
	Mead, Margaret	1901
17	Kielburger, Craig	1982

Biography Today

General Series

Biography Today General Series includes a unique combination of current biographical profiles that teachers and librarians — and the readers themselves — tell us are most appealing. The **General Series** is available as a 3-issue subscription; hardcover annual cumulation; or subscription plus cumulation.

Within the **General Series**, your readers will find a variety of sketches about:

- Authors
- Musicians
- Political leaders
- Sports figures
- Movie actresses & actors
- Cartoonists
- Scientists
- Astronauts
- TV personalities
- and the movers & shakers in many other fields!

ONE-YEAR SUBSCRIPTION

- 3 softcover issues, 6" x 9"
- Published in January, April, and September
- 1-year subscription, list price $66. **School and library price $64**
- 150 pages per issue
- 10 profiles per issue
- Contact sources for additional information
- Cumulative Names Index

HARDBOUND ANNUAL CUMULATION

- Sturdy 6" x 9" hardbound volume
- Published in December
- List price $73. **School and library price $66 per volume**
- 450 pages per volume
- 30 profiles — includes all profiles found in softcover issues for that calendar year
- Cumulative General Index, Places of Birth Index, and Birthday Index

SUBSCRIPTION AND CUMULATION COMBINATION

- $110 for 3 softcover issues plus the hardbound volume

For Cumulative General, Places of Birth, and Birthday Indexes, please see www.biographytoday.com.

"*Biography Today* will be useful in elementary and middle school libraries and in public library children's collections where there is a need for biographies of current personalities. High schools serving reluctant readers may also want to consider a subscription."

— *Booklist,* American Library Association

"Highly recommended for the young adult audience. Readers will delight in the accessible, energetic, tell-all style; teachers, librarians, and parents will welcome the clever format [and] intelligent and informative text. It should prove especially useful in motivating 'reluctant' readers or literate nonreaders."

— *MultiCultural Review*

"Written in a friendly, almost chatty tone, the profiles offer quick, objective information. While coverage of current figures makes *Biography Today* a useful reference tool, an appealing format and wide scope make it a fun resource to browse." — *School Library Journal*

"The best source for current information at a level kids can understand."

— Kelly Bryant, School Librarian, Carlton, OR

"Easy for kids to read. We love it! Don't want to be without it."

— Lynn McWhirter, School Librarian, Rockford, IL

1992

Paula Abdul
Andre Agassi
Kirstie Alley
Terry Anderson
Roseanne Arnold
Isaac Asimov
James Baker
Charles Barkley
Larry Bird
Judy Blume
Berke Breathed
Garth Brooks
Barbara Bush
George Bush
Fidel Castro
Bill Clinton
Bill Cosby
Diana, Princess of Wales
Shannen Doherty
Elizabeth Dole
David Duke
Gloria Estefan
Mikhail Gorbachev
Steffi Graf
Wayne Gretzky
Matt Groening
Alex Haley
Hammer
Martin Handford
Stephen Hawking
Hulk Hogan
Saddam Hussein
Lee Iacocca
Bo Jackson
Mae Jemison
Peter Jennings
Steven Jobs
John Paul II
Magic Johnson
Michael Jordon
Jackie Joyner-Kersee
Spike Lee
Mario Lemieux
Madeleine L'Engle
Jay Leno
Yo-Yo Ma
Nelson Mandela
Wynton Marsalis
Thurgood Marshall
Ann Martin
Barbara McClintock
Emily Arnold McCully
Antonia Novello
Sandra Day O'Connor
Rosa Parks
Jane Pauley
H. Ross Perot
Luke Perry
Scottie Pippen
Colin Powell
Jason Priestley
Queen Latifah
Yitzhak Rabin
Sally Ride
Pete Rose
Nolan Ryan
H. Norman Schwarzkopf
Jerry Seinfeld
Dr. Seuss
Gloria Steinem
Clarence Thomas
Chris Van Allsburg
Cynthia Voigt
Bill Watterson
Robin Williams
Oprah Winfrey
Kristi Yamaguchi
Boris Yeltsin

1993

Maya Angelou
Arthur Ashe
Avi
Kathleen Battle
Candice Bergen
Boutros Boutros-Ghali
Chris Burke
Dana Carvey
Cesar Chavez
Henry Cisneros
Hillary Rodham Clinton
Jacques Cousteau
Cindy Crawford
Macaulay Culkin
Lois Duncan
Marian Wright Edelman
Cecil Fielder
Bill Gates
Sara Gilbert
Dizzy Gillespie
Al Gore
Cathy Guisewite
Jasmine Guy
Anita Hill
Ice-T
Darci Kistler
k.d. lang
Dan Marino
Rigoberta Menchu
Walter Dean Myers
Martina Navratilova
Phyllis Reynolds Naylor
Rudolf Nureyev
Shaquille O'Neal
Janet Reno
Jerry Rice
Mary Robinson
Winona Ryder
Jerry Spinelli
Denzel Washington
Keenen Ivory Wayans
Dave Winfield

1994

Tim Allen
Marian Anderson
Mario Andretti
Ned Andrews
Yasir Arafat
Bruce Babbitt
Mayim Bialik
Bonnie Blair
Ed Bradley
John Candy
Mary Chapin Carpenter
Benjamin Chavis
Connie Chung
Beverly Cleary
Kurt Cobain
F.W. de Klerk
Rita Dove
Linda Ellerbee
Sergei Fedorov
Zlata Filipovic
Daisy Fuentes
Ruth Bader Ginsburg
Whoopi Goldberg
Tonya Harding
Melissa Joan Hart
Geoff Hooper
Whitney Houston
Dan Jansen
Nancy Kerrigan
Alexi Lalas
Charlotte Lopez
Wilma Mankiller
Shannon Miller
Toni Morrison
Richard Nixon
Greg Norman
Severo Ochoa
River Phoenix
Elizabeth Pine
Jonas Salk
Richard Scarry
Emmitt Smith
Will Smith
Steven Spielberg
Patrick Stewart
R.L. Stine
Lewis Thomas
Barbara Walters
Charlie Ward
Steve Young
Kim Zmeskal

1995

Troy Aikman
Jean-Bertrand Aristide
Oksana Baiul
Halle Berry
Benazir Bhutto
Jonathan Brandis
Warren E. Burger
Ken Burns
Candace Cameron
Jimmy Carter
Agnes de Mille
Placido Domingo
Janet Evans
Patrick Ewing
Newt Gingrich
John Goodman
Amy Grant
Jesse Jackson
James Earl Jones
Julie Krone
David Letterman
Rush Limbaugh
Heather Locklear
Reba McEntire
Joe Montana
Cosmas Ndeti
Hakeem Olajuwon
Ashley Olsen
Mary Kate Olsen
Jennifer Parkinson
Linus Pauling
Itzhak Perlman
Cokie Roberts
Wilma Rudolph
Salt 'N' Pepa
Barry Sanders
William Shatner

Elizabeth George Speare
Dr. Benjamin Spock
Jonathan Taylor Thomas
Vicki Van Meter
Heather Whitestone
Pedro Zamora

1996

Aung San Suu Kyi
Boyz II Men
Brandy
Ron Brown
Mariah Carey
Jim Carrey
Larry Champagne III
Christo
Chelsea Clinton
Coolio
Bob Dole
David Duchovny
Debbi Fields
Chris Galeczka
Jerry Garcia
Jennie Garth
Wendy Guey
Tom Hanks
Alison Hargreaves
Sir Edmund Hillary
Judith Jamison
Barbara Jordan
Annie Leibovitz
Carl Lewis
Jim Lovell
Mickey Mantle
Lynn Margulis
Iqbal Masih
Mark Messier
Larisa Oleynik
Christopher Pike
David Robinson
Dennis Rodman
Selena
Monica Seles
Don Shula
Kerri Strug
Tiffani-Amber Thiessen
Dave Thomas
Jaleel White

1997

Madeleine Albright
Marcus Allen
Gillian Anderson
Rachel Blanchard
Zachery Ty Bryan
Adam Ezra Cohen
Claire Danes
Celine Dion
Jean Driscoll
Louis Farrakhan
Ella Fitzgerald
Harrison Ford
Bryant Gumbel
John Johnson
Michael Johnson
Maya Lin
George Lucas
John Madden
Bill Monroe
Alanis Morissette
Sam Morrison
Rosie O'Donnell
Muammar el-Qaddafi
Christopher Reeve
Pete Sampras
Pat Schroeder
Rebecca Sealfon
Tupac Shakur
Tabitha Soren
Herbert Tarvin
Merlin Tuttle
Mara Wilson

1998

Bella Abzug
Kofi Annan
Neve Campbell
Sean Combs (Puff Daddy)
Dalai Lama (Tenzin Gyatso)
Diana, Princess of Wales
Leonardo DiCaprio
Walter E. Diemer
Ruth Handler
Hanson
Livan Hernandez
Jewel
Jimmy Johnson
Tara Lipinski
Jody-Anne Maxwell
Dominique Moceanu
Alexandra Nechita
Brad Pitt
LeAnn Rimes
Emily Rosa
David Satcher
Betty Shabazz
Kordell Stewart
Shinichi Suzuki
Mother Teresa
Mike Vernon
Reggie White
Kate Winslet

1999

Ben Affleck
Jennifer Aniston
Maurice Ashley
Kobe Bryant
Bessie Delany
Sadie Delany
Sharon Draper
Sarah Michelle Gellar
John Glenn
Savion Glover
Jeff Gordon
David Hampton
Lauryn Hill
King Hussein
Lynn Johnston
Shari Lewis
Oseola McCarty
Mark McGwire
Slobodan Milosevic
Natalie Portman
J.K. Rowling
Frank Sinatra
Gene Siskel
Sammy Sosa
John Stanford
Natalia Toro
Shania Twain
Mitsuko Uchida
Jesse Ventura
Venus Williams

2000

Christina Aguilera
K.A. Applegate
Lance Armstrong
Backstreet Boys
Daisy Bates
Harry Blackmun
George W. Bush
Carson Daly
Ron Dayne
Henry Louis Gates, Jr.
Doris Haddock (Granny D)
Jennifer Love Hewitt
Chamique Holdsclaw
Katie Holmes
Charlayne Hunter-Gault
Johanna Johnson
Craig Kielburger
John Lasseter
Peyton Manning
Ricky Martin
John McCain
Walter Payton
Freddie Prinze Jr.
Viviana Risca
Briana Scurry
George Thampy
CeCe Winans

2001

Jessica Alba
Christiane Amanpour
Drew Barrymore
Jeff Bezos
Destiny's Child
Dale Earnhardt
Carly Fiorina
Aretha Franklin
Cathy Freeman
Tony Hawk
Faith Hill
Kim Dae-jung
Madeleine L'Engle
Mariangela Lisanti
Frankie Muniz
*N Sync
Ellen Ochoa
Jeff Probst
Julia Roberts
Carl T. Rowan
Britney Spears
Chris Tucker
Lloyd D. Ward
Alan Webb
Chris Weinke

2002

Aaliyah
Osama bin Laden
Mary J. Blige
Aubyn Burnside
Aaron Carter
Julz Chavez
Dick Cheney
Hilary Duff

Billy Gilman
Rudolph Giuliani
Brian Griese
Jennifer Lopez
Dave Mirra
Dineh Mohajer
Leanne Nakamura
Daniel Radcliffe
Condoleezza Rice
Marla Runyan
Ruth Simmons
Mattie Stepanek
J.R.R. Tolkien
Barry Watson
Tyrone Willingham
Elijah Wood

2003

Yolanda Adams
Olivia Bennett
Mildred Benson
Alexis Bledel
Barry Bonds
Vincent Brooks
Laura Bush
Amanda Bynes
Kelly Clarkson
Vin Diesel
Eminem
Michele Forman
Vicente Fox
Millard Fuller
Josh Hartnett
Dolores Huerta
Sarah Hughes
Enrique Iglesias
Jeanette Lee
John Lewis
Nicklas Lidstrom
Clint Mathis
Donovan McNabb
Nelly
Andy Roddick
Gwen Stefani
Emma Watson
Meg Whitman
Reese Witherspoon
Yao Ming

2004

Natalie Babbitt
David Beckham
Francie Berger
Tony Blair
Orlando Bloom
Kim Clijsters
Celia Cruz
Matel Dawson Jr.
The Donnas
Tim Duncan
Shirin Ebadi
Carla Hayden
Ashton Kutcher
Lisa Leslie
Linkin Park
Lindsay Lohan
Irene D. Long
John Mayer
Mandy Moore
Thich Nhat Hanh
OutKast
Raven
Ronald Reagan
Keanu Reeves
Ricardo Sanchez
Brian Urlacher
Alexa Vega
Michelle Wie
Will Wright

2005

Kristen Bell
Jack Black
Sergey Brin & Larry Page
Adam Brody
Chris Carrabba
Johnny Depp
Eve
Jennie Finch
James Forman
Wally Funk
Cornelia Funke
Bethany Hamilton
Anne Hathaway
Priest Holmes
T.D. Jakes
John Paul II
Toby Keith
Alison Krauss
Wangari Maathai
Karen Mitchell-Raptakis
Queen Noor
Violet Palmer
Gloria Rodriguez
Carlos Santana
Antonin Scalia
Curtis Schilling
Maria Sharapova
Ashlee Simpson
Donald Trump
Ben Wallace

2006

Carol Bellamy
Miri Ben-Ari
Black Eyed Peas
Bono
Kelsie Buckley
Dale Chihuly
Neda DeMayo
Dakota Fanning
Green Day
Freddie Highmore
Russel Honoré
Tim Howard
Cynthia Kadohata
Coretta Scott King
Rachel McAdams
Cesar Millan
Steve Nash
Nick Park
Rosa Parks
Danica Patrick
Jorge Ramos
Ben Roethlisberger
Lil' Romeo
Adam Sandler
Russell Simmons
Jamie Lynn Spears
Jon Stewart
Joss Stone
Hannah Teter
Brenda Villa
Tyler James Williams
Gretchen Wilson

2007

Shaun Alexander
Carmelo Anthony
Drake Bell
Chris Brown
Regina Carter
Kortney Clemons
Taylor Crabtree
Miley Cyrus
Aaron Dworkin
Fall Out Boy
Roger Federer
Will Ferrell
America Ferrera
June Foray
Sarah Blaffer Hrdy
Alicia Keys
Cheyenne Kimball
Keira Knightley
Wendy Kopp
Sofia Mulanovich
Barack Obama
Soledad O'Brien
Jamie Oliver
Skip Palenik
Nancy Pelosi
Jack Prelutsky
Ivan "Pudge" Rodriguez
Michael Sessions
Kate Spade
Sabriye Tenberken
Rob Thomas
Ashley Tisdale
Carrie Underwood
Muhammad Yunus

2008

Aly & AJ
Bill Bass
Greta Binford
Cory Booker
Sophia Bush
Majora Carter
Anderson Cooper
Zac Efron
Selena Gomez
Al Gore
Vanessa Hudgens
Jennifer Hudson
Zach Hunter
Bindi Irwin
Jonas Brothers
Lisa Ling
Eli Manning
Kimmie Meissner
Scott Niedermayer
Christina Norman
Masi Oka
Tyler Perry
Morgan Pressel
Rihanna
John Roberts Jr.
J. K. Rowling
James Stewart Jr.
Ichiro Suzuki
Karen P. Tandy
Marta Tienda
Justin Timberlake
Lee Wardlaw

2009

Elizabeth Alexander
Will Allen
Judy Baca
Joe Biden
Cynthia Breazeal
Michael Cera
Miranda Cosgrove
Lupe Fiasco
James Harrison
Jimmie Johnson
Heidi Klum
Lang Lang
Leona Lewis
Nastia Liukin
Demi Lovato
Jef Mallett
Warith Deen Mohammed
Walter Dean Myers
Michelle Obama
Omarion
Suze Orman
Kenny Ortega
Robert Pattinson
Chris Paul
Michael Phelps
Rachael Ray
Emma Roberts
Robin Roberts
Grayson Rosenberger
Dinara Safina
Gloria Gilbert Stoga
Taylor Swift
Shailene Woodley